The
Catholic
Fact
Book

The
Catholic
Fact
Book

John Deedy

THE THOMAS MORE PRESS
Chicago, Illinois

ISBN 0-88347-186-8

Contents

For the extended branch:
Garrett, Jim, Janet, Donna

Foreword

FOREWORDS commonly explain what a book is about. Fine, but first let me say what this book is not.

It is not an encyclopedia, as can be guessed from its size. Encyclopedias are almost endlessly inclusive. The 1913 Gilmary Society *Catholic Encyclopedia*, for instance, comprises 16 volumes, plus supplements; the 1967 *New Catholic Encyclopedia* of the Catholic University of America has 15 volumes, plus supplements.

Rather it is a one-volume fact book, containing some encyclopedia information and some almanac data, arranged so as to be read as an informal history of its subject, the Roman Catholic Church. The book is not exhaustive of that subject, and is not meant to be. If occasionally it wanders into the offbeat, the purpose is editorial. The intention is to engage interests, while at the same time providing a certain amount of information and data about Roman Catholicism—again, by no means all, but, it is to be hoped, enough to convey something of the flavor of Roman Catholicism, what it is and how it is understood and run from official levels.

Incidentally, no one Bible translation has been used. Where possible, I have used the biblical quotes familiar to my childhood and that of the older generations of Catholics. These came from memory.

JOHN DEEDY
Rockport, Massachusetts

Section I

History

THE CATHOLIC CHURCH is that community of people who believe that Jesus, called the Christ or "anointed one," i.e. the Messiah, is God, second person of the Trinity, and savior of humankind, who intervened in history by being born of woman, and who founded a church to bring believers in his word to eternal salvation.

Catholics number more than 841,000,000, some 18 percent of the world's population of more than 4.5-billion people. An estimated 16,000,000 Catholics live in countries, mostly under Communist rule, where church leaders are unable to report figures. Statistics from ecclesial jurisdictions able to report their totals show a Catholic population of nearly 825,600,000.

The figures are contained in the *1983 Statistical Yearbook of the Church*, published by the Vatican in late 1985 and projecting 1984-1985 estimates.

The Yearbook listed Latin America as the region with the largest Catholic population: 345,500,000 people, which is 90 percent of the total population of the continent and 41 percent of all Catholics of the world.

Brazil had the largest Catholic population of any country: 116,800,000 Catholics in a population of approximately 131,300,000.

Other countries with major Catholic populations:

• Mexico, 72,000,000

- Italy, 55,700,000
- United States, 51,900,000
- France, 46,700,000

Elsewhere, Catholics comprise approximately 16 percent of the total population of Africa; 26 percent of the total population of Oceana, and some 40 percent of the total population of Europe.

Catholics are sparsest in Asia, numbering less than three percent of Asia's 2.7-billion people.

Jesus

Jesus was born in Bethlehem, a town near Jerusalem, on a day arbitrarily fixed as December 25. His birth marked the beginning of the Christian era, and for much of the world the birth of Christ became the point for the reckoning of dates. It still is. Years are designated B.C., for Before Christ, and A.D., for *Anno Domini,* the Year of Our Lord or since Christ was born. (Lately there has been a preference in some circles for use of the initials B.C.E. and C.E., standing respectively for Before the Common Era and Common Era.)

Jesus was born of a woman named Mary, known since by a variety of titles, most notably Our Lady and the Virgin Mary. Mary was the spouse of Joseph, but in Catholic understanding she miraculously conceived Jesus; that is, she begot Jesus virginally by the power of the Holy Spirit. Jesus thus had a human mother but no human father. He was born of God, and he is God; he was born of woman and is human. The process by which Christ was born is known as the Virgin Birth, a term often confused with the Immaculate Conception. The latter term refers not to Jesus' birth, but to Mary's. Jesus was virginally conceived; Mary was immaculately conceived—that is, she was born free of Original Sin and was preserved from sin through a life filled with grace from its beginning.

Joseph, Jesus' foster father, was a carpenter by trade in the Galilean town of Nazareth. It is presumed that Jesus worked as an apprentice for Joseph before beginning his public life. As a public figure in and around the area of Galilee, Jesus attracted thousands of followers by his preaching and his healing, by good works and by proclaiming the news of salvation. He spoke in the synagogues and before the elders of Judaism, and he was called Teacher and Rabbi. He challenged certain religious practices of the times, drove the money-changers out of the Temple, and upset social conventions by letting lepers and prostitutes draw near, publicans and sinners as well. His miracles were numerous, and ranged from changing water into wine (at the wedding feast of Cana) to raising people from the dead (most notably, Lazarus). His followers referred to him as the Son of David and the Messiah.

Jesus confirmed that he was the Messiah in a talk with his disciples near Caesarea Philippi (Matthew 16:13-20), and he allowed Peter to proclaim him God's holy one, the person with the words of eternal life (John 6:68-69). Authority figures viewed him suspiciously, and eventually he was condemned as a blasphemer and handed over to the Romans. The Roman procurator at the time was Pontius Pilate. After a mock trial in Jerusalem Jesus was condemned to death for the spurious crime of making himself King of the Jews.

Jesus Christ lived a total of 33 years, and died a violent death by crucifixion on Calvary. He was buried, but rose again on the third day, according to his word. For 40 days he moved widely among men and women, before ascending into heaven, where he reigns with the Father in the unity of the Trinity: Father, Son and Holy Spirit.

By word (exhortation and parable) and deed (by miracles, but more by the example of his own life), Jesus Christ gave a new shape to history and new meanings to the words love and charity. He died in disgrace, a failure, but his word was triumphant, as was he. ''He sits at the right hand of the Father, and he shall come again with glory, to judge the living and the dead, and his kingdom shall have no end"—words from the Nicene Creed, the Catholic's basic article of faith.

The Marks of the Church of Jesus Christ

Theologians may debate whether Christ consciously knew that he was divine, but there is little question that he consciously created a church. The confirmation is contained in Matthew 16:17-20: "Blessed are you, Simon son of Jonah. . . . And I say to you: 'Thou art Peter, and upon this rock I will build my church, and the gates of hell shall not prevail against it.' " Whether Christ intended that his church be so fully institutionalized as it developed to be is a separate question. In any instance, church there is, and Catholics believe theirs to be, again in the words of the Nicene Creed, "one, holy, catholic and apostolic." These words describe the four marks of the church, or its chief identifying characteristics, the signs by which it is recognized as the church founded by Christ. The four marks are understood as expressing the very intentions of Christ for his church. The church is thus:

One. Christ intended his church to be one. "There shall be one fold and one shepherd" (John 10:16). The proposition was once viewed within Catholicism as meaning that true church must be united in doctrine, worship and government, but that is a proposition that belongs to an age when the church was something of a monolith. The insistence on worship and government is not so great given new collegial and ecumenical understandings; doctrine is another matter.

Holy. Christ intended his church to be holy; that is, it must teach a holy doctrine in faith and morals, while at the same time exhorting and providing the means for members of the church to lead a holy life. "Sanctify them in truth," Christ prayed with his apostles (John 17:17).

Catholic. Christ intended that his church be universal (catholic with a lower case c); that is, he intended that it should exist for peoples of all nations and for all times, and that it teach the one faith to people everywhere. "Go into the whole world, and preach the Gospel to all creation" (Mark 16:16).

Apostolic. Christ intended that his church be propagated by the Apostles, and that authority in the church be derivative of and hold intact the doctrine and tradition of the Apostles. "You are built on a foundation of the Apostles and prophets," Paul wrote to the church at Ephesus (2:20).

The Apostles

The mandate to preach the word and sanctify people was given by Christ to the Apostles. They were the first to leave all to follow him. They were the partakers of the first eucharistic meal, which was also Christ's Last Supper. They are referred to as the first bishops of the Church. The Apostles number 12 by common count, but the precise number is more like 17.

Matthew lists 12 Apostles in his Gospel, in the following order: Peter, Andrew, James the Greater, John, Philip, Bartholomew, Thomas, Matthew, James the Less, Jude, Simon, and Judas Iscariot.

But five more are accorded the title Apostle. It extends to them, if not always in the strict, formal sense, then in the sense of having been an intimate part of the apostolic tradition, and indeed shapers in their own ways of this tradition. The five are Paul, Barnabas, Luke, Mark and Matthias.

Paul ranks as an Apostle by special call of Christ.
Barnabas was called an Apostle.

Luke and Mark were closely associated with the apostolic college, and of course were two of the four evangelists or writers of the Gospel. (The others: Matthew and John.)

Matthias was chosen to replace Judas Iscariot, after Judas' betrayal of Christ, the selection taking place in the three days between the Crucifixion and the Resurrection.

Brief biographical sketches of the 17 follow.

Peter. He was designated by Christ as first among the Apostles, and thus was the church's first head, its first pope. He was a fisherman, who was born in Bethsaida, son of Jonah. He originally bore the name Simon, but was called Peter by Christ. Peter's life was central to Christ's. He was with Jesus at the wedding feast at Cana; he witnessed the raising to life of Jairus' daughter; he witnessed the Transfiguration, and he was in the courtyard during the interrogation and sentencing of Christ. His triple denial of Christ there dramatizes the personal transformation which took place in the lives of the Apostles, changing them from hesitant, timid souls to heroes of the faith. Peter was the first to preach the Gospel in Jerusalem, and he presided over the council there in 51 A.D. Peter traveled widely throughout Judea, Samaria, Galilee, Asia Minor (he wrote two epistles to the Christians of Asia Minor), and probably Greece. A married man, some say he became widowed; others speculate that he took his wife with him on his missionary journeys. Peter established the Church in Rome and was crucified there head downwards, in 67 A.D. The crucifixion took place during the persecutions of Nero. St. Peter's Basilica was built over the site of his tomb. His feasts are June 29 and February 22 in the Roman Rite.

Andrew. He was the brother of Peter. He too was born in Bethsaida, and like his brother was a fisherman. He was the first called of the Apostles, and it was he who brought to the Lord the young boy with the five barley loaves and the two fishes for the feeding of the 5,000 at Bethsaida-Julias. Legend places Andrew as a preacher in Epirus, Achaia, Scythia and northern Greece. He was martyred in Patras, in Achaia, having been bound to a cross from which he preached in his last days. Andrew is honored as the patron of Scotland and Russia, and his feast is observed on November 30.

James the Greater. He was the son of Zebedee and the brother of John the Evangelist. His occupation was that of fisherman. With Peter and John, he witnessed the raising of Jairus' daughter, the Transfiguration and the Agony in the Garden. He preached probably as far away as Spain, and he was the first of the Apostles to be martyred, dying during a persecution of Herod Agrippa in 44 A.D. His relics are reputedly at the shrine of Santiago de Compostela in Spain. His feast is July 25 in the Roman Rite and April 30 in the Byzantine Rite.

John. With his brother James the Greater, John was known as "Son of Thunder," a title bestowed by Christ and suggesting that the brothers were impetuous and short-tempered. John was the closest of Christ's companions, and was the Apostle to whom Christ assigned the care of his mother. He lived at Ephesus in Asia Minor, and was the only one of the Twelve not to have died a violent death. He lived some 100 years, and in addition to the Fourth Gospel, he wrote three epistles and the Book of Revelation or Apocalypse. His feast is December 27 in the Roman Rite, and May 8 in the Byzantine Rite.

Philip. A native of Bethsaida, Philip was the Apostle of whom Christ inquired the cost of buying bread for the 5,000 who had gathered at Bethsaida-Julias. He told Christ that 200 *denarii* would not be enough—a problem which Christ solved with the miracle of the multiplication of the loaves and fishes. The Greeks who wished to see Jesus approached Philip, and it was Philip who, at the Last Supper, asked to see the Father and was rebuked by Jesus for being with him all this time and not knowing him. Legend has Philip preaching the Gospel in Phrygia and Scythia, and being crucified in Hieropolis. His feast is May 3 in the Roman Rite and November 14 in the Byzantine Rite.

Bartholomew. Bartholomew was listed by Matthew as one of the Twelve and is mentioned in the Acts of the Apostles, but beyond that little is known of him except that he was a friend of Philip. There is speculation that he is the Nathanael of John's Gospel. If so, he is the Apostle who engaged in the witty exchange with Jesus in John 1:45ff, which pointed up the village rivalry between Nazareth and Cana. (Nathanael was from Cana and, when admonished to regard seriously this Jesus of Nazareth, remarked, "What can you expect from Nazareth?" Exegetes see a smile behind Jesus' rejoinder that here was a man who deserves the name "incapable of deceit.") Tradition has Bartholomew preaching from Egypt across Armenia and Asia Minor to India, before being flayed and beheaded. His feast is August 24 in the Roman Rite and August 25 in the Byzantine Rite.

Thomas. Known also as Didymus, "twin," Thomas is the central figure in one of the most famous biblical stories: Jesus' resolving of Thomas' doubts about the authenticity of the Resurrection by inviting him to examine the nail wounds of his hands and to place his hand in the wound on his side, pierced by a soldier's lance (John 20:24-29). Thomas is said to have preached in Persia, Medea and India, where he was martyred near Madras. His feast is July 3 in the Roman Rite, and October 6 in the Byzantine Rite.

Matthew. Matthew was a tax collector at Capernaum, probably involved with the collecting of road tolls since Capernaum was situated along the busy Damascus road. He was one of the four Evangelists, and his gospel is seen reflecting a background in figures with its ledger-like, mathematical orderliness. Tradition locates Matthew as preacher in Judea, Ethiopia, Persia and Parthia, where he was martyred. His feast is September 21 in the Roman Rite and November 16 in the Byzantine Rite.

James the Less. He was the son of Alphaeus, and was known as the Less by way of distinguishing him from James, the brother of John. The designation likely derived from his being younger and shorter than the other James. The Acts of the Apostles identify this James as the leader of the Christian community at Jerusalem, and one epistle is credited to him. He died in 62 or 63 A.D., some say by clubbing, some from stoning, some by being cast from the pinnacle of the temple in Jerusalem. His feast is May 3 in the Roman Rite and October 9 in the Byzantine Rite.

Jude. Known also as Thaddeus, Jude was the brother of James the Less, and he is said to have preached the Gospel in Syria and Persia, where he was martyred. He is regarded as the patron of hopeless causes, possibly because it was felt devotion to him had been neglected due to the similarity of names between him and Christ's traitor, Judas Iscariot. Jude's feast is October 28 in the Roman Rite and June 19 in the Byzantine Rite.

Simon. He was known as the Cananean and the Zealot in order to distinguish him from Simon Peter. He is said to have preached in Africa and the Middle East, before being martyred in Persia, reportedly by being sawed in two. His feast is October 28 in the Roman Rite and May 10 in the Byzantine Rite. (Designation of Simon as the Zealot is said to relate to his zeal for the law.)

Judas Iscariot. This is the Apostle who betrayed Christ for 30 pieces of silver, the betrayal having been announced beforehand by Christ himself at the Last Supper. Judas was the bursar or purse-keeper of the original Twelve,

and it was he who complained during the anointing incident at Bethany about the waste of money—money, he
said, that could be better used for the poor. John attributes
the concern to Judas' being a petty thief. After the betrayal, Judas wailed that he had delivered an innocent
man. He cast away the silver pieces, went off and hanged
himself.

Matthias. It was Matthias who was chosen by the draw-
ing of lots to fill the place among the Twelve left vacant
by the betrayal and death of Judas. He was elected over
Joseph, also known as Barsabbas, whose surname was
Justus. Matthias had been a disciple of Jesus, traveling
with him from the time of his baptism by John the Baptist. He is said to have brought Christianity to Cappa-
docia, and to have been crucified at Colchis, though his
relics are now in Rome. His feast is May 14 in the Roman
Rite and August 9 in the Byzantine Rite.

Paul. A native of Tarsus in Asia Minor, Paul is known
as the Apostle of the Gentiles for his extensive missionary
journeys through Asia Minor, Cyprus, Macedonia,
Greece, Malta and Western Europe. Initially he was a foe
of Christianity, and he participated in the persecution of
Christians, until his miraculous conversion on the road
to Damascus, when he had the blinding vision of the
risen Christ. This took place about the year 43, and makes
him an Apostle by special call of Christ. Changing his
name from Saul to Paul, he quickly became a leader
of the Christian community, and wrote many epistles
which are an integral part of the Bible's New Testament.
He was martyred outside the walls of Rome during the
Neroian persecution. Death was by beheading, probably
in the year 67. His feasts are January 25 and June 29 in
the Roman Rite.

Barnabas. A Levite of Cypriot origin, he is the person in
the Acts of the Apostles (4:36-37), who sold a piece of
his land and presented the money to the Apostles. First

called Joseph, he was surnamed Barnabas by the Apostles, the new name meaning "son of encouragement." He ranks as an Apostle because of his close collaboration with Paul, notably at Antioch and Jerusalem. He is said to have been martyred in Cyprus. His feast is June 11.

Luke. Though not one of the Twelve named by Matthew, Luke is considered an Apostle by virtue of his close association with the apostolic college. As author of the Third Gospel and the Acts of the Apostles, he is the largest single contributor to the New Testament. His origins were Greek, and he was a physician by profession. He played a prominent role in the early church as a missionary companion of Paul. He was neither bishop nor priest. His Christmas narrative is so rich in detail that it is speculated his source was Mary herself. He seems to have died a peaceful death, probably in Greece about age 84. His feast is October 18.

Mark. Like Luke, Mark is closely identified with the apostolic college, as author of the second Gospel, as missionary companion of Paul and of Barnabas, and as the probable founder and first bishop of the church at Alexandria. It is speculated that he was a Levite and of a wealthy family, as his mother's house was used both as a gathering place for Christians and as a refuge for Peter after an escape from prison. Mark was martyred in Alexandria, but his relics are said to be in Venice, brought there by Venetian merchants in the 9th century. His feast is April 25.

Rites

Despite the appearance of uniformity in ritual, which use of Latin in the liturgy once conveyed, the Catholic Church is not and never has been a church of a single ritual. Since the church's earliest days, Catholics of various geographical areas have had their own local or national rites—ceremonies and prayers which, though expressions of the same fundamental truths, evolved in special fashion according to the preferences and religious instincts of particular communities of worshippers, and became separate and distinct rites in themselves. As emigration increased with the development of the New World, several of these rites took root across the Atlantic, including Canada and the United States.

One of the distinguishing marks of most of these rites historically was the use of the vernacular in the liturgy, a practice which was to be universalized in the church with Vatican Council II (1962-1965). That same Council cited the equality of rites in the church, saying: "In faithful obedience to tradition, this most sacred Council declares that holy Mother Church holds all lawfully acknowledged rites to be of equal authority and dignity; that she wishes to preserve them in the future and to foster them in every way" (Constitution on the Sacred Liturgy, 4).

The Catholic Church has two dominant rites: the Latin or Roman Rite in the Western Church, and the Eastern Rite(s) of the Eastern Catholic (Uniate) Churches. Both the Roman (Latin) and Eastern Rites have numerous subdivisions; that is, rites within the two main categories of rites.

Latin or Roman Rite. This is the rite which is prevalent in the Western Church. It draws its name from its geographical and liturgical center, which is Rome, and from the language, which from the 3rd Century until Vatican Council II, dominated its liturgy—Latin. Despite widespread use of the vernacular now in the Western Church, Latin remains the official language of the rite, and is the language commonly used for Vatican ceremonies and documents. It is the largest and the dominant rite of the Catholic Church.

There are several smaller rites within the Western Church, namely:

• *Ambrosian Rite,* an independent rite peculiar to the Archdiocese of Milan, in Italy;

• *Mozarabic Rite,* another independent rite in use in the Archdiocese of Toledo, in Spain;

• *Lyonnais Rite,* a diocesan rite centered in Lyons, France;

• *Braga Rite,* a rite fixed in the Archdiocese of Braga, in Portugal;

• *Monastic Rites,* or rites associated with religious orders, notably the Dominicans, Carthusians and Carmelites.

The preservation of these rites was insured by Pope Pius V's bull of July 19, 1570, *Quo Primum,* allowing the continuance of any rite which could prove an existence of two centuries.

Eastern Rite(s). The Eastern Church has five principal rites, serving the Byzantine, Chaldean, Coptic, Syrian, Maronite, Armenian and Malabar Uniate Churches, with their more than 12-million communicants. The rites are as follows:

• *Byzantine Rite.* This is the largest rite after the Latin or Roman Rite. It draws its name from the old city of Byzantium, later Constantinople, and now Istanbul, and is based on the rite of St. James of Jerusalem and the churches of Antioch. The rite was subsequently reformed by Saints Basil and John Chrysostom. The rite embraces Catholic Uniate Bulgarians, Albanians, Byelorussians (White Russians), Georgians, Greeks, Hungarians, Italo-Albanians, Melkites, Romanians, Russians, Ruthenians (Carpatho-Russians), Slovaks, Ukranians (Galician Ruthenians), Yugoslavs, Serbs and Croatians.

• *Alexandrian Rite.* This rite draws its name from the city of Alexandria in Egypt. Certain of its liturgical forms are from the Byzantine Rite, while others derive from the liturgies of Saints Mark, Cyril and Gregory of Nazianzen. The rite comprises in the main Egyptian

Copts and Ethiopian Uniates located in Ethiopia, Eritrea, Somalia and Jerusalem.

• *Antiochene Rite.* This rite features liturgies originally associated with the Patriarchate of Antioch, in what is now southern Turkey. Its beginnings are found in the eighth book of the *Apostolic Constitutions*, a 4th-Century collection of treatises on Christian worship, doctrine and discipline. The rite experienced development through the liturgy of St. James of Jerusalem. Members include Uniate Syrians, Maronites and Malankarese (of India).

• *Armenian Rite.* This rite embraces Uniate Armenians, and has jurisdiction in the Near East, Europe, Africa, the Americas and Austral-asia. The language of the rite is classical Armenian, but the liturgical form is that of the older Byzantine Rite, with incorporations from the Antiochene Rite.

• *Chaldean Rite.* This rite comprises Chaldean Uniates descended from Nestorians who returned to unity with Rome in the 17th Century, and Syro-Malabarese, descendants of Christians evangelized by St. Thomas in India. The Chaldeans are located across the Middle East, Europe, the Americas and Africa; the Syro-Malabarese are located mainly in India's Malabar region. The liturgy of the rite derives from the Antiochene.

With the exception of the Maronites, the Uniate communities are counterparts of separated Eastern Christian groups. The Maronites have been in communion with Rome since their community formed around monasteries founded by St. John Maro, a Syrian monk who died in the 5th Century.

The Papacy

The chief figure in the Catholic Church is the pope. The pope has several titles, including sole Patriarch of the

Western Church, but it is as Bishop of Rome that he is head of the Catholic Church. For, it is as Bishop of Rome that he is the successor of the Apostle Peter and, in turn, the person who is the direct historical link to Jesus Christ.

The word "pope" derives from the Greek word *papas*, meaning father. Catholics reserve the name for the pope, as they regard him as the father of the Christian family. The pope enjoys jurisdiction over the entire Catholic Church and its members. He is the church's supreme teacher, its supreme legislator, its supreme judge. Though in recent years the authority of the papacy has been shared through more direct consultation with the College of Cardinals and frequent convoking of Synods of Bishops, the pope's authority remains virtually total in matters pertaining to belief, to discipline and to government of the church—although, as a practical matter, many details of at least discipline and government are delegated to the various Vatican congregations or departments of the Curia, the church's central administrative body.

Election of a Pope. Current regulations concerning the election of a pope were promulgated by Pope Paul VI in the apostolic constitution *Romano Pontifici Eligendo* of Oct. 1, 1975. The principal provisions are that a new pope be elected by a two-thirds plus one majority vote of the College of Cardinals; that the vote be taken at a secret conclave or meeting convened between 15 and 20 days after the death of the predecessor pope; that the participating or voting prelates number no more than 120, and that they be under the age of 80. In other words, cardinals aged 80 or older are excluded from voting in a papal election.

Papal elections take place at the Vatican, in secluded quarters and in great secrecy. The custom is for the counting of two votes each morning and afternoon until one of the candidates receives the designated majority. Traditionally the success or failure of a vote in producing a new pope was signaled by the color of the smoke emanating from a small chimney leading from the stove where the ballots were burned—white for success; black for failure. The system was unreliable, and often led to confusion as to whether there was a new pope or not.

Word of the election of a new pope speeds rapidly beyond the conclave, probably being out before the assembled cardinals have themselves completed the mandatory pledge of obedience to the new pope. However, the name of the new pope is not known formally and widely until it is proclaimed by the senior cardinal deacon from the main balcony of the Vatican. The proclamation is made in Latin, the official language of the Church, and begins *Habemus Papam*—"We have a pope." The new pope then steps forward and imparts his blessing, *Urbi et Orbi*—"to the City and to the World."

In theory, anyone is eligible to become pope, cleric or layman. The elevation of a layman to the papacy is not unknown in Christian history; Pope Leo VIII, 963-965, was a layman. But as Leo VIII's dates indicate, the possibility belonged to another age, and is today pretty much the stuff of fiction; e.g., *Hadrian the Seventh* by Frederick Baron Corvo, the literary curiosity that first appeared in 1904 and that has been in and out of print since. The College of Cardinals elects from its own. In all probability the one elected is already a bishop, but if he is not, regulations call for his ordination as a bishop before receiving the pledge of obedience and being formally proclaimed as pope.

In difficult cases, where the cardinals are unable to arrive at a choice for a new pope by ordinary steps, alternative methods are provided, subject to the unanimous agreement of the cardinal-electors. These include election by delegation, whereby a limited number of cardinals (nine to 15) make the choice; a change in the majority requirement, from two thirds plus one to a simple majority of one; a narrowing of the candidates to the two who received the largest number of votes, short of the required majority, in the most recent balloting.

A possible but unusual election of a new pope is by acclamation, or spontaneous action on the part of the assembled cardinals.

Papal elections are perceived as being under the guidance or inspiration of the Holy Spirit, whatever the method ultimately employed in deciding on the new pope. Election is for life, although a pope may resign if he so chooses. His successor would then be elected in accordance with the foregoing provisions of *Romano Pontifici Eligendo.*

The proceedings of a papal conclave are supposed to remain absolutely secret, and thus there are prohibitions against disclosures and bans on recording machines, listening devices and other technological instruments. It is not impossible, however, for astute Vaticanologists to piece together the story of a papal conclave from scraps of information which inevitably leak from any large and important assembly.

List of the Popes. From the time of Jesus Christ, through the pontificate of John Paul II, there have been 262 popes. There have been some 37 anti-popes or false claimants to the papacy. The following list of the popes has been constructed from information in the *Annuario Pontificio,* the official yearbook of the Vatican. The exact pontificate years are not certain from the reign of St. Peter through that of Pope St. Eleutherius, the thirteenth pope. Similarly, there is uncertainty about the precise dates (months and days) of pontificates to the middle of the 11th century. In listing nationalities of the popes, the liberty is taken of locating many according to current geographical definition. For instance, Italy was a region of city-states before its consolidation in the 19th century; rather than identifying certain papal nationalities by what are now cities, these popes are identified either as Roman or Italian. Antipopes and false claimants are indicated by asterisks.

Name	Nationality	Dates of Pontificate
1. St. Peter	Galilean	29(?)-67
2. St. Linus	Tuscany	67-76
3. St. Anacletus (Cletus)	Roman	76-88

4.	St. Clement I	Roman	88-97
5.	St. Evaristus	Greek	97-105
6.	St. Alexander I	Roman	105-115
7.	St. Sixtus I	Roman	115-125
8.	St. Telesphorus	Greek	125-136
9.	St. Hyginus	Greek	136-140
10.	St. Pius I	Italian	140-155
11.	St. Anicetus	Syrian	155-166
12.	St. Soter	Italian	166-175
13.	St. Eleutherius	Greek	175-189
14.	St. Victor I	African	189-199
15.	St. Zephyrinus	Roman	199-217
16.	St. Callistus I	Roman	217-222
*	St. Hippolytus	Roman	217-235, Antipope
17.	St. Urban I	Roman	222-230
18.	St. Pontian	Roman	July 21, 230-Sept. 28, 235
19.	St. Anterus	Greek	Nov. 21, 235-Jan. 3, 236
20.	St. Fabian	Roman	Jan. 10, 236-Jan. 20, 250
21.	St. Cornelius	Roman	March 251-June 253
*	Novatian	Roman	251, Antipope
22.	St. Lucius I	Roman	June 25, 253-March 5, 254
23.	St. Stephen I	Roman	May 12, 254-Aug. 2, 257
24.	St. Sixtus II	Greek	Aug. 30, 257-Aug. 6, 258
25.	St. Dionysius	Unknown	July 22, 259-Dec. 26, 268
26.	St. Felix I	Roman	Jan. 5, 269-Dec. 30, 274
27.	St. Eutychian	Italian	Jan. 4, 275-Dec. 7, 283
28.	St. Gaius	Dalmatian	Dec. 17, 283-April 22, 296
29.	St. Marcellinus	Roman	June 30, 296-Oct. 25, 304
30.	St. Marcellus I	Roman	May 27, 308-Jan. 16, 309
31.	St. Eusebius	Greek	April 18, 309-Aug. 17, 309
32.	St. Miltiades	African	July 2, 311-Jan. 11, 314
33.	St. Sylvester I	Roman	Jan. 31, 314-Dec. 31, 335
34.	St. Mark	Roman	Jan. 18, 336-Oct. 7, 336
35.	St. Julius I	Roman	Feb. 6, 337-April 12, 352
36.	Liberius	Roman	May 17, 352-Sept. 24, 366
*	Felix II	Roman	(?) 355-Nov. 22, 365, Antipope
37.	St. Damasus I	Spanish	Oct. 1, 366-Dec. 11, 384
*	Ursinus	Roman	366-367, Antipope
38.	St. Siricius	Roman	Dec. 15, 384-Nov. 26, 399
39.	St. Anastasius I	Roman	Nov. 27, 399-Dec. 19, 401
40.	St. Innocent I	Italian	Dec. 22, 401-March 12, 417

41. St. Zosimus	Greek	March 18, 417-Dec. 26, 418
42. St. Boniface I	Roman	Dec. 28, 418-Sept. 4, 422
* Eulalius	Roman	418-419, Antipope
43. St. Celestine I	Italian	Sept. 10, 422-July 27, 432
44. St. Sixtus III	Roman	July 31, 432-Aug. 19, 440
45. St. Leo I (the Great)	Italian	Sept. 29, 440-Nov. 10, 461
46. St. Hilary	Sardinian	Nov. 19, 461-Feb. 29, 468
47. St. Simplicius	Italian	March 3, 468-March 10, 483
48. St. Felix III (II)[1]	Roman	March 13, 483-March 1, 492
49. St. Gelasius I	African	March 1, 492-Nov. 21, 496
50. Anastasius II	Roman	Nov. 24, 496-Nov. 19, 498
51. St. Symmachus	Sardinian	Nov. 22, 498-July 19, 514
* Lawrence	Roman	498; 501-5, Antipope
52. St. Hormisdas	Italian	July 20, 514-Aug. 6, 523
53. St. John I	Italian	Aug. 13, 523-May 18, 526
54. St. Felix IV (III)	Italian	July 12, 526-Sept. 22, 530
55. Boniface II	Roman	Sept. 22, 530-Oct. 17, 532
* Dioscorus	Alexandrian	Sept. 22, 530-Oct. 14, 530, Antipope
56. John II	Roman	Jan. 2, 533-May 8, 535
57. St. Agapitus I	Roman	May 13, 535-April 22, 536
58. St. Silverius[2]	Campanian	June 1, 536-Nov. 11, 537
59. Vigilius	Roman	March 29, 537-June 7, 555
60. Pelagius I	Roman	April 16, 556-March 4, 561
61. John III	Roman	July 17, 561-July 13, 574
62. Benedict I	Roman	June 2, 575-July 30, 579
63. Pelagius II	Roman	Nov. 26, 579-Feb. 7, 590
64. St. Gregory I (the Great)	Roman	Sept. 3, 590-March 12, 604
65. Sabinian	Italian	Sept. 13, 604-Feb. 22, 606
66. Boniface III	Roman	Feb. 19-Nov. 12, 607
67. St. Boniface IV	Italian	Aug. 25, 608-May 8, 615

[1]This Pope Felix should actually be Felix II, and his namesakes should be renumbered accordingly. The misnumbering of the Felix popes resulted from the erroneous insertion in some papal lists of St. Felix of Rome, a martyr.

[2]Silverius did not die as pope. Caught between contending political pressures, he was violently deposed, and banished to the island of Palmaria, where his resignation from the papacy was extorted from him on Nov. 11, 537. He died the next month, the victim of oppression and starvation. The Church honors Silverius as a martyr.

68. St. Deusdedit I (Adeodatus I)	Roman	Oct. 19, 615-Nov. 8, 618
69. Boniface V	Italian	Dec. 23, 619-Oct. 25, 625
70. Honorius I	Italian	Oct. 27, 625-Oct. 12, 638
71. Severinus	Roman	May 28-Aug. 7, 640
72. John IV	Dalmatian	Dec. 24, 640-Oct. 12, 642
73. Theodore I	Greek	Nov. 24, 642-May 14, 649
74. St. Martin I	Italian	July 649-Sept. 16, 655
75. St. Eugene I	Roman	Aug. 10, 654-June 2, 657
76. St. Vitalian	Italian	July 30, 657-Jan. 27, 672
77. Deusdedit II (Adeodatus II)	Roman	April 11, 672-June 17, 676
78. Donus	Roman	Nov. 2, 676-April 11, 678
79. St. Agatho	Sicilian	June 27, 678-Jan. 10, 681
80. St. Leo II	Sicilian	Aug. 17, 682-July 3, 683
81. St. Benedict II	Roman	June 26, 684-May 8, 685
82. John V	Syrian	July 23, 685-Aug. 2, 686
83. Conon	Unknown	Oct. 21, 686-Sept. 21, 687
* Theodore	Roman	687, Antipope
* Paschal	Roman	687, Antipope
84. St. Sergius I	Syrian	Dec. 15, 687-Sept. 8, 701
85. John VI	Greek	Oct. 30, 701-Jan. 11, 705
86. John VII	Greek	March 1, 705-Oct. 18, 707
87. Sisinnius	Syrian	Jan. 15, 708-Feb. 4, 708
88. Constantine	Syrian	March 25, 708-April 9, 715
89. St. Gregory II	Roman	May 19, 715-Feb. 11, 731
90. St. Gregory III	Syrian	March 18, 731-Nov. 741
91. St. Zachary	Greek	Dec. 10, 741-March 22, 752
92. Stephen (II)	Roman	March 23-25, 752
93. Stephen II (III)[3]	Roman	March 26, 752-April 26, 757
94. St. Paul I	Roman	April 29, 757-June 28, 767
* Constantine II	Italian	June 28, 767-69, Antipope
* Philip	Roman	768, Antipope

---

[3]A Roman named Stephen was elected pope after Zachary, but died three days later before being ordained Bishop of Rome. Another Stephen was then elected, and succeeded as a second Stephen II, since the Stephen who had died had not yet been consecrated Bishop of Rome, a necessary technicality in becoming pope. The first Stephen II is not always reckoned in the list of popes, but his inclusion in some lists makes the parenthetical number necessary in the instance of all succeeding Stephens.

95.	Stephen III (IV)	Sicilian	Aug. 1, 768-Jan. 24, 772
96.	Adrian I	Roman	Feb. 1, 772-Dec. 25, 795
97.	St. Leo III	Roman	Dec. 26, 795-June 12, 816
98.	Stephen IV (V)	Roman	June 22, 816-Jan. 24, 817
99.	Paschal I	Roman	Jan. 25, 817-Feb. 11, 824
100.	Eugene II	Roman	Feb. 824-Aug. 827
101.	Valentine	Roman	Aug.-Sept. 827
102.	Gregory IV	Roman	(?) 827-Jan. 844
*	John	Roman	Jan. 844, Antipope
103.	Sergius II	Roman	Jan. 844-Jan. 27, 847
104.	St. Leo IV	Roman	Jan. 847-July 17, 855
105.	Benedict III	Roman	July 855-April 17, 858
*	Anastasius	Roman	Aug.-Sept. 855, Antipope
106.	St. Nicholas I (the Great)	Roman	April 24, 858-Nov. 13, 867
107.	Adrian II	Roman	Dec. 14, 867-Dec. 14, 872
108.	John VIII	Roman	Dec. 14, 872-Dec. 16, 882
109.	Marinus I	Italian	Dec. 16, 882-May 15, 884
110.	St. Adrian III	Roman	May 17, 884-Sept. 885
111.	Stephen V (VI)	Roman	Sept. 885-Sept. 14, 891
112.	Formosus	Italian	Oct. 6, 891-April 4, 896
113.	Boniface VI	Roman	April 896
114.	Stephen VI (VII)	Roman	May 896-Aug. 897
115.	Romanus	Italian	Aug.-Nov. 897
116.	Theodore II	Roman	Dec. 897
117.	John IX	Italian	Jan. 898-Jan. 900
118.	Benedict IV	Roman	Jan. 900-July 903
119.	Leo V	Italian	July-Sept. 903
*	Christopher	Roman	July 903-Jan. 904, Antipope
120.	Sergius III	Roman	Jan. 29, 904-April 14, 911
121.	Anastasius III	Roman	April 911-June 913
122.	Lando	Italian	July 913-Feb. 914
123.	John X	Italian	March 914-May 928
124.	Leo VI	Roman	May-Dec. 928
125.	Stephen VII (VIII)	Roman	Dec. 928-Feb. 931
126.	John XI	Roman	Feb. 931-Dec. 935
127.	Leo VII	Roman	Jan. 3, 936-July 13, 939
128.	Stephen VIII (IX)	Roman	July 14, 939-Oct. 942
129.	Marinus II	Roman	Oct. 30, 942-May 946
130.	Agapetus II	Roman	May 10, 946-Dec. 955

131. John XII[4]	Roman	Dec. 16, 955-May 14, 964
132. Leo VIII	Roman	Dec. 4, 963-March 1, 965
133. Benedict V	Roman	May 22-June 23, 964
134. John XIII	Roman	Oct. 1, 965-Sept. 6, 972
135. Benedict VI	Roman	Jan. 19, 973-June 974
* Boniface VII[5]	Roman	June-July 974, Antipope
		Aug. 984-July 985, Antipope
136. Benedict VII	Roman	Oct. 974-July 10, 983
137. John XIV	Italian	Dec. 983-Aug. 20, 984
138. John XV	Roman	Aug. 985-March 996
139. Gregory V	German	May 3, 996-Feb. 18, 999
* John XVI	Greek	April 997-Feb. 998, Antipope
140. Sylvester II	French	April 2, 999-May 12, 1003
141. John XVII	Roman	June-Dec. 1003
142. John XVIII	Roman	Jan. 1004-July 1009
143. Sergius IV	Roman	July 31, 1009-May 12, 1012
144. Benedict VIII	Roman	May 18, 1012-April 9, 1024
* Gregory	Roman	1012, Antipope
145. John XIX	Roman	April 1024-1032
146. Benedict IX	Roman	1032-44; 1045; 1047-48
147. Sylvester III	Roman	Jan. 20-Feb. 10, 1045
148. Gregory VI	Roman	May 5, 1045-Dec. 20, 1046
149. Clement II	German	Dec. 24, 1046-Oct. 9, 1047
150. Damasus II	German	July 17-Aug. 9, 1048
151. St. Leo IX	German	Feb. 12, 1049-Apri 19, 1054
152. Victor II	German	April 16, 1055-July 28, 1057
153. Stephen IX (X)	German	Aug. 3, 1057-March 29, 1058

---

[4]This was the young Octavian, who succeeded as pope though not yet 20 years of age. It was he who instituted the custom of a pope taking a new name, selecting for himself that of John. As John XII, he was a scandal to the Church —such that the Emperor Otto I moved for the election of a new pope. Elected then, in 963, was Leo VIII. His election only complicated matters. Leo VIII was a layman in the favor of Otto, and the Romans refused to accept him, electing instead a subdeacon, Benedict, as pope. The problem of rival popes moving in and out of power was not rectified until the election of John XIII in 965. As for John XII, he reportedly was stricken by paralysis in the act of adultery, and died without the sacraments. Liutprand of Cremona adds that he was struck a blow on the temple by the devil.

[5]Neither Benedict VI nor Boniface VII, Antipope, came to happy ends. Benedict ended up in the dungeon of Castle Sant' Angelo, where he was strangled in June of 974. The Antipope Boniface, with two "reigns" to his name, was poisoned in July of 985.

*	Benedict X	Roman	April 5, 1058-Jan. 1059, Antipope
154.	Nicholas II	French	Jan. 24, 1059-July 27, 1061
155.	Alexander II	Italian	Oct. 1, 1061-April 21, 1073
*	Honorius II	Italian	Oct. 28, 1061-1072, Antipope
156.	St. Gregory VII	Italian	April 22, 1073-May 25, 1085
*	Clement III	Italian	June 26, 1080-Sept. 8, 1100
157.	Bl. Victor III	Italian	May 24-1086-Sept. 16, 1087
158.	Bl. Urban II	French	Mar. 12, 1088-July 29, 1099
159.	Paschal II	Italian	Aug. 13, 1099-Jan. 21, 1118
*	Theodoric	Roman	1100, Antipope
*	Albert	Italian	1102, Antipope
*	Sylvester IV	Roman	Nov. 18, 1105-11, Antipope
160.	Gelasius II	Italian	Jan. 24, 1118-Jan. 28, 1119
*	Gregory VIII	French	March 8, 1118-21, Antipope
161.	Callistus II	French	Feb. 2, 1119-Dec. 13, 1124
162.	Honorius II	Italian	Dec. 15, 1124-Feb. 13, 1130
*	Celestine II	Roman	Dec. 1124, Antipope
163.	Innocent II	Roman	Feb. 14, 1130-Jan. 25, 1143
*	Anacletus II	Roman	Feb. 14, 1130-Jan. 25, 1138, Antipope
*	Victor IV	Roman	March 1138-May 29, 1138, Antipope
164.	Celestine II	Italian	Sept. 26, 1143-March 8, 1144
165.	Lucius II	Italian	March 12, 1144-Feb. 15, 1145
166.	Bl. Eugene III	Italian	Feb. 15, 1145-July 8, 1153
167.	Anastasius IV	Roman	July 12, 1153-Dec. 3, 1154
168.	Adrian IV[6]	English	Dec. 4, 1154-Sept. 1, 1159
169.	Alexander III	Italian	Sept. 7, 1159-Aug. 30, 1181
*	Victor IV	Roman	Sept. 7, 1159-April 20, 1164, Antipope
*	Paschal III	Italian	April 22, 1164-Sept. 20, 1168 Antipope
*	Callistus III	Hungarian	Sept. 1168-Aug. 29, 1178 Antipope

[6]This was Nicholas Breakspear, to date the only English pope. He emerged to prominence as a papal legate to Scandinavia, and as pope, through John of Salisbury, he "gave and granted Hibernia to Henry II, the illustrious King of England, to hold by hereditary right." The suggestion exists that because he was born in England, Adrian made Ireland over to the Angevin monarch, but the allegation is said not to merit serious attention.

*	Innocent III	Italian	Sept. 29, 1179-1180, Antipope
170.	Lucius III	Italian	Sept. 1, 1181-Sept. 25, 1185
171.	Urban III	Italian	Nov. 25, 1185-Oct. 20, 1187
172.	Gregory VIII	Italian	Oct. 21-Dec. 17, 1187
173.	Clement III	Roman	Dec. 19, 1187-March 1191
174.	Celestine III	Roman	March 30, 1191-Jan. 8, 1198
175.	Innocent III[7]	Italian	Jan. 8, 1198-July 16, 1216
176.	Honorius III	Roman	July 18, 1216-March 18, 1227
177.	Gregory IX	Italian	March 19, 1227-Aug. 22, 1241
178.	Celestine IV	Italian	Oct. 25-Nov. 10, 1241
179.	Innocent IV	Italian	June 25, 1243-Dec. 7, 1254
180.	Alexander IV	Italian	Dec. 12, 1254-May 25, 1261
181.	Urban IV	French	Aug. 29, 1261-Oct. 2, 1264
182.	Clement IV	French	Feb. 5, 1265-Nov. 29, 1268
183.	Bl. Gregory X	Italian	Sept. 1, 1271-Jan. 10, 1276
184.	Bl. Innocent V	French	Jan. 21-June 22, 1276
185.	Adrian V	Italian	July 11-Aug. 18, 1276
186.	John XXI[8]	Portuguese	Sept. 8, 1276-May 20, 1277
187.	Nicholas III	Roman	Nov. 25, 1277-Aug. 22, 1280
188.	Martin IV	French	Feb. 22, 1281-March 28, 1285
189.	Honorius IV	Roman	April 2, 1285-April 3, 1287
190.	Nicholas IV	Italian	Feb. 22, 1288-April 4, 1292
191.	St. Celestine V	Italian	July 5-Dec. 13, 1294
192.	Boniface VIII	Italian	Dec. 24, 1294-Oct. 11, 1303
193.	Bl. Benedict XI	Italian	Oct. 22, 1303-July 7, 1304
194.	Clement V	French	June 5, 1305-April 20, 1314
195.	John XXII	French	Aug. 7, 1316-Dec. 4, 1334
*	Nicholas V	Italian	May 12, 1328-Aug. 25, 1330, Antipope

---

[7]The pontificate of Innocent III for some marked the apogee of the medieval papacy. Paradoxically it became associated with the nadir of Church involvement with the arts projects of the Works Progress Administration [WPA] in the 1930s, when Catholic officials in Washington charged that a panel titled "Cruelty" by artist Maurice Sterne for the library of the Department of Justice depicted Innocent III and several other clerics countenancing cruelty rather than trying to halt it. The point was pressed because Innocent III convoked Lateran Council IV in 1215, which prohibited trial by ordeal. Catholic objections to the panel prompted one Washington official to comment that "the Holy Inquisition continued unabatedly in its benign career." The panel went up anyway—without fanfare, and without negative public reaction.

[8]This pope was actually the twentieth John, but the number 20 was skipped to correct an error in numerology dating back to the 10th century. The chronology of Johannine popes thus jumps from John XIX to John XXI.

196.	Benedict XII	French	Dec. 20, 1334-April 25, 1342
197.	Clement VI	French	May 7, 1342-Dec. 6, 1352
198.	Innocent VI	French	Dec. 18, 1352-Sept. 12, 1362
199.	Bl. Urban V	French	Sept. 28, 1362-Dec. 19, 1370
200.	Gregory XI	French	Dec. 30, 1370-March 26, 1378
201.	Urban VI	Italian	April 8, 1378-Oct. 15, 1389
202.	Boniface IX	Italian	Nov. 2, 1389-Oct. 1, 1404
203.	Innocent VII	Italian	Oct. 17, 1404-Nov. 6, 1406
204.	Gregory XII	Italian	Nov. 30, 1406-July 4, 1415
*	Clement VII	French	Sept. 20, 1378-Sept. 16, 1394, Avignon Claimant
*	Benedict XIII	Spanish	Sept. 28, 1394-May 23, 1423, Avignon Claimant
*	Alexander V	Greek	June 26, 1409-May 3, 1410, Pisan Claimant
*	John XXIII	Italian	May 17, 1410-May 29, 1415, Pisan Claimant
205.	Martin V	Roman	Nov. 11, 1417-Feb. 20, 1431
206.	Eugene IV	Italian	March 3, 1431-Feb. 23, 1447
*	Felix V	Italian	Nov. 5, 1439-April 7, 1449, Antipope
207.	Nicholas V	Italian	March 6, 1447- March 24, 1455
208.	Callistus III	Spanish	April 8, 1455-Aug. 6, 1458
209.	Pius II	Italian	Aug. 19, 1458-Aug. 15, 1464
210.	Paul II	Italian	Aug. 30, 1464-July 26, 1471
211.	Sixtus IV	Italian	Aug. 9, 1471-Aug. 12, 1484
212.	Innocent VIII	Italian	Aug. 29, 1484-July 25, 1492
213.	Alexander VI[9]	Spanish	Aug. 11, 1492-Aug. 18, 1503
214.	Pius III	Italian	Sept. 22-Oct. 18, 1503
215.	Julius II[10]	Italian	Oct. 31, 1503-Feb. 21, 1513
216.	Leo X	Italian	March 9, 1513-Dec. 1, 1521

---

[9]Alexander VI was the notorious Borgia pope, who is said to have fathered at least six children, four of them by Vanozza dei Catanei. It is also recorded that he maintained a mistress after becoming pope, and that her influence resulted in her brother being named a cardinal. He was Alexander Farnese, later Pope Paul III.

[10]Julius II was the famous warrior pope, but his pontificate was of pivotal importance for art and architecture in Rome. It was Julius who commissioned Bramante to design porticoes, arcades and begin a new St. Peter's. Julius II also set Michelangelo to work on the ceiling of the Sistine Chapel and Raphael on frescoes in the papal apartments. Michelangelo sculpted a statue of Julius and suggested a book for the statue's left hand. "Nay, give me a sword," Julius is said to have replied, "for I am no scholar."

217. Adrian VI[11]	Dutch	Jan. 9, 1522-Sept. 14, 1523
218. Clement VII	Italian	Nov. 19, 1523-Sept. 25, 1534
219. Paul III	Roman	Oct. 13, 1534-Nov. 10, 1549
220. Julius III	Roman	Feb. 7, 1550-March 23, 1555
221. Marcellus II	Italian	April 9-May 1, 1555
222. Paul IV	Italian	May 23, 1555-Aug. 18, 1559
223. Pius IV	Italian	Dec. 25, 1559-Dec. 9, 1565
224. St. Pius V	Italian	Jan. 7, 1566-May 1, 1572
225. Gregory XIII	Italian	May 13, 1572-April 10, 1585
226. Sixtus V	Italian	April 24, 1585-Aug. 27, 1590
227. Urban VII	Roman	Sept. 15-Sept. 27, 1590
228. Gregory XIV	Italian	Dec. 5, 1590-Oct. 16, 1591
229. Innocent IX	Italian	Oct. 29-Dec. 30, 1591
230. Clement VIII	Italian	Jan. 30, 1592-March 3, 1605
231. Leo XI	Italian	April 1-April 27, 1605
232. Paul V	Roman	May 16, 1605-Jan. 28, 1621
233. Gregory XV	Italian	Feb. 9, 1621-July 8, 1623
234. Urban VIII	Italian	Aug. 6, 1623-July 29, 1644
235. Innocent X	Roman	Sept. 15, 1644-Jan. 7, 1655
236. Alexander VII	Italian	April 7, 1655-May 22, 1667
237. Clement IX	Italian	June 20, 1667-Dec. 9, 1669
238. Clement X	Roman	April 29, 1670-July 22, 1676
239. Bl. Innocent XI	Italian	Sept. 21, 1676-Aug. 12, 1689
240. Alexander VIII	Italian	Oct. 6, 1689-Feb. 1, 1691
241. Innocent XII	Italian	July 12, 1691-Sept. 27, 1700
242. Clement XI	Italian	Nov. 23, 1700-March 19, 1721
243. Innocent XIII	Roman	May 8, 1721-March 7, 1724
244. Benedict XIII	Italian	May 29, 1724-Feb. 21, 1730
245. Clement XII	Italian	July 12, 1730-Feb. 6, 1740
246. Benedict XIV	Italian	Aug. 17, 1740-May 3, 1758
247. Clement XIII	Italian	July 6, 1758-Feb. 2, 1769
248. Clement XIV	Italian	May 19, 1769-Sept. 22, 1774
249. Pius VI	Italian	Feb. 15, 1775-Aug. 29, 1799
250. Pius VII	Italian	March 14, 1800-Aug. 20, 1823
251. Leo XII	Italian	Sept. 28, 1823-Feb. 10, 1829
252. Pius VIII	Italian	March 31, 1829-Nov. 30, 1830

---

[11]Britain's Thomas Cardinal Wolsey was King Henry VIII's candidate in this election, but the choice went to Adrian, who heard the news of his elevation while in Spain. His epitaph sums up his attitude towards his election: "Here lies Adrian VI, who thought nothing in life more unfortunate than that he became pope." He was the last non-Italian pope until the election of John Paul II, the Polish pope, in 1978.

253. Gregory XVI	Italian	Feb. 2, 1831-June 1, 1846
254. Pius IX	Italian	June 16, 1846-Feb. 7, 1878
255. Leo XIII	Italian	Feb. 20, 1878-July 20, 1903
256. St. Pius X	Italian	Aug. 4, 1903-Aug. 20, 1914
257. Benedict XV	Italian	Sept. 3, 1914-Jan. 22, 1922
258. Pius XI	Italian	Feb. 6, 1922-Feb. 10, 1939
259. Pius XII	Roman	March 2, 1939-Oct. 9, 1958
260. John XXIII	Italian	Oct. 28, 1958-June 3, 1963
261. Paul VI	Italian	June 21, 1963-Aug. 6, 1978
262. John Paul I	Italian	Aug. 26-Sept. 28, 1978
263. John Paul II	Polish	Oct. 16, 1978-

The Avignon Papacy. From 1309 to 1377, the papacy was located at Avignon, a city in southeast France on the Rhone River. It was a period that carried through all or parts of seven papacies, and is known as the "Babylonian Captivity" of the papacy, though the popes in fact were neither captives nor prisoners of the city. The period began with the election of Clement V, a Frenchman who transformed the national composition of the College of Cardinals within months after election by naming ten cardinals, nine of whom were French. Succeeding Avignon popes followed his example, so that of 133 cardinals created during the Avignon papacy, all but ten were Frenchmen. France thus became something of a natural setting for a headquarters for the Church.

Actually, there was nothing startlingly innovative about papal headquarters being at Avignon instead of Rome, as for 75 years before the move to Avignon popes were strangers to Rome, residing instead in places like Viterbo, Siena, Florence, Anagni, Orvieto, Pisa and Perugia. Also, Innocent IV (1243-1254) lived nearly five years at Lyons and held an Ecumenical Council there (Lyons I in 1245). So did Gregory X (1271-1276) in 1274 (Lyons II).

The location of the papacy in Avignon conferred enormous status on the city, and it became a center of commerce and banking, particularly as agents of prestigious Italian banking houses moved to the city.

Concern over control of the Papal States and the defense of the temporal authority of the pope in Italy induced Urban V (1362-1370) to seek a return of the papacy to Rome, and on Oct. 16, 1367 he did indeed relocate in Rome. The return of the papacy and of the papal court brought an infusion of prosperity to Rome, but neither Urban V nor the Romans were comfortable with one another. When the pope left for Montefiascone in the summer of 1370, rumors circulated that he soon would be returning to France—which he did. On Sept. 5 he sailed for France. He died less than three months later in Avignon.

His successor, Gregory XI (1370-1378), succeeded where Urban had failed. The exhortations of two women, St. Bridgit of Sweden and St. Catherine of Siena, were instrumental in the papacy's return to Rome, but there was also a resolve born in Gregory of the recognition that he had to return to Rome if temporal sovereignty and control of the Papal States were to be retained in the papal office. Gregory XI left Avignon in September, 1376 and, traveling mostly by sea, arrived in Rome in January, 1377.

The Avignon Papacy had come to an end, but it spawned the great Western Schism, which lasted for four decades and subjected the Church to one of its most difficult trials.

The Western Schism. The great Western Schism was a period of politics and passions, which extended from 1378 to 1417, during which Christendom was divided between two and finally three papal obediences, with sympathies generally determined according to whether one was pro-French or anti-French. By some accounts, the schism was not a schism in the formal sense, but rather a "temporary misunderstanding," which found holy people, many subsequently canonized, on contending sides. But if "temporary misunderstanding" it was, it was a grievous one, which developed into a permanent blot on the Church's history.

The schism began with the election of Pope Urban VI on April 8, 1378. The electors were 16 cardinals, 11 of whom were French, four Italian and one Spanish. Urban VI was an Italian, and it is possible that he was elected under pressure from Roman mobs, who reportedly howled outside and around the Vatican, "Elect an Italian or you die." Four months later, the French cardinals declared that Urban had been falsely elected, and a new conclave was convened at Fondi, where, with French cardinals in the dominance and Italian cardinals not voting, Robert of Geneva was elected "pope." He took the name Clement VII. The date was Sept. 20, 1378.

Thus was created a situation of parallel papacies, which continued as the respective principals died, only to be succeeded by parallel popes. Scandal mounted on scandal as pope and antipope hurled excommunications at one another and threats of deposition to the princes.

In 1406 a movement began to have the respective popes —by now Gregory XII in Rome and Benedict XIII in Avignon—resign, thus clearing the way for a united, single election. The effort led to the convoking of a council at Pisa, attended by 24 cardinals, many bishops and some 300 doctors in theology and canon law. Gregory XII and Benedict XIII were summoned to appear before the council, and when they did not they were condemned in absentia for schism, heresy and perjury—and deposed. The Council of Pisa then proceeded to elect its own pope, Peter Philargi, a native of Crete, who was serving as Archbishop of Milan. He took the name Alexander V, and with him Christendom now had three persons claiming to be pope. The number stood at three when Alexander V was succeeded by the Pisan claimant who took the name John XXIII (1410-1415), the very name which Angelo Giuseppe Roncalli was to rehabilitate in 1958.

The Western Schism was finally resolved by the Council of Constance (1414-1418), which was convened irregularly but acquired authority when Gregory XII sent two representatives in 1415 to solemnly convoke it into being. The council deposed John XXIII, dismissed the claims of Benedict XIII, and accepted the resignation of Gregory XII, now 89 years of age. Twenty-three cardinals and prelates representing the nations of Italy, France, England, Germany and Spain then proceeded to elect Oddone Colonna, a Roman cardinal, who took the name Martin V.

There was a brief threat of a return to schism, when in 1439, the remnants of the Council of Basle elected as "pope" a man who had given up his kingdom for life as a contemplative, Amadeus VIII, Duke of Savoy. Amadeus took the name Felix V, but managed to obtain only small recognition in Europe. In 1449 he resigned his claim, for which he was rewarded with a pension, the rank of cardinal-bishop, and first place in the church after the pope himself, now Nicholas V. The Felix episode ended the Church's unhappy history of antipopes.

The Leadership

For many years the hierarchical structure of the Catholic Church was conceived as something of a pyramid, authority coursing from the pope at its pinnacle through widening levels of leadership to the laity, who formed a broad base for the ranks and orders which existed above them. The concept has been challenged of late, as lay persons have been invested with authority which is unique, certainly so far as the modern history of the church is concerned. Nevertheless, the church remains a closely organized society, where powers are defined according to rank and where rank, in turn, has its prerogatives. The laity may be "emerged," but the church is still firmly in the hands of the ordained and those in formal religious vows. The principal authority figure in Catholicism is, of course, the pope. Others follow in roughly descending order, namely:

Cardinals. Next to the pope, cardinals are the principal figures of the church. They are the pope-makers—which is to say that it is they who elect the pope. Theoretically they comprise the highest governing body of the Catholic Church, but since they are scattered throughout the world, their main task is the election of a new pope when the papacy falls vacant. This is so, despite efforts by recent popes to involve the cardinals as a collective group in policy matters of the Vatican; for instance, the calling together of the cardinals in 1979 to discuss the problem of budget deficits at the Vatican. For many centuries the new pope has been chosen from the ranks of the cardinals.

Cardinals are known as "Princes of the Church" and as a group they comprise what is known as the Sacred College of Cardinals. The term cardinal has been in use at least since the end of the 5th century, though it was not until the 12th century that the College of Cardinals acquired its present form and that its categories of membership were formalized under Pope Alexander III (1159-1181). These categories of membership are three:

• *Cardinal bishops.* They are the titular bishops of the six suburban sees of Rome (Ostia and Velletri, Porto and Santa Rufina, Albano, Frascati, Palestrina and Sabina) and the Eastern patriarchs. The dean of the College of Cardinals holds title to the titular see of Ostia, as well as to his other suburban see. The cardinal bishops of the six suburban sees of Rome hold full-time posts in the Roman Curia.

• *Cardinal priests.* Historically this title applied to prelates in charge of the leading churches of Rome. Today it designates those members of the college whose dioceses are outside Rome.

• *Cardinal deacons.* Formerly this title was bestowed on prelates in charge of the seven regional divisions of Rome. Today it defines titular bishops assigned to full-time posts in the Roman Curia.

Canon 351 of the new Code of Canon Law limits membership in the College of Cardinals to men who have at least been ordained to the presbyterate (priesthood).

There is, however, nothing in Catholic doctrine or in Catholic dogma which precludes lay persons from receiving the honor. It is reported that Pope Paul VI actually wanted to bestow the red hat on Jacques Maritain (1882-1973), the French philosopher and diplomat, but that Maritain refused. Present policy calls for a new cardinal to be ordained a bishop—that is, if he is not already one upon being named, which is rare. An exception to this rule was extended to the French Jesuit, Cardinal Henri de Lubac (1896-   ), who thought the practice bad theology. When he was named a cardinal in 1983, it was with papal permission to decline ordination as a bishop.

The number of cardinals has varied over the centuries. In 1586, Pope Sixtus V (1585-1590) set the number of cardinals at 70, but Pope John XXIII (1958-1963) set aside that rule, and the number of cardinals has risen dramatically since. In 1973, Pope Paul VI (1963-1978) raised the College of Cardinals to 145 members, and in 1985 Pope John Paul II brought the number to 152.

Age restrictions apply, however, according to the terms of Paul VI's apostolic letter *Ingravescentem aetatem* of November 21, 1970. At age 80, cardinals are no longer eligible to vote in papal elections, though they do remain members of the College of Cardinals with other rights and privileges. The number of cardinals entitled to participate in a papal election is restricted to 120, and full, active membership in the college is controlled accordingly. In other words, the calculation of vacancies in the college is governed by the age-80 mark. Under present policy there may be no more than 120 members under that age, however many there are who are older. At age 75, cardinals in charge of Curia and Vatican City offices are expected to submit their resignations from office to the pope, as are bishops throughout the world. At age 80, they automatically cease to be members of curial departments and offices.

Cardinals quite literally are creatures of the pope. They are named personally by him, and invested by him at a public or extraordinary consistory, though there are exceptions. Occasionally a pope will name a cardinal *in pectore;* that is, "in the breast" or secretly. Usually such appointments are governed by political considerations. The political climate of a particular country, for instance, may dictate considerations of tact or prudence about making public the name of the person honored. A cardinal *in pectore* has no title, rights or duties until such time as his appointment is made public. Once public announcement is made, the individual's seniority or precedence dates back to his secret selection.

The tendency in recent pontificates has been to internationalize the College of Cardinals, a move which in effect reduces the influence of Italian cardinals, while increasing the visibility, if not also the influence of Church leaders from third-world countries.

Patriarchs. Patriarch is an ecclesiastical title, which originates in the Eastern Church. The name derives from the Greek for father or chief of a race, clan or family, and the title designates a prelate who is second only to the pope within his particular jurisdiction. Elsewhere, cardinals have generally taken precedence over patriarchs since the reign of Pope Eugene IV (1431-1447), although on occasion this precedence has been blurred.

Originally, Canon Law identified only three bishops as patriarchs: those of Alexandria and Antioch in the East, and of Rome in the West. (To this day, one of the titles of the pope is as Patriarch of the West.) Later the bishops of Constantinople and Jerusalem were added to the list, with the bishop of Constantinople being ranked second only to the pope. Later again, the number increased further, both with the development of various rites and the formation of uniate churches.

The Eastern Rite patriarchs are those of Alexandria, for the Copts; three of Antioch, for the Syrians, Maronites and Greek and Catholic Melkites; of Babylonia, for the Chaldeans; and of Sis or Cicilia, for the Armenians—although the latter two patriarchs are more properly called *Katholikos,* prelates delegated for a universality of causes.

Patriarchs are elected by bishops of their particular rites, and are confirmed in office by the pope, from whom they receive the pallium (vestment) symbolic of their office. Latin Rite patriarchs were established at the time of the Crusades for Antioch, Jerusalem, Alexandria and Constantinople, but only one—that of Jerusalem—survives with jurisdiction. The others passed first to the status of titular patriarchs, then in 1964 were abolished entirely. Their existence had long been a matter of contention.

"Minor" patriarchates developed in the Latin Rite of the West—of Lisbon, Venice, the East Indies and, with the discovery of the Americas, of the West Indies. (In 1520, a Patriarch of the West Indies was created from among the Spanish clergy.) Similarly, bishops of Lyons, Bourges, Canterbury, Toledo and Pisa have at times been called patriarchs, although with this latter group the title was more honorary than canonically real. "Minor" patriarchates which survive (Lisbon, Venice, the East Indies) are now merely titular—which is to say, they survive in name only. The Patriarchate of the West Indies may be entirely a thing of the past; it has been vacant since 1963.

Archbishops and Bishops. The Catholic Church is divided into jurisdictional sees, called archdioceses and dioceses. An archdiocese is the principal see of a particular area, or province. Linked to it are so-called suffragan sees or dioceses. Together with the archdiocese they make up a province. Within a province are several layers of leadership, as follows:

• *Archbishop:* the title of a bishop who heads an archdiocese.

• *Metropolitan Archbishop:* the title of the head of the principal see in an ecclesiastical province. He has full episcopal powers in his own see, and certain supervisory jurisdiction over suffragan sees of the region.

• *Archbishop ad personam:* a personal title or distinction conveyed to some bishops, who do not have jurisdiction over an archdiocese.

- *Primate:* a title of honor held by the ranking bishop of a country or region.
- *Diocesan Bishop:* a bishop in charge of a diocese.
- *Coadjutor Bishop:* an assistant bishop to a diocesan bishop, with right of succession to the see.
- *Auxiliary (Titular) Bishop:* an assistant bishop to a diocesan bishop, with no rights of succession. They are given titual titles to sees which formerly existed, but now exist only in name.
- *Episcopal Vicar:* an assistant, not necessarily a bishop, designated by a bishop as his deputy for a region of his diocese.
- *Eparch, Exarch:* the titles of bishops of Eastern Rite churches.
- *Vicar Apostolic:* a bishop who is head of a missionary territory. As a rule he is a titular bishop.
- *Prefect Apostolic:* a clergyman with ordinary jurisdiction over a missionary territory.
- *Apostolic Administrator:* the temporary administrator of an ecclesiastical jurisdiction. He is usually a bishop, although not necessarily so.
- *Vicar General:* a bishop's deputy in the administration of a diocese or archdiocese. He may or may not be a bishop.
- *Monsignor:* a honorary title designating prelates of the pontifical household; that is, those singled out for papal recognition for their services to the church. Traditionally there were three ranks of monsignor: Prothonotary Apostolic, Domestic Prelate and Papal Chamberlain, the first two entitled to be called "right reverend" and the third "very reverend." In recent years the ranks were reorganized and titles simplified. Honorary prelates are now Apostolic Prothonotaries, Honorary Prelates of His Holiness the Pope, and Chaplains of His Holiness the Pope. Their common title is Reverend Monsignor. Many dioceses, including in the United States, have abandoned the practice of nominating clergymen to the ranks of monsignor, re-

garding the office as a relic of the church's age of triumphalism.

Choosing Bishops. The selection of bishops is theoretically made by the pope, but in practice a series of steps is followed, with the pope often certifying decisions actually made on other levels of administration. In the United States, the policy is for bishops to submit nominations to the metropolitan archbishop. Nominations are then considered at a meeting of the province's bishops, and the names of those receiving a favorable vote are forwarded to the office of the pronuncio in Washington, D.C., for transmission to the Sacred Congregation for Bishops at the Vatican. Official selection then follows. In proposing nominations to the episcopacy, bishops are free to consult priests, religious and laity.

Diocesan bishops, including archbishops, are required to make a periodic visit, generally every five years, to the Holy See for an audience with the pope, consultation with Vatican officials, and a visit to the tombs of SS. Peter and Paul. At this time a written report is made on conditions within their jurisdictions. This is known as the Ad Limina visit—*ad limina* meaning in Latin "to the threshold" of the Apostles.

Priests, Nuns, Brothers. The work of ministering and administering the church is advanced further by priests, sisters (nuns), religious brothers, permanent deacons, and of course lay persons who are employed either in professional or volunteer capacities.

• *Priest* is a person (male, according to the present discipline) in Holy Orders, ordained to carry out the mission of the church in both the spiritual and temporal realms. The chief supernatural powers of a priest are to celebrate Mass (and thus change bread and wine into the body and blood of Christ) and to forgive sins. In addition, he may be teacher, social worker, journalist or a host of other things in the church's broad mission to humankind.

A priest may be a member of a diocese or a religious order. A recent statistical yearbook shows a total of 408,945 priests throughout the world, 254,797 of whom are diocesan priests and 154,148 religious order priests. Religious order priests are usually specialists in some particular apostolate, such as education or evangelization. Diocesan priests are generalists in the sense that they minister to people in their everyday lives and living situations.

Parish priests (pastors) are those in charge of a defined area of an archdiocese or diocese. They receive their orders and jurisdiction from the archbishop or bishop, and are responsible to him. Their area of control is known as a parish. In larger parishes, the parish priest (pastor) will have assistants or curates.

A development since Vatican Council II (1962-1965) in some parishes has been the abandonment of the traditional pastor/curate arrangement for what is called team ministry, or the collegial management of parishes. Under this arrangement, decisions are generally arrived at by vote or consensus, so that there is less chance of parishes being autocratic institutions under the dominance of a single person. Also contributing to the collegial aspect of parishes is the introduction since Vatican II of elected parish councils, comprising religious and lay members of the parish.

Theoretically, a priest is ordained for life, but a priest can be returned to the status of a lay person through the process known as laicization. The process is controlled by the Holy See. Shortly after assuming the papacy in 1978, Pope John Paul II suspended laicization procedures in the light of the alarming number of priests seeking to be laicized. In 1980, he reinstated these procedures, but with guidelines that sharply limited the number of dispensations from what had been the case under Pope Paul VI (1963-1978). In the 1970s thousands of priests laicized, many of them in order to marry. Their actions put pressure on the church to ease the requirement of celibacy for priests (the vow of celibacy is actually taken when a man is received into the subdiaconate), but several times since the Holy See has affirmed celibacy as the glory of the church.

• *Brother* is a member of a religious community, who is in vows but not in Holy Orders; in others words, he is not a priest. There are 70,621 brothers in the world (1981 statistics)—some members of clerical communities (communities whose membership is predominantly composed of priests; e.g., the Jesuits); some members of non-clerical or lay institutes, generally known as brotherhoods (e.g., Christian Brothers, Marist Brothers, Xaverian Brothers, etc.). Brothers, who are celibate, engage in a variety of apostolates, such as education and medical work. They are individuals with distinct vocations, who are called to ministry but not to Holy Orders. At one time, brothers in "mixed communities"—that is, where the number of priests dominated—were relegated to a kind of second-class status, being the cooks, gardeners, porters and the like of the community. This has come to be less and less the case, however, as communities have moved to a peer relationship embracing all members. Some orders have reinforced the status of their brother-members by including them in a common identifying title; e.g., the Claretian Fathers and Brothers. In the instance of clerical communities, the Holy See still requires that its leaders be clerical. Brothers, properly speaking, are laymen, though they often perform similar ministries as deacons.

• *Sister* is a female religious, and there are 952,043 of them throughout the world (1981 statistics), occupied in a variety of apostolates, including teaching, nursing, social work, etc. At one time, a distinction was made between sister and nun, but now the words are used interchangeably. (See SISTER/NUN in miscellanea section.) Sisters are in vows, but, as with the case of brothers, they are much more easily dispensed from these vows than are priests. There has been a dramatic drop in the number of sisters in recent years, notably in the United States. In 1966, there were some 182,000 sisters in the United

States; in 1981, their number was down to 122,600, a decline of 31 percent. Worldwide, the drop in sisters during the same period was roughly 25 percent.

• *Permanent deacon* is an ancient office restored in the church in 1967 by way of returning the emphases originally associated with the diaconate. (See PERMANENT DEACON in miscellanea section.) There are 8,647 permanent deacons in the world (1981 statistics), most of them in the Americas. Permanent deacons may preach and perform a variety of liturgical ministries, such as officiating at baptisms, weddings, wakes and funerals. In general, their service is to a diocese or parish. Their role is expected to become more prominent, particularly if there is a continuing shortage in the number of vocations to the priesthood.

The Church of Rome

The center of the Catholic Church is a tiny city-state that is situated entirely within the city of Rome. This is the State of Vatican City, occupying precisely 108.7 acres of land and comprising about 1,000 citizens, the most prestigious of whom is the pope. The pope is the ruler of Vatican City, and through this office flows the temporal power complementing the spiritual power which the pope holds as the religious leader of the world's Catholics.

The pope has resided at the Vatican since 1377, or for more than six centuries. From 1309-1377, the pontifical court was at Avignon, in France. Before that, the papal see was headquartered in the main at the Lateran in Rome's piazza di S. Giovanni in Laterano. The Basilica of St. John in the Lateran is the cathedral church of Rome, and accordingly, the cathedral church of the pope as Bishop of Rome.

The State of Vatican City is the world's smallest nation. Though no larger than a small Iowa farm, it is nonetheless as sovereign as any of the world's largest powers. It functions with its own code of laws and government, its own import and export regulations, and its own safety and security forces—members of the latter colorfully attired in period uniforms. For instance, the Swiss Guards, the group charged with the personal safety of popes since 1506, wear bright red, yellow and blue uniforms designed by Michelangelo more than 400 years ago; traffic officers dress in early 19th-century Napoleonic uniforms.

Extraterritorial rights of the Vatican extend to more than 10 buildings in the city of Rome—mostly churches and office buildings of various Vatican congregations of its central Curia—as well as to the papal villa at Castel Gandolfo, 15 miles to the southeast. Castel Gandolfo serves as the summer residence of the pope.

Vatican Diplomatic Corps. The State of Vatican City maintains formal diplomatic relations with some 110 nations of the world, among them Finland, Ireland, Great Britain, Gabon, Greece, Sweden, Morocco, Panama, Zimbabwe and the United States. Some Marxist governments exchange diplomatic representatives with the Vatican, but as of 1985, Yugoslavia was the only purely Communist country to do so. The USSR, Peoples Republic of China, Hungary, Czechoslovakia and Poland, for instance, are not represented at the Vatican. Lithuania was represented by a first secretary.

Vatican ambassadors are designated either apostolic nuncios or pronuncios. The rank of apostolic nuncio is equivalent to that of ambassador extraordinary and plenipotentiary, and the nuncio is considered the dean of the diplomatic corps in the country to which he is accredited. To avoid diplomatic complications, nuncios are assigned only to predominantly Catholic countries. To countries which are not predominantly or officially Catholic, the Vatican sends a pronuncio. For instance, Ireland receives a nuncio; the United States a pronuncio.

Nations which have no diplomatic relations with the Vatican are assigned, where possible, an apostolic delegate. Though an apostolic delegate is a papal representative, he has no diplomatic status. His function is to serve as an intermediary between the pope, as spiritual head of the Catholic Church, and Catholics of a particular country as members of that church. It was through an apostolic delegate that the Vatican maintained contacts with Catholics of the United States during the years that there was no official exchange of diplomats between the two.

On other levels of diplomacy, the Vatican assigns permanent observers, delegates or special envoys to quasi-governmental and non-governmental international organizations, among others the United Nations, the United Nations Educational, Scientific and Cultural Organization (UNESCO), Council of Europe, Organization of American States, Universal Postal Union, International Committee for the Neutrality of Medicine, International Alliance on Tourism and World Medical Association.

Diplomatic Relations with the United States. From 1797 to 1848, United States' consuls were posted to the Papal States. In 1848, President James Knox Polk upgraded American representation to that of a mission, and resident ministers were posted until 1867, when the mission was closed after Congress failed to appropriate funds for its continuation.

In 1939, President Franklin Delano Roosevelt sent a personal representative, Myron C. Taylor, to the Vatican, and Mr. Taylor continued to serve during the presidency of Harry Truman. President Truman, in 1951, proposed that an ambassador of full diplomatic rank be sent to the Vatican and he offered the name of General Mark Clark, who had commanded the Fifth United States Army in Italy during World War II. The proposal met with intense opposition both on religious and constitutional grounds, and never materialized.

Presidents after Truman continued to name personal representatives to the Vatican. Then, in 1983, President Ronald Reagan broached anew the subject of formal diplomatic representation, this time successfully. On January 10, 1984, formal ties which had been severed 117 years before, were renewed, now on the ambassadorial level. William A. Wilson, who had been serving as Mr. Reagan's personal representative at the Vatican since 1981, was named ambassador, and the Vatican correspondingly upgraded its apostolic delegate to the Catholic Church in the United States, Archbishop Pio Laghi, to the rank of pronuncio.

The White House announced that it had taken the step to establish diplomatic relations with the Vatican and the pope in order to improve communications at a time when papacy and pope had become increasingly involved in international affairs.

Origins of the State of Vatican City. As a modern city-state, the Vatican dates only from 1929. However, its history as an independent territory traces back to the 8th century, when the papacy claimed independence for papal lands and properties. From the year 755 until the unification of the Italian peninsula in 1870 into a single country, popes controlled up to 18,000 square miles of central peninsula area. They maintained large fighting armies, which were sometimes led into battle by the pope himself. As an example, Pope Julius II (1503-1513) arranged the cannon positions during the seige of Mirandola in 1511, and is said to have amazed the troops with his courage in the face of great danger.

The military power of the papacy ended in 1870, when the forces for a united Italy under Guiseppe Garibaldi captured Rome and declared the peninsula a united kingdom under Victor Emmanuel. Pope at the time was Pius IX (1846-1878), and he so intensely disapproved of the absorption of the Papal States into the new Italy that he shut himself up in the walled section of Rome on the west bank of the Tiber River, known as the Vatican. For 59 years, he and succeeding popes regarded themselves as "prisoners of the Vatican," and refused to step beyond the bounds of St. Peter's Basilica and a small group of surrounding buildings. The situation created an impasse and spawned what became known as the Roman question, which was not settled until the signing of the Lateran Concordat of 1929. Pope at the time was Pius XI (1922-1939), while the government of Italy was headed by the Fascist dictator, Benito Mussolini. Under terms of the agreement, the Vatican received 1,750-million lira (the equivalent at the time of $100-million American dollars) in recompense for the taking over of the Papal States, and territorial sovereignty over 108.7 acres of land. Thus was born the State of Vatican City.

The Concordat of 1929 contained additional provisions which gave the Vatican extensive control over the morals and mores of Italy, but this power was markedly lessened when the concordat was updated in 1984. Under the Concordat of 1984, Roman Catholicism ceased to be the state religion of Italy, and many hitherto exclusively ecclesiastical prerogatives such as church annulments of marriages, were made subject to state confirmation. Rome lost its official designation as a "holy city," a status which allowed the Vatican to ban plays, books and films in Rome. Further religious instruction, which previously had been compulsory in the schools, became a matter of parental choice.

The Concordat of 1984 reduced greatly the influence of the Catholic Church on civil life in Italy, but in no way was the sovereignty of the State of Vatican City trimmed within its 108.7 acres.

The Curia. The Vatican's central governing body is known as the Curia. It is a network of bureaus (departments or ministries) that evolved over time from synods and advisory assemblies of the clergy, with whom the pope administered church affairs during the first 11 centuries. The Curia as an organized body has its origins in the 12th century, and except for some reforms in 1908, it existed into modern times much as Pope Sixtus V (1585-1590) had constituted it in 1588. In 1963, Pope Paul VI (1963-1978) introduced a four-year reorganization program, which both internationalized and modernized the Curia. The reorganization was formalized in the constitu-

tion *Regimini Ecclesiae Universae,* which was published
August 18, 1967 and took full effect in March, 1968. Further reorganization was implemented in 1975 and 1984.

The Curia today consists of two departments, ten congregations, three tribunals, three secretariats, and a variety of councils, commissions and offices which administer
church affairs under the authority of the pope. It is the
diplomatic arm of the church and its bureaucracy
for preserving doctrine and managing detail on a day-
to-day basis. Following is a brief description of the Curia's
bureaus:

Departments of the Curia

• *Secretariat of State.* This is the main bureau of the
Curia, and its head is both the chief diplomatic officer
under the pope and the coordinator of curial operations.
His functions are roughly similar to those of prime minister in the modern parliamentary state.

• *Council for the Public Affairs of the Church.* Formerly
the Sacred Congregation for Extraordinary Ecclesiastical
Affairs, this department along with the Secretariat of State
coordinates diplomatic and other relations with governments, and supervises nunciatures and apostolic dele-
gations, as well as the Pontifical Commission for Russia,
the latter through the department's Council for the Public
Affairs of the Church.

Congregations

• *Sacred Congregation for the Doctrine of the Faith.* This
is the old Holy Office of the Inquisition, which was

founded in the 13th century to combat heresy. The congregation was renamed in 1965, and efforts were made to correct its negative image through such steps as the abolition of the office for the censorship of books and suppression of the Roman Index of Prohibited Books. Still, the primary purpose of the congregation remains that of orthodoxy. It is charged with the responsibility of safeguarding doctrines of faith and morals.

• *Sacred Congregation for the Oriental Churches.* Its jurisdiction relates to persons and discipline of Eastern Rite Churches, and it has as many offices as there are Oriental or Eastern Rites in communion with the Holy See. It has been an autonomous congregation only since 1917, and is required to consult with the Secretariat for Promoting Christian Unity on matters relating to separated Oriental Churches and with the Secretariat for Non-Christians on those concerning Moslems.

• *Sacred Congregation For Bishops.* Established in 1588, this congregation oversees the establishment and direction of dioceses, provinces, military vicariates and other ecclesiastical jurisdictions. One of its chief functions is the naming of bishops and other prelates. The body was formerly known as the Sacred Consistorial Congregation.

• *Sacred Congregation for the Sacraments.* Instituted in 1908 as the Congregation for the Discipline of the Sacraments, it was reorganized as part of the Congregation for the Sacraments and Divine Worship in 1975, then returned to a separate congregation in 1984. The congregation supervises the discipline of the sacraments.

• *Sacred Congregation for Divine Worship.* This body evolved out of the Congregation of Rites established in 1588. For a time, it was combined with the Congregation for the Discipline of the Sacraments, then in 1984 was reestablished as a separate congregation. Its competence extends to ritual and pastoral aspects of divine worship in Roman and Western Rites.

• *Sacred Congregation for the Causes of Saints.* Established in 1588 as the Congregation of Rites, the congregation deals with beatification and canonization causes, and the preservation of relics. Its latest restructuring was in 1983, when canonization procedures were revised by Pope John Paul II.

• *Sacred Congregation for the Clergy.* Established in 1564 as the Sacred Congregation of the Cardinals Interpreters of the Council of Trent and known later as the Sacred Congregation of the Council, this body is concerned with the persons, work and ministry of clerics (deacons, priests and religious) working in dioceses of the world. Related matters concern priestly spiritual growth and formation, preaching, catechetical emphases, and the temporalities of religious life (living conditions, health insurance, etc.).

• *Sacred Congregation for Religious and Secular Institutes.* Established in 1586 as the Sacred Congregation for Consultations of Regulars, the body was absorbed in 1601 into the Sacred Congregation for Consultations of Bishops and Other Prelates, then made autonomous again in 1908. It was known more recently as the Sacred Congregation of Religious, or for the Affairs of Religious. The body handles matters dealing with institutes of religious, communal religious societies of people without vows, and secular institutes of men and women living in the world and engaged at the same time in a profession of evangelical counsel.

• *Sacred Congregation for Catholic Education.* This is the old Sacred Congregation of Seminaries and Universities. Its history dates back to 1588, with modern functions being defined and refined several times since 1915. In general, the congregation exercises supervision over institutions and works of Catholic education on all levels, including the continuing education of diocesan priests, religious and members of secular institutes. The competency of the congregation extends to Catholic universities and seminaries.

• *Sacred Congregation for the Evangelization of Peoples.* This is the former Sacred Congregation for the Propagation of the Faith. The name change was largely cosmetic. The congregation's work continues to be the directing and coordinating of Catholic missionary work throughout the world.

Tribunals

• *Sacred Apostolic Penitentiary.* A body dating back to the 12th century, this tribunal exercises jurisdiction for the so-called internal forum. The office assumed importance as the practice grew of cases being reserved to the pope or bishops. The tribunal decides on questions of conscience, and also grants absolutions, pardons, dispensations and the like.

• *Apostolic Signature.* This tribunal functions as a kind of supreme court, investigating and resolving petitions of special urgency. It determines the jurisdictional competence of lower Church courts, and is the court of appeal from decisions of the Sacred Roman Rota. The tribunal's history traces back to 1243, and exists in its present form largely as reconstituted in 1908 by Pope St. Pius X (1903-1914).

• *Sacred Roman Rota.* This is the ordinary court of appeal for cases taken to the Holy See. The origin of the name Rota is obscure, but the Rota's history is not obscure. It goes back to the 12th century (the word Rota first occurring in 1336). The tribunal was reshaped by several popes, including in 1908 by Pope St. Pius X (1903-1914) and in 1934 by Pope Pius XI (1922-1939). A primary concern of the Rota is to determine the validity of individual marriage cases.

Secretariats

• *Secretariat for Promoting Christian Unity.* This is an office which grew out of Vatican Council II (1962-1965). It was established by Pope John (1958-1963) in 1960 as a preparatory secretariat, then raised to commission status during the Council's first session. Its status was reconfirmed in 1966 by Pope Paul VI (1963-1978). The secretariat is in charge of relations with other Christian groups, and has offices both for the West and the East. Attached to the secretariat is the Commission for Catholic-Jewish Relations.

• *Secretariat for Non-Christians.* Established by Pope Paul VI in 1964, this agency handles relations with persons who are not Christians, but who profess a religious faith of some kind. Attached to the secretariat is the Commission for Catholic-Moslem Relations.

• *Secretariat for Non-Believers.* Established by Pope Paul VI in 1965, this office deals with the background and philosophy of atheism, and is in charge of dialogue with non-believers.

Councils, Commissions, Offices

A number of pontifical councils, commissions and offices round out the Curia—some minor in importance; others of such significance as one day likely to merit elevation in organizational status. The major ones follow. In most cases their names summarize their focus:

• Council for the Laity
• Commission for Justice and Peace
• Commission for Catholic-Jewish Relations
• Commission for Catholic-Moslem Relations
• Commission for the State of Vatican City
• Commission for Latin America
• Commission for the Authentic Interpretation of the Code of Canon Law
• Commission on Migration and Tourism

- Council for the Family (separate but closely related to the Council for the Laity)
- Commission for the Protection of the Historical and Artistic Monuments of the Holy See
- Commission for the Works of Religion
- Council of Cardinals for the Study of Organizational and Economic Problems of the Holy See
- Theological Commission
- Biblical Commission
- Council on Culture
- Commission for Russia
- Prefecture of the Economic Affairs of the Holy See
- Prefecture of the Pontifical Household
- Central Statistics Office
- Commission for Social Communications
- Cor Unum Council (to coordinate information and services of Catholic aid and human development agencies throughout the world)

Additional divisions of the Curia deal with the Code of Oriental Canon Law; revision and emandation of the Vulgate; archeology, historical science and sacred art in Italy; the ecclesiastical archives of Italy; the preservation of the faith and erection of new churches in Rome; discipline; and the holy sanctuaries of Pompeii, Loreto and Bari.

The office known as the Apostolic Chamber administers the temporalities of the Holy See between the death of one pope and the election of a new pope, while the office for Administration of the Patrimony of the Apostolic See handles the estate of the Apostolic See.

Vatican Museums and Tourist Attractions. More than 4,000 persons work at the Vatican, four times the number of people who actually live there. Most of them are priests and religious. However, thousands more visit the Vatican daily and millions over a year's time—scholars, students, tourists. They come for many reasons: to worship, to study, to do research, to admire masterpieces of art accumulated over many centuries, to see the pope and to receive his blessing.

Papal audiences are held in the Audience Hall, opened in 1971 on the south side of St. Peter's Basilica with accommodations for as many as 12,000 persons, or, weather permitting, in St. Peter's Square, the pope either appearing on his balcony overlooking the square or moving among the people, although not so freely and unshielded since the attempted assassination of Pope John Paul II in 1981.

General papal audiences are scheduled weekly, and may last, depending upon circumstances, from approximately an hour to an hour-and-a-half. Wednesday is audience day. Arrangements are under the supervision of the Prefecture of the Apostolic Household.

Americans seeking admission tickets to general audiences may apply to the Bishops' Office for United States Visitors to the Vatican at the Casa Santa Maria, via dell' Umilita, 30, 00187 Rome.

General audiences are also held at Castel Gandolfo, when the pope is in residence there.

Major attractions at the Vatican are:

• St. Peter's Basilica, built between 1506 and 1626; the largest and, very probably, the most significant church in Christendom.

• The Bernini colonnade, the massive twin structure completed about 1667, which reaches out from St. Peter's like giant arms to enfold the visitor.

• The Vatican Library, one of five, with a collection of 70,000 manuscripts, 770,000 volumes, and 7,500 incunabula.

• The Sistine Chapel, with its famous ceiling painted by Michelangelo, and recently cleaned and restored.

• The Chapel of Nicholas V, featuring paintings by Fra Angelico of St. Stephen, St. Lawrence, the four Evangelists and other saints.

• The Loggias designed by Raphael and painted by his pupils.

• The Church of St. Ann, parish church of residents of Vatican City.

• The Vatican Post Office, where one may purchase Vatican stamps, prized by collectors for the beauty of their design.

• The Vatican Numismatics Office, where Vatican coins are available in denominations of 10, 20, 50, 100, 200, 500 and 1,000 lire.

In addition there are exotic fountains, museums, art galleries, gardens, and other amenities of the modern city. The Vatican has a clinic, pharmacy, bookstore, souvenir shops, astronomical observatory, printing plant (among other products, the daily newspaper *L'Osservatore Romano*), fire department, radio station (with broadcasts in 34 languages), and railway station for the convenience of the pope—though like most other long-distance travelers today, popes now use planes more than they do trains. Vatican City is too small to have its own airport, so departure point for most papal trips is from a commercial airport serving Rome.

Ecumenical Councils

Ecumenical Councils are assemblies of the college of bishops from all over the world, convoked under the presidency of the pope, for purposes of discussing and regulating matters of church doctrine and discipline. As such, Ecumenical Councils are regarded as the mind of the church in action, the *sensus ecclesiae* taking form and shape through discussion and deliberation, and finally being set in place through the promulgation of dogmatic definitions and authoritative decrees, which in turn are binding on the church.

Ecumenical Councils are momentous events in the history of the church. Only 21 have been called, and inevitably they have figured significantly in giving the church its directions through the centuries. The first eight Ecumenical Councils were held in the East; the last 13 in the West. Most of the separated Eastern churches (Orthodoxy) recognize the validity of the first seven councils, but Monophysite Armenians, Syrians and Copts limit recognition to the first three, and Nestorians to the first two.

Following is a brief sketch of the Church's 21 Ecumenical Councils:

1. *Nicaea I* (325). Lasted two months and 12 days, and comprised 318 bishops with Bishop Hosius of Cordova assisting as legate of Pope St. Sylvester. Emperor Constantine was also present. The Council gave formulation to a Nicene Creed; condemned Arianism (which denied the divinity of Christ); fixed the date for Easter; and adopted as the model of the church's organization the civil division of the Empire.

2. *Constantinople I* (381). Lasted three months and brought together 150 bishops under Pope St. Damasus I and Emperor Theodosius I. The council condemned new forms of Arianism, such as Macedonius' impugning of the divinity of the Holy Spirit; added clauses to the Nicene Creed referring to the Holy Spirit (*qui simul adoratur*) and what follows to the end; and designated the Bishop of Constantinople as the ranking prelate of the East, with primacy next to the pope.

3. *Ephesus* (431). Extending over five sessions between June 22 and July 17, it involved more than 200 bishops presided over by St. Cyril of Alexandria representing Pope St. Celestine I. The council condemned Nestorianism (which denied the real unity of the divine and human natures in Christ); condemned Pelagianism (which denied original sin and questioned the means to salvation); and conveyed to Mary the title *Theotokos* (Bearer of God), thus declaring her the Mother of God.

4. *Chalcedon* (451). In session between October 8 and November 1, the council convened 150 bishops under Pope St. Leo the Great and Emperor Marcian. It defined the two natures, divine and human, in Christ, while con-

demning Monophysitism (Eutychianism), which denied Christ's humanity. Eutyches was excommunicated.

5. *Constantinople II* (553). Brought together 165 bishops between May 5 and June 2 under Pope Vigilius and Emperor Justinian I. It condemned the errors of Origen and *The Three Chapters* of Theodoret of Cyrus, Theodore of Mopsuestia and Ibas of Edessa, and it confirmed the first four councils, particularly that of Chalcedon, whose authority was being contested.

6. *Constantinople III* (680-681). Convened under Pope Agatho and Emperor Constantine Pogonatus, the council was attended by the Patriarchs of Constantinople and Antioch, the Emperor and 174 bishops. It condemned Monothelitism (which denied the human will in Christ); defined the two wills (divine and human) in Christ as distinct principles of operation; and censured Pope Honorius I for a letter to Bishop Sergius of Constantinople containing an ambiguous statement relating to the unity of wills in Christ. Several heretics were anathematized.

7. *Nicaea II* (787). Convoked by Emperor Constantine VI and his mother, Empress Irene, under Pope Adrian I, the council sat for eight sessions between September 24 and October 23, and was presided over by legates of Adrian. Between 300 and 367 bishops attended. The council condemned Iconoclasm (which regarded the use of sacred images as idolatrous); condemned Adoptionism (which held Christ to be the Son of God by adoption rather than nature); and regulated the veneration of holy images.

8. *Constantinople IV* (869-870). Convened under Pope Adrian II and Emperor Basil, it comprised 102 bishops, three papal legates and four patriarchs. It condemned an irregular council *(conciliabulum)* summoned by Photius and disposed him as Patriarch of Constantinople, restoring Ignatius to the patriarchate. Photius had called his council in opposition to Pope Nicholas and Ignatius. Photius' schism prevailed in the Greek Church, and no more Ecumenical Councils were held in the East. In fact,

it was not until the end of the 11th Century that Constantinople IV was termed ecumenical by canonists.

9. *Lateran I* (1123). Convened by Pope Callistus II, this was the first Ecumenical Council held in Rome, some 900 bishops and abbots meeting between March 18 and April 6. The council abolished the right of lay princes to investiture with ring and crosier and ecclesiastical benefices; voted reform measures in 25 canons; and focused on the recovery of the Holy Land.

10. *Lateran II* (1139). Convoked by Pope Innocent II, the council brought together some 1,000 prelates and the Emperor Conrad. It met three times in April, and adopted 30 disciplinary measures and canons, one holding holy orders to be an invalidating impediment to marriage. Measures were also adopted to counter the schism involving the antipope Anacletus.

11. *Lateran III* (1179). Convened by Pope Alexander III, Frederick I being emperor, the council met three times between March 5 and 19, with 302 bishops present. It condemned the Waldenses and Albigenses for doctrinal positions relating to the sacramental system, the nature of good and evil, *et al.*, and adopted numerous reforms. One was to provide that popes be elected by a two-thirds vote of the cardinals.

12. *Lateran IV* (1215). Regarded as the most important council of the Middle Ages, Lateran IV was convened by Pope Innocent III and brought together the Patriarchs of Constantinople and Jerusalem, 71 archbishops, 412 bishops, 800 abbots, among others. Seventy important decrees were issued, one defining the term "transubstantiation" and another stipulating the obligation of annual confession and Communion.

13. *Lyons I* (1245). Presided over by Pope Innocent IV, the council included three patriarchs, 140 bishops; Baldwin II, Emperor of the East, and St. Louis, King of France, assisted. The council excommunicated Emperor Frederick II; approved more than 20 canons; and directed the launching of a new crusade under the command of Louis against the Saracens and Mongols.

14. *Lyons II* (1274). Called by Pope Gregory X, the council included the Patriarchs of Antioch and Constantinople, 15 cardinals, 500 bishops and some 1,000 other dignitaries. It accomplished a reunion of the Greek Church with Rome, but one that was only temporary. Thirty-one canons were approved; rules were laid down for papal elections; and means were discussed for recovering Palestine from the Turks. There were six sessions between May 7 and July 17.

15. *Vienne* (1311-1312). This council was called by Clement V, the first of the Avignon popes, and it involved three sesisons held between October 16, 1311 and May 6, 1312. Three kings—Philip IV of France, Edward II of England and James II of Aragon—joined with from 114 to 300 bishops (the exact number is in dispute) in attendance. The council suppressed the Knights Templar, a military order dedicated to the defense of the Christian kingdom; enacted clerical reforms; and provided for the teaching of Oriental languages in the church's universities.

16. *Constance* (1414-1418). This council involved two pontificates, those of Gregory XII and Martin V, and 45 sessions extending over four years. Its main purpose was to end the Western Schism, and this it accomplished. The council issued decrees against Wycliff and Hus. Another decree asserting the superiority of an ecumenical council over the pope was rescinded on its reconsideration.

17. *Florence* (1438-1445). This council actually convened at Basle in 1431, Eugene IV being pope and Sigismund emperor. Its object was the religious pacification of Bohemia. Quarrels with the pope, however, caused the council to be shifted first to Ferrara (1438) and then to Florence (1438), the event thus being also known as the Council of Basle-Ferrara-Florence. Many Eastern-Rite bishops were in attendance, and the council effected reunions with the Greeks, Armenians and Jacobites, all of which proved to be short-lived however. Reaffirmed was the concept of papal primacy over an ecumenical council.

18. *Lateran V* (1512-1517). This council extended over the pontificates of Julius II and Leo X, Maximillian I be-

ing emperor, and engaged 15 cardinals and some 80 archbishops and bishops. Its decrees were mainly disciplinary.
The council closed as the Reformation budded, and
though during its years of deliberation it reflected concern for abuses in the Church, it failed to take decisive
action to blunt the blow that was coming. A proposal for
a new crusade against the Turks foundered on the upheaval in Germany caused by Martin Luther.

19. *Trent* (1545-1563). This was the longest of the
Ecumenical Councils, extending over 15 years, five pontificates (Paul III, Julius III, Marcellus II, Paul IV and
Pius IV), and two emperorships (Charles V and Ferdinand). It involved some 300 prelates and 160 doctors of
divinity, brought together in the church's reaction to the
Reformation and the challenges of Luther and other reformers. The council issued a record number of reforms
and dogmatic decrees, and gave the church its essential
direction and mindset for some 400 years. Its definitions
covered subjects ranging from faith, grace and the
sacraments, to the jurisdiction of the pope and the education of priests, and set in motion the movement known
as the Counter-Reformation.

20. Vatican I (1869-1870). Called by Pope Pius IX and
involving more than 800 prelates, the council is famous
for its declaration of papal infallibility—the proposition
that the pope cannot err in defining matters of faith and
morals. The decisive vote on the issue came on Monday,
July 18, 1870, one day before the outbreak of the Franco-
German war. A number of prelates had fled Rome in an-
ticipation of the war; still 435 assembled for the vote.
Despite months of intense debate pro and con, the
measure carried with only two voting *non placet*, "it does
not please"—Bishop Aloisio Riccio of Cajazzo, Italy, and
Bishop Edward Fitzgerald of Little Rock, Arkansas. The
new dogma was promulgated by the pope as a spectacular
thunder and lightning storm swept over the Vatican, and
elicited comparisons of the pope to Moses promulgating
the law on Mount Sinai. The council adjourned and was
never officially closed.

21. *Vatican II* (1962-1965). Convoked by Pope John XXIII and concluded by Pope Paul VI, the council ran through four fall sessions, and produced two dogmatic and two pastoral constitutions, nine decrees and three declarations, which were to change dramatically religious practice and life in the church. The council introduced the vernacular to the liturgy, revamped liturgical practices generally, underscored the legitimacy of the individual conscience, and encouraged theological exploration of hitherto sacrosanct beliefs and practices, including the exercise of authority in the church. The council advanced the idea of collegiality—that power should be shared by the pope with the bishops, and to an extent with lay Catholics. A total of 2,600 fathers participated in the proceedings.

Heresies

The church has grappled with heresy—persistence in error, or obstinate denial or doubt by Christians of some doctrine of belief—since its very founding. Among the first heretics were converts from Judaism in the early church—some of whom held that circumcision and the observance of the Mosaic Law were necessary for salvation, and thus obligatory also for Gentile converts; others of whom considered circumcision and the Mosaic Law at least obligatory for Jewish Christians. They are known in history as Judaizers, and their positions were condemned at the Council of Jerusalem (A.D. 51), prototype of church's later ecumenical councils. Procedures of the Council of Jerusalem are described in Acts 15:1ff.

Heresies have presented formidable problems for the church and some have disrupted the unity of faith over many years. The Arian heresy presented 55 years of direct and several centuries of indirect difficulty; the Acacian heresy, 35 years; the Monothelite heresy, 41 years; Iconoclasm, portions of two centuries. Though heresies have been painful experiences for the church's central administration, some actually have resulted in clarification and development of church doctrine. The names of a few heresies have passed into the language and acquired meanings only distantly related to the theological controversies which gave them birth.

Some of the major heresies:

Montanism, a 2nd-Century heresy originating with Montanus of Phrygia and two so-called prophetesses, Maximilla and Prisca, also called Priscilla, which held that the Second Coming was imminent and that the end of the world was approaching. It proposed a rigorous code of morality, including new fasts and abstinences—what St. Jerome described as three Lents, "as though three Saviours had suffered." Tertullian was the heresy's most famous advocate. The heresy was condemned by Pope St. Zephyrinus (199-217).

Gnosticism is a collective name applied to theories which up to the 5th Century built on the Platonic principle that reason was superior to faith, and which attributed to adherents a deeper insight into the doctrines of Christianity. These persons accordingly comprised an intellectually elitist class; they were "people who knew." The Gnostic school was without any central leader or authority, but it developed a large literature, and for two centuries presented a serious danger to Christianity before losing its impetus. Among other things, Gnosticism enveloped the Docetist theory that Christ merely appeared or seemed to be a man, to have been born, lived, suffered and died.

Arianism is a 4th-Century heresy which denied the divinity of Christ. It took its name from the priest Arius of Alexandria and was born of the question of how God the Son was related to God the Father. Arianism described the Son as a second or inferior God, posed midway between the First Cause and creatures, who once had not existed. The proposition was condemned by the

First Council of Nicaea (325), but forms of Arianism spawned over several centuries, presenting the church with continuing problems.

Acacianism was a spin-off from Arianism, and owes its name to Acacius, a 4th-Century bishop of Caesarea. Essentially it claimed that the Son was similar, not identical in essence, with the Father. The theory evolved out of public debate following the First Council of Nicaea and its condemnation of Arianism. Acacianism was condemned by the Semi-Arian Synod of Lampsacus in 365. Acacius was deposed from his see, and his influence waned with his loss of power.

Priscillianism was a 4th-Century Spanish heresy which viewed marriage as diabolical and believed in the dualism of a Kingdom of Light and a Kingdom of Darkness, both represented in the individual and in conflict in terms of the person's salvation. The heresy questioned elements of the Scriptures, such as the creation narrative, and imposed a rigorous asceticism, such as fasting on Sundays and Christmas Day. Further, because people in general allegedly could not understand higher subtleties, it was permitted for enlightened Priscillianists to tell lies for a holy end. It was because of the latter proposition that Augustine is said to have written his celebrated *De mendacio*.

Nestorianism is traced to Nestorius, a 5th-Century Patriarch of Constantinople, who denied the real unity of the divine and human natures in Christ, and by extension the tenet that Mary is the mother of Second Person of the Trinity, or Mother of God *(theotokos)*. Part of the reasoning: "No one can bring forth a son older than herself." The heresy was condemned by the Councils of Ephesus (431) and Chalcedon (451).

Pelagianism originated in the 5th Century with the Breton monk Pelagius, who denied original sin, insisted on the naturalness of concupiscence and the death of the body, and ascribed the existence and universality of sin to the negative example which Adam set by the first sin.

Pelagius further claimed that salvation could be attained through free will and an individual's natural powers, thus bringing into question the meaning and importance of grace. St. Augustine vehemently opposed Pelagianism, and the heresy was condemned by the Council of Ephesus (431). Semi-Pelagianism, a doctrine of grace which aimed at a compromise between the positions of Pelagius and Augustine, was condemned by the Second Synod of Orange (529).

Monophysitism, known also as Eutychianism, was a 5th-Century heresy which rejected the two natures of Christ, divine and human, and argued instead for a single composite nature. In essence this amounted to a denial of Christ's human nature. The heresy's name derived from Eutyches, head of a monastery near Constantinople, although it is alleged he contributed little or nothing to Monophysitism's theory and influence. The heresy was condemned by the Council of Chalcedon (451).

Monothelitism, a 7th-Century modification of Monophysitism, denied the human will in Christ. Proponents acknowledged a divine will, but their denial of a human will posited an incompleteness for Christ's human nature. Severus of Antioch and Patriarch Sergius of Constantinople were leading advocates of Monothelitism. The heresy was condemned by the Council of Constantinople (680-1).

Donatism was a 4th-Century heresy which arose in the African Church and concerned the validity of Baptism and other sacraments when administered by heretics and sinners. The name derived from Donatus the Great, and was around for some 100 years, until the conference of Carthage of 411, after which its influence waned. One effect of the heresy was to clarify the principle that sacraments derive their efficacy from Christ, not from their human ministers.

Iconoclasm was an 8th- and 9th-Centuries heresy that involved the destruction of holy pictures, crosses and relics as idolatrous. The heresy originated in the East, and probably reflected Moslem influence—any kind of representation of the human form being of course abominable to Moslems, whether in form of picture, statue or otherwise. The heresy touched the West, and there were dramatic cases of Iconoclasm, as in the Diocese of Turin, where the Bishop Claudius in 824 ordered all holy pictures and crosses in the diocese destroyed, proscribed pilgrimages, and forbade veneration of relics, intercession of saints and use of candles except for practical purposes. Iconoclasm was widely denounced, then formally condemned at the Second Council of Nicaea (787). It continued to persist, however, for some years.

Berengarius' heresy involved the denial of transubstantiation and the real presence of Christ in the Eucharist. Berengarius (c. 999-1088), a native of Tours and an archdeacon, held instead that Christ's was an intellectual or spiritual presence. It was the first of the clearly Eucharistic heresies, and was condemned by two Lateran councils (1078 and 1079). Berengarius accepted, and signed the profession of faith that "after the consecration, the bread is the true body of Christ, the very body born of the Virgin";—that "the bread and wine on the altar, by the mystery of the sacred prayer and words of our Redeemer, are substantially converted into the very flesh and blood of our Lord Jesus Christ, true and life-giving..."

Jansenism originated with Cornelius Jansenius (1585-1638), a Bishop of Ypres, and was based on the proposition that human nature was corrupted by original sin. The will was mastered by concupiscence, and could not escape the attraction of evil except when aided by the movement of grace superior to the force of concupiscence. The heresy also branched into predestination, holding that Christ died only for those predestined to heaven. Others were to go to hell. The heresy was condemned by Urban VIII in 1642, Innocent X in 1653 and Clement XI in 1713, among other popes, but its spirit lived on, particularly in France, where its rigorous moral and ascetic codes long dominated the practice of the administration of the sacraments and the teaching of moral theology.

Quietism originated with a Spanish priest living in Rome in the 17th Century, Father Michael Molinos, and built on the principle of self-annihilation of powers and passive resignation. The soul should resign itself to the devil's intrusions, and not regard as sin untoward happenings, including carnal actions performed alone or with others. When temptations occurred, one was to let the demon have its way. Scruples and doubts were to be set aside. Consequent carnal actions were not to be mentioned in confession. By not confessing them, the soul overcame the demon, acquired a "treasure of peace," and attained a closer union with God. Molinos was arrested by the Inquisition in 1685 and after a long trial was sentenced in 1687 to life imprisonment. He confessed to personal aberrations and to having taught that impure and carnal acts were licit to those who prayed, as only the lower, sensual self was affected by them. It is said that he directed "a whole army of pious souls."

Patron Saints

The Catholic Church has had very many members who have achieved historical positions in science, the arts, government, exploration—all fields of human endeavor. But its special heroes remain its saints, individuals of exceptional holiness of life, of virtue and benevolence, whose place in heaven the church deems to be assured. Some achieved heaven by martyrdom for the faith; some by the ecclesiastical process of canonization (see Miscellanea). But in heaven the church says they are.

Throughout history, the church has encouraged the veneration of the memory of saints, and thus saints have evolved as intercessors before the throne of God in favor of prayerful petitions, and as role models for those who hope to emulate their saintly and heroic virtues. Veneration of the saints at times has indeed become so strong and so dominant a cult among Catholics as to eclipse the liturgy in some areas of the worship and shroud the preeminent place of God and Christ in Catholic devotion. It was this phenomenon that prompted the Fathers of Vatican II to urge "all concerned to work hard to prevent or correct any abuses, excesses, or defects which may have crept in here or there, and to restore all things to a more ample praise of Christ and of God" (Dogmatic Constitution on the Church, *Lumen Gentium*—51).

One result of the conciliar recommendation was the apostolic letter *Mysterii paschalis celebrationem* issued by Pope Paul VI on February 14, 1969, revising the calendar of the saints. Four broad principles were to be implemented: (1) the histories of the lives of the saints found then in the calendar were to be subjected to critical study; (2) the number of devotional feasts should be lessened; (3) only saints of universal significance should be chosen for the universal calendar; (4) saints on the universal calendar should be chosen from every race and period of time. The principles were directly derivative of the instruction of Vatican II that the feasts of the saints not take precedence over feasts which commemorate the very mysteries of salvation.

With the revising of the calendar of the saints, many saints dropped from sight—some because their authenticity was questioned; others because their feasts were deemed redundant on an otherwise crowded calendar. Among saints who passed into obscurity were Canute, Valentine, Alexius, Christopher, Eustace and Philomena, though for convenience's sake their names may remain associated with churches, orders, patronages and the like, for or to which they were named earlier.

Several feasts were also suppressed, such as the Name of Mary (September 12), a feast included in the Roman calendar in 1684 to celebrate the victory over the Turks at Vienna in 1683. The ruling of the Sacred Congregation of Rites was that the Feast of the Name of Mary duplicated the Feast of the Birth of Mary.

The revising of the calendar of saints does not mean

that saints are less important to Catholic Christian history; it means only that the scales have been adjusted to balance the priorities of worship. The revision also results in the introduction of new saints to Catholic consciousness, through the broadening of feasts to include, among others, the names of SS. Paul Miki and Companions (February 6), St. Maximilian Maria Kolbe (August 14), St. Turibius of Mogrovejo (March 23) and St. Charles Lwanga and Companions, the Ugandan martyrs (June 3).

The association of specific saints with particular occupations or life-situations of people has been common to Catholicism for centuries. Thus there exist patron saints—saints whose designation it is to provide inspiration, example, hope to people who feel an affinity with them for a variety of reasons. The church itself has officially named patron saints, but in many instances the title has been bestowed by tradition arising out of popular veneration or reverence. Some patron saints:

Accountants: St. Matthew
Actors: St. Genesius
Acolytes (altar boys): St. John Berchmans
Advertising: St. Bernadine of Siena
Alpinists: St. Bernard of Menthon
Anesthetists: St. Rene Goupil
Archers: St. Sebastian
Architects: St. Barbara; St. Thomas the Apostle
Armorers: St. Dunstan
Art: St. Catherine of Bologna
Artillerymen: St. Barbara
Artists: St. Luke
Astronomers: St. Dominic
Athletes: St. Sebastian
Authors: St. Francis de Sales
Automobiles: St. Frances of Rome; St. Christopher
Aviators: St. Joseph of Cupertino; St. Therese of Lisieux; Our
    Lady of Loreto
Bakers: St. Elizabeth of Hungary: St. Honoratus; St. Nicholas
Bankers: St. Matthew
Barbers: SS. Cosmas and Damian; St. Louis

Barren women: St. Anthony of Padua; St. Felicitas
Basketmakers: St. Anthony of Egypt
Blacksmiths: St. Dunstan
Blind persons: St. Odilia; St. Raphael
Blood banks: St. Januarius
Bodily ills: Our Lady of Lourdes
Bookbinders: St. Peter Celestine
Bookkeepers: St. Matthew
Booksellers: St. John of God
Brewers: St. Augustine of Hippo; St. Luke; St. Nicholas of Myra
Bricklayers: St. Stephen
Brides: St. Nicholas of Myra
Brushmakers: St. Anthony, Abbot
Builders: St. Vincent Ferrer
Butchers: St. Anthony, Abbot; St. Hadrian; St. Luke
Cabdrivers: St. Fiacre
Cabinetmakers: St. Anne
Cancer patients: St. Peregrine
Canonists: St. Raymond of Penafort
Carpenters: St. Joseph
Catechists: St. Charles Borromeo; St. Viator; St. Robert
  Bellarmine
Catholic Action: St. Francis of Assisi
Candlemakers: St. Ambrose; St. Bernard of Clairvaux
Charities: St. Vincent de Paul
Children: St. Nicholas of Myra
Children of Mary: St. Agnes; St. Maria Goretti
Choirboys: St. Dominic Savio
Clerics: St. Gabriel of Our Lady of Sorrows (St. Francisco
  Possenti)
Comedians: St. Vitus
Confessors: St. Alphonsus Liguori; St. John Nepomucene
Convulsions in children: St. Scholastica
Cooks: St. Lawrence; St. Martha
Coopers: St. Nicholas of Myra
Coppersmiths: St. Maurus
Dairy workers: St. Brigid
Deaf persons: St. Francis de Sales
Dentists: St. Apollonia
Desperate circumstances: St. Gregory of Neocaesarea; St. Jude
  Thaddeus
Dietitians (hospital): St. Martha

Domestic animals: St. Anthony, Abbot
Druggists: SS. Cosmas and Damian; St. James the Less
Dyers: SS. Maurice and Lydia
Dying: St. Joseph; St. Barbara
Ecologists: St. Francis of Assisi
Editors: St. John Bosco
Emigrants: St. Frances Xavier Cabrini
Engineers: St. Ferdinand III
Eucharistic congresses and societies: St. Paschal Baylon
Expectant mothers: St. Gerard Majella; St. Margaret;
    St. Raymond Nonnatus
Eye trouble: St. Lucy
Falsely accused: St. Raymond Nonnatus
Farmers: St. Isidore; St. George
Farriers (Blacksmiths): St. John the Baptist
Firefighters: St. Florian
Fire prevention: St. Barbara; St. Catherine of Siena
First communicants: St. Tarcisius; Blessed Imelda
Fishermen: St. Andrew
Florists: St. Dorothy; St. Therese of Lisieux
Forest workers: St. John Gualbert
Founders: St. Barbara
Foundlings: Holy Innocents
Fullers: St. Anastasius; St. James the Less
Funeral directors: St. Joseph of Arimathea; St. Dismas
Gardeners: St. Adelard; St. Fiacre; St. Dorothy; St. Tryplon;
    St. Phocas
Girls: St. Agnes
Glassworkers: St. Luke
Goldsmiths: St. Dunstan; St. Anastasius
Gravediggers and graveyards: St. Anthony, Abbot
Grocers: St. Michael
Gunners: St. Barbara
Hatters: St. Severus of Ravenna; St. James the Less
Haymakers: SS. Gervase and Protase
Headaches: St. Teresa of Avila
Heart ailments: St. John of God
Hospital administrators: St. Basil the Great; St. Frances
    Xavier Cabrini
Hospitals: St. Camillus de Lellis; St. John of God;
    St. Jude Thaddeus
Housewives: St. Anne

Hunters: St. Eustachius; St. Hubert
Infantrymen: St. Maurice
Innkeepers: St. Amand
Invalids: St. Roch
Jewelers: St. Eligius, St. Dunstan
Journalists: St. Francis de Sales
Jurists: St. Catherine of Alexandria; St. John Capistran
Laborers: St. Isidore; St. James; St. John Bosco
Lawyers: St. Ivo; St. Genesius; St. Thomas More
Learning: St. Acca; St. Ambrose
Librarians: St. Jerome
Lighthouse keepers: St. Venerius
Locksmiths: St. Dunstan
Lost articles: St. Anthony of Padua
Lovers: St. Raphael
Maids: St. Zita
Marble workers: St. Clement I
Mariners: St. Michael; St. Nicholas of Tolentino
Medical-record librarians: St. Raymond of Penafort
Medical social workers: St. John Regis
Medical technologists: St. Albert the Great
Medically ill: St. Dympna
Merchants: St. Francis of Assisi; St. Nicholas of Myra
Messengers: St. Gabriel
Metalworkers: St. Eligius
Millers: St. Arnulph; St. Victor
Missions: foreign: St. Francis Xavier, St. Therese of Lisieux;
    black: St. Peter Claver, St. Benedict the Moor
Mothers: St. Monica
Motorcyclists: Our Lady of Grace
Motorists: St. Christopher; St. Frances of Rome
Mountaineers: St. Bernard of Menthon
Musicians: St. Cecelia; St. Dunstan
Nail makers: St. Cloud
Notaries: St. Luke; St. Mark
Nurses: St. Agatha; St. Camillus de Lellis; St. John of God;
    St. Raphael
Nursing and nursing services: St. Catherine of Siena;
    St. Elizabeth of Hungary
Old maids: St. Andrew
Orators: St. John Chrysostom
Organ builders: St. Cecelia

Orphans: St. Jerome Aemilian
Painters: St. Luke
Paratroopers: St. Michael
Pawnbrokers: St. Nicholas of Myra
Pharmacists: SS. Cosmas and Damien; St. James the Greater;
    St. Gemma Galgani (hospital pharmacists)
Philosophers: St. Justin; St. Catherine of Alexandria
Physicians: SS. Cosmas and Damien; St. Luke; St. Panteleon;
    St. Raphael
Pilgrims: St. James
Plasterers: St. Bartholomew
Poets: St. Cecelia; St. David
Poisoning: St. Benedict
Police officers: St. Michael
Poor: St. Anthony of Padua; St. Lawrence
Poor souls: St. Nicholas of Tolentino
Possessed: St. Bruno; St. Denis
Postal workers: St. Gabriel
Priests: St. Jean Baptiste Vianney
Printers: St. Augustine of Hippo; St. Genesius; St. John of God
Prisoners: St. Barbara; St. Dismas
Prisons: St. Joseph Cafasso
Protector of crops: St. Ansovinus
Publicity agents: St. Bernardine of Siena
Public relations (hospitals): St. Paul the Apostle
Radiologists: St. Michael
Radio workers: St. Gabriel
Retreats: St. Ignatius Loyola
Rheumatism: St. James the Greater
Saddlers: SS. Crispin and Crispinian
Sailors: St. Brendan; St. Cuthbert; St. Erasmus; St. Eulalia;
    St. Peter Gonzales
Scholars: St. Brigid
Schools (Catholic): St. Joseph Calasanctius; St. Thomas Aquinas
Scientists: St. Albert
Sculptors: St. Claude
Seafarers: St. Francis of Paolo
Secretaries: St. Genesius
Seminarians: St. Charles Borromeo
Servants: St. Zita; St. Martha
Shoemakers: SS. Crispin and Crispinian
Sick: St. John of God; St. Michael; St. Camillus de Lellis

Silversmiths: St. Andronicus
Singers: St. Gregory; St. Cecelia
Skaters: St. Lidwina
Skiers: St. Bernard
Social workers: St. Louise de Marillac
Soldiers: St. Hadrian; St. George; St. Ignatius; St. Joan of Arc;
   St. Sebastian; St. Martin of Tours
Speleologists (cave explorers): St. Benedict
Stenographers: St. Cassian; St. Genesius
Stonecutters: St. Clement
Stonemasons: St. Stephen; St. Barbara
Students: St. Catherine of Alexandria; St. Thomas Aquinas
Surgeons: SS. Cosmas and Damian
Swordsmiths: St. Maurice
Tailors: St. Homobonus
Tanners: SS. Crispin and Crispinian; St. Simon
Tax collectors: St. Matthew
Teachers: St. Catherine of Alexandria; St. Gregory the Great;
   St. John Baptist de la Salle (principal patron)
Telegraph and telephone employees: St. Gabriel
Television workers: St. Gabriel
Television: St. Clare of Assisi
Tertiaries: St. Louis of France; St. Elizabeth of Hungary
Theologians: St. Alphonsus Liguori; St. Augustine
Throat: St. Blaise
Travelers: St. Anthony of Padua; St. Christopher; St. Nicholas of
   Myra; St. Raphael
Travel hostesses: St. Bona
Universal Church: St. Joseph
Universities: Blessed Contardo Ferrini
Vocations: St. Alphonsus
Watchmen: St. Peter of Alcantara
Weavers: St. Anastasia; St. Anastasius; St. Paul the Hermit
Wheelwrights: St. Catherine of Alexandria
Winegrowers: St. Vincent
Wine merchants: St. Amand
Women in labor: St. Anne
Women's Army Corps: St. Genevieve
Workingmen: St. Joseph
Writers: St. Francis de Sales; St. Lucy
Yachters: St. Adjutor
Youth: St. Aloysius Gonzaga; St. Gabriel Possenti;
   St. John Berchmans

Patron Saints of Countries and Geographical Areas

Alsace: St. Odilia
Americas: Our Lady of Guadalupe; St. Rose of Lima
Argentina: Our Lady of Lujan
Armenia: St. Gregory the Illuminator; St. Bartholomew
Asia Minor: St. John the Evangelist
Australia: Our Lady Help of Christians
Belgium: St. Joseph
Bohemia: St. Wenceslaus; St. Ludmilla
Borneo: St. Francis Xavier
Brazil: Immaculate Conception; Nossa Senhora de Aparecida;
    St. Peter of Alcantara
Canada: St. Anne; St. Joseph
Chile: Our Lady of Mt. Carmel; St. James
China: St. Joseph
Colombia: St. Louis Bertrand; St. Peter Claver
Corsica: Immaculate Conception; St. Alexander Sauli
Crete: St. Titus
Cyprus: St. Barnabas
Czechoslovakia: St. John Nepomucene; St. Procopius;
    St. Wenceslaus
Denmark: St. Canute; St. Ansgar
Dominican Republic: Our Lady of High Grace; St. Dominic
East Indies: St. Francis Xavier; St. Thomas the Apostle
Ecuador: the Sacred Heart
England: St. Augustine of Canterbury; St. George;
    St. Gregory the Great
Ethiopia: St. Frumentius
Europe: St. Benedict; SS. Cyril and Methodius
Finland: St. Henry
France: Our Lady of the Assumption; St. Denis; St. Joan of Arc;
    St. Martin of Tours; St. Remigius; St. Therese of Lisieux
Gaul: St. Irenaeus
Germany: St. Boniface; St. Michael; St. Peter Canisius;
    St. Suitbert
Gibraltar: Our Lady of Europe
Greece: St. Andrew; St. Nicholas of Myra
Holland: St. Willibord; St. Plechelm
Hungary: King St. Stephen; St. Gerard; Blessed Virgin Mary
    under the title Great Lady of Hungary
India: Our Lady of the Assumption
Ireland: St. Patrick; St. Brigid; St. Columba

Italy: St. Catherine of Siena; St. Francis of Assisi;
St. Bernardine of Siena
Japan: St. Francis Xavier; St. Peter Baptist
Lesotho: Immaculate Heart of Mary
Lithuania: St. Casimir; Blessed Cunegunda
Malta: St. Paul; Our Lady of the Assumption
Mexico: Our Lady of Guadalupe; St. Martin de Valencia and
Companions
Monaco: St. Devota
Moravia: SS. Cyril and Methodius
New Zealand: Our Lady Help of Christians
North America: St. Isaac Jogues and Companions
Norway: St. Olaf
Papua New Guinea and the northern Solomon Islands:
St. Michael the Archangel
Paraguay: Our Lady of the Assumption
Peru: St. Joseph
Philippines: Sacred Heart of Mary
Poland: St. Casimir; Blessed Cunegunda; St. Stanislaus of
Cracow; Our Lady of Czestochowa; St. Hyacinth
Portugal: Immaculate Conception; St. Francis Borgia;
St. Anthony; St. Vincent; St. George
Roumania: St. Nicetas
Rome: St. Philip Neri
Russia: St. Andrew; St. Nicholas of Myra; St. Therese of Lisieux
Scandinavia: St. Ansgar
Scotland: St. Andrew; St. Columba; St. Palladius
Silesia: St. Hedwig
Slovakia: Our Lady of Sorrows
South Africa: Our Lady of the Assumption
South America: St. Rose of Lima
Spain: St. Teresa of Avila; St. James the Greater; St. Felix;
St. Euphrasius
Sri Lanka (Ceylon, formerly): St. Lawrence
Sweden: St. Bridget; St. Eric; St. Ansgar
Switzerland: St. Andeol
United States: Immaculate Conception
Uruguay: Our Lady of Lujan
Wales: St. David
West Indies: St. Gertrude

Saints: Their Symbols in Art

St. Agatha: tongs, veil

St. Agnes: lamb
St. Ambrose: bees, dove, ox, pen
St. Andrew: transverse cross
St. Angela Merici: ladder, cloak
St. Anne: door
St. Anthony of Egypt: bell, hog
St. Anthony of Padua: Christ child, bread, book, lily
St. Augustine of Hippo: dove, child, shell, pen
St. Barbara: tower, palm, chalice, cannon
St. Barnabas: stones, ax, lance
St. Bartholomew: knife, flayed skin
St. Benedict: broken cup, raven, bell, crozier, bush
St. Bernard of Clairvaux: pen, bees, instruments of the Passion
St. Bernadine of Siena: chrism
St. Blaise: wax taper, iron comb
St. Bonaventure: ciborium, cardinal's hat
St. Boniface: oak, ax, book, fox, scourge, fountain, raven, sword
St. Bridget of Kildare: cross, candle, flame over head
St. Bridget of Sweden: book, pilgrim's staff
St. Bruno: chalice
St. Catherine of Alexandria: wheel, lamb, sword
St. Catherine di Ricci: ring, crown, crucifix
St. Catherine of Siena: stigmata, cross, ring, lily
St. Cecelia: organ
St. Charles Borromeo: Eucharist, coat of arms with the word
   Humilitas
St. Christopher: giant, torrent stream, tree, Christ Child
St. Clare of Assisi: monstrance
St. Colette: lamb, birds
SS. Cosmas and Damian: phial, box of ointment
St. Cyril of Alexandria: pen, Mary holding Christ Child
St. Cyril of Jerusalem: purse, book
St. Dominic: rosary, star
St. Dorothy: flowers, fruit
St. Edmund: arrow, sword
St. Elizabeth of Hungary: alms, flowers, bread, pitcher
St. Francis of Assisi: deer, wolf, birds, fish, stigmata
St. Francis Xavier: crucifix, bell, ship
St. Genevieve: bread, keys, herd, candle
St. George: dragon
St. Gertrude: crown, taper, lily
SS. Gervase and Protase: scourge, club, sword

St. Giles: crozier, hind, hermitage
St. Gregory the Great: tiara, crozier, dove
St. Helena: cross
St. Hilary: pen, stick, child
St. Ignatius Loyola: Eucharist, chasuble, book
St. Isidore: bees, pen
St. James the Greater: pilgrim's staff, shell, key, sword
St. James the Less: square rule, halbred, club
St. Jerome: lion
St. John Berchmans: cross, rosary
St. John Chrysostom: bees, dove, pen
St. John of God: alms, heart, crown of thorns
St. John the Baptist: lamb, skin of animal, head on platter
St. John the Evangelist: eagle, chalice, kettle, armor
St. Josephat Kuncevyc: chalice, crown, winged deacon
St. Joseph: lily, rod, plane, carpenter's square
St. Jude: sword, square rule, club
St. Justin Martyr: ax, sword
St. Lawrence: cross, gridiron, book of the Gospels
St. Leander of Seville: pen
St. Liborius: pebbles, peacock
St. Longinus: lance
St. Louis IX of France: crown of thorns, nails
St. Lucy: cord, eyes
St. Luke: ox, book, brush, palette
St. Margaret: dragon
St. Mark: lion, book
St. Martha: holy water sprinkler, dragon
St. Mary Magdalene: ointment box
St. Mathias: lance
St. Matilda: purse, alms
St. Matthew: winged man, purse, lance
St. Maurus: scales, spade, crutch
St. Meinrad: two ravens
St. Michael: scales, banner, sword, dragon
St. Monica: sash, tears
St. Nicholas: boy in boat, anchor, three purses
St. Patrick: shamrock, cross, harp, baptismal font, serpents
St. Paul: sword
St. Peter: keys, boat, cock
St. Philip the Apostle: column
St. Philip Neri: altar, chasuble, vial

St. Rita: rose, crucifix, thorn
St. Roch: bread, angel, dog
St. Rose of Lima: crown of thorns, anchor, city
St. Sebastian: arrows, crown
SS. Sergius and Bacchus: military garb, palm
St. Simon: cross, saw
St. Simon Stock: scapular
St. Teresa of Avila: heart, arrow, book
St. Therese of Lisieux: roses entwined around a crucifix
St. Thomas the Apostle: lance, ax
St. Thomas Aquinas: chalice, monstrance, dove, ox
St. Ursula: ship, clock, arrow
St. Vincent: gridiron, boat
St. Vincent de Paul: children
St. Vincent Ferrer: pulpit, cardinal's hat, captives, trumpet

The Church's Influence

The Catholic Church is one of the great success stories of recorded history, but at the same time it is a church which in secular context has failed its full promise. The church began in seeming failure, its founder dying an ignominious death on the cross. It endured the most intense persecutions, its adherents at one time being fed to the lions for the amusement of the mobs. But this church grew and prospered, and when Constantine accepted the Christian faith in 337 A.D. the new faith had in fact triumphed over the old paganism and newly popular Oriental faiths, such as the cult of Mithra. Christianity became entrenched as the state religion. Given the dominance of the Roman Empire in the then-known, so-called civilized world, it was inevitable that Christianity's place should also be dominant. The church's interest in art, medicine and education fortified its preeminence as a religion and as an institutional entity, so that after the disintegration of the Roman Empire, it was uniquely positioned to survive while the Empire itself went down.

At the opening of the 9th century of the Christian Era, Charlemagne was crowned successor in the West to the old Roman emperors by Pope Leo III (795-816). The time was Christmas Day in the year 800. Charlemagne was to unify most of Europe, of course, and with this achievement there came into being the Holy Roman Empire, a centralized political and religious unity modeled on the ideal spelled out in St. Augustine's *City of God*. The political and religious spheres thus were joined into a harmony. There were occasional differences about who took precedence, pope or emperor, but by and large for centuries, the church's position was secure. Catholicism was not only the "true" religion, it was the one religion, and the future belonged to it.

Or so it seemed. A number of factors worked against the church, including, it developed, its close, indeed intimate connection with Western culture. The connection was natural to be sure, the church being a prime shaper of this culture. However, the identification of church with a particular geographical area (Western Europe and those parts of the world absorbing Western emigrees) and a particular race (white) created difficulties that were never fully overcome, and which indeed returned to haunt when the world shrank and the church reached out to other peoples, blacks and Asiatics notably. (Notwithstanding, one of the great growth areas for the church at the present time is black Africa.) Some blame for this circumstance has been unfairly laid upon the church. On the other hand, it must be conceded that many problems were of the church's own doing—as when in 1704, it repudiated Jesuit Father Matteo Ricci, the celebrated missionary to China who adopted Chinese manners, customs and dress, and tolerated as a part of Catholic practice Chinese customs and beliefs considered alien and inimical to Christianity. Less Western precommitments and more tolerant attitudes towards the cultures of others might have changed religious history in the Far East, but with the insistence on the universality and absoluteness of practice in the Western or Latin Church, a bright evangelical opportunity was lost, likely forever. (Ironically, Ricci's repudiation was due in major degree to intramural ecclesiastical rivalries, specifically the involvement of the Dominicans, who were severely critical of the Jesuits for the Ricci initiative.)

Father Ricci was vindicated in 1939, when Rome finally allowed certain indigenous Chinese codes within the Catholic prescript, by recognizing, for instance, the regard in which Confucius is held by the Chinese and by accepting the reverence which Chinese have for their ancestors. By then it was much too late for the evangelization of the Far East, but at least it indicated a new respect for the culture of others. Today there seems a caution that the mistake that was made in China in the 18th century is not repeated in the 20th in the area which Rome regards as brimming with evangelical promise, Africa. Hence, the apparent acceptance of a certain "inculturation" or Africanization of the liturgy, an acceptance underscored by Pope John Paul II's willingness to join in liturgical services which feature native dances and in which drums are substituted for pipe organs and tribal chant for traditional hymns.

The Fracturing of Christianity. Two cataclysmic events occurred, which were to effectively shatter Christian unity and limit the sphere and scope of the Roman Catholic Church's influence. The first was the separation of the Eastern Churches, the so-called great Eastern Schism, now more decorously called the East-West Schism. The second was the Protestant Reformation, dramatically initiated on the continent by Martin Luther and having an independent but parallel scenario across the English Channel in England.

East-West Schism. The definitive break between Eastern and Western Christianity, a break which resulted in the formation of the Eastern Orthodox Churches, occurred in 1054 and is popularly thought to have exclusively concerned theological disagreement on the procession of the Holy Spirit—the so-called *filioque* dispute. The dispute involved the addition of *filioque* to the Nicene Creed, a word expressing the double procession of the Holy Spirit from the Father and the Son. The Latin or Western Church sponsored the addition; the Eastern or Greek Church rejected the addition as heretical.

Though the 1054 date and the *filioque* issue are historical landmarks, neither in its respective context defines the East-West dispute with total accuracy. The roots of the East-West Schism actually go back centuries before 1054 and involve a number of issues besides *filioque*.

There was, to begin with, the development of different political philosophies between East and West—the one essentially Hellenic; the other essentially Roman. Also, the adaptation of the organized church to the West-East political divisions of the Roman Empire set the stage for competition between Rome and the principal cities of the East, notably Constantinople, Alexandria and Antioch. Tensions were alleviated for a time by conveyance of the ecclesiastical rank of patriarch to the heads of these sees, but when the title "ecumenical patriarch" was introduced in the East, Rome saw this as a serious challenge to the primacy which the Bishop of Rome had traditionally enjoyed. The iconoclasm controversy involving Emperor Leo and Pope Gregory III (731-741) exacerbated feelings between East and West, and Rome bristled as the Emperor detached the Province of Illyricum from its jurisdiction and declared it subject to the Patriarchate of Constantinople, now the dominant see in the East. The Emperor likewise confiscated the pontifical estates in that part of Italy under Byzantine influence, agitating matters further.

The rivalry between East and West, until now largely political and geographical, took a theological turn, when the *filioque* issue cropped up during the reign of Pope Leo III (795-816). Leo had seriously strained East-West relations when he proclaimed Charlemagne emperor of the Romans, an initiative which challenged the claim of the Byzantine emperors to be the legitimate heirs of the classical Empire. But Leo III recouped respect in the East when he refused to add *filioque* to the Nicene Creed. The *filioque* concept originated largely through Spanish and Frankish usage, and came to Rome along with the Frankish hegemony. Leo III agreed with the *filioque* theology but questioned the propriety of its addition to the Creed, as Frankish theologians had wanted. Several succeeding popes concurred with Leo III. Not so Pope Sergius IV (1009-1012), however. On his election, he included a copy of the Nicene Creed incorporating *filioque*, along with the customary announcement to the Patriarch of Constantinople containing the papal profession of faith. The Patriarch of Constantinople refused to recognize Sergius' election and excommunicated him. It was the true beginning of the East-West Schism, although the breach did not become final until 1054.

The climactic incident was fomented by a delegation sent to Constantinople by Pope Leo IX (1049-1054), ostensibly in conjunction with moves initiated by the Emperor to settle controversies and effect a reconciliation. The delegation was headed by Cardinal Humbert of Silva Candida, who, it is recorded, conducted himself with "tactless arrogance." The Patriarch of Constantinople, Michael Cerularius, refused to accept a letter from Humbert, among other reasons because it expressed doubt about the legitimacy of Michael Cerularius' elevation. Offended by the refusal, Humbert lashed out, offending Eastern sensibilities with a series of actions, including an attack on Greek Christians for rejecting the *filioque* theology. In an ultimate expression of embitterment, Humbert deposited a bull of excommunication against the Patriarch on the altar of the Hagia Sophia ("Divine Wisdom"), the famed church, now a mosque, built by Justinian. Humbert then took his leave of Constantinople. Michael Cerularius countered by convoking a synod, which condemned Humbert and his bull, and excommunicated the legates.

For Rome, the schism was now formal, but for Greeks the culmination came later with the diverting of the Fourth Crusade, the cruel sacking of Constantinople, and the establishment of a Latin Empire of Constantinople, complete with Latin patriarch, in 1204.

The East-West Schism was thus a long process, involving many causes. Indisputable is that the loss to Rome was enormous, as virtually the whole Christian East aligned with the Eastern patriarchs, and formed into what was to become known as the Orthodox Church (the obvious suggestion in the choice of name being that the Western or Latin Church was *un*orthodox).

According to a 1970 estimate of the Eastern Orthodox World Foundation, there are more than 200-million Orthodox Christians. They are grouped into several jurisdictions, the principal ones being the Greek and Russian Orthodox Churches. The Greek Orthodox Church has patriarchates of Constantinople, Alexandria, Antioch and Jerusalem. The Russian Orthodox Church is under the Patriarchate of Moscow. Other jurisdictions include the Patriarchates of Serbia, Rumania and Bulgaria, the Katholikate of Georgia in the Soviet Union, Byelorussians and Ukranian Byzantines, the Orthodox Churches of Albania, China, Czechoslovakia, Estonia, Finland, Hungary, Japan, Latvia, Lithuania and Poland, and small Orthodox communities elsewhere in the world.

Protestant Reformation. Fundamental in any discussion about the Protestant Reformation is recognition that in the 16th century there was much to protest about in the Western Church and much reforming needing to be done. Abuses were rampant, not only in terms of ecclesiastical privileges, but also so far as clerical formation, preaching, the administration of the sacraments and devotional practices in general were concerned. At the same time, there were the lingering negative effects of the Avignon papacy, when rival popes were excommunicating one another and all their adherents, and when the papal court had secularized itself to marked degree. The Western Church was vulnerable for an upheaval of some sort.

There were a number of concerned, papally loyal bishops anxious to institute reforms, but the catalyst for change turned out to be an Augustinian friar, Martin

Luther. On October 31, 1517, he nailed 95 theses deal-ing with the sale of indulgences and matters of Catholic belief and practices on the door of the cathedral at Wit-tenberg, and what originated as something of a conven-tional challenge to scholastic debate escalated into a declaration of independence from "authoritarian" Rome. Western Christendom rapidly chose sides between Luther and Rome. Pope Leo X (1513-1521) condemned 41 of Luther's theses, then formally excommunicated him in June, 1520. When Luther burned the bull of excommu-nication the following December, his break with Rome was complete and the stage was set for what was to be-come known historically as the Protestant Reformation, or just plain Reformation.

Interestingly enough, Luther seldom used the word Reformation, and the word Protestant did not come into wide usage until 1529, when seven Lutheran princes and 14 imperial cities protested against the decrees of the Diet of Speyer, their protest popularizing the word Protest-ant. In any instance, the Protestant Reformation was now a fact of history, and the Catholic Church, which a few cen-turies before saw its unity fractured in the East, now ex-perienced a fracturing in the West. Whole geographical areas of central and northern Europe were peeled away from the church by the Reformation, and the hegemony of the Catholic Church was reduced to the countries of southern Europe, with the notable exceptions of Ireland, Poland, Hungary and scattered pockets of Catholicism across the Continent.

About the same time that continental Europe was go-ing through its religious trauma, England was undergo-ing a "reformation" of its own. The catalytic factor there was Pope Clement VII's (1523-1534) refusal to grant King Henry VIII a decree of nullity invalidating his marriage to Catherine of Aragon and freeing him to marry Anne Boleyn. Henry VIII, who had been accorded the title Defender of the Faith by Rome in 1521 for his defense of the church against the claims of Martin Luther with the book *Assertio septem sacramentorum*, retaliated in due course by absorbing the legal authority claimed by the church into the authority of the State and declaring himself "under God, the Supreme Head" of the church in England. The Act of Supremacy of 1534 formalized the renunciation of papal jurisdiction and the ecclesiastical ascendancy of the King. By then, Henry VIII had been officially excommunicated by Clement VII, and gone now was another area of influence for the Western Church.

It is interesting to note that whereas the Reformation on the Continent concerned matters of doctrine, in England, personal, political and economic considerations were the issues of primary importance. (One issue was control over the appointment to benefices, a lucrative papal privilege which eventually passed to the state.) Thus did Henry VIII not only reject basic theological tenets of continental reformers, but he remained firm in the conviction that the traditional sacramental system was the efficacious avenue of salvation.

The Reformation gained impetus on the continent as princes and governments lent it support, often for political reasons. For many, it was the opportunity to weaken control of the Emperor, to loosen the grip of the church in civil affairs, and to secularize vast and wealthy holdings of the church.

As all this was transpiring, reformers such as John Calvin and Ulrich Zwingli came along with doctrinal principles of their own, and their principles led to the formation of creedal churches beyond Lutheranism. These generally became known as Reformed Churches, and not infrequently confessional statements were formulated for believers according to national boundaries. The consequence was further religious division of the formerly united Western Church. There were now three contentious and often combative religious factions: Catholic, Lutheran and Reformed. Anglicanism in England added a fourth division.

Time has healed many old animosities between Catholics and Protestants in most parts of the world (there are painful exceptions, as in Northern Ireland), and impressive ecumenical advances have been made in the last 20 years on a number of theological and disciplinary interfaith issues. Still the possibility of a reunited Western Christendom remains very much a remote possibility. One reason is the number of Protestant Churches now in existence. In the United States alone, there are more than 250 Protestant church bodies. It is unlikely in the extreme that a reconciliation could ever be effected between Rome and that many Church groups. Religious division, in a word, seems a permanent part of the Western Church's future. The Roman Catholic Church's influence is certain to be limited accordingly.

Post-Reformation Catholicism. The Council of Trent (1545-1563) initiated many internal reforms aimed at the correction of problems within the Western Church. There were refined definitions of the sacraments; decrees of reform on the discipline of the clergy and matters respecting ecclesiastical benefices; decrees of reform on the mode of life of cardinals and bishops, monks and nuns; and new stipulations regarding the education and formation of priests, among much else. The Council of Trent did not settle religious differences within the now sundered Western Church, but it demonstrated the viability of the church as it drew on the reservoirs of spiritual strength that were and are the church's.

As the Council of Trent gave Roman Catholicism a renewed church, so did the mobilization of the Counter-Reformation give it a revived church. The Counter-Reformation extended from the pontificate of Pope Pius IV in 1560 to the close of the Thirty Years' War in 1648, and was spearheaded by three great reforming popes: St. Pius V (1566-1572), Gregory XIII (1572-1585) and Sixtus V (1585-1590). It was a period of enormous spiritual zeal that saw the founding of a number of new religious orders, whose efforts were crucial in salvaging vast areas of Europe for Roman Catholicism. The Franciscan reform spun off the Capuchins, who were instrumental in securing Italy, France and sizable parts of Germany for Roman Catholicism. The new Theatine order supplied energetic and effective parish priests for the dioceses of Italy. The new Ursuline order provided badly needed religious women for the works of the church.

Especially conspicuous in the Counter-Reformation period, however, were the Jesuits, members of the Society of Jesus approved in 1540 by Pope Paul III (1534-1549). The Jesuits preserved Roman Catholicism in Bavaria and the southern part of the Netherlands; rescued Poland, which seemed headed into Calvinism; ministered to the pockets of Catholics who defied the persecutions in England; and embarked on missionary work in India, China, and among the Indians of North and South America, notably in Brazil, Paraguay and what was known then as the missions of New France (upper New York State and lower Canada). In a sense, the Jesuits personified the vitality of Roman Catholicism and its ability to survive in the face of the worst imaginable adversities. But it was almost as if they had a mirror on their own history of adversities, for Pope Clement XIV (1769-1774) suppressed the Jesuits in 1773 and it was not until 1814 that they were restored to the church's good graces by Pope Pius VII (1800-1823).

The fortunes of the Latin Church ebbed and flowed in the centuries after the Reformation. The age of exploration gave the church a strong foothold in vast areas of the New World, as missionaries accompanied explorers and planted the faith with marked success, particularly in South and Central America. On the other hand, the struggles in Europe between royal absolutism and popular nationalism often cost the church dearly, most noticeably in France, where the French Revolution led to persecutions, then severe regulation of the church. Still the church entered the 20th Century in firm control of itself and of the geographical areas in the Old World that continued to be loyal to it after the Reformation, and in the New World, the lands over which it acquired hegemony in the era of discovery and emigration. In many countries, Catholicism was the state religion still, where the will of the church had for all practical purposes the force of constitutional law. This was especially so in countries such as Italy, Ireland, Spain and Portugal.

But that too was to change, as countries became more aware of their pluralistic compositions and more respectful of the rights of conscience of their religious minorities. By the same token, the Declaration on Religious Freedom (*Dignitatis Humanae*) of Vatican Council II (1962-1965) changed forever the church's place in the broader society when it pronounced the ethical doctrine of religious freedom as a human right, personal and collective. In its own way it set the stage for the deestablishment of Catholicism as the official religion in many countries where the formality had lingered. This in turn loosened the church's influence over both the mores and the morals of the people of those countries. Not that the latter necessarily followed the former. In some instances, it was the reverse: the newly asserted religious independence of Catholics presaging the deestablishment of Catholicism as the state religion. By way of example, Catholicism did not cease to be the state religion of Italy until 1984. However, the grip of the church over the country and its people had been slipping away for years, to such an extent where in 1981, the church could not win a referendum on the issue which had come to be regarded as the ultimate test of Catholic loyalty and allegiance: abortion. That year, Italian voters rejected by 68 to 32 percent a proposal that would have restricted abortions to cases in which the mother's life or physical health was endangered. The vote was considered a major defeat for the church.

It remains to be seen whether the influence of the church will be weaker or stronger under the now nearly universal arrangement of separation of the church from state—the Moslem world excluded. The experience of the church in the United States provides reason for optimism. On the other hand, the United States is not the world, and what combined for strength and growth here may prove to be less salutary in places where the church has been so protected as to leave it enervated when required to stand on its own.

As for the Moslem or Islamic world, the Catholic Church's influence there is minimal, in part because of East-West political rivalries and the common association by Moslems of Catholicism with Western culture and political motivations. The Church spoke conciliatorily of Islam in the Vatican II document on non-Christian religions *(Nostra Aetate)*, stressing the things which Catholicism and Islam share in common. Islam, for instance, acknowledges Jesus as one of the six great prophets (the others: Adam, Noah, Abraham, Moses and Mohammed, the greatest of all), and it honors Mary, calling on her with devotion. But friendly as the Vatican II document was, it did not undo what the Council itself admitted were centuries of quarrels and misunderstandings, nor did it open doors to meaningful dialogue. In fact, when Pope John Paul II visited Africa in August, 1985, he felt compelled to call for an end of the "era of polarization" between the two religions. Moslems and Christians must seek a dialogue, he said during a later stop in Cameroon. He made a similar point in a later stop in Morocco, which regards itself as the "Land of Islam." The Pope's words did not bring any rush to parley, however.

Section II

The Basic Tenets of Belief

The Ten Commandments

THE BASIC MORAL CODE of the Church is rooted in the Old Testament's Ten Commandments, or Decalogue, which came from God through Moses. The Ten Commandments were written, the Scriptures inform, by the finger of God on two tablets of stone, and received by Moses on Mount Sinai. He made them the basis of what we know as Mosaic Law. The Commandments are twice recorded in the Pentateuch (first five books of the Bible): In Exodus and in Deuteronomy. They are frequently alluded to by Christ in the New Testament, and they are summarized in the double precept of charity (love of God and love of neighbor) as well as in the Beatitudes (sometimes described as the positive application of the essentially negative Commandments). The Ten Commandments were adopted by Christianity with only one notable variation from the ancient law of Jewish tradition: the day to be kept holy under the Third Commandment. The Jewish tradition holds to Saturday, the last day of the week; the Christian tradition holds to Sunday, the first day of the week.

The Ten Commandments sum up the fundamental obligations of religion and morality. The first three Commandments involve the individual's relationship to God; the other seven, the individual's relationship with neighbor. All Ten Commandments are conditioned by love—the first three, love of God directly; the remaining seven, the love which in the ideal order should flow to family and neighbor through love of God, thereby becoming the basis for justice among peoples.

The Ten Commandments are as follows:

1. I am the Lord, your God, you shall not have other gods before me. (Ex. 20:2-3)
2. You shall not take the name of the Lord, your God, in vain. (Ex. 20:7)
3. Remember to keep holy the Sabbath day. (Ex. 20:8-9)
4. Honor your father and your mother. (Ex. 20:12)
5. You shall not kill. (Ex. 20:13)
6. You shall not commit adultery. (Ex. 20:14)
7. You shall not steal. (Ex. 20:15)
8. You shall not bear false witness against your neighbor. (Ex. 20:16)
9. You shall not covet your neighbor's wife. (Ex. 20:17)
10. You shall not covet your neighbor's house. (Ex. 20:17)

The Beatitudes

The Beatitudes, expostulated by Christ in the Sermon on the Mount, are more hortatory than admonishing, and speak of the happiness that is possible on earth and in heaven for those who live by their precepts. The Beatitudes are mentioned 26 times in the Psalms and in other portions of the Old Testament, as well as in the Gospel accounts of Matthew (5:3-11) and Luke (6:20-22). Their most familiar form comes through Matthew, and they are repeated here in the wording familiar to Catholics of a certain age:

1. Blessed are the poor in spirit, for theirs is the kingdom of heaven;
2. Blessed are the meek, for they shall inherit the land;
3. Blessed are they who mourn, for they shall be comforted;
4. Blessed are they who hunger and thirst for justice, for they shall be satisfied;
5. Blessed are the merciful, for they shall obtain mercy;
6. Blessed are the poor of heart, for they shall see God;
7. Blessed are the peacemakers, for they shall be called the children of God;
8. Blessed are they who suffer persecution for justice's sake, for theirs is the kingdom of heaven.

The Beatitudes allow of expansion and contraction (Luke has a decidedly shorter version than Matthew), and there are almost as many translations as there are editions of the Bible. Whatever the translation, the Beatitudes contain in substance God's law and the rule of evangelical perfection.

The Nicene Creed

Dogmatic developments in the Church, along with the problem of heresies, brought with them the necessity of a composite statement which constituted a profession of faith. This became known as the Nicene Creed, as its formulation began with the Council of Nicaea in 325 A.D. The creed was not completed, however, until the Council of Constantinople in 381 A.D. It was recited by candidates for baptism, personally or by proxy according to age, and it remains to this day an essential element of the formally celebrated Mass. The Nicene Creed is as follows:

"I believe in one God, the Father almighty, creator of heaven and earth, and of all things visible and invisible. And in one Lord Jesus Christ, the only-begotten Son of God, born of the Father before all ages; God of God, light of light, true God of true God; begotten, not made; consubstantial with the Father; by whom all things were made. Who for us men and our salvation, came down from heaven, and was incarnate by the Holy Spirit of the Virgin Mary, and was made man. He was crucified also for us, suffered under Pontius Pilate, and was buried. On the third day he arose again, according to the Scriptures, and ascended into heaven. He sits at the right hand of the Father, and he shall come again in glory to judge the living and the dead; and his kingdom will have no end. I believe in the Holy Spirit, the Lord and Giver of life, who proceeds from the Father and Son. Who, together with the Father and the Son, is adored and glorified. Who spoke by the prophets. I believe in the one, holy, catholic and apostolic Church. I confess one baptism for the remission of sins, and I expect the resurrection of the dead, and the life of the world to come. Amen."

The Sacraments

The primary channels of grace from God through his church to his people are the sacraments. The sacraments are outward signs of inward grace, instituted by Christ, for the individual's sanctification. They can be perceived by the senses; they signify the graces they actually give; and under no circumstances are they superfluous, although it is not necessary for all Catholics to receive all the sacraments. In fact, it is impossible for some Catholics to receive all the sacraments under the present discipline, Holy Orders being barred to women. Actually it is rare for a male to receive all the sacraments, since in the Western or Latin Rite, marriage and Holy Orders are mutually exclusive sacraments, except for widowers. (In the Eastern Rite, marriage is permitted for priests under defined circumstances.)

The sacraments number seven: Baptism, Confirmation, Holy Eucharist, Penance (Reconciliation), Extreme Unction (Anointing of the Sick), Holy Orders and Matrimony. Baptism and Penance (Reconciliation) are called sacraments of the dead, because they give life through sanctifying grace, called "first grace," to those considered spiritually dead for reason of Original Sin and actual sin. The remaining five—Confirmation, Holy Eucharist, Extreme Unction (Anointing of the Sick), Holy Orders and Matrimony—are called sacraments of the living, because their reception presupposes in the ordinary sense that the recipient is in the state of grace. These sacraments give what is termed "second grace."

Certain Protestant denominations distinguish between greater and lesser sacraments, but there is no such distinction in Catholicism. The Council of Trent (1545-1563) ruled agianst theological innovators in the sacramental area, declaring: "If any one says that the sacraments of the New Law do not contain the grace which they signify, or that they do not confer grace on those who place no obstacle to the same, let him be anathema."

A brief description of each of the sacraments follows:

Baptism is the sacrament of spiritual regeneration and initiation into the Christian community. It confers sanctifying grace and cleanses the soul of original sin—and, in the instance of older recipients, of actual sins and the punishment due them. Baptism is accomplished with the pouring of water, and the recitation of the words: "I baptize you in the name of the Father and of the Son and of the Holy Spirit." Immersion in water is also an approved method of conferral, depending on custom and appropriate approval. The sacrament is received but once, and is considered necessary for salvation. Christians have baptized from the beginning, but the practice was not unique to them. Converts to Judaism were also initiated at times by immersion in water, water again being the symbol of that which cleanses. The usual minister of baptism is a bishop, priest or deacon, although in cases of emergency anyone can validly baptize.

Confirmation by earlier definition is the sacrament by which the Holy Spirit enters persons in a special way enabling them to profess their faith as true and perfect Christians and soldiers of Jesus Christ. Vatican Council II (1962-1965) described it as a sacrament by which individuals are bound more intimately to the church and endowed by the Holy Spirit with special strength so that they can "spread and defend the faith both by word and by deed as true witnesses of Christ." Confirmation is conferred through the anointing with chrism, the imposition of hands, and the recitation of the words: "N...., receive the seal of the Holy Spirit, the gift of the Father" (or, "Be sealed with the gift of the Holy Spirit"). The ordinary minister is a bishop, although priests may be delegated for the purpose and confirm in times of emergency. Confirmation was once linked to baptism. It did not have a separate sacramental ritual before the 3rd Century, and did not become a regular practice until after the 5th Century. The sacrament completes the Christian initiation begun with baptism, but is not essential for salvation. It is received but once.

Holy Eucharist is the sacrament by which Christ is present and is received by believers under the appearances of bread and wine. The consecration of bread and wine into the body and blood of Christ takes place at Mass. The consecrator must be a priest, but the sacrament can then be administered by deacons and approved eucharistic ministers, both religious and lay. The words of consecration are the familiar, "This is my body. . . . This is the cup of my blood." The Eucharist may be received under one species, bread alone, or both species, bread and wine, depending on the occasion and authorization. The Mass is the usual setting for reception of the Eucharist, and it may be received once a day—although there are exceptions to both norms. Conditions for its reception are a state of grace, right intention, and observance of the Eucharist fast. Catholicism holds that the consecrated species are the actual body and blood of Christ, but much of Protestantism, on the basis of the same biblical texts on which Catholic belief is based, holds that Christ is only symbolically present in the Eucharist. The origin of the sacrament is traced to the Last Supper.

Penance (Reconciliation) is the sacrament by which sins committed after baptism are forgiven through absolution by a priest and the person is reconciled with God and the Church. The basic elements of the sacrament are sorrow for one's sins because of a supernatural motive; confession to a duly authorized minister of previously unconfessed grave or mortal sins (minor or venial sins need not of necessity be confessed); and reparation by means of the penance (prayer or other act) imposed by the priest. The traditional words of absolution are: "I absolve you from your sins in the name of the Father, and of the Son, and of the Holy Spirit." Methods for administering the sacrament have taken various forms over the centuries. Private confession evolved during the Middle Ages, and became dominant in the modern church, though new rituals have emerged in recent years. Still, individual and integral confession and absolution remain the ordinary means for the administration of the sacrament. The priest is the minister of the sacrament.

Extreme Unction (Anointing of the Sick) is the sacrament by which those of advanced age or in danger of death from sickness or accident are anointed with blessed oil and prayed over by a priest. The sacrament is seen as giving health and strength to the soul, and sometimes to the body. Grace is conferred, and sins are forgiven, including inculpably unconfessed grave or mortal sins. The sacrament may be received more than once, and may be administered in a communal ritual, as in a home for the aged, regardless of whether the individuals are in imminent danger of death. The anointing is usually to the forehead and hands, with the prayer: "Through this holy anointing and his most loving mercy, may the Lord assist you by the grace of the Holy Spirit so that, when you have been freed from your sins, he may save you and in his goodness raise you up." The first formal ritual for the sacrament dates from the 9th Century. Prior to that the blessed oils were regarded as a sacramental substance through which God could effect physical cures. Sacramental promulgation is based on the letter of St. James the Apostle, 5:13-15.

Holy Orders is the sacrament through which individuals receive the power and grace to perform the sacred duties of bishops, priests and deacons. Under the present discipline of the church, Holy Orders is reserved to males, but there is pressure to extend the availability of the sacrament to women. Among the powers of the priesthood are consecration of the Eucharist, forgiveness of sins, celebration of other sacraments, and the right to perform a range of pastoral and ecclesiastical functions. The priesthood is achieved by advancing through the minor orders of porter, lector, exorcist and acolyte, to the major orders of subdiaconate, diaconate, and finally to ordination as priest.

Ordination (formerly called consecration) as bishop is considered the fullness of the sacrament. In hierarchal union with the pope and their brother-bishops, bishops are regarded as successors of the Apostles and pastors of the church. The power to ordain others belongs to bishops. They are the primary teachers of the church and the custodians of doctrine, although priests also do preach and teach the word of God.

In ascending order, the steps to the priesthood and the functions of its initiates are:

Porter, to protect the entrance to the Christian assembly and to turn away undesirables; it is an order of early origin and use in the Church, but presently without particular significance.

Lector, to read the scriptural passages and other prayers and messages of the liturgy; it is a function now commonly performed by lay persons, called commentators.

Exorcist, to perform services of exorcism, or explusion of evil spirits; it is a responsibility now reserved to specially designated priests.

Acolyte, to serve in minor roles at liturgical worship; it is a function now largely fulfilled by altarboys or other servers at the Mass.

Subdeacon, to serve in secondary but nevertheless important capacities in liturgical worship, notably the Mass. In the West, this is regarded as a major order, but not so in the East. The order dates from the middle of the 3rd century and was upgraded to major order in the Western Church in the 13th century.

Deacon, to serve in the ministry of the liturgy, of the word, and of charity. There are two kinds of deacons: those who receive the order while advancing to ordination, and those who receive the order and remain in it permanently (see Permanent Deacon).

Priest, as described.

The essential matter of the rite of ordination is the imposition of hands on the heads of the *ordinandi* by the ordaining bishop. The essential form is the accompanying prayer in the preface of the ordination rite. Other elements of the rite include the presentation of the implements of sacrifice—the chalice of wine and the paten with host—along with prescribed prayers.

Matrimony is a sacrament by which a man and woman bind themselves together for life in a lawful union, and receive the grace to discharge their duties as husband and wife. It is the one sacrament that is administered by the principals themselves. The priest is present as a witness for the church and generally also for the state. (A deacon may fulfill this function.) Two other witnesses are likewise required, roles performed by the maid-of-honor and best-man (matron-of-honor, if the female witness happens to be married).

Church legislation governing marriage is explicit and detailed, and is spelled out in 111 canons of the Code of Canon Law. The canons address matters of consent (a marriage must be rational, free, true and mutual), age (marriage is prohibited before age of puberty), pastoral preparation, impediments, mixed marriages, secret marriages, form, separation of spouses, convalidation, etc.

In instances of troubled marriages, civil divorce is permitted for civil purposes, but it is the Church's position that a civil divorce does not break the bond of a valid marriage.

The Church does grant annulment—which is not to be confused with divorce. An annulment is the Church's declaration that from the beginning there has been no marriage, because of a lack of validity traceable to an unknown or concealed impediment, an essential defect in consent, or a condition placed by one or both of the partners against the nature of the sacrament. A decree of nullity declares that no marital bonds ever existed.

The Golden Rule

This is a principle sometimes regarded as non-theological, as the guiding rule of humanism. In fact, it is thoroughly grounded in Christianity and in the scriptures themselves. Luke situates the Golden Rule immediately after the Beatitudes, in the passage where Jesus urges love of enemies. The variations are as multiple as translations of the Bible, but most of us know the Golden Rule as "Do unto others as you would have them do unto you" (Luke 6:31). The admonition catches its echo in John 13:34, when, at the Last Supper, Jesus said: "I give you a new commandment: Love one another, that as I have loved you, you also love one another." In a real sense, love is the fulfilling of the law, the ingredient without which belief, creed have no meaning.

What Must Be Believed?

The basics of the church's doctrine of belief are spelled out in the Nicene (Nicene-Constantinople) Creed and in the Apostle's Creed, which most Catholics learn with their first prayers and which is the introductory prayer to the popular Marian rosary. But the doctrine of the church has expanded from that which the Apostles and early Father knew, as the church refined and expanded its understanding of belief and the responsibilities of faith. As recently as 1950, for example, the Assumption of Our Lady (body and soul) into heaven—long a revered feast of the church—was formally declared a truth of faith and a dogma of the church by Pope Pius XII (1939-1958).

The exaltation of a feast such as the Assumption to the level of official doctrine was accomplished with remarkable ease, primarily because the teaching authority of the church at the time enjoyed unquestioning acceptance with the church's membership. Thus, to the question "What must be believed?" the answer as recently as 1950 was, "Everything is to be believed"—and further, could be believed and was believed, for the church's membership was so disposed. Today it sometimes seems that the opposite is the case—that little is believed or, at the very least, that Catholics pick and choose what they want to believe.

The cause of this development is still a matter of debate, but it appears likely, from timing if nothing more, that the roots of dogmatic independence among Catholics can be traced to Vatican Council II's Declaration on Religious Freedom *(Dignitatis Humanae)*. The document addressed religious freedom in the broad sense, and was not conceived as a "white paper" for intramural consumption. However, it speedily became an expression of large intramural significance, as Catholics applied the precepts of the declaration to their individual spiritual lives in such areas as birth control, divorce, second marriages and clerical and religious discipline. If that development was not altogether predictable to the Council Fathers, it was to the priest who was a principal architect of the document, Father John Courtney Murray, S.J. (1904-1967). Shortly after the declaration was voted, Father Murray declared, "Inevitably, a second great argument will be set afoot—now on the theological meaning of Christian freedom." For, he continued, those who receive this freedom "assert it within the church as well as within the world."

This application is not something to which the official church is reconciled. In essence, the position of the church is that Catholics are bound to believe revealed truths, including those proposed or defined by the church and thus entered into the church's dogmatic treasury. They are bound to believe these revealed truths both as a matter of salvation and in order to maintain the bonds of the family of faith, which is the Catholic Church. The church's position derives of scriptural authority (John 20:21, Luke 10:16, Matthew 18:17, Mark 16:16, etc.), and the doctrine of infallibility ratified at the Council of Trent (1545-1563). At the same time, it is conceded that some revealed truths are fundamental to the faith, while others are non-fundamental, and accordingly may be doubted or even lawfully denied. This is another way of saying that some dogmas of faith are more necessary than others, and further that an explicit knowledge of some dogmas is necessary to salvation, while an implicit faith in others is considered sufficient.

Worship

Practice as a Catholic—The Mass. The principal act of worship of the Catholic faith is the celebration of the

Mass. In the traditional sense, the Mass is the sacrifice of the New Law in which Christ, through the ministry of the priest, offers himself to God in an unbloody manner under the appearances of bread and wine. While not rejecting this understanding, Vatican Council II (1962-1965) expanded the sense of the Mass to accent the concepts of community and love, or *agape*—which in the Greek translates to "love, love feast." Pertinent declarations of the Council:

"Acting in the person of Christ, and proclaiming his mystery, they [priests] join the offering of the faithful to the sacrifice of their Head. Until the coming of the Lord (cf. 1 Cor. 11:26), they represent and apply in the Sacrifice of the Mass the one sacrifice of the New Testament, namely the sacrifice of Christ offering himself once and for all to his Father as a spotless victim (cf. Heb. 9:11-28)." (Constitution on the Church, 28)

"At the Last Supper, on the night when he was betrayed, our Savior instituted the Eucharistic Sacrifice of his Body and Blood. He did this in order to perpetuate the sacrifice of the Cross throughout the centuries until he should come again, and so to entrust to his beloved spouse, the church, a memorial of his death and resurrection: a sacrament of love, a sign of unity, a bond of charity (cf. St. Augustine, "In Ioannis Evangelium, tractatus 26"), a paschal banquet in which Christ is consumed, the mind is filled with grace, and a pledge of future glory is given to us." (Constitution on the Sacred Liturgy, 47)

At the same time, the Council Fathers decreed that the rite of the Mass should be revised "in such a way that the intrinsic nature and purpose of its several parts, as also the connection between them, can be more clearly manifested, and that devout and active participation by the faithful can be more easily accomplished" (Constitution on the Sacred Liturgy, 50).

Thus it is that a new order of the Mass was introduced after Vatican Council II.

Order of the Mass. Under the old formula, the Mass had two essential divisions: the Mass of the Catechumens, which consisted of the preliminary prayers and readings of the service, and the Mass of the Faithful, which consisted of the central elements of the service involving the consecration of the species of bread and wine into the Body and Blood of Christ. Under the new formula, the essential divisions of the Mass are the Liturgy of the Word, which consists of the readings, homily, recitation of the Nicene Creed and the prayers of the faithful, and the Liturgy of the Eucharist, which consists of the offering of the gifts, the central act of sacrifice which is the Consecration, and the Eucharistic banquet, involving the reception of Communion. The Liturgy of the Word and the Liturgy of the Eucharist are preceded by brief introductory rites and followed by concluding rites. Mass can be celebrated only by a priest. The faithful, by their presence, assist at the Mass.

Catholics are required under church law to attend Mass on Sundays and holy days of obligation. The priest is encouraged to celebrate Mass daily, whenever possible. On Sundays and holy days of obligation, priests may celebrate Mass twice (bination) or three times (trination), according to the circumstances of need and necessity. On given feasts (Christmas and All Souls' Day), three Masses are customary. Until relatively recent years, the practice was to restrict the celebration of Mass to morning (prenoon) hours. Today, Mass may be celebrated at any hour, and Sunday Mass may be anticipated with a ceremony in the evening hours of Saturday. The only day of the year on which Mass is not celebrated is Good Friday. The liturgy for that day calls for a Celebration of the Lord's Passion, consisting of a Liturgy of the Word, veneration of the cross, and Holy Communion (the Eucharist having been previously consecrated). The ordinary site for the Mass is a church or chapel, but home and outdoor Masses have become common with the easing of regulations governing rituals.

Vestments of the Mass. Liturgical vestments in their every component are not absolutely necessary for the celebration of Mass, but custom and decorum dictate their use. These vestments derive of clothing in popular use in the early church, and over the years they have acquired a sacred symbolism. The vestments are as follows:

• Amice: a small linen cloth, which covers the priest's shoulders.

• Alb: a white linen tunic of full-body length.

• Cincture or girdle: a cord used to fasten the alb at the waist.

• Maniple: a strip of cloth, which hangs from the left arm.

• Stole: a long narrow cloth worn about the neck and crossed on the breast.

• Chasuble: the outer garment, which hangs from the shoulders.

• Dalmatic: the outer garment worn by deacons in place of a chasuble.

The material, style and ornamentation of liturgical vestments may vary, according to episcopal norms and latitudes allowed by the Holy See. The vestments customarily ornamented are the chasuble, dalmatic and stole.

The alb, stole and chasuble are cited as the minimal vestments required for a priest celebrating Mass.

Liturgical Colors. The outer liturgical vestments vary in color according to the liturgical season, feast day or occasion. The colors used at Mass are:

• Green, the color of hope and growth. Barring exceptions, it is used from mid-January until the eve of Septuagesima Sunday, and from the day after Trinity Sunday until the eve of the First Sunday of Advent. This is the period known as "per annum," throughout the year, or Ordinary Time.

• Purple, or violet, the penitential color. It is used mainly during Advent and Lent. It may also be used in Masses for the dead.

• Red, the color of fire and blood. It is used on the feasts of the Apostles and martyrs, as well as on feasts connected with the passion and death of Christ, including Pentecost, or Votive Mass of the Holy Spirit.

• Rose, the color of joy anticipated. It is used in place of purple, or violet, on such feasts as Gaudete Sunday (Third Sunday of Advent) and Laetare Sunday (Fourth Sunday of Lent).

• White, the color of purity and joy. It is the color of Christmas and Easter, as well as the feasts and commemorations of the Virgin Mary, angels, saints who were not martyrs, All Saints and specified feasts. It is often substituted for other colors, including at funeral Masses.

• Black, the color of mourning. It may be used in offices and Masses for the dead, although with the new emphases of the Mass of Christian Burial and the rite of passage to eternal life, white may be used. White vestments have traditionally been used at the funerals of infants and children who died before reaching the age of reason (7).

(Gold, strictly speaking is not a liturgical color, but gold vestments may be used on solemn occasions, even though the color does not conform to the requirements of the day.)

Liturgical Vessels. The principal vessels of the Mass are:

• Chalice, or the cup; used for the consecration of the wine.

• Paten, or plate; used for holding the bread of consecration.

(Both of the above vessels should be made of strong, noble materials, not given to corrosion or easy breakage. Gold plating is required of interior parts subject to rust, and the cup should be of nonabsorbent composition.)

• Ciborium, shaped like a chalice; used to hold the hosts distributed to the faithful at the communion.

• Cruets; containers for the water and wine used at Mass.

Other liturgical vessels:

• Monstrance, or ostensorium; a portable container or receptacle used to display the Blessed Sacrament at Benediction or in the course of processions.

• Luna, Lunula or Lunette; a small receptacle used to hold the Blessed Sacrament in an upright position in the monstrance.

• Pyx, a vessel the size of a pocketwatch; used in carrying the Blessed Sacrament to the sick.

Liturgical Linens. The principal linens used in the Mass are:

• Corporal, a square linen cloth, placed on the altar, and used as a resting place for the sacred species during the Liturgy of the Eucharist.

• Altar cloth, a white cloth, often linen, used to cover the altar table.

• Pall, a square piece of starched or stiff material, usually linen, used to cover the chalice.

• Purificator, an oblong piece of cloth, again usually linen, used for cleaning the sacred vessels after the reception of Communion.

• Burse, a square, stiff case, flat and open at one end, used for carrying the corporal.

Other Forms of Worship

The Mass, as said, is the principal form of worship in the Catholic Church. But there exists alongside the Mass a range of devotional options for the devout Catholic. Following are devotionals traditional to the prayer life of many Catholics.

The Rosary. One of the most popular Catholic devotions has historically been the rosary. The rosary is a prayer in honor of the Virgin Mary, consisting of 150 Hail Marys, 15 Our Fathers, 15 Doxologies, preceded ordinarily by the Apostles' Creed, one Our Father, three Hail Marys and a Doxology said for the increase of faith, hope and charity. The rosary is prayed to meditation on the life, passion and glory of Jesus, and as such is divided into three sets of mysteries. As a rule, only one-third of the rosary is said at a time, and the prayers are counted in decades on a string of blessed beads. The sets of the rosary's mysteries are as follows:

The Five Joyful Mysteries:
1. The Annunciation
2. The Visitation
3. The Birth of Our Lord
4. The Presentation of Our Lord
5. The Finding of Our Lord in the Temple

The Five Sorrowful Mysteries:
1. The Agony of Our Lord in the Garden
2. The Scourging at the Pillar
3. The Crowning with Thorns
4. The Carrying of the Cross
5. The Crucifixion and Death of Our Lord

The Five Glorious Mysteries:
1. The Resurrection
2. The Ascension
3. The Descent of the Holy Spirit
4. The Assumption of Our Blessed Mother into Heaven
5. The Coronation of Our Blessed Mother

The origin of the rosary is attributed to St. Dominic in the 13th Century and, over the centuries, has been regarded as a powerful prayer of intercession in times of danger and calamity. The victory of Lepanto (1571) and the deliverance of Vienna (1683) from the Turks are connected to the praying of the rosary. In thanksgiving the Church marks October 7 as the Feast of Our Lady of the Rosary.

The Angelus. The Angelus is a prayer recited morning, noon and evening (6 a.m., 12 noon and 6 p.m.) in honor of Mary and in commemoration of the Incarnation of Christ. The prayer is named from its first word in the Latin, "Angelus." It consists of three versicles, three Hail Marys and concluding prayer, as follows:

V. The angel of the Lord declared unto Mary.
R. And she conceived of the Holy Ghost.
   Hail Mary, etc.
V. Behold the handmaid of the Lord.
R. Be it done unto me according to thy word.
   Hail Mary, etc.
V. And the Word was made flesh.
R. And dwelt among us.
   Hail Mary, etc.
V. Pray for us, O holy Mother of God.
R. That we may be made worthy of the promises of Christ.

   Let us Pray

Pour forth, we beseech Thee, O Lord, Thy grace into our hearts, that we to whom the Incarnation of Christ, Thy Son, was made known by the message of an angel, may by His passion and cross be brought to the glory of His resurrection, through the same Christ Our Lord. Amen.

The Angelus owes its origins to the Franciscans. The custom of ringing the bell for the Angelus dates from the 13th Century, when the practice was introduced as an admonishment to Catholics to pray for the victory of the crusades.

During the Easter Season, the "Regina Coeli" commemorating the joy of Mary at Christ's Resurrection is substituted for The Angelus.

The Regina Coeli. Queen of heaven, rejoice. Alleluia.
For He whom thou didst deserve to bear.
Alleluia.

Hath risen as He said. Alleluia.
Pray for us to God. Alleluia.
V. Rejoice and be glad, O Virgin Mary!
Alleluia.
R. Because Our Lord is truly risen. Alleluia.
Let us Pray
O God, who by the resurrection of Thy Son, Our Lord
Jesus Christ, hast vouchsafed to make glad the whole
world, grant, we beseech Thee, that, through the in-
tercession of the Virgin Mary, His Mother, we may at-
tain the joys of eternal life. Through the same Christ
Our Lord. Amen.

Stations of the Cross. The devotion of the Stations of the
Cross, known also as the Way of the Cross, is a series
of 14 meditations on the Passion and Death of Christ. The
devotion traces the path followed by Christ from the pal-
ace of Pilate to Calvary and burial. Tradition holds that
it was the Blessed Mother who originated this devotion
by retracing the steps of Jesus and pausing at spots along
the way marked by special incidents. It is more likely,
however, that the devotion began with pilgrims to
the Holy Land, who visited and prayed at scenes of the
passion.

Depictions of these scenes are mounted in most Catholic churches. The practice is to move from station to station, meditating at each and reciting an Our Father, Hail
Mary and a Gloria. If a group of persons is involved, it
is only necessary for the leader to move about. The Stations of the Cross may also be said on a specially blessed
cross, known as a Stations Crucifix.

The Stations of the Cross developed widely along with
devotion to the Passion in the 12th and 13th Centuries.
The Franciscans were instrumental in this development,
but it was a Redemptorist, St. Alphonsus Liguori (1696-
1787), who gave the devotion its modern impetus with
meditations that became standard in many churches.
These meditations and a listing of the stations follow:

FIRST STATION: Jesus is Condemned to Death

Consider how Jesus, after having been scourged and crowned with thorns, was unjustly condemned by Pilate to die on the cross.

My adorable Jesus, it was not Pilate, no, it was my sins that condemned You to death. I beg You, by the merits of this sorrowful journey, to assist my soul in its journey toward eternity. I love You, Jesus my love, I love You more than myself; I repent with my whole heart for having offended You. Never permit me to separate myself from You again. Grant that I may love You always and then do with me as You will.

SECOND STATION: Jesus Takes Up His Cross

Consider how Jesus, in making this journey with the cross on His shoulders, thought of us, and for us offered to His Father the death He was about to undergo.

My beloved Jesus, I embrace all the tribulations You have destined for me until death. I beg You, by the merits of the pain You suffered for me in carrying Your cross, to give me the necessary help to carry mine with perfect patience and resignation.

I love You, Jesus my love...

THIRD STATION: Jesus Falls the First Time

Consider this first fall of Jesus under His cross. His flesh was torn with scourges, His head crowned with thorns, and He had lost a great quantity of blood. He was so weakened He could scarcely walk, and yet He had to carry this great load upon His shoulders. The soldiers struck Him rudely, and thus He fell several times in His journey.

My beloved Jesus, it is not the weight of the cross, but my sins, which have made You suffer so much pain. Ah, by the merits of this first fall, deliver me from the misfortune of falling into mortal sin.

I love You, Jesus my love...

FOURTH STATION: Jesus Meets His Afflicted Mother

Consider the meeting of the Son and the Mother, which took place on this journey. Jesus and Mary looked at each other, and their looks became as so many arrows to wound those hearts which loved each other so tenderly.

My most loving Jesus, by the sorrow You experienced in this meeting, grant me the grace of a truly devoted love for Your most holy Mother. And you, my Queen, overwhelmed with sorrow, obtain for me, by your intercession, a continual and tender remembrance of the Passion of your Son.

I love You, Jesus my love...

FIFTH STATION: Simon of Cyrene Helps Jesus

Consider how the Jews, seeing that at each step Jesus from weakness was on the point of expiring, and fearing that He would die on the way, when they wished Him to die the ignominious death of the cross, constrained Simon the Cyrenian to carry the cross behind Our Lord.

My most sweet Jesus, I will not refuse the cross as the Cyrenian did; I accept it, I embrace it. I accept in particular the death You have destined for me; with all the pains that may accompany it; I unite it to Your death, I offer it to You. You have died for love of me; I will die for love of You and to please You. Help me by Your grace.

I love You, Jesus my love...

SIXTH STATION: Veronica Wipes the Face of Jesus

Consider how the holy woman named Veronica, seeing Jesus so afflicted, and His face bathed in sweat and blood, presented Him with a towel with which He wiped His adorable face, leaving on it the impression of His holy countenance.

My most beloved Jesus, Your face was beautiful before, but in this journey it has lost all its beauty, and wounds and blood have disfigured it. Alas, my soul was once beautiful, when it received Your grace in Baptism; but I have disfigured it since by my sins; You alone, my Redeemer, can restore it to its former beauty. Do this by Your passion; O Jesus. I repent of having offended You. Never permit me to offend You again.

I love You, Jesus my love...

SEVENTH STATION: Jesus Falls the Second Time

Consider the second fall of Jesus under the cross—a fall which renews that pain of all the wounds of the head and members of our afflicted Lord.

My most gentle Jesus, how many times You have pardoned me, and how many times I have fallen again, and begun again to offend You! Oh, by the merits of this new fall, give me the necessary help to persevere in Your grace until death. Grant that in all temptations which assail me, I may always commend myself to You.

I love You, Jesus my love...

EIGHTH STATION: Jesus Comforts the Women of Jerusalem

Consider how these women wept with compassion at seeing Jesus in such a pitiable state, streaming with blood, as He walked along. But Jesus said to them, "Weep not for me but for yourselves and for your children."

My Jesus, laden with sorrows, I weep for the offenses I have committed against You, because of the pains they have deserved, and still more because of the displeasure. they have caused You who have loved me so much. It is Your love, more than the fear of hell which causes me to weep for my sins.

I love You, Jesus my love...

NINTH STATION: Jesus Falls the Third Time

Consider the third fall of Jesus Christ. His weakness was extreme, and the cruelty of his executioners excessive, who tried to hasten His steps when He had scarcely strength to move.

Ah, my outraged Jesus, by the merits of the weakness You suffered in going up Calvary, give me strength sufficient to conquer all human respect and all my wicked passions which have led me to despise Your friendship.

I love You, Jesus my love...

TENTH STATION: Jesus is Stripped of His Garments

Consider the violence with which the executioners stripped Jesus. His inner garments adhered to His torn flesh, and they dragged them off so roughly that the skin came with them. Compassionate your Savior thus cruelly treated and say to Him:

My innocent Jesus, by the merits of the torment You felt, help me to strip myself of all affection to things of earth, in order that I may place all my love in You who are so worthy of my love.

I love You, Jesus my love...

ELEVENTH STATION: Jesus is Nailed to the Cross

Consider how Jesus, after being thrown on the cross, extended His hands and offered to His eternal Father the sacrifice of His death for our salvation. These barbarians fastened Him with nails, and then, raising the cross, allowed Him to die with anguish on this infamous gibbet.

My Jesus! loaded with contempt, nail my heart to Your feet, that it may ever remain there, to love You and never quit You again.

I love You, Jesus my love...

TWELFTH STATION: Jesus Dies on the Cross

Consider how your Jesus, after three hours' agony on the cross, consumed at length with anguish, abandons himself to the weight of His body, bows His head and dies.

O my dying Jesus, I kiss devoutly the cross on which You died for love of me. I have merited by my sins to die a miserable death, but Your death is my hope. Ah, by the merits of Your death, give me grace to die embracing Your feet and burning with love for You. I yield my soul into Your hands.

I love You, Jesus my love...

THIRTEENTH STATION: Jesus is Taken Down from the Cross

Consider how, after the death of Our Lord, two of His disciples, Joseph and Nicodemus, took Him down from the cross, and placed Him in the arms of his afflicted Mother, who received Him with unutterable tenderness, and pressed Him to her bosom.

O Mother of Sorrow, for the love of this Son, accept me as your servant and pray to Him for me. And You, my holy Redeemer, since You have died for me, permit me to love You, for I wish but You and nothing more. I love You, Jesus my love...

FOURTEENTH STATION: Jesus is Laid in the Tomb
Consider how the disciples carried the body of Jesus to bury it, accompanied by His Holy Mother, who arranged it in the sepulcher with her own hands. They then closed the tomb and all withdrew.

O my buried Jesus, I kiss the stone that encloses You. But You rose to life again on the third day. I beg You, by Your Resurrection, make me rise glorious with You at the last day, to be always united with You in heaven, to praise and love You forever.
I love You, Jesus my love...

Some modern Stations of the Cross include a fifteenth station on the Resurrection-Ascension, out of an awareness of the relation of the Passion to these events.

Novenas. Novenas are public or private devotions spaced over a period of nine days or, alternatively, over a period of nine weeks, during which one day each week is set aside for the devotions. The practice is said to have originated with the Apostles and disciples as, along with the Virgin Mary, they awaited the coming of the Holy Spirit (Pentecost) after the Ascension.

Novenas are commonly made to God or to him through Mary, the angels or the saints. Prayers vary according to the novena.

At one time, novenas were among the most popular devotions of the church, notably certain novenas to the Blessed Virgin and to saints like St. Francis Xavier (March 4-12). However, their popularity has waned in recent years.

Missions. In the devotional sense, a mission is a series

of sermons and spiritual exercises, conducted under the leadership of a competent religious person, usually male but sometimes female, as by a nun, for purposes of renewing and deepening one's religious life. Parish missions were once a common feature of Catholic life. Generally they lasted a week, and included a course of talks, meditation, self-examination of faith and conscience, and devotional exercises such as daily Mass and Communion.

Retreats. In the devotional sense once again, a retreat is a series of spiritual exercises and religious services held in convent, school or, as is generally understood, in a place specially designated as a retreat house. A retreat is similar to a mission, but its exercises and services are usually more particularized, since retreat groups, as distinct from parish missions, tend to be more homogeneous, bringing together people of a kind (e.g., priests, nuns) or from an occupation (e.g., doctors, nurses, communications workers). A retreat may be as short as three days. When it is held in a retreat house, the practice is for the participant to remain day and night.

Benediction of the Blessed Sacrament. Benediction (Exposition) of the Blessed Sacrament is a devotion in which the Sacred Host (Blessed Sacrament) is placed in a monstrance and displayed to the faithful for adoration. A ciborium may be used in place of a monstrance. This devotion too has lessened in popularity, but at one time it was solemn practice to expose the Blessed Sacrament at evening services on Sundays and holy days, on the eves of First Fridays, and on special feasts, such as that of Corpus Christi. The Forty Hours' devotion and the Holy Hour devotion were derivitive of this act of worship. Coincident or not, the popularity of Benediction of the Blessed Sacrament waned as the church deemphasized triumphalism in Catholic life and worship after Vatican Council II (1962-1965).

Traditional Prayers

The Sign of the Cross

In the name of the Father, and of the Son, and of the Holy Spirit. Amen.

The Lord's Prayer

Our Father who art in heaven, hallowed be Thy name; Thy kingdom come; Thy will be done on earth as it is in heaven.

Give us this day our daily bread; and forgive us our trespasses as we forgive those who trespass against us; and lead us not into temptation, but deliver us from evil. Amen.

The Hail Mary

Hail Mary, full of grace! the Lord is with thee; blessed art thou among women, and blessed is the fruit of thy womb, Jesus.

Holy Mary, Mother of God, pray for us sinners, now and at the hour of our death. Amen.

Doxology (The Gloria)

Glory be to the Father, and to the Son, and to the Holy Spirit. As it was in the beginning, is now, and ever shall be, world without end. Amen.

The Apostles' Creed

I believe in God, the Father Almighty, Creator of heaven and earth; and in Jesus Christ, His only Son, Our Lord; who was conceived by the Holy Spirit, born of the Virgin Mary, suffered under Pontius Pilate, was crucified, died, and was buried. He descended into hell; the third day He arose again from the dead; He ascended into heaven, sitteth at the right hand of God, the Father Almighty; from thence He shall come to judge the living and the dead. I believe in the Holy

Spirit, the Holy Catholic Church, the communion of saints, the forgiveness of sins, the resurrection of the body, and life everlasting. Amen.

The Confiteor

I confess to Almighty God, to blessed Mary ever Virgin, to blessed Michael the Archangel, to blessed John the Baptist, to the holy Apostles Peter and Paul, and to all the Saints, that I have sinned exceedingly in thought, word, and deed through my fault, through my fault, through my most grievous fault. Therefore, I beseech the blessed Mary ever Virgin, blessed Michael the Archangel, blessed John the Baptist, the holy Apostles Peter and Paul, and all the Saints, to pray to the Lord our God for me.

May the Almighty God have mercy on me, and forgive me my sins, and bring me to everlasting life. Amen.

May the almighty and merciful Lord grant me pardon, absolution, and remission of all my sins. Amen.

Act of Contrition

O my God, I am heartily sorry for having offended Thee, and I detest all my sins, because of Thy just punishments (the loss of heaven and the pain of hell), but most of all because they offend Thee, my God, who art all-good and deserving of all my love. I firmly resolve, with the help of Thy grace, to confess my sins, to do penance, and to amend my life. Amen.

Act of Faith

O my God, I firmly believe that Thou art one God in three Divine Persons, Father, Son, and Holy Spirit; I believe that Thy Divine Son became man, and died for our sins, and that He will come to judge the living and the dead. I believe these and all the truths which the Holy Catholic Church teaches, because Thou hast revealed them, who can neither deceive nor be deceived.

Act of Hope

O my God, relying on Thy almighty power and infinite mercy and promises, I hope to obtain pardon of my sins, the help of Thy grace, and life everlasting, through the merits of Jesus Christ, my Lord and Redeemer.

Act of Love

O my God, I love Thee above all things, with my whole heart and soul, because Thou art all-good and worthy of all love. I love my neighbor as myself for the love of Thee. I forgive all who have injured me, and ask pardon of all whom I have injured.

The Divine Praises

Blessed be God.
Blessed be His Holy Name.
Blessed be Jesus Christ, true God and true Man.
Blessed be the Name of Jesus.
Blessed be His Most Sacred Heart.
Blessed be His Most Precious Blood.
Blessed be Jesus in the Most Holy Sacrament of the Altar.
Blessed be the great Mother of God, Mary most holy.
Blessed be her holy and Immaculate Conception.
Blessed be her glorious Assumption.
Blessed be the name of Mary, Virgin and Mother.
Blessed be St. Joseph, her most chaste spouse.
Blessed be God, in His angels and in His saints.

The "Hail, Holy Queen"

Hail, Holy Queen, Mother of Mercy, our life, our sweetness, and our hope. To thee do we cry, poor banished children of Eve; to thee do we send up our sighs, mourning and weeping in this valley of tears. Turn, then, most gracious advocate, thine eyes of mercy toward us; and after this our exile, show unto us the blessed fruit of thy womb, Jesus, O clement, O loving, O sweet Virgin Mary.

Pray for us, O Holy Mother of God.

That we may be worthy of the promises of Christ.

The Memorare

Remember, O most gracious Virgin Mary, that never was it known that any one who fled to thy protection, implored thy help, and sought thy intercession, was left unaided. Inspired with this confidence, I fly unto thee, O Virgin of virgins, my Mother! To thee I come, before thee I stand, sinful and sorrowful. O Mother of the Word Incarnate, despise not my petitions, but, in thy mercy, hear and answer me. Amen.

Prayer Before a Crucifix

Look down upon me, O good and gentle Jesus, while before Thy face I humbly kneel, and with burning soul pray and beseech Thee to fix deep in my heart lively sentiments of faith, hope, and charity, true contrition for my sins, and a firm purpose of amendment; while I contemplate with great love and tender pity Thy five wounds, pondering over them within me, calling to mind the words which David Thy prophet said of Thee, my good Jesus: "They have pierced My hands and My feet; they have numbered all my bones."

De Profundis

Out of the depths I have cried unto Thee, O Lord! Lord, hear my voice.

Let Thine ears be attentive to the voice of my supplication.

If Thou, O Lord, wilt mark iniquities:

Lord, who shall abide it!

For with Thee there is merciful forgiveness; and by reason of Thy law I have waited for Thee, O Lord.

My soul hath relied on His word; my soul hath hoped in the Lord.

From the morning watch even until night; let Israel hope in the Lord.

Because with the Lord there is mercy: and with Him plenteous redemption. And He shall redeem Israel from all his iniquities.

Eternal rest give unto them, O Lord, and let perpetual light shine upon them.

May they rest in peace. Amen.

O God, the Creator and Redeemer of all the faithful, grant to the souls of Thy servants departed the remission of all their sins, that through pious supplications they may obtain that pardon which they have always desired: Who livest and reignest for ever and ever. Amen.

The Anima Christi

Soul of Christ, sanctify me; Body of Christ, save me; Blood of Christ, inebriate me; Water from the side of Christ, wash me; Passion of Christ, strengthen me. O good Jesus, hear me; Within your wounds hide me; Separated from you, let me never be; From the evil one protect me; At the hour of my death, call me; And close to you bid me; That with your saints I may be, praising you forever and ever. Amen.

Prayer of St. Ignatius

Take, O Lord, and receive my entire liberty, my memory, my understanding and my whole will. All that I am and all that I possess You have given me: I surrender it all to Your love and Your grace; with these I will be rich enough, and will desire nothing more.

Prayer of St. Francis of Assisi for Peace

Make me, O Lord, an instrument of your peace.
Where there is hatred, let me sow love;
Where there is injury, pardon;
Where there is doubt, faith;

Where there is despair, hope;
Where there is darkness, light;
Where there is sadness, joy.

O Divine Master, grant that I may not so much seek to be consoled as to console; to be understood as to understand; to be loved as to love;

For it is in giving that we receive; it is in pardoning that we are pardoned, and it is in dying that we are born to eternal life. Amen.

Morning Offering

O my God, I offer Thee all my prayers, works, and sufferings of this day in union with the Sacred Heart of Jesus, for the intentions for which He pleads and offers Himself in the Holy Sacrifcice of the Mass, in thanksgiving for Thy favors, in reparation for my offenses, and in humble supplication for my temporal and eternal welfare, for the wants of our holy Mother the Church, for the conversion of sinners, and for the relief of the poor souls in purgatory.

I wish to gain all the indulgences attached to the prayers I shall say and to the good works I shall perform this day.

Blessing Before Meals

Bless us, O Lord, and these Thy gifts, which we are about to receive from Thy bounty, through Christ Our Lord. Amen.

Grace After Meals

We give Thee thanks for all Thy benefits, O Almighty God, who livest and reignest forever; and may the souls of the faithful departed, through the mercy of God, rest in peace. Amen.

Ejaculations (Short Exclamations of Prayer)

Jesus, Mary and Joseph, have mercy on us.
Blessed be God.
Mary of Mercy, pray for us.

My Jesus, Mercy.
Most Sacred Heart of Jesus, have mercy on us.
My Lord and my God.
Jesus, meek and mild, make my heart like to thine.

Obligations As A Practicing Catholic

The obligations of the practicing Catholic fall into moral and ecclesiastical categories. The moral category embraces respect for and observance of the Ten Commandments, and their fulfillment in the precepts of love of God and neighbor embodied in the Beatitudes and the Golden Rule. The ecclesiastical category embraces what is expected in church law of the average Catholic in the normal course of events. The expectation can be stated briefly, but its range is such as to govern Catholics as a whole in their total lives.

The average practicing Catholic is expected under ecclesiastical law to:

• Attend Mass on Sundays and holy days of obligation;
• Fulfill one's Easter duty;
• Observe the laws of fast and abstinence;
• Observe the Commandments of the Church.

This, of course, is the bare minimum. Catholics are also expected to live the principles of the church (e.g., its social doctrine), although latitudes here are elastic, since certain principles are subject to individual interpretation and application.

Works of Mercy. The principles of the Church are bound in the main by the Corporal and Spiritual Works of Mercy.

The Corporal Works of Mercy are seven:

• To feed the hungry;
• To give drink to the thirsty;

- To clothe the naked;
- To visit the imprisoned;
- To shelter the homeless;
- To visit the sick;
- To bury the dead.

The Spiritual Works of Mercy, likewise seven, are:

- To admonish the sinner;
- To instruct the ignorant;
- To counsel the doubtful;
- To comfort the sorrowful;
- To bear wrongs patiently;
- To forgive all injuries;
- To pray for the living and the dead.

Holy Days. Holy days are special days of devotion, established by the church to remind Catholics of the mysteries of their religion, of important events in the lives of Jesus Christ and of Mary, and to recall to them the virtues of the saints together with the rewards of a life lived close to God. The church asks that holy days be observed reverentially, and therefore imposes the obligation of attendance at Mass and abstinence from servile work, to the extent that this is possible.

Technically, all Sundays of the year are holy days. In addition, the church specifies ten feasts as holy days, although by indult of the Holy See the number observed varies from country to country. In the United States, the number of holy days of obligation has stood at six since late in the 19th century.

Holy Days in the United States. The six holy days of obligation for American Catholics were determined at the Third Plenary Council of Baltimore (1884). They are:

- *Christmas,* December 25, the feast marking the birth of Jesus Christ in Bethlehem;
- *The Solemnity of Mary,* January 1, the feast exalting the motherhood of Mary (formerly known as the Feast

of the Circumcision or the Octave of the Birth of Our
Lord);

• *Ascension*, the feast observed on the sixth Thursday
after Easter to mark Christ's ascension into heaven, 40
days after his Resurrection;

• *Assumption*, August 15, the feast commemorating the
taking of Mary, body and soul, into heaven after her death
on earth;

• *All Saints*, November 1, the feast commemorating all
the saints in heaven, but in particular those without any
specified feast day of their own;

• *Immaculate Conception*, December 8, the feast celebrating the freedom from sin of Mary the Mother of Jesus
from the moment of conception, and thus her preservation from original sin.

The remaining four holy days of the church are
Epiphany and Corpus Christi (rescheduled when necessary to coincide with a Sunday), and the Feast of St.
Joseph and Feast of Saints Peter and Paul (observed on
their respective dates—March 19 and June 20—but with
no Mass obligation applicable to American Catholics).

Holy Days, Their Status. In recent years, there has been
considerable speculation that the number of holy days
would be reduced. The American bishops at least twice
entertained thoughts of trimming the number to three—
either Christmas, the Solemnity of Mary and the Ascension, or Christmas, All Saints and the Immaculate Conception. Each time, they were dissuaded by popular
reaction.

The draft of the new Code of Canon Law would have
reduced the number of holy days to two: Christmas and
a Marian feast day to be determined by individual national hierarchies. However, Pope John Paul II struck out
the proposal and retained the number of holy days at ten
in approving the final form of the new Code (1983).

Certain confusion occurs when a holy day of obligation falls on a Saturday and is thus back-to-back with Sun-

day, also a day when attendance at Mass is obligatory. Does attendance at the Saturday Mass satisfy the obligation for both days? The answer is no, unless one attends two Saturday Masses: one in the earlier hours marking the holy day feast and one in the evening hours anticipating the Sunday obligation. Recently bishops in dioceses in Ohio, Michigan and Hawaii dispensed Catholics from attendance at a holy-day Mass when the feast backed up to a Sunday. Reasons were pastoral and practical. One consideration was the problem of health and travel for priests who minister to more than one community, sometimes miles apart from one another, as in the case of parishes and missions of rural areas.

It is also common to dispense from the holy-day obligation, when the feast occurs on a Monday. The same logic applies.

Easter Duty. Church law prescribes that Catholics receive Communion at a minimum of once a year by way of complying with the divine injunction to partake of the body and blood of Christ, and also by way of preserving the life of grace in the individual soul. The requirement is a serious one binding Catholics of the Roman Rite, and in the United States is to be fulfilled during the period designed as the Easter Time: the period extending from the first Sunday of Lent to Trinity Sunday, which is the Sunday after Pentecost, eight weeks after Easter. The Sacrament of Penance (Reconciliation) is not an absolute prerequisite for reception of the Eucharist, and thus is not a necessary part of one's Easter Duty. However, reception of the sacrament is encouraged in conjunction with the fulfillment of the Easter Duty requirement.

Church law prescribing the reception of the Eucharist during the Easter Time was promulgated by the Fourth Lateran Council (1215), and mitigated an earlier prescript which made it obligatory for Catholics to receive three times a year (Christmas, Easter and Pentecost). The Council of Trent (1545-1563) repeated the obligation of receiving during the Easter season. Paradoxically, one result of the emphasis on annual reception of the Eucharist was to reduce the number of times it was received during the rest of the year by fostering a rigorism about penitential disposition and worthiness to receive the sacrament more often than once a year. These attitudes persisted into the 20th century before being rooted out by Pope St. Pius X (1903-1914), who is known as the pope of frequent communion. Pius X encouraged frequent Communion by requiring but two conditions for its reception: state of grace and pious intention. There was also the necessity of observing the Eucharistic fast, which then involved abstinence from food and water from the previous midnight.

Fast and Abstinence. The church has greatly eased its fast and abstinence requirements in recent years, including that of Friday abstinence. Under the new Code of Canon Law, Fridays remain days of abstinence from meat except when the Friday occurs with a solemnity like Christmas, but the discipline is subject to the directives of the appropriate episcopal conference. The bishops of France, for instance, reinstated the practice of Friday abstinence in 1984, but extended the abstinence options from meat to tobacco or alcohol.

In the United States, Ash Wednesday and Good Friday are days of fast (limiting oneself to one full meal and two lighter meals) and abstinence (refraining from eating meat). The Fridays of Lent are days of abstinence in the United States. The obligation of abstinence begins with age 14 and extends throughout life. The obligation of fast begins with age 18 and extends to age 59. Eating between meals is not permitted on fast days, but liquids, including milk and fruit juices, are allowed. Catholics are urged to take these obligations seriously.

The church's discipline with respect to fast and abstinence derives of a desire to bring a spirit of penance into the life of Catholics individually, this in accord with the counsel of St. Mark: "Reform your lives and believe in the Gospel" (1:15). In the church's view, self-denial is bound up with reform and repentance, and a fundamental form of self-denial is fasting and abstaining. Historically, many saints linked fasting to prayer, believing that it helped prepare the mind for entering into the presence of God with alertness and clarity.

Eucharistic Fast. Norms of the new Code of Canon Law repeat the general requirement that communicants fast from foods and liquids for at least one hour before receiving the Eucharist. However, whereas the old norms said "with the exception of water," new norms add with the exception of "water and medicine."

In instances of the elderly and the sick, they are exempted entirely from the Eucharistic fast, along with those who care for them. The old norm was flexible, but called for a fast of "about a quarter of an hour."

A priest offering two or three Masses during the one day can eat food and drink liquids before the second and third Mass without regard for the hour's time limit.

Commandments of the Church. The commandments of the church, such as they remain in the post Vatican Council II church, are without the theological or moral authority of the Ten Commandments of God. The church, in fact, has defined nothing regarding the form, organization and number of the commandments of the church, and though the Council of Trent (1545-1563) recommended the church's commandments in a general way, it said nothing concerning them as a particular body of laws. The commandments of the church evolved slowly through history, and it was not until the 19th century that they were finally fixed at six. This was done by the bishops of England, and their enumeration was adopted by the fathers of the Third Plenary Council of Baltimore (1884), and prescribed for the United States. The six commandments of the church as learned by American Catholics are:

1) To assist at Mass on Sundays and holy days of obligation;
2) To fast and abstain on the days appointed;
3) To confess one's sins at least once a year;

4) To receive Holy Communion during the Easter season;
5) To contribute to the support of one's pastor;
6) To observe the laws of the Church concerning marriage.

(The English discipline was actually more specific on the sixth commandment. Its wording: "Not to marry within a certain degree of kindred nor to solemnize marriage at the forbidden times.")

Rules and Regulations

The Eucharist. As it is Baptism which identifies a person as a Christian, so is it the qualification to receive the Eucharist according to the rite of the Catholic Church which formalizes one's standing as a communicant of the Catholic Church.

For born Catholics, First Holy Communion—initiation as a communicant—commonly occurs on attainment of the age of reason or discretion, which is about 7. The practice in most places is to precede First Communion with First Confession (the Sacrament of Penance or Reconciliation). The necessity for First Confession in such instances has been the subject of controversy in recent years. Opponents argue that the commission of serious sin is impossible before the age of reason, since the individual lacks maturity both of reflection and will in order to commit serious sin—or, for that matter, to sin at all; which, in turn, obviates the need, much less the necessity for confession in the Sacrament of Penance (Reconciliation). In other words, can sin be confessed which does not exist in the first place, and does not the exercise of early confession under the circumstances become something of a mockery of the seriousness of the sacrament? The Holy See rejects this position. On May 24, 1973, it issued the document *Sanctus Pontifex*, approved by Pope Paul VI (1963-1978), which stated a preference for First Confession *before* First Communion, and ordered an end to experiments to the contrary. The admonition was repeated in 1977. Despite the Vatican advisory, however, experiments deferring the Sacrament of Penance continue in some dioceses. The practice is justified on grounds that the Vatican document is disciplinary rather than doctrinal, and accordingly subject to pastoral interpretation by individual bishops. Notwithstanding, Canon 914 of the new Code of Canon Law reiterates the 1973 position of *Sanctus Pontifex* that sacramental confession should precede First Communion.

The problem is generally academic in instances of converts to Catholicism, since conversion presumes maturity, and maturity involves different levels of reflection, will and responsibility for one's actions. Converts to Catholicism in most cases make a sacramental confesison before receiving their First Communion.

Conditions for receiving the Eucharist require that the recipient be in the state of grace, possess a proper disposition and observe the Eucharistic Fast.

Ordinarily, Communion is received under one species— bread. However, with instructions issued by the Congregation for Divine Worship on May 25, 1967 and June 29, 1970, and directives of episcopal conferences (including the U.S. Bishops' Conference) and individual bishops, Communion may now be received under the species of both bread and wine. Because convenience is a factor, the practice is generally limited to special liturgical occasions, such as weddings or jubilees, or restricted to Masses where attendance is small and dual reception of the species thus more manageable. In instances where reception is under both species, the wine may be received either by sharing the cup or by intinction (dipping the consecrated host into the consecrated wine).

Ordinarily, again, it is the custom to receive Communion but once a day, but reception a second time in the one day is permitted within a eucharistic celebration, as in the cases of persons attending morning Mass and then a wedding, funeral or evening Mass later in the day. Persons in danger of death are urged to receive the Eucharist a second time in the one day, even apart from Mass. The sick and shut-ins may also receive Communion apart from the Mass, with the sacrament administered either by priests or extraordinary ministers of the Eucharist (authorized laity). The purpose in allowing Communion more than once a day is to promote full participation in every eucharistic liturgy in which the individual joins.

Intercommunion. Catholics may not request Communion from clergy of other Christian churches who have not been validly ordained to the priesthood.

Within the Catholic Church intercommunion is possible for certain qualified non-Catholics. The criteria are contained in "Instruction on the Admission of Other Christians to the Eucharist," dated June 1, 1972, and issued July 8, 1972, and framed in the context of Vatican Council II's Decree on Ecumenism and the 1967 "Directory of Ecumenism" of the Secretariat for Promoting Christian Unity. The guiding principles are:

• "There is an indissoluble link between the mystery of the church and the mystery of the Eucharist, or between ecclesial and Eucharistic communion; the celebration of the Eucharist of itself signifies the fullness of profession of faith and ecclesial communion" (Instruction, 1972).

• "Eucharistic communion practiced by those who are not in full ecclesial communion with each other cannot be the expression of that full unity which the Eucharist of its nature signifies and which in this case does not exist; for this reason such communion cannot be regarded as a means to be used to lead to full ecclesial communion" (Instruction, 1972).

• The matter of reciprocity "arises only with those churches which have preserved the substance of the Eucharist, the sacrament of orders and apostolic succession" (Directory, 1967).

Catholic policy with respect to Intercommunion distinguishes between separated Eastern Rite Christians and other Christians, as follows:

• Separated Eastern Rite Christians may be given Communion (as well as receive the sacraments of Penance/Reconciliation and Anointing of the Sick) at their request. Catholics, in turn, may receive these same sacraments from priests of separated Eastern Rite Churches under conditions of spiritual necessity and benefit, and when access to a Catholic priest is physically or morally impossible. This reciprocity derives of the recognition that separated Eastern Rite Churches have maintained apostolic succession through their bishops and have valid priests and sacramental belief and practice. Generally speaking, these are the Eastern Orthodox Churches.

• Other Christians—generally speaking, those who are members of Reformation-related Churches—may receive the Eucharist but on a more limited basis, reception being "confined to particular cases of those Christians who have a faith in the sacrament in conformity with that of the church, who experience a serious spiritual need for the Eucharistic sustenance, who for a prolonged period are unable to have recourse to a minister of their own community, and who ask for the sacrament of their own accord; all this provided that they have proper dispositions and lead lives worthy of a Christian" (Directory, 1967). "Spiritual need" is defined as "a need for an increase in spiritual life and a need for a deeper involvement in the mystery of the church and its unity." The circumstances for reception of the Eucharist under this allowance extend to persecution, imprisonment and danger of death, coupled with the lack of availability of a minister of one's own denomination.

Matrimony. In simplest Catholic understanding, Matrimony is a sacrament by which a man and woman are bound together for life in lawful wedlock, and receive the grace to discharge their duties as husband, wife and parents. Among the chief effects of the sacrament are the special help of God to love one another faithfully; to bear one another's faults; to rear one's children properly.

Eligibility for the sacrament is determined by a number of factors, including:

Age: For a marriage to be valid, the woman must have completed her 14th year; the man, his 16th. These are minimum ages; in practice the Church insists on a much greater maturity of years.

Consent: The exchange of marriage vows must be rational, free, true and mutual. Fear or force, or the presence of conditions or intentions contrary to the nature of marriage can render matrimonial consent invalid.

Freedom from Impediments: Impediments can range from impotency, to blood relationship, to legal relationship resulting from adoption. Direct blood relationship (father-daughter, mother-son) is an impediment to marriage, as is a collateral relationship to the fourth degree (brother-sister, first, second and third cousins). Other impediments include the presence of Holy Orders, an existing valid marriage, and affinity (a kinship or close relationship resulting from a valid marriage). Dispensations from many impediments are possible. Some are reserved to the Holy See, but many can be obtained from local episcopal authority.

Because of escalating divorce rates, most dioceses now require instruction periods of up to six months to prepare couples entering a marriage.

For a Catholic marriage to be valid and lawful, it must be performed in the presence of a competent priest or deacon, and two witnesses. This is the one sacrament that the recipients administer to themselves; the priest is present as witness and to bring the blessing of the church to the union. The sacrament per se consists in the mutual expression of the contracting parties to take one another as husband and wife. A Roman Catholic (as of March 25, 1967) or an Eastern Rite Catholic (as of November 21, 1964) may contract marrriage validly in the presence of a separated Eastern Rite priest, provided other requirements of Canon Law are met.

The ordinary place for a marriage ceremony is the parish church of either party, or in the instance of a mixed marriage, in the parish church of the Catholic party. Exceptions to this rule are common.

Divorce and Remarriage. Church law regards as valid all marriages contracted according to its laws and falling within its jurisdiction. It holds Catholics to be bound by all the marriage laws of the church, and, in instances of mixed marriages, it considers the non-Catholic partner, whether baptized or not, to be bound by the same ecclesiastical laws governing the marriage. Among other things, this includes openness to the birth of children and rejection of artificial birth control as a method for determining the size of one's family. Natural birth control (e.g., the rhythm system) is permitted.

For married couples in troublesome unions, the church for reasons spiritual and humanitarian allows recourse to alternatives, including legal separation and civil divorce. Neither of these alternatives is regarded, however, as vitiating the marriage bond itself. This bond the church holds to be permanent, presuming the consummation of the valid marriage, and barring the existence of a diriment impediment or radical defect in place prior to the attempt to contract the particular marriage. Of course, with the death of one or the other spouse, the marriage ceases to exist and the surviving party is free to remarry.

In a limited number of circumstances, a valid but unconsummated marriage of baptized persons, or of a baptized and unbaptized person, can be dissolved, as by dispensation by the pope or with the solemn religious profession of one of the parties to the marriage. The latter must be made with the permission of the pope. The bond is dissolved coincidental with the religious profession, and the other party may then remarry.

Other dispensations are possible under what are known popularly as the Pauline Privilege and the Petrine Privilege.

Pauline Privilege: This is a dispensation granted in the instance of unbaptized persons in a legitimate, even consummated marriage, one of whom subsequently receives baptism in the church. That person can seek the dissolution of the legitimate marriage and remarry in the Catholic Church. The granting of this privilege is based on St. Paul (1 Cor. 7:12-16): "If a brother has a wife who is an unbeliever, and she is content to live with him, let him not put her away. And if a woman has an unbeliever for a husband, and he is content to live with her, let her not put him away....However, if the unbelieving partner does not consent, they may separate. In these circumstances, the brother or sister is not tied...." The conditions for receiving the Pauline Privilege are those of the scripture passage: A marriage prior to the baptism of one of the parties; reception of baptism by one of the parties; refusal of the other party, unbaptized, to live peacefully with the baptized party with respect to the matter of faith. The Pauline Privilege is meant to protect the faith of converts to Christianity.

Petrine Privilege: This is a dispensation granted in the instance of a legitimate, even consummated marriage of a baptized and an unbaptized person, freeing the baptized person to marry again. The name derives of the fact that the dispensation is granted by the pope, the successor to St. Peter, in virtue of the privilege of faith. There are no formally prescribed conditions for receiving the Petrine Privilege, as with the Pauline Privilege, but the reasons must be grave and involve considerations of faith.

With respect to marriages of non-Catholics, the Church recognizes these as valid, both those contracted before ministers of religion and civil officials, unless the marriages are rendered null and void on other grounds.

Civil Divorce: The Church regards civil divorce strictly as a legal arrangement, which does not affect the bond of a valid marriage. This bond is held to be indissoluble, whether the parties to the marriage are both Catholics, Catholic and non-Catholic, or both non-Catholics. The church permits the aggrieved party in a troublesome marriage to obtain a civil divorce out of such considerations as family, health, custody of children and property. But it does not concede that civil divorce breaks the bond of a valid marriage. The church prefers that permission for civil divorce be obtained from proper church authority, but the reality is that many Catholics take this as a liberty unto themselves.

In recent years the theology and ecclesiastical regulation of Catholic marriage have moved away from uniform legalisms, and have tended to become more person-oriented both in theory and practice. This development has brought with it certain liberalizing tendencies in favor of divorce and "good conscience" second marriages. A school of thought, for instance, has formed around the proposition that a marriage that is without marital affection, that is emotionally and psychologically dead, is dead in fact. The church rejects such theorizing, but has relaxed its position in a number of directions. For instance, the excommunication formerly in force against Catholics who married before a non-Catholic minister was abrogated March 18, 1966 by the Congregation for the Doctrine of the Faith. At the same time, the church has broadened its pastoral ministry to divorced and remarried Catholics, under the realization that civil divorce is a dramatically increasing fact of Catholic life and that not infrequently second marriages are considerably happier than the valid first marriage.

Annulment: This is the church's declaration that an apparently valid marriage was in fact no marriage at all because of the existence, unknown or concealed, from the outset of a diriment impediment or radical defect to the supposed marriage. (See "Freedom from Impediments"; also, "Annulment" in the Miscellanea section.) Annulments (formally called decrees of nullity) are not easily acquired. The process requires much time and paper work. After the Council of Trent (1545-1563), the grounds for annulments were carefully defined and generally enforced quite strictly. Annulments were granted only if one of the parties did not fully consent (e.g., out of fear or coercion), or was unable to fulfill one's marital obligations (e.g., if one was impotent), or if the proper dispensation had not been given to one of the canonical impediments to a valid marriage (e.g., blood relationship or affinity). New pastoral and psychological understandings, however, have led to an easing of interpretations with respect to what constitutes a valid or invalid marriage, so that combined with new administrative procedures annulments have become more common. In 1968, American diocesan marriage tribunals issued 450 annulments; in 1981, the number was around 48,000.

Mixed Marriages. Until recently, the church was strenuously opposed to a marriage between a Catholic and a non-Catholic, on grounds that a mixed marriage brought about family discord, jeopardized the faith of the Catholic partner, and led to neglect of the religious training of the children of the union. Its position has softened in recent years, however, under considerations of ecumenism and the realities of the pluralistic society. Today the emphasis is on the preparation and religious support of the parties to mixed marriages, including programs of mutual pastoral care involving ministers of different faiths. The Holy See's position on mixed marriages is spelled out in the March 31, 1970 letter of Pope Paul VI, *Matrimonia Mixta* (Mixed Marriages), while policy in the American Catholic Church is contained in the November 16, 1970, statement, "Implementation of the Apostolic Letter on Mixed Marriages."

Among the principal considerations or requirements in a mixed marriage are the following:

• The Catholic party must declare his/her intention to continue to practice the Catholic faith, and promise to do all in his/her power to see that children of the marriage are baptized and raised as Catholics. (At one time the non-Catholic partner was required to agree to this arrangement in writing or by oral declaration, but now the practice is merely to inform the non-Catholic partner of the Catholic partner's promise.)

• The ordinary principal witness to a mixed marriage is an authorized priest, and the ordinary place for a mixed marriage is the parish church of the Catholic party. However, dispensations may be obtained with respect to both. With appropriate dispensations, a mixed marriage can take place in the church of the non-Catholic party, with a non-Catholic minister as the officiating witness. A Catholic priest may attend such a ceremony, and may also address, pray with and bless the marrying couple. Similarly, a non-Catholic minister may take part in a mixed marriage ceremony in a Catholic church, addressing, praying with and blessing the couple.

• A mixed marriage can take place at a Nuptial Mass. (The Church once showed its disapproval of mixed marriages by not publishing the banns and not extending the nuptial blessing even at those mixed marriages for which it had extended dispensation.)

• Pastoral counseling or instruction is advised to minimize the problems of a mixed marriage, including instruction of the non-Catholic partner in the essentials of the Catholic faith. This is for purposes of understanding, not proselytism.

Marriage and the Family. For many generations, the responsibilities of marriage were built around the same emphases as the Catholic parish, those involving children. The parish had its Catholic school (often built before the parish church itself); the family had its children. And as the parish school commonly became the focus of parish life, so were children the focus of family life. Thus it was that various Vatican offices, old instruction books and manuals unqualifiedly identified the primary purpose of marriage as "the begetting and rearing of children."

Change with respect to marriage and the family began to evolve with Pope Pius XII (1939-1958) and the recognition of interpersonal values in the marital relationship. Though such values as commitment and fulfillment may be secondary in Christian marriage, they were, in Pius XII's opinion, nevertheless vital to a happy and blessed marriage. Pius XII's personalist approach to marriage has since been expanded, with the result that the church, though not repudiating traditional teaching on marriage, has moved to a more integrated approach with respect to marital values. Some theologians have even dropped the traditional distinction between primary and secondary ends of marriage. The church itself has not done so officially, although, as discourses of Pope John Paul II (1978-   ) make clear, it has adopted a more personalistic perspective with respect to Christian marital values, including the use of sex within marriage. This reflects certain emphases of Vatican Council II (1962-1965). Vatican II spoke of marriage as a union in love, and intimate partnership, a social and divine institution enriching the expressions of body and mind and advancing the perfection of the individuals' personalities; marriage is thus a community, a covenant. The Council added that marriage does not exist solely for procreation, but for a whole manner and communion of life (Constitution on the Church in the Modern World, 50). Nevertheless, in speaking of the mission of parents, the Council specified the old traditional responsibilities to transmit human life and to educate those to whom life has been transmitted. In the latter context, it counseled parents to train children from childhood to recognize God's love for all persons, and to see "energetically" to their children's religious education. Means for meeting religious-education responsibilities include support and patronage of Catholic schools, and the enrolling of children attending public or other non-Catholic schools in parish Confraternity of Christian Doctrine or related religious-education programs.

Birth Control. Historically, the church has regarded artificial birth control as immoral and contrary to both divine law and natural law. Proscribed therefore is the use of medications, drugs, instruments, devices, douches, pills and other mechanical or "artificial" means aimed at preventing conception. Artificial birth control is held to be a contravention of the primary purpose of marriage, and being a violation of the natural law, its use is regarded as morally wrong, not only for Catholics, but all persons.

On the other hand, natural birth control, performed with mutual consent and for serious reasons, may be practiced morally. Principal forms of natural birth control are the rhythm method (intercourse restricted to the "safe" period in the spouse's ovulation cycle) and periodic continence or self-restraint. *Coitus interruptus,* or the interruption of the marital act and the spilling of the seed outside the vagina, is held to be morally wrong.

The church's position on birth control is based on the principle that each and every marital act *(quilibet matrimonii usus)* must remain open to the transmission of life or its possibility. This position came under rigorous reexamination during the pontificate of Paul VI (1963-1978), and a papal commission was named to study and recommend on the possibility of change. The commission included theologians, legal experts, historians, sociologists and family members, and it produced by 64 to 4 majority a report advising the pope that a change in the church's position was both possible and advisable. Paul VI, however, chose not to accept the recommendation, and on July 24, 1968 he issued the encyclical *Humanae Vitae* condemning contraception and reaffirming the principle that "each and every marriage act" must remain open to the transmission of life (paragraph 11). Though surveys indicate that large numbers of Catholics reject this teaching it remains the official policy of the church. Pope John Paul II has several times echoed the themes of *Humanae Vitae,* including at a general audience July 11, 1984, when he said, "We are reminded of the church's teaching that every marriage act must remain open to the transmission of life." Insistence of this point is seen by some as a rejection of Vatican Council II's teaching in the context of marriage that the morality of a human act had to be taken from "the nature of man and his actions" and not only from the biological structure of the individual.

Abortion. Since its earliest days, the church has admitted no doubt about the immorality of abortion, holding that it is an evil act to destroy the life of an innocent child. Not acceptable is the plea that the child is an unjust aggressor or that the rights of an individual give a mother the right and authority to terminate a pregnancy. Abortion is classed as a violation of the Natural Law, which forbids any attempt at destroying fetal life, and the Fifth Commandment, "Thou shall not kill." The church's position is thus consistent with books attributed to Hippocrates, who required physicians to bind themselves by oath not to give women drinks fatal to life in the womb. The 4th-century Council of Eliberis decreed that the Eucharist should be refused for the rest of her life, including on her deathbed, to an adulteress who had procured the abortion of her child, and the sixth ecumenical council (Constantinople III, 680-681) ruled that those procuring an abortion should bear all the punishments inflicted on murderers. Excommunication for abortion was specified in the bull *"Apostolicae Sedis"* of Pope Pius IX (1846-1878).

Vatican Council II (1962-1965) condemned abortion in its Constitution on the Church in the Modern World:

"Whatever is opposed to life itself, such as any type of murder, genocide, abortion, euthanasia, or willful self-destruction, whatever violates the integrity of the human person....; whatever insults human dignity....; All these things and others of their like are infamies indeed" (27).

"....From the moment of conception life must be guarded with greatest care, while abortion and infanticide are unspeakable crimes" (51).

Direct abortion is always wrong. Indirect abortion, however, may be permissible under the principle of the Double Effect. Indirect abortion would be one that occurs as a consequence of medical treatment or surgical operation to save the life of the mother, and from which the death of the fetus occurs as a regretted but unavoidable consequence. The evil is permitted, but only if four criteria are met: (1) the evil effect is not wished and every reasonable effort is taken to avoid it; (2) the immediate effect must be good in itself (e.g., saving the life of the woman); (3) the evil is not made a means in obtaining the good effect (else the end would be justifying the means, an immorality all its own); (4) the good effect must be at least as important as the evil effect which follows.

Therapeutic abortions—including abortions to avoid the birth of an abnormal child; abortions for social, familial or community considerations; and abortions for the physical and/or psychological well-being of the mother—are forbidden.

Accidental abortions, as in the instance of non-induced miscarriages, are without moral blame.

Pius IX's bull *"Apostolicae Sedis"* applied excommunication to those who actually and efficaciously procured an abortion. Current policy, however, extends the penalty of excommunication to all who are party to an abortion, including doctors, nurses, clinical technicians, counselors, etc. Pius IX's bull held those voluntarily aiding in an abortion in any way to have done a moral wrong, but did not apply excommunication to them.

Section III

The Teaching Church

THE MESSAGE OF SALVATION in the Catholic church is rooted in three sources: Tradition, the Bible and the teaching authority of the Church—which, with respect to the last, is to say pope, bishops and, more recently, conferences of bishops. This tripartite arrangement of divine and human origination was reaffirmed by the Fathers of Vatican Council II (1962-1965) in the Dogmatic Constitution on Divine Revelation *(Dei verbum)*:

> "It is clear that sacred tradition, sacred Scripture, and the teaching authority of the Church, in accord with God's most wise design, are so linked and joined together than one cannot stand without the others, and that all together and each in its own way under the action of the one Holy Spirit contribute effectively to the salvation of souls" (10).

The task of conveying the message of salvation and of authentically interpreting the word of God is claimed and exercised by the church in the name of Jesus Christ. This does not necessarily subvert the individual conscience to the institution (although in some cases this may happen), nor does it necessarily exalt the teaching office of the

Church above all else, including the word of God. However, it does make within Catholicism for a delicate and often difficult balancing. For as the deposit of faith flows from a trinity of realities—Tradition, Scripture and Authority—so is it assimilated by a variety of responses, including those of conscience, intellect, obedience and the loyalties of faith.

Sacred Tradition

Sacred Tradition is bound up in Catholic understanding with the living magisterium, or teaching authority, of the Church, and results in the church's essential differentiation from much of Protestantism. The theological reference point, and thus point of departure from much of Protestantism, is the Catholic tenet that not all of Revelation and the truths of religion are contained in Holy Scripture—the Bible—and that alongside Scripture as a source of Revelation and of dogmatic truth is Tradition.

Tradition is the transmission from one generation to another of some doctrine, account or custom which is not necessarily found in the Bible. Therefore it is Tradition—Sacred Tradition—which accounts for many details of Catholicism, including the precise number of sacraments, the time of institution of some sacraments, the inclusion of certain books in the Bible, the timing and method of Baptism, and the day to be maintained holy according to Divine Law; in other words; why Sunday instead of Saturday?

Sacred Tradition is oral by derivation, and its validity as process in the Catholic understanding of things is based on the oral origins of Christianity itself. Christ preached; he did not write. Christ commanded the Apostles to preach all nations; he did not order them to sit down and write books for all nations.

That Christ's Revelation goes beyond the Bible, and that therefore there is a depository of Sacred Tradition, is traced to Biblical references. There is Paul's first letter to the church at Corinth: "You have done well in remembering me and in holding fast to the traditions just as I have handed them to you" (11:2). There is also the second letter of John: "There is much more I have to tell you, but I do not intend to convey it by pen and ink. I hope rather to visit you and talk with you person to person, so that our joy may be full" (12).

Tradition inevitably conveys to the Catholic magisterium, and the pope as the church's principal authority figure and teacher, a preeminence in guiding the minds and hearts of the faithful. Tradition is intimately related to the progress or development of dogma, theology and the faith itself, and it is the living magisterium that confirms specific points of Tradition. It was such in the time of the Fathers, from Clement of Rome, through Justin, to Caesarius of Arles; it was such in the time of the Doctors of the church, from those of the early church, like Athanasius and Gregory Nazianzen, through those of the Middle Ages, including Thomas Aquinas, Bonaventure and John of the Cross; it is such in modern times, from the conciliar declaration of infallibility in 1870 through the declaration of the Assumption of Mary as dogma by Pope Pius XII in 1950.

Using the latter by way of example: The dogmatic definition that Mary, the Mother of God, was assumed "body and soul, to heavenly glory" derived not from whim or the personal piety of a particular pope. It derived rather from Tradition, the living belief of the church, in this instance supplementing certain theological conclusions based on Mary's motherhood and immaculate conception. Tradition with respect to the Assumption reached back at least to the time of St. Gregory of Tours, who in the 6th century noted: "The Lord took Mary's holy body and conveyed it on a cloud to paradise; there it was united with her soul, and glorified with the elect, it enjoys the eternal blessings that shall have no end."

By the end of the 6th century, Mary's assumption was a feast observed throughout the universal church. In the 20th century, Pope Pius XII used Tradition to assert the dogmatic character of that which the feast commemorated.

The Fathers of Vatican Council II addressed the topic of Tradition in the Dogmatic Constitution on Divine Revelation *(Dei verbum)*, chapter II, entitled ''The Transmission of Divine Revelation'':

''In his gracious goodness, God has seen to it that what he had revealed for the salvation of all nations would abide perpetually in its full integrity and be handed on to all generations. Therefore Christ the Lord, in whom the full revelation of the supreme God is brought to completion (cf. 2 Cor. 1:20, 3:16, 4:6), commissioned the apostles to preach to all men that Gospel which is the source of all saving truth and moral teaching, and thus to impart to them divine gifts. This Gospel had been promised in former times through the prophets, and Christ himself fulfilled it and promulgated it with his own lips. This commission was faithfully fulfilled by the apostles who, by their oral preaching, by example, and by ordinances, handed on what they had received from the lips of Christ, from living with him, and from what he did, or what they had learned through the prompting of the Holy Spirit. The commission was fulfilled, too, by those apostles and apostolic men who under the inspiration of the same Holy Spirit committed the message of salvation to writing.

''But in order to keep the Gospel forever whole and alive within the Church, the apostles left bishops as their successors, 'handing over their own teaching role' to them. This sacred tradition, therefore, and sacred Scripture of both the Old and the New Testament are like a mirror in which the pilgrim Church on earth looks at God, from whom she has received everything, until she is brought finally to see him as he is, face to face'' (cf. 1 John 3:2) (7).

"And so the apostolic preaching, which is expressed in a special way in the inspired books, was to be preserved by a continuous succession of preachers until the end of time. Therefore the apostles, handing on what they themselves had received, warn the faithful to hold fast to the traditions which they have learned either by word of mouth or by letter (cf. 2 Thessalonians 2:15)...Now what was handed on by the apostles includes everything which contributes to the holiness of life, and the increase in faith of the People of God; and so the Church, in her teaching, life, and worship, perpetuates and hands on to all generations all that she herself is, all that she believes" (8).

Tradition and Scripture. The same Vatican II document *Dei verbum,* spoke about Tradition and the sacred Scripture, or Bible:

"Hence there exists a close connection and communication between sacred tradition and sacred Scripture. For both of them, flowing from the same divine well-spring, in a certain way merge into a unity and tend toward the same end. For sacred Scripture is the word of God inasmuch as it is consigned to writing under the inspiration of the divine Spirit. To the successors of the apostles, sacred tradition hands on in its full purity God's word, which was entrusted to the apostles by Christ the Lord and the Holy Spirit. Thus, led by the light of the Spirit of truth, these successors can in their preaching preserve this word of God faithfully, explain it, and make it more widely known. Consequently, it is not from sacred Scripture alone that the Church draws her certainty about everything which has been revealed. Therefore both sacred tradition and sacred Scripture are to be accepted and venerated with the same sense of devotion and reverence (9).

"Sacred tradition and sacred Scripture form one sacred deposit of the word of God, which is committed to the Church... (10).

Tradition and the Church's Teaching Authority. Finally, with respect to Tradition and the teaching authority of the Church, *Dei verbum* continued as follows:

"...[The] task of authentically interpreting the word of God, whether written or handed on, has been entrusted exclusively to the living teaching office of the Church, whose authority is exercised in the name of Jesus Christ. This teaching office is not above the word of God, but serves it, teaching only what has been handed on, listening to it devoutly, guarding it scrupulously, and explaining it faithfully by divine commission and with the help of the Holy Spirit; it draws from this one deposit of faith everything which it presents for belief as divinely revealed.

"It is clear, therefore, that sacred tradition, sacred Scripture, and the teaching authority of the Church, in accord with God's most wise design, are so linked and joined together that one cannot stand without the others, and that all together and each in its own way under the action of the one Holy Spirit contribute effectively to the salvation of souls" (10).

The Place of the Bible

The Bible is the fundamental source of Catholic dogma and, of course, is central to Catholic thought and teaching, but at the same time, the Bible is a book curiously neglected by Catholics. The lessons of the Mass are drawn from the Bible, and Catholic behavioral codes are based on the Bible. Yet unlike much of Protestantism, Catholicism has never seen the development among its adherents of what might be called a popular Biblical spirituality, this despite encouragement from church leadership, from popes down, to read the Bible and the attachment of special indulgences to such reading. The Bible is the all-time best-seller since the invention of movable type by Johannes Gutenberg and the first printed Bible in 1455.

The Catholic Fact Book

Most every Catholic home has a Bible, but in many Catholic homes, again, the Bible remains an unread book, certainly on a regular basis.

That a different condition may exist in much of Protestantism was virtually conceded by the Fathers of Vatican Council II (1962-1965), in their Decree on Ecumenism *(Unitatis redintegratio):*

> "A love, veneration, and near cult of the sacred Scriptures lead our brethren (in the separated Churches) to a constant and expert study of the sacred text. For the gospel 'is the power of God unto salvation to everyone who believes, to Jew first and then to Greek.' " (Rom. 1:16)
>
> "Calling upon the Holy Spirit, they seek in these sacred Scriptures God as He speaks to them in Christ, the One whom the prophets foretold, God's Word made flesh for us. In the Scriptures they contemplate the life of Christ, as well as the teachings and the actions of the Divine Master on behalf of men's salvation, in particular the mysteries of His death and resurrection" (21).

What Is the Bible? The Bible, or sacred Scripture, is the record of God's revelation in history, written by persons under the inspiration of the Holy Spirit. In Catholic editions, the Bible embodies 72 sacred books divided into the traditional Old and New Testaments. The original languages of the Bible are Hebrew, Aramaic and Greek, and the period of composition covers some 1,300 years, from Moses through John the Evangelist.

The common groupings of the Biblical books is as follows:

The Old Testament comprises:

The Pentateuch: The Books of Genesis, Exodus, Leviticus, Numbers, Deuteronomy.

The Historical Books: The Books of Joshua, Ruth, Samuel I and II, Kings I and II, Chronicles I and II, Ezra, Nehemiah, Tobias, Judith, Esther, Maccabees I and II.

The Wisdom Books: The Books of Job, Psalms, Proverbs, Ecclesiastes, Song of Songs, Wisdom, Sirach (Ecclesiasticus).

The Prophetic Books: The Books of Isaiah, Jeremiah, Lamentations, Baruch, Ezekiel, Daniel, Hosea, Joel, Amos, Obadiah, Jonah, Micah, Nahum, Habakkuk, Zephaniah, Haggai, Zechariah, Malachi.

Protestant editions of the Bible usually omit seven books (Tobias, Judith, Wisdom, Sirach/Ecclesiasticus, Baruch and Maccabees I and II), and portions of books (Esther, X, 4-xvi, 24, and Daniel iii, 24-90; xiii, 1-xiv, 42) which are not found in Jewish editions of the Old Testament.

The New Testament comprises:

The Gospel according to Matthew, Mark, Luke and John; the Acts of the Apostles; the Epistle of Paul to the Romans; the Epistles of Paul, one and two, to the Corinthians; the Epistles of Paul to the Galatians, Ephesians, Philippians, Colossians; the Epistles, one and two, of Paul to the Thessalonians; the Epistles, one and two, of Paul to Timothy; the Epistles of Paul to Titus, Philemon, Hebrews; the Epistle of James; the Epistles, one and two, of Peter; the Epistles, one, two and three, of John; the Epistle of Jude; and Book of Revelation.

The four Gospels are historical in the main, and encompass what is called the "good news" of salvation.

The Acts of the Apostles record the history of the Apostles after the Ascension of Christ into heaven.

The 21 epistles are strongly doctrinal in character, while the Apocalypse is prophetical, dealing with events hidden in the future, including the world's end and a vision of a new heaven and earth.

Protestant editions usually omit the Epistle of St. James, the Epistle of Paul to the Hebrews, the Epistle of St. Jude and the Apocalypse.

Popes and the Bible. The importance of the Bible in the life of the church and its people has been stressed time and again by the Holy See, beginning in modern times notably with the encyclical letter *Providentissimus Deus* of Pope Leo XIII (1878-1903). The letter was issued Nov. 18, 1893, partly in response to rationalists who, as knowledge of antiquity expanded, attacked the truthfulness and divine origin of the Bible. Scientists at the same time were pointing out the literal impossibility of certain Biblical passages, such as the creation of humankind. (Evolutionary theories were then making their initial impressions.) Leo XIII made a strong defense of the inerrancy of the Bible, while conceding that "a certain religious obscurity" may surround certain of the sacred writings. He urged use of the Bible by the faithful, but counseled on misinterpretations and seeming conflicts relating to scientific developments. Some pertinent passages of the encyclical (footnotes omitted):

   " . . . . [The] watchful care of the Church shines forth conspicuously. By admirable laws and regulations, she has always shown herself solicitous that 'the celestial treasure of the sacred books, so bountifully bestowed upon many by the Holy Spirit, should not lie neglected.' She has prescribed that a considerable portion of them shall be read and piously reflected upon by all her ministers in the daily office of the sacred psalmody. She has ordered that in cathedral churches, in monasteries, and in other convents in which study can conveniently be pursued, they shall be expounded and interpreted by capable men; and she has strictly commanded that her children shall be fed with the saving words of the Gospel at least on Sundays and solemn feasts. Moreover, it is owing to the wisdom and exertions of the Church that there has always been continued, from century to century, that cultivation of Holy Scripture which has been so remarkable and has borne such ample fruit. . .
   " . . . [Since] the divine and infallible magisterium of the Church rests also on the authority of Holy Scripture, the first thing to be done is to vindicate the trustworthiness of the sacred records, at least as human

documents, from which can be clearly proved, as from primitive and authentic testimony, the divinity and misison of Christ our Lord, the institution of an hierarchical Church, and the primacy of Peter and his successors. It is most desirable, therefore, that there should be numerous members of the clergy well prepared to enter upon a contest of this nature, and to repulse hostile assaults, chiefly trusting in that armor of God recommended by the Apostle (Eph. 6:13-17), but also not unaccustomed to modern methods of attack....

"In order that all these endeavors and exertions may really prove advantageous to the cause of the Bible, let scholars...loyally hold that God, the Creator and Ruler of all things, is also the Author of the Scriptures—and that, therefore, nothing can be proved either by physical science or archaeology which can really contradict the Scriptures. If then, apparent contradiction be met with, every effort should be made to remove it. Judicious theologians and commentators should be consulted as to what is the true or most probable meaning of the passage in discussion and the hostile arguments should be carefully weighed. Even if the difficulty is after all not cleared up and the discrepancy seems to remain the contest must not be abandoned; truth cannot contradict truth, and we may be sure that some mistake has been made either in the interpretation of the sacred words or in the polemic discussion itself; and if no such mistake can be detected, we must then suspend judgment for the time being....

"Finally, We admonish, with paternal love, all students and ministers of the Church always to approach the sacred writings with reverence and piety; for it is impossible to attain to the profitable understanding thereof unless the arrogance of 'earthly' science be laid aside, and there be excited in the heart of the holy desire for that wisdom 'which is from above.'...."

Providentissimus Deus was followed by a number of important Bible-related documents, including:

• A letter of Leo XIII to the Minister General of the Friars Minor, Nov. 25, 1898, containing directives on the use of the Bible in preaching.

• A decree of Leo XIII, Dec. 13, 1898, granting an indulgence of 300 days for reading the Gospels for at least 15 minutes, and, under the usual conditions, a plenary indulgence once a month for the daily reading of the Gospels. (This indulgence has been gradually increased. Present provision is a plenary indulgence for devout reading of the sacred Scriptures for at least one half-hour.)

• An encyclical letter of Leo XIII, *Depuis le jour,* to the bishops and clergy of France, Sept. 8, 1899, recalling the directives of *Providentissimus Deus* in the context of education of the clergy.

• A apostolic letter of Pope St. Pius X on March 27, 1906, detailing instructions on Scripture studies in seminaries.

• The encyclical *Pascendi dominici gregis* of Pius X, Sept. 8, 1907, apropos doctrines of the Modernists, containing passages explaining and condemning Modernists' attitudes toward sacred Scripture.

• An apostolic letter of Pius X establishing in Rome the Pontifical Biblical Institute, May 7, 1909.

• *Spiritus paraclitus,* an encyclical letter by Pope Benedict XV, Sept. 15, 1920, marking the 1500th anniversary of the death of St. Jerome, and citing St. Jerome's love for the Bible and explaining the principles he used to understand it. The encyclical reaffirmed and further clarified points of Leo XIII's *Providentissimus Deus.*

• *In praeclara summorum,* an encyclical letter by Benedict XV, April 30, 1921, marking the 600th anniversary of Dante's death and commending Dante's appreciation of sacred Scripture.

• A *motu proprio* of Pope Pius XI on April 27, 1924, specifying that academic degrees in sacred Scripture were to enjoy the same rights and canonical status as degrees in theology and canon law.

A major document in the promotion of Biblical studies in the church was Pope Pius XII's encyclical of Sept. 30, 1943, *Divino afflante Spiritu*. The encyclical used the 50th anniversary of Leo XIII's *Providentissimus Deus* to remark on the restoration of "confidence in the authority and historical value" of the Bible, and encouraged scholars to further research and studies, including into the life and times of the human authors of the Bible. Following are some key passages from the encyclical (footnotes omitted):

"Inspired by the Divine Spirit, the sacred writers composed those books, which God, in His paternal charity towards the human race, deigned to bestow on them in order 'to teach, to reprove, to correct, to instruct in justice: that the man of God may be perfect, equipped for every good work.' This heaven-sent treasure Holy Church considers as the most precious source of doctrine on faith and morals. No wonder therefore that, as she received it intact from the hands of the Apostles, so she kept it with all care, defended it from every false and perverse interpretation and used it diligently as an instrument for securing the eternal salvation of souls, as almost countless documents in every age strikingly bear witness. . . .

"Moreover we may rightly and deservedly hope that our time also can contribute something towards the deeper and more accurate interpretation of Sacred Scripture. For not a few things, especially in matters pertaining to history, were scarcely at all or not fully explained by the commentators of past ages, since they lacked almost all the information which was needed for their clearer exposition. How difficult for the Fathers themselves, and indeed well-nigh unintelligible, were certain passages is shown, among other things, by the often-repeated efforts of many of them to explain the first chapters of Genesis; likewise by the reiterated attempts of St. Jerome so to translate the Psalms that the literal sense, that, namely which is expressed by the words themselves, might be clearly revealed....

"Let those who cultivate biblical studies....neglect none of those discoveries, whether in the domain of archaeology or in ancient history or literature, which serve to make better known the mentality of the ancient writers, as well as their manner and art of reasoning, narrating and writing. In this connection Catholic laymen should consider that they will not only further profane science, but moreover will render a conspicuous service to the Christian cause if they devote themselves with all due diligence and application to the exploration and investigation of the monuments of antiquity and contribute, according to their abilities, to the solution of questions hitherto obscure.

"For all human knowledge, even the non-sacred, has indeed its own proper dignity and excellence, being a finite participation of the infinite knowledge of God, but it acquires a new and higher dignity and, as it were, a consecration, when it is employed to cast a brighter light upon the things of God."

Vatican II and the Bible. The centrality of the Bible in the conveying of the "good news" of salvation was stressed repeatedly in the documents of Vatican Council II (1962-1965). Following are a few of the more notable passages:

"The Church has always venerated the divine Scriptures just as she venerates the body of the Lord, since from the table of both the word of God and of the body of Christ she unceasingly receives and offers to the faithful the bread of life, especially in the sacred liturgy. She has always regarded the Scriptures together with sacred tradition as the supreme rule of faith, and will ever do so. For, inspired by God and committed once and for all to writing, they impart the word of God Himself without change, and make the voice of the Holy Spirit resound in the words of the prophets and apostles. Therefore, like the Christian religion itself, all the preaching of the Church must be nourished and ruled by sacred Scripture. For in the sacred books, the Father who is in heaven meets His children with great love and speaks with them; and the force and power in the word of God is so great that it remains the support and energy of the Church, the strength of faith for her sons, the food of the soul, the pure and perennial source of spiritual life. Consequently, these words are perfectly applicable to sacred Scripture: 'For the word of God is living and efficient' (Heb. 4:12) and is 'able to build up and give the inheritance among all the sanctified' (Acts 20:32; cf. 1 Th. 2:13).''

Dogmatic Constitution on Divine Revelation
(Dei verbum), 21

''Sacred Scripture is of paramount importance in the celebration of the liturgy. For it is from Scripture that lessons are read and explained in the homily, and psalms are sung; the prayers, collects, and liturgical songs are scriptural in their inspiration, and it is from Scripture that actions and signs derive their meaning. Thus if the restoration, progress, and adaptation of the sacred liturgy are to be achieved, it is necessary to promote that warm and living love for Scripture to which the venerable tradition of both Eastern and Western rites gives testimony.''

Constitution on the Sacred Liturgy
(Sacrosanctum concilium), 24

''In the study of sacred Scripture, which ought to be the soul of all theology, students should be trained with special diligence. After a suitable introduction to it, they should be accurately initiated into exegetical method, grasp the pre-eminent themes of divine revelation, and take inspiration and nourishment from reading and meditating on the sacred books day by day.''

Decree on Priestly Formation
(Optatem totius), 16

Infallibility

The church exercises its teaching authority with a confidence born of infallibility. Infallibility, in its most elementary terminology, is the doctrine that the church by divine favor is preserved from error in its definitive, dogmatic teaching on matters of faith and morals. Further, in common Catholic understanding the church is preserved not only from actual error, but also from liability to error and possibility of error. The Biblical basis for this tenet is Mathew 28:18-20, wherein Jesus commissions the apostles to go and make disciples of all nations, promising them that "I will be with you all days." Thus it is that the church regards God as the source and author of its infallibility, an understanding which allows infallibility to course through human and perhaps sometimes unworthy agents.

Contrary to certain impressions, infallibility is not regarded as a vehicle for the pronouncement of new doctrine, even in those few instances—the definition of the Immaculate Conception by Pope Pius IX in 1854 and of the Assumption of Mary by Pope Pius XII in 1950—where the exercise of infallibility was seeming bound up with the proclamation of new doctrine. The rationale is that these proclamations were merely the formal confirmation of articles of faith which existed from the beginning. Accordingly their formal definings are viewed as actions which clarified a particular dogma and its place in the deposit of faith, not as actions which gave birth to something which previously did not exist.

Organs of Infallibility. The Church by exercise of its ordinary teaching authority *(magisterium ordinarium)* is said to be infallible, but the practical organs of infallibility are (1) the Ecumenical Councils and (2) the papacy in the person of the reigning pope.

Ecumenical Councils are assemblies of the world's bishops, which juridically represent the church universal as hierarchically constituted by Jesus Christ. Ecumenical Councils are discussed in detail earlier in this book, but it is important to recall that certain conditions are essential in order for them to qualify as infallible assemblies. They must be summoned by the pope (although a pope can give *ante* or *post factum* consent to a council, as was the case in some early councils when the summons was issued in the name of a ranking civil authority); the presidency of a council belongs to the pope or his representative; papal ratification is required to authenticate any and all conciliar decrees. (Unanimous vote is not a precondition to ratification.)

Papal infallibility is based on Scripture (e.g., "Thou art Peter, and upon this rock I will build my church. And the gates of hell shall not prevail against it" (Matthew 16:18-19); on Tradition (e.g., Clement's letter to the Corinthians at the end of the 1st Century; the Ecumenical Councils from Nicaea I, 325, onwards; and on the explicit definition of Vatican Council I in 1870 that "the Roman Pontiff, when he speaks *ex cathedra* that is, when in the exercise of his office as pastor and teacher of all Christians he defines, by virtue of his supreme Apostolic authority, a doctrine of faith or morals to be held by the whole church—is, by reason of the Divine assistance promised to him in blessed Peter, possessed of that infallibility with which the Divine Redeemer wished his church to be endowed in defining doctrines of faith and morals; and consequently that such definitions of the Roman Pontiff are irreformable of their own nature *(ex sese)* and not by reason of the Church's consent." The definition is contained in Vatican I's dogmatic constitution *Pastor aeternus.*

Pastor aeternus described papal authority as ordinary, immediate, and episcopal. The term *ordinary* was used to indicate that papal authority or power is not delegated, but belongs to the office by reason of its function. *Immediate* signified that the pope can exercise authority and power directly over the faithful without any intermediary. *Episcopal* meant that the pope has the pastoral authority to teach, sanctify and rule, and that his authority over the church universal is the same as a bishop's authority in his own diocese.

Though the prerogative of papal infallibility was defined in 1870, it was not intentionally, consciously and specifically used by a pope until the defining of the dogma of the Assumption of Mary into heaven by Pius XII in 1950. (Pius IX's defining of the dogma of the Immaculate Conception preceded *Pastor aeternus* by 16 years.) There have been no explicit uses of infallibility since 1950 by a pope acting on his own authority and apart from an Ecumenical Council. For instance, Pope Paul VI did not specifically invoke infallibility when pronouncing condemnation of artificial birth control in the 1968 encyclical *Humanae Vitae.*

Conditions of Papal Infallibility. For a pope to speak infallibly, he must (1) pronounce himself on a matter of faith or morals; (2) he must speak as the vicar of Christ, in his office as pope, and to the Church universal; (3) he must make clear his intention to speak *ex cathedra* ("from the chair" of Peter), as with the use of such terms as "we/I proclaim," "we/I define," etc.

Strictly speaking, infallibility applies to only that portion of document or pronouncement which is specified as such. The definition of the doctrine of the Immaculate Conception, for instance, is contained in the lengthy constitution *Ineffabilis Deus* of Dec. 8, 1854, but only the few sentences pronouncing and defining that Mary from the moment of her conception was preserved exempt from all stain of Original Sin, are construed as being infallible. The same is true in many documents of conciliar status.

Encyclicals

A primary method for implementing the church's teaching authority is through the papal encyclical. By etymological definition, an encyclical letter means simply a circular letter. Though great significance is attached within Catholicism to encyclicals, they are actually a recent development of church history. They came into common usage only in the 18th century, when they acquired status as important messages of a pope on issues of moment to the church. In the early centuries of church history, the term encyclical had applied not only to papal letters, but also to letters and pastoral documents addressed by archbishops and bishops to their diocesans or to other bishops. These latter documents are now referred to as pastorals or pastoral letters, with the word encyclical reserved to papal-level documents of a major kind.

An encyclical letter deals in the main with matters of doctrine, morals or discipline with broad application in the church. As such, an encyclical letter differs from an encyclical epistle, which is addressed to a particular part or section of the church, as for instance a letter from the pope to a national hierarchy. In general, encyclicals are intramural documents, although a few—e.g., John XXIII's *Pacem in Terris* and Paul VI's *Ecclesiam Suam*—have sought broader audiences by being addressed to "all men of good will."

Encyclicals are very formal documents, and appear in the Latin language, with few exceptions. For example, the 1907 encyclical (more specifically, encyclical epistle) of Pope Pius X to the bishops, clergy and people of France on the separation of church and state was written in French, bearing the title *Une Fois Encore*.

Encyclicals take their title from the opening words of their texts. As a specimen both of the derivation of title and the formality of address, one might consider the 1943 encyclical letter of Pope Pius XII on biblical studies, *Divine afflante Spiritu:*

LITTERAE ENCYCLICAE

Ad venerabiles Patriarchas, Primates, Archiepiscopos, Episcopos aliosque locorum Ordinarios pacem et communionem cum Apostolica Sede habentes, itemque ad universum clerum et Christifideles Catholici orbis: De Sacrorum Bibliorum Studiis Opportune Provehendis.

PIUS PP. XII
Venerabiles Fratres, Dilecti Filii
Salutem et Apostolicam Benedictionem
Divino afflante Spiritu, illos Sacri Scriptores
exararunt libros, quos Deus, pro sua erga hominum
etc., etc., etc.

The Authority of Encyclicals. The binding force or authority of encyclicals is a matter of interpretation.

Pope Pius XII addressed the subject in his encyclical *Humani Generis* of August 12, 1950:

> "Nor must it be thought that what is contained in encyclical letters does not of itself demand assent, on the pretext that the popes do not exercise in them the supreme power of their teaching authority. Rather, such teachings belong to the ordinary magisterium, of which it is true to say: 'He who hears you, hears me' (Lk. 10:16); for the most part, too, what is expounded and inculcated in encyclical letters already appertains to Catholic doctrine for other reasons. But if the supreme pontiffs in their official documents purposely pass judgment on a matter debated until then, it is obvious to all that the matter, according to the mind and will of the same pontiffs, cannot be considered any longer a question open for discussion among theologians."

The fact remains, however, that encyclicals per se are not *ex cathedra* documents invested with the infallible authority of the issuing pontiff. An encyclical, in other words, is a weighty document expressing the mind of the church as reflected in the thinking of the reigning pope, but the contents of an encyclical do not become dogma merely by fact of being included in an encyclical.

The *Catholic Encyclopedia* (New York, 1913) states: "The degree to which the infallible magisterium of the Holy See is committed [in an encyclical] must be judged from the circumstances, and from the language used in the particular case."

Some Major Encyclicals. Not all encyclicals have had a strong and lasting impact on church history, but very many have set the church's course for periods of generations. The following list contains the titles, subject matter and dates of some of the more notable encyclical letters and encyclical epistles. The difference between the latter two forms can be determined from the scope of the subject matter, as summarized. In parentheses is the total number of encyclicals credited to the particular pope.

Pope Benedict XIV, 1740-1758 (13)

1740: *Ubi Primum*, on the duty of bishops; Dec. 3.

1741: *Quanta Cura*, forbidding traffic in alms; June 30.

1751: *A Quo Primum*, to the bishops of Poland, on Jewish people and Christians living in the same place; June 14.

1754: *Quod Provinciale*, to the bishops of Albania, on Christians using Mohammedan names; Aug. 1.

1755: *Allatae Sunt*, to missionaries to the Orient, on the observance of Oriental rites; July 26.

Pope Clement XIII, 1758-1769 (6)

1758: *A Quo Die*, on unity among Christians; Sept. 13.

1759: *Appetente Sacro*, on the spiritual advantages of fasting; Dec. 20.

1761: *In Dominico Agro*, on instruction in the faith; June 14.

1766: *Christinae Reipublicae*, to the bishops of Austria, on the dangers of anti-Christian writings; Nov. 25.

Pope Clement XIV, 1769-1774 (4)

1769: *Decet Quam Maxime,* to the bishops of Sardinia, on abuses in taxes and benefices; Sept. 21

Pope Pius VI, 1775-1799 (2)

1775: *Inscrutabile,* on the problems of the pontificate; Dec. 25.

1791: *Charitas,* to the bishops of France, on the matter of the civil oath in France; April 13.

Pope Pius VII, 1800-1823 (1)

1800: *Diu Satis,* to the bishops of France, on a return to the Gospel principles; May 15.

Pope Leo XII, 1823-1829 (3)

1824: *Ubi Primum,* to the bishops of the world, on Leo's assuming of the papacy; May 5.

Pope Pius VIII, 1829-1830 (1)

1829: *Traditi Humilitati,* detailing Pius' program for the pontificate; May 24.

Pope Gregory XVI, 1831-1846 (9)

1832: *Summo Iugiter Studio,* to the bishops of Bavaria, on mixed marriages; May 27.

Cum Primum, to the bishops of Poland, on civil obedience; June 9.

Mirari Vos, on liberalism and religious indifference; Aug. 15.

1835: *Commissum Divinitus,* to the clergy of Switzerland, on Church and State; May 17.

1840: *Probe Nostis,* on the propagation of the faith; Sept. 18.

1841: *Quas Vestro,* to the bishops of Hungary, on mixed marriages; April 30.

1844: *Inter Praecipuas*, on biblical societies; May 8.

Pope Pius IX, 1846-1878 (37)

1846: *Qui Pluribus*, on faith and religion; Nov. 9.

1847: *Praedecessores Nostros*, on aid for Ireland and the Irish; March 25.

1849: *Ubi Primum*, on the Immaculate Conception; Feb. 2.

Nostis et Nobiscum, to the bishops of Italy, on the Church in the Papal States; Dec. 8.

1852: *Nemo Certe Ignorat*, to the bishops of Ireland, on clerical discipline; March 25.

Probe Noscitis Venerabiles, to the bishops of Spain, on clerical discipline; May 17.

1853: *Inter Multiplices*, to the bishops of France, on unity of spirit; March 21.

1854: *Neminem Vestrum*, to the clergy and faithful of Constantinople, on the persecution of Armenians; Feb. 2.

Optime Noscitis, to the bishops of Ireland, on the proposed Catholic university for Ireland; March 20.

Apostolicae Nostrae Caritatis, on peace; Aug. 1.

1856: *Singulari Quidem*, to the bishops of Austria, on the Church in Austria; March 17.

1858: *Amantissimi Redemptoris*, on priests and the care of souls; May 3.

1859: *Qui Nuper*, on the Pontifical States; June 18.

1860: *Nullis Certe Verbis*, on the need for civil sovereignty; Jan. 19.

1863: *Incredibili*, to the bishops of Bogota, on persecution in New Granada; Sept. 17.

1864: *Maximae Quidem*, to the bishops of Bavaria, on the Church there; Aug. 18.

Quanta Cura, on errors in modern society, to which was attached the famous Syllabus of Pius IX listing and condemning 80 errors; the Syllabus was intended as a defense of the rights of the Church and of "truth" against the abuses of freedom and culture in a liberalizing world, but in historical perspective it was rather a reactionary rejection of modern culture and a declaration of opposition to the modern State; Dec. 8.

1867: *Levate*, on the afflictions of the Church; Oct. 27.

1870: *Respicientes*, protesting the taking over of the Papal States; Nov. 1.

1871: *Ubi Nos*, to all bishops, on the Papal States; May 15.

1873: *Quartus Supra*, to the bishops and people of the Armenian Rite, on the Church in Armenia; Jan. 6.

1874: *Vix Dum a Nobis*, on the bishops of Austria on the Church there; March 7.

1875: *Quod Numquam*, to the bishops of Prussia, on the Church there; Feb. 5.

Graves ac Diuturnae, to the bishops of Switzerland, on the Church there; March 23.

Pope Leo XIII, 1878-1903 (88)

1878: *Inscrutabili Dei Consilio*, on the evils of society; April 21.

Quod Apostolici Muneris, on socialism; Dec. 28.

1879: *Aeterni Patris*, on the restoration of Christian philosophy; Aug. 4.

1880: *Arcanum*, on Christian marriage; Feb. 10.

1881: *Diuturnum*, on the origin of civil power; June 29.

Licet Multa, to the bishops of Belgium, on the Church in that country; Aug. 3.

1882: *Etsi Nos*, to the bishops of Italy, on conditions in that country; Feb. 15.

Cum Multa, to the bishops of Spain, on conditions in that country; Dec. 8.

1883: *Supremi Apostolatus Officio*, on the devotion of the Rosary, Sept. 1.

1884: *Nobilissima Gallorum Gens*, to the bishops of France, on the religious question in that country; Feb. 8.

Humanum Genus, on Freemasonry; April 20.

Superiore Anno, on recitation of the Rosary; Aug. 30.

1885: *Immortale Dei*, on the role of the Catholic citizen of the modern state; Nov. 1.

Spectata Fides, to the bishops of England, on the importance of Christian education; Nov. 27.

1886: *Iampridem*, to the bishops of Prussia, on Catholicism in Germany; Jan. 6.

Quod Multum, to the bishops of Hungary, on the freedom of the Church; Aug. 22.

Pergrata, to the bishops of Portugal, on the Church in that country; Sept. 14.

1887: *Vie Ben Noto*, to the bishops of Italy, on the Rosary and public life; Sept. 20.

Officio Sanctissimo, to the bishops of Bavaria on the Church there; Dec. 22.

1888: *In Plurimis*, to the bishops of Brazil on the abolition of slavery; May 5.

Libertas, on the nature of human freedom; June 20.

Saepe Nos, to the bishops of Ireland on the issue of boycotting; June 24.

Quam Aerumnosa, to the bishops of America on Italian immigrants; Dec. 10.

Etsi Cunctas, to the bishops of Ireland on the Church in that country; Dec. 21.

Exeunte Iam Anno, on the correct ordering of Christian life; Dec. 25.

1889: *Magni Nobis*, to the bishops of the United States, on the Catholic University of America; March 7.

Quamquam Pluries, on devotion to St. Joseph, foster father of Jesus; Aug. 15.

1890: *Sapientiae Christianae*, on Christians as citizens; Jan. 10.

Dall'Alto Dell'Apostolicio Seggio, to the Church in Italy on Freemasonry in that country; Oct. 15.

Catholicae Ecclesiae, on slavery in mission lands; Nov. 20.

1891: *In Ipso,* to the bishops of Austria, on episcopal gatherings in that country; March 3.

Rerum Novarum, on capital and labor, specifically in the context of the poor conditions of the working person and the right of the worker to organize labor unions; May 15.

Pastoralis Officii, to the bishops of Germany and Austria, on the morality of dueling; Sept. 12.

Octobri Mense, on October as the month of the Rosary; Sept. 22.

1892: *Au Milieu des Sollicitudes,* to the bishops, clergy and Catholics of France, on the matter of Church and State in their country; Feb. 16.

Quarto Abeunte Esaeculo, to the bishops of Spain, Italy and North and South America, on the quadricentennial of Columbus' voyages to the New World; July 16.

Magnae Dei Matris, on the Rosary; Sept. 8.

Inimica Vis, to the bishops of Italy, once again on Freemasonry; Dec. 8.

Custodi di quella Fede, to the Italian people, also on the issue of Freemasonry; Dec. 8.

1893: *Ad Extremas,* on seminaries for native clergy; June 24.

Constanti Hungarorum, to the bishops of Hungary, on the Church in that country; Sept. 2.

Laetitiae Sanctae, on devotion to the Rosary; Sept. 8.

Providentissimus Deus, on the study of the Scriptures; Nov. 18.

1894: *Caritatis,* to the bishops of Poland, on the Church there; March 19.

Inter Graves, to the bishops of Peru, on the Church there; May 1.

Praeclara Gratulationis, to the Eastern churches, expressing reverence for their venerable rites and inviting them to return to communion with Rome; June 20.

Litteras a Vobis, to the bishops of Brazil, on the clergy of that country; July 2.

1895: *Longinqua Oceani*, to the bishops of the United States, on Catholicism in the United States, with stress on the necessity of unity and harmony; the encyclical defended and explained the establishment of an Apostolic Delegation in Washington, and cited the progress of the Catholic University of America, founded in 1889; Jan. 6.

Permoti Nos, to the bishops of Belgium, on social conditions in that country; July 10.

1896: *Insignes*, to the bishops of Hungary, on the Hungarian millennium; May 1.

Satis Cognitum, on the unity of the Church; June 29.

1897: *Divinum Illud Munus*, on the Holy Spirit; May 9.

Affari Vos, to the bishops of Canada, on the Manitoba school issue; the encyclical lauded the bishops for their vindication of the Catholic principles of education, but advised union and charity when claiming justice; Dec. 8.

1898: *Caritatis Studium*, to the bishops of Scotland, on the Church in that country; July 25.

Spesse Volte, to the bishops and people of Italy, on the suppression of Catholic institutions; Aug. 5.

Quam Religiosa, to the bishops of Peru, on civil marriages; Aug. 16.

1899: *Testem Benevolentiae*, to Cardinal James Gibbons of Baltimore, concerning the errors of Americanism, the "phantom heresy" which amounted, in retrospect, to little more than ideological separatism from Rome in adapting the Church's teachings to popular manners and modes; Jan. 22. (Some sources classify this document as an apostolic letter, but it is designated an encyclical by John Tracy Ellis in *Documents of American Catholic History*; Milwaukee, 1962.)

Depuis le Jour, to the hierarchy and clergy of France, on the subject of education of the clergy; Sept. 8.

Paternae, to the bishops of Brazil, also on the subject of education of the clergy; Sept. 18.

1900: *Omnibus Compertum,* to the Patriarch and bishops of the Greek-Melkite Rite, on unity among Greek Melkites; July 21.

1901: *Graves de Communi,* on Christian Democracy; Jan. 18.

Reputantibus, to the bishops of Bohemia and Moravia, on the language issue in Bohemia, Aug. 20.

1902: *In Amplissimo,* to the bishops of the United States, in which Leo praises their success in spreading the faith, in establishing a school system, in developing missions to "the negro and the Indian," and in exploiting the liberty granted the Church by American law; also mentioned is the generosity of American Catholics in relieving "the penury of the Holy See"; April 15.

Mirae Caritatis, on the Eucharist; May 28.

Dum Multa, to the bishops of Ecuador, on marriage legislation; Dec. 24.

Pope/Saint Pius X, 1903-1914 (16)

1903: *E Supremi,* on restoring all things in Christ; Oct. 4.

1904: *Ad Diem Illum Laetissium,* on the Immaculate Conception; Feb. 2.

1905: *Acerbo Nimis,* on the teaching of Christian Doctrine; April 15.

Il Fermo Proposito, to the bishops of Italy, on Catholic Action in that country; June 11.

1906: *Vehementer Nos,* to the bishops, clergy and faithful of France, on France's Law of Separation; Feb. 11.

Gravissimo Officio Munere, to the bishops of France, on French associations of worship; Aug. 10.

1907: *Une Fois Encore,* to bishops, clergy and people of

France, on the separation of Church and State; Jan. 6.

Pascendi Dominici Gregis, on the doctrines of the Modernists; the encyclical acted as a Syllabus of Errors for the early 20th Century, by formalizing the decree _Lamentabili Sane Exitu_ (July 3, 1907), which condemned numerous propositions of Modernism, and specified penalties for those "refusing obedience to ecclesiastical authority" as well as for those "who show a love of novelty in history, archaeology or biblical exegesis" and those who "neglect the sacred sciences or appear to prefer the secular sciences to them"; Sept. 8.

1911: _Iamdudum_, on the Law of Separation in Portugal; May 24.

1912: _Lacrimabili Statu_, to the bishops of Latin America, on Indians of the South American continent; June 7.

Singulari Quadam, to the bishops of Germany, on labor organizations; Sept. 24.

Pope Benedict XV, 1914-1922 (13)

1914: _Ad Beatissimi Apostolorum Principis_, an appeal for peace between nations; Nov. 1.

1918: _Quod Iam Diu_, on the approaching peace conference; Dec. 1.

1919: _Paterno Iam Diu_, on the children of Central Europe; Nov. 24.

Maximum Illud, on missionary activity in the postwar world; Nov. 30.

1920: _Pacem Dei Munus Pulcherrimum_, on the peace conference and Christian reconciliation; May 23.

Annus Iam Plenus, on the children of Central Europe; Dec. 1.

1921: _In Praeclara Summorum_, to professors and students

of fine arts in Catholic institutions of higher learning; April 30.

Pope Pius XI, 1922-1939 (30)

1923: *Studiorum Ducem*, on St. Thomas Aquinas and Thomism as the basis of Christian philosophy; June 29.

1924: *Maximam Gravissimamque*, to the bishops, priests and people of France, on French diocesan associations; Jan. 18.

1926: *Iniquis Afflictisque*, on the persecution of the Catholic Church in Mexico; Nov. 18.

1928: *Mortalium Animos*, on religious unity and the pre-eminence of Rome as the one true Church; the document, which remained substantially in force until the pontificate of John XXIII, had a strong negative impact on the ecumenical movement; Jan. 6.

Rerum Orientalium, on the promotion of Oriental studies; Sept. 8.

1929: *Rappresentanti in Terra*, on Christian education; Dec. 31.

1930: *Casti Connubii*, on family life and the sanctity of Christian marriage; the encyclical denounced the abuses of the communications media, including theatrical productions, books, periodicals, movies and radio, in what was seen as an effort "to trample and deride the sanctity of marriage and to extol or so depict divorce, adultery and all the basest vices as to make them appear free of all reproach and infamy"; Dec. 31.

1931: *Quadragesimo Anno*, on reconstruction of the social order; issued to mark the 40th anniversary of Leo XIII's *Rerum Novarum* encyclical on capital and labor; May 15.

Non Abbiamo Bisogno, a defense of Catholic Action in Italy and a criticism of the youth program of the

Fascists; June 29. (This was the encyclical spirited out of Italy by Msgr. Francis Spellman, future Cardinal-Archbishop of New York, in order for the document to escape Fascist censorship. The encyclical was released to the world from Paris.)

1932: *Acerba Animi,* to the bishops of Mexico, on the continuing persecution of the Church in that country; Sept. 29.

1933: *Dilectissima Nobis,* to the bishops, clergy and people of Spain, on the oppression of the Church in that country; June 3.

1936: *Vigilanti Cura,* to the bishops of the United States, on motion pictures; June 29.

1937: *Mit Brennender Sorge,* to the bishops of Germany, on the Church and the German Reich, protesting that the Church's rights were being violated, but that the situation could be relieved if the Concordat were properly applied; March 14.

Divini Redemptoris, on the intrinsically evil nature of atheistic Communism, with which no Catholic could collaborate; March 19.

Nos Es Muy Conocida, to the bishops of Mexico, on religious conditions in that country; March 28.

Pope Pius XII, 1939-1958 (41)

1939: *Summi Pontificatus,* on the unity of human society; Oct. 20.

Sertum Laetitiae, to the bishops of the United States, on the progress of the Church in America; the encyclical warned against the dangers to good morals in American society because of the prevalence of divorce and birth control, the weakening of respect for authority, and a public educational system that ignored religious values; Nov. 1.

1943: *Mystici Corporis Christi,* on the Mystical Body of Christ; the document identified the Mystical Body of Christ with the Roman Catholic Church; June 29.

Divino Afflante Spiritu, on promoting biblical studies; the document commemorated the 50th anniversary of Leo XIII's *Providentissimum Deus*, and is said to have been drafted by Fr. Augustin Bea, S.J., one of the great ecumenists of John XXIII's pontificate; Sept. 30.

1945: *Communium Interpretes Dolorum*, to the world's bishops, on prayers for peace during the month of May; April 15.

1946: *Quemadmodum*, on the care of the world's destitute children; Jan. 6.

Deiparae Virginis Mariae, to bishops of the world, on the possibility of defining the Assumption of Mary as a dogma of faith; May 1.

1947: *Mediator Dei*, on the sacred liturgy, its nature, laws and possible adaptations; for many years the encyclical was a kind of Magna Carta of the liturgical apostolate, and it was on the basis of this encyclical that Rome gradually eased the fast before Communion, allowed evening Masses for the convenience of the faithful, and revised the Easter liturgies; Nov. 20.

Optatissima Pax, on public prayers for social and world peace; Dec. 18.

1948: *Auspicia Quaedam*, on public prayers for world peace and the solution of the Palestine question; May 1.

In Multiplicibus Curis, on peace in Palestine; Oct. 24.

1949: *Redemptoris Nostri Cruciatus*, on the holy places of Palestine; April 15.

1950: *Anni Sacri*, on the combatting of atheistic propaganda in the world; March 12.

Summi Maeroris, on prayers for peace; July 19.

Humani Generis, on false opinions and attempts to destroy Catholic truths by undermining the foundations of Catholic doctrine; the encyclical was considered to be aimed strongly at France's progressive theologians, and it cost several prominent writers, seminary professors and provincial superiors there their positions of authority; most were later rehabilitated, but for the time being, a wave of intellectual repression born of the encyclical swept through seminaries and religious orders; Aug. 12.

1951: *Evangelii Praecones*, on the promotion of Catholic missions; June 2.

1952: *Orientales Ecclesias*, on the persecutions of the Eastern Church; Dec. 15.

1953: *Fulgens Corona*, announcing a Marian Year to commemorate the centenary of the definition of the dogma of the Immaculate Conception; Sept. 8.

1954: *Sacra Virginitas*, on consecrated virginity; March 25.

Ad Sinarum Gentem, to the bishops, clergy and people of China, on the supranationality of the Church; Oct. 7.

Ad Caeli Reginam, proclaiming the Feast of the Queenship of Mary; Oct. 11.

1955: *Musicae Sacrae*, on the matter of sacred music; Dec. 25.

1956: *Luctuosissimi Eventus*, on events in Hungary and asking prayers for peace and freedom for the Hungarian people; Oct. 28.

Laetamur Admodum, on peace in Poland, Hungary and the Middle East; Nov. 1.

Datis Nuperrime, condemning the ruthless application of force in Hungary; Nov. 5.

1957: *Le Pelerinage de Lourdes*, on the centenary of the apparitions at Lourdes (1858) and the need to be on guard against materialism; July 2.

Miranda Prorsus, on motion pictures, radio and television; Sept. 8.

1958: *Ad Apostolorum Principis*, to the bishops of China, on Communist efforts to drive the Church in China into schism; June 29.

Meminisse Juvat, appealing for prayers for the per-
secuted Church; July 14.

Pope John XXIII, 1958-1963 (8)

1959: *Ad Petri Cathedram,* on truth, unity, peace and a
spirit of charity; the encyclical was firmly anti-Communist, admonitory towards mass media, and in-
sistent on obedience; June 29.

Princeps Pastorum, on the missions and issued to
commemorate the 40th anniversary of Benedict
XV's *Maximum Illud* reorganizing missionary work;
Nov. 28.

1961: *Mater et Magistra,* addressed to the world; the encyclical cited the needs of underdeveloped countries, the depressed state of agriculture, the
pressures of an expanding population, and stressed
the obligation of wealthy nations to assist nations
less fortunate; the document thus broadened out
from previous papal social encyclicals, which had
dealt principally with industrial relations and
distributive justice in developed industrial countries; May 15.

1963: *Pacem in Terris,* addressed also to the world; the
encyclical discussed human rights, the dignity of
the individual, and order between peoples, from
the level of the family to that of international councils; it denounced racism, defended the right of the
individual to worship according to conscience,
urged an end to the arms race and a ban on nuclear
weapons, and supported the concept of a world
body "endowed with a breadth of powers, structure, and means" to solve problems of worldwide
dimensions (interpreted as a call for a strong United
Nations); extraordinary in scope, the encyclical became John XXIII's last will and testament, as he
died of stomach cancer the following June 3;
April 11.

Pope Paul VI, 1963-1978 (7)

1964: *Ecclesiam Suam,* on the Church and the dialogue which was the Church's duty to conduct with itself, with other Christians, and with believers and non-believers of all the world; Aug. 6.

1965: *Mense Maio,* on peace, and for prayers during the month of May for that end; April 29.

Mysterium Fidei, on the Eucharist; Sept. 3.

1966: *Christi Matri,* on peace, and for prayers during the month of October for that end; Sept. 15.

1967: *Populorum Progressio,* on the development of peoples, and the need to take drastic action to close the growing imbalance between rich nations and poor nations; March 26.

Sacerdotalis Caelibatus, on priestly celibacy; June 24.

1968: *Humanae Vitae,* on the regulation of birth; the encyclical reiterated the Church's traditional ban on the use of artificial contraceptives, and held that "every conjugal act must be open to the transmission of life," thus serving as catalyst to a wide protest in which large numbers of priests and people disagreed publicly with the pope; the encyclical produced the greatest clash between authority and conscience in modern Church history; July 25.

Pope John Paul II, 1978-   ( )

1979: *Redemptor Hominis,* on the connection between the Redemption and the dignity of the individual; the encyclical broached the pope's philosophy of Christian humanism, and offered an exposition and explanation of Vatican Council II's Declaration on Religious Freedom; March 4.

1980: *Dives in Misericordia,* on the mercy of God, with stress on the role of God and the impingement of the Divine on human values; Nov. 30.

1981: *Laborem Exercens,* on human work and the place of

labor unions as "an indispensable element" of modern industrial society and a vehicle "for the struggle for social justice"; Sept. 14. (The encyclical was originally scheduled for release May 15, the 90th anniversary of Leo XIII's *Rerum Novarum*, but was delayed because of the assassination attempt on the pope's life in St. Peter's Square, May 13, 1981, and the pope's convalescence.)

1985: *Slavorum Apostoli*, on "solidarity" among Slavic people, religious tolerance in Eastern Europe, and closer ties between Roman Catholicism and Eastern Orthodoxy; July 2.

1986: *Dominum et Vivificantem*, on the evils of materialism; May 30.

Bishops as Teachers

The episcopacy, as stated earlier, is the fullness of the priesthood. To belong to the episcopacy is to be a bishop. To be a bishop is to be a successor of the Apostles. By way of emphasis, the very first of the traditional papal titles is that of the pope as bishop. The pope is: "*Bishop of Rome* and Vicar of Jesus Christ, Successor of St. Peter, Prince of the Apostles, Supreme Pontiff of the Universal Church, Patriarch of the West, Primate of Italy, Archbishop and Metropolitan of the Roman Province, Sovereign of Vatican City." But, again, the first of his titles is as bishop. As Bishop of Rome, the pope is the direct successor of St. Peter, to whom Christ consigned the future of his Church. Peter, of course, preached and was crucified in Rome. The Bishop of Rome enjoys an unchallenged primacy in Catholicism; he is "bishop of bishops."

The word "bishop" derives from the Greek word for "overseer." Thus, in hierarchical union with the pope and with fellow bishops, bishops as a body are overseers or pastors of the Church. A bishop can administer all the sacraments; he alone can administer Holy Orders. A bishop consecrates holy oils, churches, the vessels of the liturgy, etc. Individually, bishops are responsible for the care of the local Church (archdiocese, diocese, missionary see, etc.); collectively, bishops are responsible for the care of the universal Church. The latter point was emphasized by Vatican Council II (1962-1965) in the context of collegiality:

"Just as, by the Lord's will, St. Peter and the other apostles consituted one apostolic college, so in a similar way the Roman Pontiff as successor of Peter, and the bishops as the successors of the Apostles are joined together. The collegial nature and meaning of the episcopal order found expression in the very ancient practice by which bishops appointed the world over were linked with one another and with the Bishop of Rome by the bonds of unity, charity and peace; also, in the conciliar assemblies which made common judgments about more profound matters in decisions reflecting the views of many. The ecumenical councils held through the centuries clearly attest this collegial aspect" (Dogmatic Constitution on the Church, *Lumen gentium*, 22).

In the hierarchical order there are many ranks: pope, cardinal, patriarch, archbishop, bishop; consecrated prelates, abbots, apostolic administrators, vicar apostolics, prefect apostolics, etc. The ecclesiastical powers of these ranks vary greatly according to the responsibilities involved. But so far as Holy Orders are concerned, full power belongs to those ordained bishops. The Pope, in other words, would have no fuller power of orders than the bishop of an anonymous missionary territory.

By the same token, however, the authority which a bishop has in his own episcopal jurisdiction does not intrude upon the authority which the pope has, by virtue of his office as Roman Pontiff, of reserving cases to himself or some designated representative. When problems arise in a particular diocese, a usual practice is for the pope to dispatch another bishop as apostolic visitor to examine the ministry of the bishop brought into question. An instance of such an action was the dispatching of Archbishop James A. Hickey of Washington, D.C., in 1983 to Seattle, Washington, to study charges brought by individuals against Seattle Archbishop Raymond Hunthausen. The investigation into the ministry of Archbishop Hunthausen extended over two years, and was closed November 27, 1985 with praise for many aspects of his leadership, but also with an admonishment calling for "greater vigilance" in upholding the church's teaching in several areas, including divorce, contraceptive sterilization and homosexuality. A week later Archbishop Hunthausen was assigned an auxiliary bishop, Donald W. Wuerl of Pittsburgh, a former secretary in the Roman Curia. The incident dramatized the close, sometimes zealous watch on discipline and orthodoxy which Rome maintains even over bishops.

The orthodoxy of bishops is considered of vital importance because of the charge laid upon them by Christ himself, and summarized in its fullest implications in Vatican II's Decree on the Bishop's Pastoral Office in the Church, *Christus Dominus:* "Christ gave the Apostles and their successors the command and the power to teach all nations, to hallow men in the truth, and to feed them. Hence, through the Holy Spirit, who has been given to them, bishops have been made true and authentic teachers of the faith, pontiffs, and shepherds" (2).

Conferences of Bishops. The 18th and first-half of the 19th Centuries saw the development within the church of an exaggerated notion of papal primacy and infallibility, traceable in major degree to the formal declaration of papal infallibility as dogma at Vatican Council I (1869-1870). Unilateral exercise of authority became the virtual norm within Catholicism. The bishops looked to Rome for lead in all things, and Rome in turn spoke authoritatively and for all on all matters, from war and peace to social justice, from clerical discipline to marital behavior. There was, in sum, no regular collaboration with the bishops of the world in the exercise of the teaching office.

Vatican Council II (1962-1965) acted to restore ancient balances between the pope and the bishops by reactivating the concept of collegiality—which is to say that as St. Peter and the other Apostles constituted one apostolic college, so in similar fashion are the Roman Pontiff, the pope, and the bishops as successors of the Apostles joined together. The concept is spelled out in Vatican II's Dogmatic Constitution on the Church *(Lumen gentium)*.

Thus it is that, though the authority of the pope remains primal, the situation no longer is that of the pope apart or on a pedestal with the bishops as ecclesiastical inferiors, but rather of a College of Bishops with the pope as its head. Thus the episcopacy and the papacy, each existing by divine right and each with its own legitimate authority, form the one communion with responsibilities that are both mutual and separate.

The notion of collegiality is validated historically by the fact of the church's 21 Ecumenical Councils. The reactivation of the concept with Vatican Council II has been marked by more frequent structured consultations between the pope and the College of Cardinals on matters such as church and Vatican finances, and by the formation of a Synod of Bishops, a central ecclesiastical institute which is convened periodically as a kind of mini-council to deal with topics of concern in the broader Church (see "Synod of Bishops" in Miscellanea).

On the regional or national level, collegiality has spawned conferences of bishops, or official bodies of bishops of a particular country or geographical area. Conferences of bishops operate under norms and statutes approved by the Holy See. Their particular advantage is to enable bishops of a country or a territorial area to act together as pastors of their local church on matters of urgency in their region. This has quickened the church's response to problems. At the same time it has pointed up the variety of opinions possible within the church on given topics.

A dramatic example of the latter is found in the peace

messages that issued in 1983-4 from the various national hierarchies. The United States Conference of Bishops ratified a pastoral letter ("The Challenge of Peace: God's Promise and Our Response") which, while refraining from declaring that nuclear weapons could never be used as a means of retaliation, asserted nonetheless that the bishops could not imagine a situation that would justify their use. The West German bishops, on the other hand, supported the NATO (North Atlantic Treaty Organization) policy of "flexible response"; that is, nuclear weapons might be needed to halt an overwhelming enemy attack employing conventional weapons. The French bishops aligned themselves with the West Germans, while the Dutch bishops stopped just short of urging unilateral disarmament as a means of controlling and reducing nuclear arsenals. The Irish bishops, meanwhile, declared that unilateral disarmament was a "strict moral obligation" if elements of a country's nuclear strategy were immoral.

The dramatic significance of these messages was that here were conferences of bishops addressing a topic which before 1962 would have been reserved to Rome. The actions attested both to the growth of the concept of collegiality on the level of the local church and to the local church's new-found independence, or at least its release from monolithic thought which had previously obtained on most topics within the church.

It should be noted, however, that Rome exercised the privilege of reviewing beforehand the pastoral letter of the American bishops, the first and potentially most consequential of the peace messages. The review could itself be justified as an expression of collegiality, Rome wishing to share in the thought of the local bishops. But more likely the review was authoritative rather than collegial, Rome being concerned that the American bishops might be too pacifist in their leanings. Pacificism, in a word, might be tolerable in the instance of a small hierarchy in a militarily insignificant country; for example, The Netherlands. It would be less tolerable in the instance of a large hierarchy in a country, like the United States, whose military strength is bound up with the balance of power in the world.

Whatever the considerations, it is clear that national conferences of bishops are not totally independent of Rome, and that collegiality is not so much a prerogative or exclusive right as it is an entitlement subject to the dispositions of Rome and ultimately the reigning pope. This, in turn, would appear to confirm the ambiguousness of collegiality as principle in the church, its application and the extent of its relativeness being dependent on the tolerance and will of the dominant authority in the Church.

It goes almost without saying that statements of conferences of bishops do not have the same authority as those issued by the pope or by Vatican agencies in the pope's name or with his authority. It could not be otherwise when, as the peace messages indicate, one conference of bishops can hold to one position and another episcopal conference to a position which is utterly different.

The large importance of conferences of bishops (aside from obvious organizational considerations) is that they are in a position to provide guidelines on local or national problems consistent with the principles of faith—which guidelines in turn may vary from national situation to national situation. These guidelines would not be binding in conscience in the absolute sense as would be a guideline from the pope. For instance, what gives the message of *Humanae Vitae* its force as guideline on sexual conduct within marriage is that it derives from a pope as a papal encyclical; it would not have the same force, either in a country or a geographical region, if it originated with a conference of bishops.

Conscience and the Catholic

Conscience is the intrinsic faculty by which an individual arrives at a judgment concerning the rightness or wrongness of a particular act. Historically the church has honored the primacy of conscience, while holding that the best-formed conscience was one aided by good will, by the right use of the emotions, by the external experience of living, and by certain external helps. Among the latter is the authoritative teaching office of the Church—the magisterium or teaching authority. Thus a dichotomy is set up. Conscience is the "voice of reason" or the "voice of God," and in Catholic understanding a person who follows/obeys the dictates of conscience shall never offend God. At the same time, however, Catholic understanding ties conscience to obedience, and further exalts obedience to a virtue when the individual subjects his/her will to that of another for God's sake. Conscience is absolute, but conscience is also subject to obedience.

The dichotomy is glimpsed in successive paragraphs in Vatican II's Pastoral Constitution on the Church in the Modern World *(Gaudium et spes)*, section 16 on the dignity of the moral conscience:

"In the depths of his conscience, man detects a law which he does not impose upon himself, but which holds him to obedience...."

"Conscience is the most secret core and sanctuary of a man. There he is alone with God, whose voice echoes in his depths. In a wonderful manner conscience reveals that law which is fulfilled by love of God and neighbor...."

The Correct Conscience. The church so respects conscience that it holds free from guilt wrongful acts arising from a certain but erroneous conscience. This is not to say that the wrongful act is made itself good by the erroneous conscience, but rather that the individual is not held responsible for the wrongful act because the individual's conscience knows no better. The point is made succinctly in the just cited Pastoral Constitution on the Church in the Modern World: "Conscience frequently errs from invincible ignorance without losing its dignity" (16).

That conscience can err accounts for the church's emphasis on a properly formed conscience—or, in church parlance, a correct conscience. A correct conscience is one which is in harmony with church teaching, which is to say that the individual Catholic is responsible for knowing and following the position of the church, and conforming his/her conscience to that position. Once upon a time the act of conforming was almost automatic within Catholicism, but in recent years this is less so. Large numbers of Catholics take different readings of conscience from the teaching authority's, as on the morality of artificial birth control, and have made their individual moral decisions—in the name of supremacy of the individual conscience.

Accordingly, whereas obedience to the teaching authority had stabilized the Church for centuries, the exaltation of conscience introduced displays of independence which were dramatically new for Catholicism. These displays of independence have been both in the behavioral and moral realms, and though they are deplored by some, others regard them as signs of the vibrancy of the church and the latitudes of belief and expression now possible within Catholicism.

The Release of Conscience. Many factors were at work in the release of Catholic conscience—some secular, the church of course not existing in a vacuum; some reactionary, as in disappointment or anger over particular papal actions or pronouncements, notably *Humanae Vitae*, the 1968 birth-control encyclical. But mostly the new spirit of independence evolved out of Vatican Council II (1962-1965) with its conciliar emphases on religious freedom and the dignity of the individual, both as a human and religious right, personal and collective. In this context, the principal influence by far was the Declaration of Religious Freedom *(Dignitatis humanae)*, the opening

words of which, however otherwise intended, became
a kind of manifesto for large numbers of Catholics:

> "A sense of the dignity of the human person has been
> impressing itself more and more deeply on the con-
> sciousness of contemporary man. And the demand is
> increasingly made that men should act on their own
> judgment, enjoying and making use of a responsible
> freedom, not driven by coercion, but motivated by a
> sense of duty" (1).

The Declaration on Religious Freedom was addressed
to the broad family of humankind, rather than to internal Catholicism *per se*, but its impact within Catholicism
was enormous, as individual Catholics applied the principles of religious freedom to their individual lives, both
as Christian believers and practicing Catholics. This is not
precisely what the Fathers of Vatican II had intended, but
the development was predictable, certainly in the eyes
of the person who was a principal architect of the document, American Jesuit Father John Courtney Murray.
"Inevitably, a second great argument will be set afoot—
now on the theological meaning of Christian Freedom,"
he said, adding that those who receive this freedom
"assert it within the church as well as within the world."
The words were prophetic. Vatican II settled long-stand-
ing ambiguities between the People of God and the People Temporal, but it also bequeathed to the church of the
1980s the concept of a released conscience.

Expectations Regarding Conscience. However widespread the assertions of individual conscience in modern
Catholicism, the position of the church with regard to conscience remains constant. Individuals are obliged (1) to
obey a certain and correct conscience; (2) to obey a certain conscience even when it is erroneous out of ignorance
or faulty knowledge; (3) to disregard and correct a conscience known to be erroneous or derelict; (4) to rectify

a scrupulous conscience, which sees error where there is none; (5) to resolve a doubtful conscience before acting. Points four and five direct the individual conscience towards the teaching authority of the Church.

Probabilism. If, after attempts to resolve a doubtful conscience, the conscience remains doubtful regarding the morality of a particular action, the Church provides that indecision may be settled by the invocation of probabilism. Probabilism as moral system holds that, when there is question of the lawfulness or unlawfulness of an act, it is permissible to follow a genuinely probable opinion in favor of liberty, even though the opposing position is more probable.

Probabilism as moral system developed towards the end of the 16th century, though it is apparent from history that earlier problems in the church were resolved by principles which were probabilist in tendency. St. Augustine, for instance, declared that marriage with infidels was not to be regarded as unlawful since it was not specifically condemned in the New Testament, and St. Thomas Aquinas held that a precept did not bind except through the presence of knowledge. Both were applications of probabilism.

Movements, Artifacts, Institutions, Orders, Organizations and Communications

Centers of Pilgrimage

THE PILGRIMAGE INSTINCT is one that predates Christianity, extending back to primitive times and belief in multiple gods, when individuals would travel to one place or another to pay honor at the shrine of the deity said to control the destiny of people or the movement of nature. Incorporated into Christianity, the pilgrimage rationale is much the same. Devout Christians have historically wished to visit locations hallowed by the birth, life or death of someone holier than themselves. The church has encouraged this, regarding pilgrimages not only as a religious exercise, but also as a purifying act; thus the practice of attaching to pilgrimages remission of canonical penalties or, for those not under a particular sanction, graces to be applied to their spiritual lives.

Pilgrimages became so much a part of the Christian tradition that time-schedules were once provided for them within civil and ecclesiastical law. The canons of Hereford Cathedral, for example, allowed its clergy three weeks each year for visiting a shrine within the English kingdom; seven weeks for a pilgrimage to the tomb of St. Denis in Paris; eight weeks for a pilgrimage to the tomb of St. Edmund in Pontigny; sixteen weeks to go to Rome or to the shrine of St. James at Compostela in Spain; one year for going to the Holy Land. No clergyman was expected to make more than one foreign pilgrimage in his lifetime.

Following are some—far from all—historically popular pilgrimage points. Some of the ancient shrines no longer retain the popularity nor the focus that they did once-upon-a-time, but their places have been taken by more modern shrines, so that a tradition continues, which is as old as the visit made to the tomb of Christ on the third day after the Crucifixion by Mary Magdalene, Mary the mother of James, and their female companions. They went to anoint the body only to find the tomb empty.

Holy Land

Jerusalem and its environs have been held holy from earliest days, and not only by Christians, but by Jews and Moslems as well. This is the land where for members of three religions—Christianity, Judaism, Islam—God chose to intervene in history. For Christians and Jews this land is the Holy Land. Arabia, with its Mecca and Medina, is Islam's Holy Land. (Both cities are in western Saudi Arabia.) But for Moslems Jerusalem is also a holy place, as it was from Jerusalem, the Koran declares, that the Prophet Mohammed rose to heaven. This establishes a potentially important tie between Moslems and people of the other two faiths, the more so since on Mohammed's instructions Moslems venerate the patriarchs and saints of the Bible, along with Jesus and his mother Mary.

For Christians the Holy Land is a special place, because it was here that Christ was born (Bethlehem is south of Jerusalem in the occupied region known as the Left Bank), where he lived, preached and died by crucifixion—and accordingly the place from where he resurrected into heaven. To walk in the footsteps of Christ has been a Christian impulse from at least the third century. That was when the first pilgrimages to the Holy Land were recorded. But the Holy Land was a world away, quite literally, in days of travel by foot or horse. There were many who wished to go there who never could. Some provided for their hearts to be buried there after their deaths; others made pilgrimages to nearer shrines. Indeed it was the Holy Land's virtual inaccessibility to pilgrims of the West which initially gave impetus to Rome as a pilgrimage center.

Still the Holy Land never lost its grip on Christian piety, which helps explain the Crusades of the Middle Ages, launched for the purpose of wresting the Holy Land from so-called infidels. Over the centuries Rome has worried for the safety and preservation of the shrines associated with Christ, but the shrines have survived by and large, despite wars and persecutions and the excesses of Christians themselves, who among other things removed many Holy Land relics to the West.

Italy

Rome ranks with the Holy Land as the principal pilgrimage objective of Catholic Christians. It has been such since earliest centuries, so much so that the city gave its name to the verb expressing the very notion of traveling or wandering; in English, the verb is roam.

Rome's attraction to the devout rested then as now in its being the burial place of the apostles Peter and Paul, and not even danger of death deterred early Christians from making pilgrimages to their tombs. SS. Constantine and Victoria are said to have made straight for the tomb of Peter on their arrival in Rome, where they were caught by Roman soldiers and put to death. It is a safer place now.

St. Peter was buried at the Circus Neronianus, where he was crucified during Nero's persecution. Over his tomb was erected the basilica bearing his name, which would become one of the wonders of the world. Peter's tomb rests beneath the high altar of St. Peter's Basilica. Soaring overhead is the dome of Michelangelo.

St. Paul, another of Nero's victims, is buried in the Basilica of St. Paul Outside the Walls, one of Rome's most illustrious churches. Under the papal altar, in the Confession, is a marble sacrophagus containing his remains.

In earlier ages it was practice for pilgrims to wear a sign identifying them as such. These were known as pilgrim signs, and commonly they were in the form of badges sewn to the hat, pinned on outer garments, or hung about the neck. Paradoxically, though the chief shrines of Rome were the tombs of Peter and Paul, the pilgrim sign for those who went to Rome in the Middle Ages seems to have been the "vernicle" or reproduction of St. Veronica's veil. Chaucer indicates as much in describing the pardoner:

> "That strait was comen from the Court of Rome
> A vernicle had he served upon his cappe."

Assisi in East Umbria in central Italy is the site of the Portiuncula, the famed shrine-chapel of Our Lady of the Angels, which the Benedictines gave to St. Francis of Assisi in the early 13th century, and which he renovated and made into the first church of the Franciscan Order. The Portiuncula is enshrined now in Assisi's Basilica of St. Mary of the Angels. Rich indulgences (known as the Portiuncula Indulgence or Pardon of Assisi) were attached to pilgrimages to the chapel by Pope Honorius III (1216-1227), the pope who confirmed the rule of St. Francis. These may now be gained in other Franciscan and parish churches.

Loreto, a small town south of Ancona and near the Adriatic Sea, claims pilgrim attention as the location of the "Holy House of Loreto"—the alleged house in which Mary was born; where she was hailed by an angel; and where the Word was made Flesh. Legend has it that the house was conveyed by angels from Palestine to the town of Tersato in Illyria in 1291, and a few years later carried off again by angels, at last achieving a final resting place in Loreto. The authenticity of the Holy House is debunked by many, but it is interesting to note that on October 4, 1962, seven days before the opening of Vatican Council II, Pope John XXIII visited Loreto and Assisi to pray for the success of the event.

Mantua in the northern Italian province of Lombardy, boasts the beautiful church of Santa Maria delle Grazie outside the city walls. The church enshrines a painting on wood of the Madonna, which is attributed to St. Luke. Reproductions of the painting are found in religious-goods stores worldwide. August 15, the Feast of the Assumption, is the high point of the shrine's pilgrimage season.

Naples has been a pilgrimage center for several centuries because of its two famous shrines—Madonna del Carmine and Santa Maria della Grotta—and also because in the cathedral church are preserved the head of St. Januarius and two ampullae (flasks) of his blood. Januarius was a 4th century martyr, whose relics were brought to Naples from Montevergine in 1479. Several times each year the head of St. Januarius is exposed on the altar. The larger of the ampullae is brought within sight of the head and the congregation, whereupon the blood, which had appeared as a dark and solid mass, liquefies. The event is regarded locally as being miraculous.

Padua, near Venice in northeast Italy, is famed as the resting place of St. Anthony. The city's outstanding church is the Basilica of St. Anthony of Padua, begun in 1232.

The saint's body reposes under the high altar. A chapel called "Capella del Santo" features nine bas-reliefs by Lombardi depicting miracles of St. Anthony. Pilgrimages to Padua continue year-round.

Turin is the main community of Piedmont, and was once the capital of the Duchy of Savoy and the Kingdom of Sardinia. For years pilgrims have flocked there because in the Chapel of Santissimo Sudario attached to the cathedral is preserved the Holy Shroud of Turin, the burial cloth in which Joseph of Arimathea is said to have wrapped the body of Jesus. The cloth, about 13½ feet long and 4¼ feet wide, contains the likeness of a human form, front and back. The devout believe this to be the likeness of Jesus himself. Expositions of the cloth are the occasions of large pilgrimages. In 1983 the Vatican accepted the gift of the shroud, it having been willed to Pope John Paul II by the former King Umberto of the House of Savoy.

Ireland

Downpatrick in County Down, Northern Ireland, is revered as the most sacred of Irish cities, for in the cathedral church there are the relics of St. Patrick, St. Brigid and St. Columba. Curiously, none of the three died there. St. Patrick died at Saul in 493 and was buried at Down, which did not even have a church at the time. St. Brigid was originally buried in Kildare, but her remains were moved to Downpatrick around 878 to protect them from defilement by Scandinavian raiders. St. Columba's remains were brought to Downpatrick from Iona, again for reasons of safety, the island being subject to periodic invasions by Norsemen and Danes. The presence of the remains of Ireland's three greatest saints in the one resting place has made Downpatrick a center of devotion for centuries.

St. Patrick's Purgatory on Donegal's Lough Derg has drawn pilgrims from all parts of Ireland for hundreds of years. Lough Derg, 13 miles in circumference, has 11 islands, the principal of which are Saints Island and Station Island. St. Patrick's Purgatory is on Station Island and draws its name from the tradition that St. Patrick was the first to establish the three-day penitential vigil of praying and fasting that constitutes yet the basis of pilgrimage there.

Knock in County Mayo, in the northwest Province of Connaught, experienced an apparition in 1879, when on the wet evening of August 21 the Blessed Virgin, St. Joseph and John the Evangelist were said to appear on the wall of the parish church. The apparition lasted more than two hours and was witnessed by 15 villagers. Knock became a popular place of pilgrimage when persons begain claiming miraculous cures after touching the wall. In 1976 a grander church dedicated to Our Lady, Queen of Knock, was erected near the orignial parish church. Pope John Paul II visited Knock in 1979 to mark the centennial of the apparition, and 450,000 pilgrims flocked to the village for the occasion. Currently an international airport is being developed to promote pilgrimages to the site.

England

Most of the ancient shrines of England passed from Catholic to Anglican control following King Henry VIII's break with Rome in 1534. Some shrines were dismantled and destroyed during the accompanying tensions. Others survived, although with different devotional emphases.

Canterbury has ranked as the most famous of English shrines since medieval times. It is, thanks to the evangelizing of St. Augustine, the birthplace of Saxon Christianity. St. Augustine is buried here; St. Thomas a Becket was martyred here. Seventeen of Canterbury's archbishops were sainted, nine became cardinals, and 12 became lord chancellors of England before the Roman Catholic control of the shrine was ended with the accession to the throne of Queen Elizabeth I in 1558. Canterbury is now the seat of Anglicanism's ranking archbishop, and it is, as Belloc once described it, the spiritual center yet of England. For many, however, Canterbury's spiritual roots essentially remain in Roman Catholicism. Pope John Paul II visited Canterbury in 1982, and prayed there with Anglican Archbishop Robert Runcie.

Chichester in Sussex has drawn pilgrims for centuries to its cathedral, wherein is the tomb of St. Richard, a 13th-century figure who entered Oxford as a poor scholar and later became its chancellor. Richard was elected bishop of Chichester in 1244 and served until his death in 1253. He had been a model bishop, and pilgrims thronged to his shrine in emulation of the devotion of King Edward I. By 1478, the crowds were so great that regulations were posted so that pilgrims could approach the shrine in more orderly manner. (Parish priests were advised to give notice of their coming, and enter by the west door in pre-scribed order.) The principal pilgrimage dates were Whit-sunday (seventh Sunday after Easter) and April 3 (the Feast of St. Richard).

Durham, in the north of England along the Scottish border, is a center of devotion for possessing the relics of St. Cuthbert and St. Bede. Cuthbert was a Bishop of Lindisfarne, whose remains were transferred to the "new" Durham Cathedral in 1104. There they are en-shrined in a reliquary completed by John, Lord Nevill of Raby, in 1372. Bede, a contemporary and biographer of Cuthbert, was a writer and teacher of such renown as to win the accolade in his lifetime of "the Venerable Bede." He was formally canonized in 1899. The authen-ticity of the relics of Cuthbert and Bede has been ques-tioned in relatively recent years, but people still visit Durham to marvel at what Dr. Samuel Johnson termed the cathedral's appearance of "rocky solidity and of in-determinate duration."

Edmundsbury in Suffolk is famed as the burial place of St. Edmund, king and martyr, to whom are attributed many miracles. Edmund lived in the 9th century and died at the hands of invading Danes, whose demands he felt offended his Christian beliefs. He was killed in 870 and buried at Hoxne, but his relics were moved in the 10th century to Beodricsworth, thenceforth known as Edmundsbury. A famous abbey was built there, and St. Edmund's shrine in the abbey church became a pilgrimage point for kings such as Canute and Henry VI, and ordinary folk as well.

Ely in Cambridgeshire is a center of devotion as the shrine to St. Etheldreda, a queen of Northumbria of holy reputation. Etheldreda became a nun and founded a monastery on the site of what became Ely's famous cathedral. She is buried there, although a hand of the saint is venerated in the Church of St. Etheldreda in Ely Place, London. The London Church was the first of the pre-Reformation places of worship in England which was restored to Catholic worship.

Glastonbury in Somerset boasts legends that trace back to 63 A.D., when St. Joseph of Arimathea arrived in Britain with 11 companions, having been sent by the apostle Philip. The names of St. Patrick and St. David are associated with Glastonbury, as well as King Arthur and St. Dunstan. Then too there is the celebrated Glastonbury Thorn, a variety of hawthorn, which flowers at Christmastime as well as in May. The legend is that the original tree grew from the staff of St. Joseph of Arimathea, which took root upon being thrust into the ground, and blossoms at Christmas, mindful of the Lord's birthday. Botanists have other, non-miraculous explanations for the origin and endurance of the curious thorn tree.

Lincoln, a cathedral city in East England, has roots that go back to St. Theodore and the founding of the see in 678. The present cathedral was begun by St. Hugh shortly after being named Bishop of Lincoln in 1186. It was England's first Gothic building and it introduced the architectural feature of the pointed arch. St. Hugh was buried here, but his shrine was destroyed during the Reformation. That action lessened Lincoln's attraction as a pilgrimage place, but visitors are still numerous.

Oxford is thought of as a university center, but it was long a popular pilgrimage center because of its shrine of St. Frideswide. Twice a year—in mid-Lent and on the Feast of the Ascension—the university community, headed by the chancellor, marched in solemn procession to her shrine. Remnants of this practice survive in ceremonies connected with the saint's feastday, October 19.

Pembrokeshire in Wales is the site of the shrine of St. David, considered so holy at one time that William the Conqueror hastened there immediately after his conquest of England. That was in the 11th century. By papal decree, two pilgrimages to St. David's were equal to one to Rome.

Walsingham in Norfolk was the site of England's most famous Marian shrine. The shrine dated from 1061, and numerous kings went on pilgrimages there, among them Henry III in 1241, Edward I in 1280 and 1296, Edward II in 1315, Henry VI in 1455, Henry VII in 1487 and Henry VIII in 1513. Twenty-five years later, in 1538, Henry VIII tolerated its destruction. The shrine of Our Lady of Walsingham was dismantled and the statue of Our Lady was sent to London, where it was burned. A private home was erected on the spot. Of the medieval buildings, all that remain are the eastern gable and base of the church's west tower, much of the refectory and part of the prior's lodge. The site was excavated in 1855 and again in 1955. This has helped draw pilgrimages back to Walsingham.

Westminster Abbey in London enshrines the relics of St. Edward the Confessor, the monarch who endowed Westminster Abbey. The abbey was consecrated in 1065. Edward grew up in Normandy. After the Norman Conquest of England in 1066—an event which opened the English

Church to European influence—Edward's memory and
his shrine were zealously conserved by the Norman
kings. An imposing new shrine was built for his relics
in 1163 by King Henry II, at the suggestion of St. Thomas
a Becket. Immediately the shrine became a pilgrimage objective and has remained so, though on a far less organized basis than in the so-called ages of faith.

France

Argenteuil, a city in northern France on the Seine, claims
to have in its parish church the Holy Coat of Christ, the
coat for which the soldiers cast lots at the Crucifixion.
Tradition has it that it was brought to Argenteuil by Charlemagne. (The cathedral of Trier, on the Moselle in West
Germany, makes the same claim, alleging that the Holy
Coat was sent to the city by Empress St. Helena.) A verifiable claim by Argenteuil is that its abbey once had as
abbess the famous Heloise, the pupil and wife of Pierre
Abelard; their star-crossed romance is one of the great
romantic tragedies of history. Whatever the authenticity
of the relic of the Holy Coat, Argenteuil has known pilgrims since the 13th century.

Chartres is a major cathedral city southwest of Paris, with
a famous sanctuary dedicated to the Blessed Virgin. Pilgrimages have continued here for centuries, attracting
kings of France and England, Mary Queen of Scots and
saints such as Bernard of Clairvaux, Anselm of Canterbury, Thomas a Becket, Vincent de Paul and Francis
de Sales.

La Salette in southeast France is celebrated as the place
where the Blessed Virgin, sorrowful and weeping, appeared to two young shepherds, Melanie Calvat and
Maximin Giraud, on September 19, 1846. Reportedly, the
Virgin complained about the impiety of Christians, and
threatened chastisement if they persisted in evil, mercy
if they amended their ways. The authenticity of the ap-

parition has been questioned, but Bishop de Bruillard of Grenoble declared the apparition as credible in 1851 and authorized the cult of Our Lady of La Salette. A shrine church was erected on the mount of La Salette, and subsequently given the title of minor basilica.

Le Puy in the Haute-Loire region claims another Marian apparition, this one to a sick widow converted by St. Martial, a 3rd-century saint. In the Middle Ages, no French shrine drew more pilgrims than Le Puy. Charlemagne came there twice, as did several kings and the mother of Joan of Arc. The popular hymn, "Salve Regina," was written by a Bishop of Le Puy, Adhemar of Monteil, and was once known as the anthem of Le Puy.

Lisieux in the Province of Calvados in northwest France is famed as the home of St. Therese of Lisieux, the extraordinarily pious Carmelite, whose autobiography became a best seller after her death in 1897 and whose "Little Way" was hailed by Pope Benedict XV as containing "the secret of sanctity for the entire world." The Basilica of St. Therese of Lisieux, one of the largest monuments in all of France, was completed in 1954 and quickly became a center of pilgrimage.

Lourdes in the Pyrenees is far and away the most popular French shrine of our time, attracting pilgrims from all over the world year-round. Pope John Paul II himself went there in 1983 to point up his concern for the sick and the crippled. The shrine commemorates the appearance of the Blessed Virgin on 18 occasions in 1858 to a 14-year-old girl, Bernadette Soubirous, at the grotto of Massabielle. The waters at Lourdes are said to possess miraculous qualities. The shrine thus attracts many who are infirm and invalid. Accounts of cures are many.

Mont-St.-Michel in Normandy is one of the quaintest of pilgrimage objectives, with its medieval architecture and fortified Benedictine abbey piled on a conical outcropping of rock in the Atlantic. Legend has it that the abbey was built on direct command of the Archangel Michael, who appeared on three occasions to the Bishop of Avranches, St. Aubert, about the year 708. The site is now primarily a tourist spot, but for many years pilgrims visited there to honor the Archangel Michael and seek his intercession in times of war and distress.

Pontigny in Yvonne contains the relics of St. Edmund of Canterbury, and once was a favorite visiting place for English pilgrims. The shrine was despoiled during the Huguenot troubles, but the relics were saved and preserved in a large reliquary of 18th-century craftswork.

Tours is known for its shrine containing the remains of St. Martin. Before the Revolution it was one of the most famous and popular pilgrimage centers in Christendom. Clovis came here in 507 after his victory over the Visigoths. A basilica was built over the tomb of St. Martin, and many miracles were associated with the place. The kings of France preserved Martin's cape *(cappa, chape)*, hence the word chapel for the shrine where it was reserved.

Spain

Compostela is noted for its shrine of St. James the Greater, the apostle who was the brother of John the Evangelist. James' relics are believed to be here, thus explaining the shrine's renown in medieval times. Pilgrims to Compostela bore back with them the sign of scallop shells as testimony of their trip, thereby establishing a custom which eventually extended to pilgrimages in general. Pilgrimages to the shrine are recorded as early as the 8th century.

Montserrat is the most popular center of pilgrimages to the Blessed Virgin in Spain, with a history going back to the 10th century. The shrine church was dedicated in 1562.

Puche in Valencia boasts a famous sanctuary dedicated to Our Lady of Mercy, in whose honor the Order of Mercy came into being. The Feast of Our Lady on September 24 is observed there with special devotion.

Saragossa in Aragon has another famous shrine dedicated to the Blessed Virgin, under the title Neustra Senora del Pilar. Tradition has it that its Marian statue was set in place by directive of the apostle James, while Mary was still living—a detail which, if true, would date Catholic Marian devotion back to earliest Christian times. Many miracles are said to have been performed there.

Toledo in central Spain has a famous cathedral which enshrines a statue of the Blessed Virgin in a heavily ornamented chapel of jasper, a variety of quartz. It became a center of devotion as pilgrims were drawn by the legend of the apparitions of St. Ildephonus. Ildephonus, it is alleged, was visited by the martyr-saint Leocadia, who rose from her tomb to thank him for the devotion he had shown to Mary. Among other things, Ildephonus wrote tracts on the perpetual virginity of Mary. On another occasion, it is said, Mary herself appeared to him and presented him with a priestly garment in thanks for his zeal in honoring her. Ildephonus, an Archbishop of Toledo, died in 667.

Portugal

Fatima, north of Lisbon, ranks with Lourdes as the most noted of modern shrines of the Blessed Virgin. Here Mary is said to have appeared six times to three peasant children between May 13 and October 13, 1917, recommending among other things frequent recitation of the rosary, devotion to Mary under the designation of her Immaculate Heart, and the consecration of the Russian people to her under this title—a request implemented by Pope Pius XII in 1952 in an apostolic letter addressed to them. In 1930 the apparitions at Fatima were pronounced worthy of belief. Reportedly a "secret" was conveyed during the Fatima apparitions. Although there has been enormous speculation about what the secret of Fatima might be, it has never been revealed. Pope John Paul II visited Fatima in 1982 in thanksgiving for having survived the attempt on his life the year before. The assassination attempt took place on May 13, the anniversary of the first of the Fatima apparitions, prompting the Pope to link his survival to the intervention of Our Lady of Fatima.

Belgium

Beauraing near Namur is the site of more reported Marian apparitions, 33 in all occurring between November 29, 1932, and January 3, 1933: Mary visiting five children in the garden of their convent school. A chapel was built on the site as a pilgrimage center. The Bishop of Namur extended approbation to the events in 1949.

Bruges in West Flanders claims to possess a relic of the Holy Blood, shed during the Passion and which may have adhered to one of the instruments of the Passion. According to tradition, the relic was presented to Thierry of Alsace during the Second Crusade by his cousin Baldwin, King of Jerusalem. It was brought to Bruges in 1150. Verifiable or not, the relic was long venerated with great devotion and was carried in solemn procession on the Monday following the first Sunday in May, with the Flemish nobility and thousands of pilgrims taking part. Several other places claim to have relics of the Holy Blood, including Saintes and Mantua, but it is impossible to verify their authenticity. A different age is more skeptical about the relic.

Oostacker, near Ghent, became a place of pilgrimage in the 19th century, after the Marquise de Calonne de Courtebourne built an aquarium on her estate in the form of an artificial grotto or cave. It was the time of great enthusiasm over the apparitions at Lourdes, and the parish priest suggested that a statue of Our Lady of Lourdes be placed among the rocks. That was in 1871. Two years later the shrine was opened to the public on Sunday afternoons, and throngs of pilgrims made their way there. Eventually a large Gothic church was erected adjacent to the shrine, and a long avenue was built to the shrine and Stations of the Cross erected. The shrine became known as the Lourdes of Flanders.

Austria

Mariazell in Austria's Styria province has a 10th-century statue of the Madonna that has attracted pilgrims for many years. Virtually every important Habsburg visited the shrine, and Maria Theresa left behind medallions of her husband and children. June and July were the favorite pilgrimage months. At one time, the government decreed the day on which pilgrims from Vienna would process to Mariazell. The pilgrims would meet at Vienna's famed Cathedral of St. Stephen (Karlskirche) and then begin their four-days' pilgrimage.

The imposing Karlskirche is itself a center of devotion, having been built between 1716 and 1739 as thanksgiving for the liberation of Vienna from the plague.

Germany

Cologne, ancient Rhine city in West Germany, was a popular pilgrimage center in a more credulous age for its shrine of the Three Kings—the Magi who paid homage to the Infant Jesus at Bethlehem. Tradition records that the relics of the three were brought by St. Helena to Constantinople, then transferred to Milan, and in the 12th century to Cologne, to which they were carried in triumph by Frederick Barbarossa—Emperor Frederick I of the Holy Roman Empire. The relics were encased in a reliquary by Nicholas of Verdun. It is considered a remarkable example of the art of the medieval goldsmith.

Poland

Cracow claims a miraculous statue of the Virgin Mary brought to the city by St. Hyacinth. At one time it was the object of devout pilgrimages.

Czestochowa with its Black Madonna—an icon on which the images of Mary and Child have been darkened as if by smoke and fire—is the holiest of Polish shrines. It is a shrine associated both with faith and, for non-Communist Poles, with national patriotism. The icon is made of cypress wood, and legend has it that the images were painted by St. Luke on a panel made by St. Joseph for display in the home of Jesus, Mary and Joseph in Nazareth. Reportedly it was transported to Constantinople, where in 988 it came into possession of Anna, the wife of Vladimir of Kiev. The icon arrived in Czestochowa in 1382, and has been the object of great devotion since. Some sources suggest the icon is of 9th-century Greek-Italian origin, but the possiblity that the icon is less old than the legend holds has not dulled the fervor of Polish respect for the icon. The Black Madonna is enshrined on the Hill of Light, Jasna Gora, above the city itself. Czestochowa is in south-central Poland, and is the principal pilgrimage center of the country.

Canada

Ste. Anne de Beaupre on the St. Lawrence River above Quebec City boasts one of the great shrine churches of Canada. Its history dates back to 1658 and the reportedly miraculous cure of Louis Guimont, a cripple, on the day work was to start on a small chapel to St. Anne. The present structure is a large Romanesque-Gothic basilica, featuring an eight-foot oaken statue and major relic of St. Anne—a portion of her forearm. Also on display are medical appliances, such as canes and crutches, left behind by persons who were ostensibly cured at the shrine.

Trois-Rivieres, also on the St. Lawrence but below Quebec

city, is the site of the shrine of Our Lady of the Cape, Queen of the Most Holy Rosary. Its history dates from 1714 and the construction of a fieldstone church, preserved yet as the oldest stone church in North America. A remarkable over-sized rosary winds around a portion of the grounds in the manner of a fence. The church was declared a pilgrimage shrine in 1909 by the First Plenary Council of Quebec.

Montreal, further down the St. Lawrence, has its Notre Dame Basilica, patterned after Notre Dame of Paris, but the major pilgrimage objective is St. Joseph's Oratory, a minor basilica overlooking the city from the heights of Mount Royal. The shrine began as a small chapel erected in 1904 by Blessed Andre Bessette, C.S.C. The shrine grew to immense proportions with the start of work on the basilica church in 1924. A belfry with a 60-bell carillon marks the site of the original chapel.

Ontario province has a shrine honoring several of the Jesuit Martyrs of North America, killed by Mohawk Indians between 1642 and 1649. The shrine, situated on the site of the old Fort Sainte Marie, is a counterpart to the shrine of the North American Martyrs at Auriesville, New York.

United States

Auriesville in Montgomery County in up-state New York is the place where Jesuit Father Isaac Jogues and his companions were martyred by Mohawks in the 17th century. Jogues was tomahawked and beheaded; the others died equally cruel deaths. They were canonized by Pope Pius XI in 1930. The site of the Mohawk village where the martyrdoms occurred was purchased in 1884 and a small shrine erected under the title Our Lady of Martyrs. The shrine was developed and the grounds extended, as pilgrimages grew and Rome confirmed the cult of the martyrs. The martyrs were Jogues, Anthony Daniel, John de Brebeuf, Gabriel Lalemant, Charles Garnier and Noel Chabanel, all Jesuit priests, and Rene Goupil and John Lelande, lay missionaries. Auriesville is on the New York State Thruway, not far from Amsterdam.

Washington, D.C., is the location of the Shrine of the Immaculate Conception, honoring the Blessed Virgin under the title by which she was declared patroness of the United States in 1846. The national shrine is the seventh largest religious structure in the world, and the largest in the Western Hemisphere. It can accommodate up to 6,000 worshippers. The shrine abuts the campus of the Catholic University of America and draws some one-million pilgrims annually.

Mexico

Guadalupe near Mexico City is the site of the famous apparitions of the Blessed Virgin to Juan Diego, an Indian in his 50s, between December 9 and 12, 1531. They took place at Tepeyac, a hill northwest of Mexico City. In her first appearance the Virgin instructed Juan Diego to have the bishop, a man named Zumarraga, build a church on the site. To convince the bishop of Juan Diego's credentials, the Virgin told him on another appearance to go up to the rocks, pick flowers, and take them to the bishop. Juan Diego followed instructions, and when he presented them, magnificent out-of-season roses fell from his mantle. Beneath them was a painted image of the Virgin. This is the image of Our Lady of Guadalupe that Catholics worldwide know so well today. The first sanctuary was erected in 1533, but this has been succeeded by a grander edifice. Our Lady of Guadalupe was declared patroness of "New Spain" by Pope Benedict XIV in 1754. In 1910 Pope St. Pius X declared her patroness of Latin America, and in 1945 Pope Pius XII named her patroness of the Americas.

Notable Edifices, Institutions

Catholic life is centered about its places of worship—its basilicas, cathedrals, churches.

Basilica designates a place of worship celebrated for its antiquity, historical importance, architectural dignity and association with development of the faith. There are two classes: major and minor. *Major Basilicas* possess a papal throne and altar, and a holy door opened and closed in connection with Jubilee Years. *Minor Basilicas* possess certain ceremonial privileges which confer on it a precedence over other places of worship of a particular locality, although not the cathedral of the area.

Cathedral is the principal or chief church of a diocese or archdiocese. It is the place of worship in which the bishop of a diocese, or archbishop of an archdiocese, has his seat *(cathedra)*. A see customarily has one cathedral, although in instances of combined or multi-city dioceses (Galveston-Houston, Texas; Kansas City-St. Joseph, Missouri, etc.) a *co-cathedral* is customarily designated. Pro-cathedral is the designation given to a place of worship used as a cathedral. The Archdiocese of Dublin, Ireland, has a pro-cathedral (St. Mary's off of O'Connell Street), a designation which registers continuing Catholic dissent in Ireland over the accession of Christ Church Cathedral (formerly Holy Trinity Cathedral) and St. Patrick's Cathedral during the Anglican Reformation.

Church is the ordinary place of Christian worship for a parish or community of believers.

Basilicas

Major basilicas have also been known as patriarchal basilicas, being representative in a sense of the early evolving ecclesiastical provinces of Christendom. The preeminent major basilica is St. John Lateran in Rome, the cathedral church of the pope as Bishop of Rome, and Patriarch of the West. As such it is the highest-ranking church in the world, the "mother church." It was not until after the return of the papacy from Avignon that St. Peter's became the center of papal ceremonies.

The other major basilicas of Rome and their historical patriarchal associations are St. Peter's (Constantinople), St. Paul Outside the Walls (Alexandria), and St. Mary Major (Antioch). St. Lawrence Outside the Walls, attributed to the Patriarch of Jerusalem, ranks as a minor basilica. Among other structures enjoying the designation of major basilica is that associated with St. Francis and the Portiuncula in Assisi.

The principal basilicas of Rome:

• *St. John Lateran* was destroyed and rebuilt many times. Its history goes back to Constantine, and during the time of Pope Sylvester I (314-335) the church was known as the Basilica of the Savior. The present structure, which follows the lines of the classical basilica with a nave and four aisles, dates from the 17th century. Its facade was built in 1735 by Alexander Galilei. Among the basilica's showpieces is a statue of Constantine, found at the Quirinal, and bronze doors, which were requisitioned from the Curia at the Forum by Pope Alexander VII (1655-1667). Also here is the tomb of Sylvester II (999-1003), the French pope, who was the first to proclaim the "necessity" of the Crusades for the "rescue" of the Holy Land. The Lateran was the residence of the popes before the papacy was moved from Rome to Avignon.

• *St. Peter's Basilica* succeeds a structure that was begun by Constantine in 323 and that for centuries was regarded as one of the marvels of the world. Like other Roman churches, however, it fell into decay during the years that the papacy was at Avignon. The neglect necessitated its razing. Pope Nicholas V (1447-1455) decided that a new basilica should be built, but it was Pope Julius II (1503-1513) who initiated the project in a serious way. It took

176 years to complete the basilica. Popes, architects and designs tumbled one upon another, and the project bogged down amid such controversies as whether the design of the basilica should be in the form of a Greek cross or the nave extended in order to form a Latin cross. Michelangelo favored a Greek cross with a dome. The magnificent dome was indeed built, but Pope Paul V (1605-1644) revised other designs so that the basilica would assume the form of a Latin cross after all. It was not until 1626 and the papacy of Urban VIII (1623-1644) that St. Peter's could finally be dedicated. The basilica is of heroic proportions. Its length is 693.8 feet—longer than two football fields, endzones included—and as such is the largest church in Christendom. It overshadows St. Paul's, London (520.3 feet), the Florence cathedral (490.4 feet), Milan cathedral (444.2 feet), and St. Sophia's in Constantinople (354 feet). St. Peter's is a veritable museum, with treasures such as Michelangelo's Pieta and a bronze baldachino by Bernini, some 95-feet high. But the holiest treasure of all is the tomb of St. Peter the Apostle, which rests beneath the high altar.

• *St. Paul Outside the Walls* is another Roman church which owes its origins to Constantine. He built a church over the tomb of the apostle Paul. This was succeeded by a basilica begun in the 4th century and completed during the reign of Pope Leo the Great (440-461). For some 1,400 years the basilica retained its original character. Then in 1823, it was destroyed by fire—the fire being caused, it is said, by the negligence of a worker who was repairing the lead of the roof. The basilica was restored according to its old design, with much of the world rallying behind the work. The Khedive of Egypt, for instance, contributed pillars of alabaster, while the Emperor of Russia sent malachite and lapis lazuli (a deep-blue mineral), used in the decoration of the tabernacle. The mosaics of the chancel arch date from the 5th century; they were salvaged from the fire and restored, but, it is said, not well. Later they were reset, and they now comprise one of the glories of the structure. The relics of the apostle Paul are in an area under the main altar.

• *St. Mary Major,* the so-called fourth church of Rome, is the largest dedicated to the Virgin Mary and the only Roman church retaining its original form and character, some later decorations notwithstanding. The basilica dates from the time of Pope Sixtus III (432-440), and was dedicated to Mary to commemorate her formal definition as Mother of God. It was restored and embellished during the papacy of Benedict XIV (1740-1758). Fernando Fuga, a Florentine architect, was in charge, and his hand is to be seen in the facade with its portico and loggia, and the 36 restored marble columns of the central nave. The ceiling, by Julian Sangallo, was gilded with the first gold brought from the New World. A feature of the basilica is a series of 5th-century mosaics reproducing scenes from the Old and New Testaments.

• *St. Lawrence Outside the Walls,* the fifth patriarchal basilica, though a minor basilica, is another of Constantine's churches. The church was vandalized by Alaric and the Visigoths after their capture of Rome in 410, but was rebuilt by Pope Pelagius II (579-590). Next the Longobards ravaged the church, and it was necessary to restore it again. Some credit the second restoration to Pope Hadrian I (772-795); others to Pope Honorius III (1216-1227). During the World War II aerial bombardment of July 19, 1943, the basilica sustained extensive damage, particularly to the nave and facade. These were repaired, but lost were a number of paintings by Cesare Fracassini commissioned by Pope Pius IX (1846-1878).

Minor Basilicas.

The number of minor basilicas has increased markedly in recent years, as popes have extended to the world the rank and "privileges" belonging to the minor basilicas of Rome. These privileges are largely honorific and include such things as the right of the canons or pastors of the place of worship to wear the *cappa magna*, a vestment ordinarily reserved to bishops and cardinals. Other privileges cover the use of an umbrella *(conopoeum)* and ceremonial bell, but most have given way in most places to the latter-day de-triumphalizing of liturgical rites.

There are some 30 minor basilicas in the United States alone. Alphabetically by state, they are:

- *Alabama:* Cathedral of the Immaculate Conception, Mobile.
- *California:* Mission Dolores, San Francisco; Old Mission of San Carlos, Carmel; St. Joseph, Alameda; Mission San Diego de Alcala, San Diego.
- *Colorado:* Cathedral of the Immaculate Conception, Denver.
- *Florida:* Cathedral of St. Augustine, St. Augustine.
- *Illinois:* Our Lady of Sorrows, Chicago; Queen of All Saints, Chicago.
- *Indiana:* St. Francis Xavier (Old Cathedral), Vincennes.
- *Iowa:* St. Francis Xavier, Dyersville.
- *Kentucky:* Our Lady of Gethsemani (Trappist), Gethsemani; Cathedral of the Assumption, Covington.
- *Louisiana:* St. Louis Cathedral, New Orleans.
- *Maryland:* Assumption of the Blessed Virgin Mary, Baltimore.
- *Massachusetts:* Our Lady of Perpetual Help ("Mission Church"), Roxbury.
- *Michigan:* St. Adalbert, Grand Rapids.
- *Minnesota:* St. Mary's, Minneapolis.
- *Missouri:* Immaculate Conception, Conception; St. Louis, St. Louis.

- *New York:* Our Lady of Perpetual Help, Brooklyn; St. James Cathedral, Brooklyn; Our Lady of Victory, Lackawanna; Blessed Virgin Mary of the Rosary of Fatima, Youngstown.
- *Ohio:* Lady of Consolation, Carey.
- *Pennsylvania:* St. Vincent's, Latrobe (Benedictine Archabbey); Sacred Heart, Conewago; SS. Peter and Paul, Philadelphia.
- *Texas:* St. Mary's, Galveston.
- *Wisconsin:* St. Josephat, Milwaukee.

The Cathedral of San Juan in San Juan, Puerto Rico, is also ranked as a minor basilica.

Canada has 14 minor basilicas, as follows:
- *Alberta:* Cathedral of St. Joseph, Edmonton.
- *Manitoba:* Cathedral of St. Boniface, St. Boniface.
- *Newfoundland:* Cathedral of St. John the Baptist, St. John's.
- *Nova Scotia:* St. Mary's, Halifax.
- *Ontario:* Notre Dame, Ottawa; St. Peter's Cathedral, London.
- *Prince Edward Island:* St. Dunstan, Charlottetown.
- *Quebec:* Cathedral of St. Michael, Sherbrooke; Cathedral of Our Lady, Queen of the World, Montreal; St. Joseph's on Mount Royal, Montreal; Notre Dame, Montreal; Our Lady of the Cape, Trois-Rivieres; Notre Dame, Quebec; St. Anne de Beaupre, Beaupre.

Among other notable minor basilicas are the Basilica of the Grotto at Lourdes, the Church of the Sacred Heart on Montmartre in Paris, and the Church of Marienthal in Alsace.

Cathedrals.

The metaphorical marriage has long been a part of Catholic rationale; the nun as bride of Christ, for instance. At one time canonists even spoke of the union of bishop and church as a spiritual marriage, and although this was understood in the broad sense (Church with a capital c), it has been applied on occasion to express the affinity that ideally exists between a bishop and his cathedral church. As an old *Catholic Encyclopedia* (The Gilmary Society, 1913) expressed it, "...the bishop should love his cathedral, adorn and embellish it, and never neglect it."

The concept of a metaphorical or spiritual marriage is likely a strained one, certainly where bishops and cathedrals may be concerned, but the pride which bishops and Catholic communities have taken in the chief church of their see has resulted in many magnificent cathedrals. Following is a selection of them:

• Notre Dame of Paris, on an isle of the Seine, is one of the landmark churches of Christendom. The cornerstone was laid in 1163; the facade completed in 1218; the towers in 1235. By the early 14th century, the cathedral was completed, and it has since withstood revolution and wars with remarkable grace and endurance. The cathedral's treasury was raided during the French Revolution, and many precious objects were removed for melting down at the mint. Catholic worship was interrupted for a time, but resumed in 1802. Three years later the cathedral was designated a minor basilica. Notre Dame is famous for its stained glass, notably the west rose window which dates from around 1220, as well as for its gargoyles, stone carvings of birds of prey, wild boars and feline forms which act as water spouts about the structure.

• *Chartres Cathedral*, southwest of Paris, was begun in 1020, when the bishop Fulbert invited the sovereigns of Europe to contribute towards the rebuilding of a church that had been destroyed by fire. Fires continued to plague Chartres, seriously interfering with construction in 1030, 1134 and 1194. In 1220, however, work was advanced to a point where Guillaume le Breton was able to write: "Entirely rebuilt in dressed stone and terminating in a vault that may be compared to the shell of a tortoise, the cathedral of Chartres need fear nothing further from temporal fire until the Day of Judgment." The cathedral was dedicated in 1260. Chartres Cathedral too is famous for its stained glass. Its windows date from the 13th century and contain some 3,889 figures. One of the principal themes is the glorification of Mary.

• *Reims Cathedral* in northeast France also replaced a church destroyed by fire in 1211. It was built in exactly 100 years' time, and stands as one of the most notable examples of Gothic architecture. In its treasury is the famous chalice of St. Remigius, the cup from which kings of France drank the wine of communion during their solemn coronation ceremonies. In 1886, Reims Cathedral was affiliated to the Lateran Basilica in Rome, thereby gaining for it the indulgences and favors attached to the Lateran.

• *Westminster Cathedral* in London was built following the restoration of the hierarchy in England in the 19th century. The project originated in 1865, but it was not until 30 years later that construction actually began. Work continued into this century. The main structural components of the cathedral are brick and concrete. The cathedral covers some 54,000 square feet, and features an uninterrupted nave 60-feet wide, with domical vaulting. Especially remarkable are the stations of the cross, imposing a 5'-8" square carvings of Hoptonwood stone by Eric Gill, the celebrated British sculptor and artist, who died in 1940. The stations are set above eye-level on the massive brick piers of the nave. Each has a differently designed border, a Latin inscription among the figures, and a title in English at the base. They were executed between 1914 and 1918. The last station was installed in March, 1918.

• *St. Mark's* in Venice dates from 829 and draws its name by virtue of its possessing the relics of St. Mark (purchased by Venetian merchants at Alexandria, where Mark was martyred). In the 11th century the structure was remodeled after the style of the Basilica of the Apostles at Constantinople, now Istanbul. St. Mark's was lavishly decorated over several centuries, particularly the 14th. It is said that Venetian vessels of the time seldom returned from their distant voyages without bringing something for the ornamentation of St. Mark's—a column, capital, frieze, etc. The four horses of gilded bronze above the main doorway, for instance, once adorned the Arch of Trajan; they were removed to the Hippodrome at Constantinople, then brought to Venice in 1204 by Enrico Dandolo. The facade features mosaics, Byzantine sculptures and carvings of the Evangelists and the Saviour. St. Mark's has basilica status. Since 1807 it has also been Venice's cathedral.

• *Milan Cathedral* was begun in 1386 under Giovanni Galeazzo Visconti and completed under Napoleon in 1805. It is a remarkable example of Italian Gothic architecture, distinguished by 98 needle-like turrets, on the main one of which is a gilded bronze statue of the Madonna. The cathedral is of white marble. The interior has no less than five naves and 4,000 statues. Outside are another 2,000 statues. The tomb of St. Charles Borromeo, the saint whose spirit is said to have mirrored the ideals of the Counter-Reformation, is under the cupola; he was a Cardinal-Archbishop of Milan. The high altar of the cathedral was a gift of Pope Pius IV (1559-1565).

• *St. Patrick's Cathedral* on New York City's fashionable Fifth Avenue is of geometric Gothic design, after the manner of the cathedrals of Reims, Amiens and Cologne. Its cornerstone was laid on the Feast of the Assumption in 1858, and work continued into this century with the construction of the Lady Chapel in an apsidal recess. The chapel was completed in 1906. The cathedral is 386 feet in length, which made St. Patrick's at the time of its construction eleventh in size among churches of the world. Its towers soar 330 feet into the sky. The cathedral is built of granite and white marble. With the archbishop's residence at its rear, the cathedral occupies the city block between 50th and 51st Streets. Lexington Avenue is to the rear.

National Shrine.

The National Shrine of the Immaculate Conception is located at 4th Street and Michigan Avenue in northeast Washington, D.C., adjacent to the campus of the Catholic University of America. Contemporary in style, yet with strong Byzantine-Romanesque lines, the shrine is built in the fashion of medieval cathedrals without any steel skeleton and framework. Construction materials are of stone, brick, tile and concrete.

The project of a shrine honoring Mary under her title as patroness of the United States was initiated in 1914, and the foundation stone was laid in 1920. For years, visitors worshipped in an underground crypt, while work proceeded on the upper church and superstructure. These were dedicated in 1959, though work remained to be done on the shrine. In its finished state, the shrine has a seating capacity of 3,000 and a total capacity of 6,000. The mosaics of the shrine are especially noteworthy.

The Shrine of the Immaculate Conception is 459 feet in length and rises to an interior height under its dome of 159 feet. It is the largest church in the United States, and the seventh largest in the world. In addition to the main altar, there are another 50 inside chapels honoring, among others, St. Pius X, St. Louise de Marillac, St. Vincent de Paul and the Blessed Mother under a variety of titles.

The bell tower, featuring a 56-bell carillon, was the gift of the Knights of Columbus.

The shrine is open daily and attracts more than a million visitors annually.

Museums.

A museum, purely and simply, is a building or place where works of art or other objects of permanent value are preserved and displayed. Once upon a time, Catholic officials applied the interesting subdivisional term Christian Museums, using it to identify those museums which specialized in Christian objects of art antedating the Middle Ages. As such, the first Christian Museum was that of the Vatican, its origin dating from Pope Benedict XIV (1740-1758), who established it under the title "Museum Christianum." The problem, however, with the qualifying adjective was that so-called "Christian Museums," at the Vatican as elsewhere, conveniently accommodated art that was pre-Christian, pagan and secular so long as the object was considered a work of art per se. Today, one does not encounter the term Christian Museum, which is as well. The term would apply in the strict sense to the Roman catacombs (Christian Museums in the real sense) and to little else. It would certainly not apply to the Gallery of Contemporary Art opened at the Vatican Museum in 1973 under the sponsorship of Pope Paul VI, and which includes work which is neither Christian nor religious, though art nonetheless.

The principal museums under Catholics auspices are those of the Vatican. The Vatican museums are several, among them:

• *Pio Clementino Museum,* so called because it is the accomplishment of two popes: Clement XIV (1769-1774) and Pius VI (1775-1799). Among its treasures are the Torso of Heracles, the Belvedere Apollo and the Laocoon group. (Laocoon was the priest of Apollo of Troy, who warned the Trojans against admitting the wooden horse into their city. With his two sons he was killed by serpents sent by Athena.)

• *Chiaramonti Museum,* named for Pope Pius VII (1800-1823), who was born Barnabo Chiaramonti. Divided into 60 sections, the museum displays some 800 Greek-Roman works: statues, busts, sarcophagi, reliefs, etc. Included among them are the Daughters of Niobe, a relief in Boeotian limestone, and a head of Neptune.

• *Braccio Nuovo,* a museum featuring statuary, including the statue of Augustus of Prima Porta, the Group of the Nile, and the Doriforos, an early representation of an athlete which shows a profound knowledge of human anatomy on the part of the sculptor.

• *Egyptian Museum,* opened during the pontificate of Gregory XVI (1831-1846), it houses statues, papyrus manuscripts, sarcophagi and other ancient Egyptian works and objects. It is a spectacular collection, but of lesser importance than Egyptian museums elsewhere.

• *Etruscan Museum,* in which are collected antiquities— statues, sarcophagi, bowls, vessels, mosaics, lamps, etc.— excavated between 1828 and 1836 in western Etruria, an ancient country located between the Arno and Tiber Rivers in what today is the Tuscany area of Italy.

For many centuries (e.g., the Renaissance, 14th to the 17th centuries) the Church was an industrious sponsor of the arts. It follows that the theme for much of this art should be religious. Notable examples. . . .indeed, so many thousands of notable examples have found their way into the great public museums of the world that to visit and view them is to experience something of a religious moment.

Universities

The modern university was born in the Middle Ages, when a revival of interest in learning led to the founding of major schools of education, notably in Salerno, Bologna and Paris, which became centers for the study of medicine, law and theology, respectively. The Catholic Church was very much a part of this movement, but not exclusively so. Popes did indeed affix their authority to the founding of universities, but the power to establish these institutions belonged also to civil rulers, including emperor, king and queen. Prior to the Reformation, some

81 universities were established. Of that number, 33 held papal charter; 15 were founded by imperial or royal license; 20 had both papal and imperial/royal charter; and 13 had no charter, having developed independently of official charter. Though the origins of these universities were several, they were nonetheless strongly Catholic in character, because the developing civilization, particularly in the West, was essentially Catholic.

In the beginning the word university was not used to designate a community focusing on a collection of the sciences and their study. Rather it was a legal term associated with the corporate entity of an institution. It was only in the 13th century that the words *universitas* (totality) and *studium* (study) began to be applied to institutions of learning as such. In the instance of Oxford in England, both *Universitas Oxoniensis* and *Studium Oxoniese* were used.

The term *alma mater* (nourishing, dear, mother) evolved in roughly the same period. Around 1300, the Oxford masters were using the expression *mater universitas*, perhaps having adopted it from a document of Pope Innocent IV (1243-1254), in which he spoke of Oxford as *foecunda mater* (fruitful mother). Later the expression became *alma mater*, the usage probably having been suggested by the hymn beginning "Alma redemptoris mater." In any instance, the expression is recorded in Paris in 1389, in Cologne in 1392, and in Oxford in 1411.

In the Middle Ages, popes contributed substantially to the development and prosperity of Europe's universities, intervening at times to protect their personnel against encroachments of local populaces. (Town and gown tensions are as old as universities themselves.) The Reformation brought a "new learning" to universities, most immediately in Germany and England, while in France the inroads of Gallicanism and Jansenism, and controversy involving the university and the Jesuits became factors in the substitution of royal for papal influence at the University of Paris. Eventually, of course, the

University of Paris was completely secularized, this by the end of the 16th century.

No longer was theology the mistress of sciences. Intellectual life was turned about. Emphases were on rationalism and humanism. Latin ceased to be the primary language of instruction; freedom of research became the operative code. By the 19th century, many universities which had been Catholic, and often papal institutions as well, had disappeared or been taken over by the state, including some in Catholic Spain and Italy. They were then reconstituted as centers for the exploration and exposition of the so-called natural branches of learning. Concessions were made in some places—Austria and Germany, for instance—so that Catholic faculties of theology could exist as part of state universities, but as has been noted, the presence of a faculty of Catholic theology did not and does not make the university Catholic as a whole.

(As an example of how the latter system works, Swiss theologian Father Hans Kung was a ranking professor on the Catholic faculty at the state-run University of Tubingen in West Germany. When the feud between Kung and the Vatican over such tenets as papal infallibility, the Virgin Birth and the divinity of Christ, reached the desk of Pope John Paul II in 1980, pressure was brought by Rome to have Kung removed from the faculty. The action ended with a compromise which allowed Kung to remain on the faculty of the university, while no longer being responsible to its Catholic theology department and no longer being involved in examining candidates for the priesthood.)

The reverses, which resulted in the loss of direct Catholic influence in university centers such as Paris, Bologna, Coimbra, Alcala, Douai and Salamanca, did not bring about a retreat of the church from interest in the university. Quite the opposite. In 1876, Pope Pius IX issued a charter to what is now Laval University in Quebec; Pope Leo XIII issued one in 1881 to St. Joseph University of Beirut, in Lebanon, and another in 1889 to St. Paul University (formerly the University of Ottawa) in Ontario.

Pope Leo XIII strongly encouraged the establishing of the University of Fribourg in Switzerland in 1889.

Today there are Catholic colleges and universities, pontifical universities and ecclesiastical faculties in countries in many parts of the world, erected, authorized and supervised by the Vatican's Sacred Congregation for Catholic Education. However, the eminence that was the Church's in university life and learning is markedly less than it was in the so-called ages of faith, when the word "thought" was virtually synonymous with Catholic thought.

A further factor diminishing the church's influence in education was the Iron Curtain that descended on Eastern Europe in the post-World War II ideological split between the communist governments of the East and democracies of the West. The character of many universities changed, so that by 1985 there was only one Catholic university in Eastern Europe—in Lublin, Poland.

Pontifical Universities. In 28 countries of the world there are 46 pontifical universities; that is, universities which have been canonically erected and which are authorized by the Vatican's Sacred Congregation for Catholic Education to confer degrees in specific fields of study.

Three are in the United States: Catholic University of America and Georgetown University, both in Washington, D.C., and Niagara University in Niagara Falls, New York.

Three are in Canada: Laval University in Quebec; St. Paul University (formerly the University of Ottawa) in Ottawa, and the University of Sherbrooke in Sherbrooke.

The pontifical university in Cuba—the Catholic University of St. Thomas of Villanueva in Havana—was taken over by the Castro regime in 1961.

Other pontifical universities are in Argentina, Belgium, Brazil, Chile, Colombia, Ecuador, Ethiopia, France, Germany, Guatemala, Ireland, Italy, Japan, Lebanon, The Netherlands, Panama, Paraguay, Peru, Philippine

Islands, Poland, Portugal, Puerto Rico, Spain, Taiwan and Venezuela.

Ecclesiastical Faculties. In 22 countries of the world there are 51 ecclesiastical faculties; that is, faculties in Catholic universities and seminaries, which again have been canonically erected and which are authorized by the Vatican's Sacred Congregation for Catholic Education to approve degrees in specific fields of study.

Five are in the United States: the School of Theology at St. Mary's Seminary and University of Baltimore; St. Mary of the Lake Faculty of Theology in Chicago; the Jesuit School of Theology at Berkeley; the Weston School of Theology in Cambridge, Massachusetts; and the theologate and college at the Pontifical College Josephinum in Columbus, Ohio. (Unlike the others, the latter is immediately subject to the Vatican.)

Four are in Canada: the Pontifical Institute of Medieval Studies in Toronto; the Dominican Faculty of Theology of Canada in Ottawa; Regis College—Toronto section of the Jesuit Faculty of Theology in Canada, in Toronto; and the College of the Immaculate Conception—Montreal section of Jesuit Faculties in Canada, in Montreal.

Other ecclesiastical faculties are in Argentina, Australia, Austria, Brazil, France, Germany, England, India, Israel, Italy, Ivory Coast, Lebanon, Madagascar, Malta, Mexico, Nigeria, Peru, Poland, Spain and Switzerland.

An ecclesiastical faculty existed in Vietnam with the erection in 1965 of the Theological Faculty of the Pontifical National Seminary of St. Pius X, in Dalat. Its activities have been suppressed, however, by the Communist regime.

Rome

A number of pontifical universities and institutes are located in Rome. Among them are:

- The Pontifical Gregorian University and its associate

institutions, the Pontifical Biblical Institute and the Pontifical Institute of Oriental Studies

- The Pontifical Lateran University
- The Pontifical Urban University
- The Pontifical University of St. Thomas Aquinas (popularly known as the Angelicum)
- The Pontifical University Salesianum and its associated institution, the Pontifical Institute of Higher Latin Studies (known as the Faculty of Christian and Classical Letters)
- The Pontifical Athenaeum of St. Anselm
- The Pontifical Athenaeum 'Antonianum'
- The Pontifical Institute of Sacred Music
- The Pontifical Institute of Christian Archeology
- The Pontifical Theological Faculty 'St. Bonaventure'
- The Pontifical Theological Faculty, Pontifical Institute of Spirituality 'Teresianum'
- The Pontifical Theological Faculty 'Marianum'
- The Pontifical Institute of Arabic and Islamic Studies
- The Pontifical Faculty of Educational Science 'Auxilium'
- The Pontifical Institute 'Regina Mundi'

Also headquartered in Rome is the *Pontifical Academy of Sciences*, a body reconstituted by Pope Pius XI in 1936 to promote research and the freedom of pure science, and to honor its practitioners. The academy has a normal membership of 70 members, although the total may vary with honorary and supernumerary appointees. Members may be Catholic or otherwise, and they are often called upon to make special studies and reports. One such was the study of the American strategic defense initiative known as "Star Wars," requested by Pope John Paul II. The study, critical of the "Star Wars" system, was leaked to the public in July, 1985, to the embarrassment of the

Vatican, the Pope having not yet taken a public stand on the issue.

The Pontifical Academy of Sciences evolved out of the *Linceorum Academia* (Academy of the Lynxes), established in 1603 by Pope Clement VIII (1592-1605). Pius XI gave it its present name in 1936.

United States

The suggestion of a Catholic University of America was broached at the Second Plenary Council of Baltimore in 1866, and finalized at the Third Council of 1884. The statutes of the Catholic University of America were approved by Pope Leo XIII in 1889 with his apostolic letter *Magni Nobis*, and the university that year opened with 46 students. In 1985 the enrollment was 7,057.

But even before the establishment of a Catholic University of America there was a flourishing Catholic higher-educational system in the United States, one that dated back to the founding of Georgetown University in 1789 by the Catholic Clergy of Maryland, Incorporated. In 1805 Georgetown was entrusted to the direction of the Society of Jesus (Jesuits), the order which was to give the Catholic college/university system so much of its shape in the United States through the establishment of such institutions of higher learning as St. Louis (1818), Holy Cross (1843), Marquette (1881), Boston College (1863), John Carroll (1886), Gonzaga (1887), St. Peter's (1872), and in the current century LeMoyne (1946) and Fairfield (1942), among others. As of 1986, there were 28 Jesuit colleges and universities in the United States, with an enrollment of 178,500 students.

(Fordham, one of the best known Jesuit universities, developed out of St. John's College, founded in 1841 by the then-Diocese of New York; the Jesuits took the property and college over in 1846. Notre Dame University, the best known of American Catholic universities, is occasionally mistakenly identified as a Jesuit institution; it was founded in 1842 by the Congregation of the Holy Cross, and is still operated by that order.)

The *Official Catholic Directory* for 1985 listed 242 Catholic colleges and universities in the United States with an enrollment of 549,940 students.

In order to satisfy eligibility requirements for receiving public funds, Catholic colleges and universities in some states (New York, for example) have reconstituted themselves as independent institutions by procedures such as the legal incorporation of the Jesuit resident community as separate from the educational institution. In most instances, however, these were *pro forma* legal exercises, which changed the status of the institution in law, but not in religious or denominational character.

University Presses. A number of American universities operate university presses for the publication of scholarly books. Among them are the Catholic University of America, Loyola University of Chicago, Fordham, Notre Dame, St. John's Abbey and University, and Gergetown University.

Elsewhere, the Catholic University of the Sacred Heart in Milan and Coimbra University in Portugal maintain important university presses.

Orders and Organizations

The Catholic Church is an organism. It is also an organization made up of orders, associations and groups—thousands of them, gathered under a number of headings. In some respects, the church is the most systematized (if not also systematic) of entities. There exists an order of organization for everyone, it seems. Many are religious; for example, the orders of priests, brothers and nuns. Many are fraternal, recreational, apostolic, social, devotional—a host of things.

Many Catholics choose not to be a part of the church's organized or bureaucratic life, confining their involvements and contacts instead to the requirements of worship or the dictates of conscience and will. But for those who prefer a more intimate, closer relationship, there is much from which to choose. The sections following deal with the organizational life of the church with particular focus on the United States. Much of what exists in the United States can be found in one form or another in many other parts of the world where the church is strongly situated.

Lay Organizations

One of the largest and perhaps the most visible of lay organizations in the United States is the *Knights of Columbus,* a fraternal and insurance (benefit) society of men with headquarters in New Haven, Connecticut (One Columbus Plaza, 06507), and council halls in cities across the United States and elsewhere. The Knights of Columbus has 1.4-million members enrolled in more than 1,700 councils. Most are in the United States; others are in Canada, the Philippines, Cuba, Mexico, Panama, Puerto Rico, Guam, Guatamala, the Dominican Republic and Virgin Islands. The Knights of Columbus still is primarily an American society. The organization has assets of some $1.3-billion (it once owned and leased the land on which Yankee Stadium stands), and has insurance in force of more than eight billion dollars. The organization is known for its generosity to Catholic causes. Among other things, it supports and maintains seven playgrounds in Rome (a project suggested to the group by Pope Benedict XV), and it pays for the ''up-link'' to the satellites of the International Telecommunications Satellite Consortium (INTELSAT), which carry important Vatican events to the world. The organization sponsors scholarship funds, and runs a variety of programs for the elderly, for youths, for the retarded and people in emergency situations. Its colorfully garbed Fourth Degree members are familiar sights at formal Catholic ceremonies, such as the installation of bishops and ground-breakings for new Catholic buildings. The organization was founded in 1882.

At one time, by far the most visible lay association in

the United States was the *Holy Name Society,* an organization for men founded in Europe in 1274 by the master general of the Dominicans, Blessed John Vercelli, for the promoting of reverence for the Holy Name of Jesus. The society was introduced into the United States in 1870-1871. In the early decades of this century the Holy Name Society could rally tens of thousands of men for candlelight processions and rallies in cities like Boston and Pittsburgh, and its annual communion breakfasts were often media as well as membership events. (One of the most celebrated and controversial of communion breakfasts had Senator Joseph McCarthy speaking April 4, 1953, before wildly cheering Holy Namers of the New York Police Department.) The Holy Name Society claims about 5-million members on diocesan and parochial levels, but it is now largely a paper organization— certainly in many areas of the United States. In the 1950s, many dioceses began to replace parish Holy Name Societies with parish units of the National Council of Catholic Men. One effect was to diminish further the strength of the society without at the same time providing a parochially viable substitute.

Following is a list of some of the better-known lay organizations:

• *National Council of Catholic Men* (4712 Randolph Drive, Annandale, Va. 22003), a constituent organization of the National Council of Catholic Laity. As a federation of organizations, it provides programs of information and action, conferences, leadership training seminars, etc., through which Catholic men may be heard nationally on issues of common interest.

• *National Council of Catholic Women* (1312 Massachusetts Ave., N.W., Washington, D.C. 20005), a federation of some 10,000 organizations of women in the United States. Like its counterpart male organization, it sponsors programs of information and action aimed at giving American

Catholic women a voice in community, national and international affairs.

• *National Council of Catholic Laity* (P.O. Box 14525, Cincinnati, Ohio 45214), a federation of national, diocesan and parish lay groups, plus individuals. It serves as a clearinghouse for ideas and projects assisting the laity.

• *St. Vincent de Paul Society* (4140 Lindell Blvd., St. Louis, Mo. 63108), an association devoted to service to the poor and the needy. The society was founded by St. Vincent de Paul in Paris in 1833, and was introduced into the United States in 1845. There are now some 4,700 conferences with 36,000 members in the U.S. Since 1969, American conferences have admitted women members, but the society remains yet a men's organization by and large in the United States. One of the rules of the society is anonymity; the works of the society may be publicized, but the members must not. Over the past half-century, American Vincentians have distributed goods and provided assistance valued at $400-million.

• *Catholic Worker Movement* (36 E. First St., New York, N.Y. 10003), an apostolate providing food and shelter for the homeless. Founded in New York in 1933 by Peter Maurin and Dorothy Day, the movement has houses of hospitality in some 60 cities of the country and communal farms in several rural areas. Emphases are on service, voluntary poverty, pacifism and a kind of political anarchism.

• *The Christophers* (12 E. 48th St., New York, N.Y. 10017), a movement (as distinct from organization) promoting personal initiative and responsible action in Christian contexts in areas of government, education, industrial relations, communications and the like. The movement was founded by a priest (Fr. James G. Keller, M.M.) and is currently headed by a priest (Fr. John Cantoir), but focus of interest is essentially on the laity. Christopher radio and television programs are carried by more than

1,500 stations, and a publication, *Christopher News Notes*, appears seven times a year with a circulation of 750,000.

• *Serra International* (22 W. Monroe St., Chicago, Ill. 60603), an association of 15,200 members in 490 clubs in 33 countries. The group promotes vocations to the priesthood and to religious life, while also encouraging responsible Catholic lay leadership.

• *Pax Christi USA* (6337 W. Cornelia St., Chicago, Ill. 60634), an organization of lay persons and religious concerned about world peace and a just world order. The group is an expression of the International Catholic Movement for Peace founded at Lourdes in 1948. Pax Christi USA was founded in 1973 and has a membership of some 10,000, including several bishops.

• *Catholics United for the Faith* (222 North Ave., Box S, New Rochelle, N.Y. 10801), an organization concerned about preservation of the fundamentals of faith. The organization was founded in response to Vatican Council II's call for the involvement of the laity. It opposes many post-conciliar directions in and of the church.

• *Morality in Media, Inc.* (475 Riverside Drive, New York, N.Y. 10115), a group concerned about the eroticization of society, and particularly media's role in this development. Morality in Media was founded and long headed by a priest (the late Fr. Morton A. Hill, S.J.), but lay persons make up the bulk of its 50,000 members. The group aims to stop traffic in pornography through the enforcement of laws already on the books. One project is the National Obscenity Law Center, which supplies information for attorneys and public prosecutors likewise concerned about pornography.

Religious Orders

There were 180,247 women and men in religious life in the United States, according to *The Official Catholic*

Directory for 1985. Of the total, 35,052 were diocesan or so-called secular priests. The others—sisters, priests, brothers—belonged to one or another religious order or community.

Sisters. The number of sisters in the United States totaled 115,386 in 1985. The figure is imposing, but, as mentioned earlier, it is dramatically below the highs of two decades ago. (In 1966 there were 182,000 sisters in the United States.) The decline is due in the main to departures from religious life and a dearth of new vocations, and is a matter of worry and study in the church, from the Vatican to the individual religious community. Nonetheless, the number of nuns is impressive.

Women religious are engaged in education, nursing, social work, service ministries, and various other forms of individual and collective witness, including contemplative life. Many are also engaged in the care of the sister-religious, as the number of aged nuns has increased without the concomitant increase in new vocations needed to handle what has always been an internal task of young novices in convent and religious life.

American women religious are gathered into more than 300 religious institutes. This number too is impressing, and would be much larger still if one chose to count some sisterhoods—specifically the Benedictines, Dominicans and Franciscans—by their individual federations, communities and orders, rather than, as here, single institutes. For example, there are nine different Dominican sisterhoods and over 80 that are Franciscan (Franciscan Sisters of the Immaculate Conception, Franciscan Sisters of the Sacred Heart, Franciscan Sisters of Christian Charity, Sisters of St. Francis of the Holy Cross, etc.).

Concerned about their collective welfare, including, for some nuns, their seeming status as second-class members in an essentially male-dominating church, sisters in the United States have formed a number of inter-order associations, most of them in the years since Vatican Council II, to promote common goals. These associations range the ideological gamut. Among them:

• *Consortium Perfectae Caritatis*, or Partnership of Perfect Love. This group takes its name from the Vatican II Decree on the Appropriate Renewal of the Religious Life (*Perfectae Caritatis*), and has as its objective the development of religious life in concert with the guidelines and directives of Vatican II, beginning with the document from which it derives its name. As its name suggests, the group is traditional (some would say conservative) in focus. It was founded in 1971.

• National Coalition of American Nuns is in some respects a counterpart organization to Consortium Perfectae Caritatis. Founded in 1969, it is concerned for the role of women in the church and in the larger society. It is an advocate of social activism, and frequently takes positions that are liberal and ecclesiastically controversial.

• Leadership Conference of Women Religious was organized in the 1950s as the Conference of Major Superiors of Women, and was extended official Vatican approval in 1962 by the Congregation for Religious and Secular Institutes. It took its present name in 1971. It was the group's official status which accounted for the invitation to its then-president, Mercy Sister M. Theresa Kane, to deliver a greeting to Pope Paul II during his visit to the National Shrine of the Immaculate Conception in Washington, D.C., in the course of his 1979 visit to the United States. Sister Kane proceeded to stun the Pope and millions of others with a call to the church to demonstrate concern for human dignity "by providing the possibility of women as persons being included in all ministries of our Church."

• *National Black Sisters' Conference* was established in 1968 to determine and promote priorities in service to black people, to encourage vocations among black people, and to deepen the practice and experience of religious life by quickening knowledge and appreciation of black culture and lifestyle. Membership includes 700 black sisters in 123 religious communities.

• *National Assembly of Religious Women* was founded in 1970 as the National Assembly of Women Religious "to live and communicate the meaning of woman's life in the church and the world today; to commit themselves to a Ministry of Justice by the continuous use of their organized power for the liberation of all peoples from oppression; to work actively to promote respect for all human life and to insure effective participation of people in decisions which affect their lives." The group's name was changed in 1982 to broaden its feminist and feminine appeal.

Other associations of women religious include the Association of Contemplative Sisters, the National Sisters' Vocation Conference, the International Union of Superiors General, and the Religious Formation Conference. The last named was founded in 1953 as the Sister Formation Conference, but its name was changed in 1976 so as to include men and persons belonging to non-canonical religious groups within its purview.

• *Brothers.* According to 1985 figures, there were 7,544 religious brothers in the United States. This too is a dramatically smaller number than was once the case, being some 60 percent less than what it was in 1966. Brothers are grouped in the main into 28 institutes (Christian Brothers, Xaverian Brothers, Franciscan Brothers, Alexian Brothers, etc.); some fewer belong to "mixed communities," where membership is comprised mostly of priests (Jesuits, Trappist, etc.).

The decline in the number of brothers is, like that of sisters, an issue of concern at the Vatican. Thus, brotherhoods were included in the special study ordered by

Pope John Paul II in 1983 focusing on religious orders in the United States, with particular attention being paid to their sharp losses in memberships.

The principal inter-institute organization for brothers is the *National Assembly of Religious Brothers*, founded in 1972 as a membership group for brothers in the United States and elsewhere, notably Canada. Purposes of the assembly include publicizing the unique vocations of brothers and quickening awareness among brothers themselves of their ministerial potential and role in the church and society.

- *Order Priests.* Of the 57,317 ordained priests counted in the United States in 1985, diocesan (secular) priests totaled 35,052. The remainder—22,265—belonged to some 107 religious institutes of men (religious orders). Membership in religious orders has decreased in the years since Vatican Council II, but the dip has been far less drastic than in the sisterhoods and brotherhoods.

Some of the better known religious orders are: the Society of Jesus (Jesuits); Order of St. Benedict (Benedictines); Order of Cistercians of the Strict Observance (Trappists); Order of Friars Preachers (Dominicans); Order of Friars Minor (Franciscans); Order of Friars Minor Capuchin and Order of Friars Minor Conventual (both also Franciscan); Society of Mary (Marists); Missionary Oblates of the Immaculate Conception (OMI Fathers); Catholic Missionary Society of America (Maryknollers); Congregation of the Oratory of St. Philip Neri (Oratorians); Missionary Society of St. Paul the Apostle (Paulists); Congregation of the Most Holy Redeemer (Redemptorists); Society of Priests of St. Sulpice (Sulpicians); Congregation of the Mission (Vincentians, Lazarists); and Congregation of the Holy Cross (C.S.C.s)

Order priests are active in education, hospital ministries, home and foreign missions, retreat work, pastoral duties, social services and a variety of apostolates, such as communications and witnessing for peace.

A principal association for order priests is the *Conference of Major Superiors of Men,* established in 1956 and officially recognized in 1960 by the Vatican's Congregation for Religious and Secular Institutes. It is an association of some 263 major superiors of religious communities and institutes, having a membership of nearly 30,000. The group exists to promote the spiritual and apostolic welfare of their priests and brothers.

For diocesan (secular) priests, a principal association is the *National Federation of Priests' Councils,* an organization which was born of a controversial grassroots meeting of priests in Chicago in 1968 and which has since gained general national recognition and acceptance. The organization, for instance, is now listed in the *Official Catholic Directory.* Purposes of the group are to facilitate communication among priests' councils, official or unofficial; to provide a forum for the discussion of pastoral matters; to enable priests' councils to speak with a common, representative voice; to promote and collaborate in programs of pastoral research and action; to implement norms for the renewal of priestly life; and to provide means for nationally united priests' councils to cooperate with other church groups to address the church's needs. The organization represents more than 100 priests' councils (mostly diocesan senates of priests), religious congregations and other associations of priests, formal and independent. Among the latter are PADRES, an association of Hispanic priests, brothers and deacons, and the National Black Catholic Clergy Caucus.

PADRES is an acronym for the Spanish "Padres Asociados para Derechos Religiosos, Educativos y Sociales." The group was founded in 1970 by 55 Mexican-American priests in southwestern United States to help the church identify better with the pastoral, social, educational and economic needs of Spanish-speaking people. The scope of the organization broadened nationally and embraced Hispanic people generally, as Hispanic emigration accelerated and the American church began to appreciate more acutely the demographic change that was taking place in its membership.

The National Black Catholic Clergy Caucus was founded in Detroit in 1968 for the dual purpose of fostering the spiritual and theological growth of its members and of counteracting institutional racism in the American church. It numbers over 700 black priests, permanent deacons and brothers. Black Catholics in the United States number about one million, thus comprising two percent of the American Catholic population. As of 1985, there were 10 black American bishops. As a group, they issued a pastoral letter September 9, 1984, "What We Have Seen and Heard." It was the first pastoral of its kind in American Catholic history, and it charged that "racism, at once subtle and masked, still festers within our church as within our society." The pastoral pointed to "a richness in our Black experience," and discussed black spirituality by its four major characteristics: contemplative, holistic, joyful and communitarian.

Schools

One of the principal apostolates of those in religious orders, both of women and men, is education. The apostolate is considerably smaller in the United States than it was in the record years of the early 1960s, but it is nevertheless an awesome effort.

Figures for 1985 showed a total of 9,942 separate Catholic educational institutions in the United States. Besides colleges and universities, already mentioned, there were 90 diocesan seminaries; 228 religious-order seminaries, novitiates and scholasticates; 870 diocesan and parish high schools; 555 private high schools; 7,658 parish elementary schools; 299 private elementary schools; and 91 protective institutions.

Their faculties comprised 4,600 priests, 138 scholastics, 2,678 brothers, 30,223 sisters and 134,520 lay persons, for a grand total of 172,159.

Under their instruction were 549,940 students in colleges and universities; 2,100,578 in parish elementary schools; 62,377 in private elementary schools; 8,296 in protective institutions.

Meanwhile, 895,168 Catholic high-school pupils in public schools and 3,157,008 Catholic students in public elementary schools were receiving religious instruction under released time, in religious vacation schools and other classes.

All told there were 7,578,423 American youths of all grades under Catholic instruction of one sort or another during the year.

Health-Care Institutions

The modern hospital is not a Christian invention. From the day that ancient tribes stopped putting to death their sick, infirm and aged, peoples have been concerned for those among them who were ailing. In ancient Greece and Rome, for instance, the sick would spend a night at the temple of Asclepius (Aesculapius), the god of medicine and healing, and hope for a dream. The ideal dream, interpreted in turn by priests, would theoretically contain directions from God for the patient's recovery.

Christ himself provided numerous examples of his concern for the sick and ailing, working cures on the deaf, the blind, the halt, the leper, the hemorhaging woman. He further counseled the apostles to cure those who are sick (Luke 10:9; Mark 16:18).

When and where the first traditional hospital was opened is a question. (The word hospital derives from the Latin *hospes*, guest, and *hospitium*, guest house or guest room.) The presumption is that it was in the East, not the West, since so many words used to describe particular health-care institutions are of Greek rather than Latin origin. An institution for the care of the aged, for instance, was a *gerontochium;* for the orphaned, a *orphanotrophium;* for poor and infirm pilgrims, a *xenodochium.*

By the 10th century monasteries were prominently associated with hospital work, as they became centers for the care of the sick and the needy of their immediate neighborhoods. Dioceses were joined into the apostolate, as bishops established hospitals in connection with their collegiate churches. These hospitals took their names from the churches, thus rooting the practice of hospitals under church auspices bearing the patronal name of a heavenly protector. The practice has continued into modern times with only relatively few exceptions.

Hospitals have multiplied and the care provided has improved enormously, of course, with scientific progress and under attendant influences ranging from economics to social imperatives. Still the church's hand has remained strong in the work, continuing to bring a Christian dimension to a professional specialty which reflects the humanist instinct at its noblest.

United States. There are more than 1,500 health-care institutions of one sort or another under Catholic auspices in the United States. Of the total 731 are Catholic hospitals (637 general; 94 special) with a total bed capacity of 178,101. There are 170 orphanages and infant asylums (institutions), and 607 homes for the aged and invalid. The figures are those of *The Official Catholic Directory* for 1985.

Patients treated in Catholic hospitals during 1984 numbered 37,369,448. The number cared for in the orphanages and infant asylums was 11,246 (another 14,928 children were cared for in foster homes). Homes for the aged and invalid had facilities for 74,844 guests.

In addition there were 129 nursing schools under Catholic auspices with an enrollment of 22,297 student nurses.

The coordinating service organization for most of these health-care institutions is the *Catholic Health Association of the United States* (formerly the Catholic Hospital Association). The group was founded in 1915 to assist church-related health-care organizations to provide optimal health services and programs to the communities they serve, this in conjunction with the healing mission of the church. The group is based in St. Louis, Missouri.

Communications

The Catholic church has been interested in the formal
avenues of communication since Apostolic times. We do
not know that Christ ordered the apostles to get his story
down in writing. We know that he commanded them to
teach all nations, and perhaps implicit in that directive
was the suggestion that the record be gotten down on
paper. In any instance, Christ's story and the story of
the infant church were committed to paper, and that record is known as the New Testament. It represents the
church's first and, in retrospect, most important venture
into communications.

For centuries monasteries maintained scriptoriums,
rooms for the writing or copying of manuscripts, including the four Gospels. Many astonishingly beautiful
documents emanated from monastic scriptoriums, such
as the Book of Kells, the early-Middle Ages (7th century)
illuminated book of the Gospels which, since the 17th
century, has been in the library of Trinity College, Dublin.
The decorations in this book are so intricate that it is said
one-page's work was enough to occupy the talents of the
illuminator for a lifetime. The contention is likely an ex-
aggeration, but it does testify to the brilliance and splen-
didness of the illumination.

Other important manuscripts of the period are the 9th-
century Book of Armagh, also at Trinity College; the 9th-
century Rushworth Gospels at the Bodleian Library at Oxford; the 8th-century Lindisfarne Gospels in the British
Library, London; a Gospel-book in the Vatican Library
signed by the Abbot Uigbald, who presided at Lindisfarne
in the late-8th, early-9th centuries; a Gospel-book in the
State Public Library in Leningrad, also attributed to
monks at Lindisfarne of the same period; and a number
of manuscripts from the Anglo-Irish foundation at Echternach in Luxembourg, including the Echternach Gospels,
a Book of the Prophets and a Martyrologium.

Of course such hand-lettered and decorated books as
these were not for general handling or for circulation. It

was not only that the public at the time was largely illiterate. There was also the problem of the scarcity of books. They were just too valuable for general handling. When the first public library was opened in Dublin—Marsh's library, beside St. Patrick's Cathedral (Church of Ireland)—books were placed on a leash-chain to protect against their removal.

The Age of Print. Everything changed, to be sure, with Johannes Gutenberg's invention of printing from movable type in the 15th century. The immediate effect of the invention was to make more accessible the books of religion (Gutenberg's first product was a printed Bible, followed shortly by a Latin *Psalterium*), and also the literature of Greece and Rome. By 1493, broadsides (sheets printed on one side for posting and reading) had made their appearance in Germany and soon thereafter in Italy. (In Italy they were called *Gazetta* after the coin, *gazeta*, paid for reading them. Hence the popular newspaper name "Gazette.") These were the forerunners of the modern newspaper. Broadsides were succeeded by "relations," which were narratives or accounts of peoples and events; for example, the *Relations de la Nouvelle-France*, more popularly known as the *Jesuit Relations*, begun in 1616 and detailing the work of the Jesuits among the Indians of North America.

The most obvious benefit in Gutenberg's invention was facilitation of the spread of ideas, a benefit which attracted church authorities and accounts for the church's interest in printing and the published word from the beginning of the revolutionary era opened up by the printing press. The church has energetically used the press as a complement to its evangelical and social missions. At different stages in history, emphases have varied to meet the challenges posed, but generally the aspiration has been to have that portion of the press under ecclesiastical control and auspices function as an educational and instructional tool, certainly so far as books are concerned, and as a sort of modern Gospel, so far as newspapers and magazines are concerned, chronicling and promoting the activity of the Mystical Body of Christ (the church) as the four Gospels chronicled the activity of the physical Christ.

Over the centuries, the record has been at best uneven. On occasion the church's press has risen, almost literally, to great heights; at other times it has been so negative and defensive as to be an embarrassment. The problem was not always that of writers, editors and staff. The church itself has displayed an almost consistent ambiguity with respect to the printed word, encouraging its use and then placing it under restraints of censorship by long requiring the official clearance of manuscripts (the *imprimatur/nihil-obstat* system) and maintaining a black-list of authors and titles *(The Index of Prohibited Books)* whose ideas it found objectionable. The censoring activities of the church have eased markedly in recent years, but they still exist, as certain European and Latin American theologians (Father Hans Kung, Father Edward Schillebeeckx, Father Leonardo Boff, *et al.*) can testify.

The church's own official record is contained in the *Acta Apostolicae Sedis*, a publication established at the Vatican in 1908 for detailing the activities of the Holy See and printing the decrees and acts of the papacy and the congregations and tribunals of the Roman Curia. The *Acta* differs from *L'Osservatore Romano,* the Vatican daily newspaper. *L'Osservatore Romano* is an authoritative voice of the Vatican, but only those items are official which are specifically designated as such. What appears in the *Acta* ordinarily takes effect three months following the date of its appearance there. The usual language of the *Acta* is Latin; of *L'Osservatore,* Italian.

United States. Nothing contributed more immediately to the development of a Catholic press in the United States than the fact that Catholics were strangers in a strange land, and often unwelcome strangers at that. The initial purpose of a church press was to conserve the faith of Catholics and to represent their rights in an atmosphere where social and political bias was strong, even sometimes hostile. It is not surprising, therefore, that the Catholic press should have evolved with something of a polemical character. The American Catholic press largely outgrew that aspect of its past, as Catholics were accepted in the mainstream of American life, but tinges remain, and can flare up when subjects intimately interconnect with Catholic interests. One saw this in the 1950s on aid to education issues; one sees it in the 1980s on certain women's-rights issues. Shrillness does not infect every Catholic publication when causes preoccupy, then shape editorial judgments, including those of the bishop-publishers of diocesan papers. There are always exceptions. These, however, tend to be lost sight of. The point is that the Catholic press in the United States is anything but an editorial monolith. Opinions abound, though to be sure most conform to official lines.

Newspapers. According to the 1985 *Catholic Press Directory*, there were 161 English-language newspapers in the United States with a total circulation of 5,384,695. Five were national newspapers (*Our Sunday Visitor*, 208,816; *The National Catholic Reporter*, 47,676; *Catholic Twin Circle*, 57,857; *The National Catholic Register*, 56,630; *The Wanderer*, 34,354). The remainder (156) were diocesan newspapers; their circulation: 4,979,362. In addition there were more than 25 foreign-language papers, several with national circulations, such as *El Visitante Dominical* (Spanish, 31,000) and *Jednota* (Slovak and English, 36,651).

Among the largest diocesan newspapers were *The Long Island Catholic* (Rockville Centre), 140,989; *Catholic New York* (New York), 129,261; *The Chicago Catholic* (Chicago), 118,220.

Notable diocesan newspapers: *The Catholic Messenger* (Davenport, Iowa), 25,572; *The Church World* (Portland, Maine), 9,578; *The Catholic Free Press* (Worcester, Mass.), 25,169.

Diocesan newspapers are the official publications of the sees where they are published. Rather than publish their own newspapers, at least three American dioceses purchase space for their announcements and news in secular newspapers of their areas: Anchorage, Alaska; St. Augustine, Florida; Lake Charles, Louisiana.

Magazines. There were 344 English and other-language Catholic magazines circulating in the United States during 1985 with more than 20-million readers. The largest circulation belonged to *Columbia* (1,367,402), the membership magazine of the Knights of Columbus. General-interest magazines with large circulations: *Catholic Digest* (620,530); *Liguorian* (525,000); *St. Anthony's Messenger* (384,754); *U.S. Catholic* (90,000).

Notable Catholic magazines: *America* (31,221); *The Critic* (3,000); *Commonweal* (17,228); *Salt* (10,251); *Cross Currents* (5,200); *U.S. Catholic* (63,000).

Combining the statistical totals of Catholic publications in the United States with those of their sister-publications in Canada, one arrives at the mighty figures of 179 newspapers, 354 magazines, 41 publications in languages other than English—with an overall circulation of 27,043,126.

The interests of the Catholic press in North America are represented by the Catholic Press Association of the United States and Canada. Executive director is James A. Doyle. The association is based in Rockville Centre, New York.

Publishers. Including the university presses, there are some 65 Catholic-oriented general publishers in the United States, according to the 1985 *Catholic Press Directory*. The total includes Doubleday & Company of New York, which is really a secular publishing house, but which maintains a department for issuing books for the religious market, notably Bibles and paperback reprints in its Image Books series. These houses published more than 900 religious titles in 1984, ranging from textbooks, to books focusing on marriage and the family, to books on religious aspects of the human condition generally.

Some notable publishing houses and the number of titles published during 1984: Ave Maria Press, 15; Benziger Publishing Company, 57; Crossroad Publishing Company, 40; Dimension Books, 16; Doubleday, 40; Franciscan Herald Press, 48; Ignatius Press, 12; Liguori Publications, 45; The Liturgical Press, 42; Orbis Books, 35; Our Sunday Visitor, 24; Paulist Press, 90; Resource Publications, 12; St. Anthony Messenger Press, 12; Silver Burdett Company, 14; Templegate Publishers, 11; The Thomas More Association, 12; Thomas Nelson Publishers, 100; Twenty-Third Publications, 18; USCC Office of Publishing Services, 36; U.S. Catholic Historical Society, 15; Winston Press, 26.

The Sheed & Ward imprint, once among the most respected in the publishing industry, underwent a series of vicissitudes after the deaths of its founders, Frank Sheed and Maisie Ward. At one time the name was combined with Andrews and McMeel, publishers, to form the house of Sheed Andrews and McMeel, Inc. Later the name disappeared completely, only to be revived recently in Kansas City, Missouri, as a service of the *National Catholic Reporter*'s Publishing Co., Inc.

As the communications industry entered the era of electronics, a number of Catholic publishers and visual-service organizations kept pace, broadening into such areas as audio- and video-cassettes, slide programs, filmstrips, records, tapes, spot programs for radio and television, and the like. Publishers limit themselves pretty much to the production of cassettes. Catholic radio and television organizations handle cassettes as well as multiple other electronic services.

Radio and Television. When communications entered the age of radio and telecommunications, the church entered with it, but in neither area has its influence been as strong nor its role as prominent as in the area of print.

Vatican Radio was designed by Guglielmo Marconi (1874-1937), the native of Bologna who invented the radio and shared the Nobel Prize for physics with Ferdinand

Braun in 1909. The station was inaugurated in 1931 and was supervised by Marconi until his death. The station broadcasts in 34 languages and is on the air some 280 hours a week, its short-wave programs carrying throughout the world. However, in many areas—the United States, for instance—it is quoted for its opinions more than it is listened to by radio audiences. One reason why is the absence of shortwave bands from most American radio sets.

The Vatican also has television facilities, and important Vatican ceremonies and events are beamed to the world, as mentioned, via INTELSAT, the International Telecommunications Satellite Consortium, with the help of funding from the Knights of Columbus.

The church has traditionally encouraged press, radio and television in countries of the world, but in some places the apostolates are insignificant or non-existent because of governmental repressions.

United States. The electronics-communications apostolate in the United States has evolved through the notorious period of the Father Charles E. Coughlin radio talks of the 1930s, through the spectacular period of the Bishop (later Archbishop) Fulton J. Sheen radio and television show "Life Is Worth Living" of the 1950s, and has settled into a quiet but efficient present and a mission of service to millions of listeners and viewers. Most dioceses maintain communications' offices, and these are instrumental in arranging such programs locally as the radio rosary and the television Mass. In addition, a number of orders and organizations sponsor or cooperate in the production of specialty programs which are heard and seen nationwide. Some of these follow:

• *Christopher Closeup* (radio), a 15-minute interview-discussion program heard weekly on 236 stations, and sponsored by The Christophers. (The Christophers also air a one-minute "Christopher Thought for the Day" daily on some 1,500 stations.)

- *Christopher Closeup* (television), half-hour and 15-minute interviews in color seen weekly on 52 commercial stations, 41 cable systems, the American Armed Forces network and other outlets.

- *Crossroads* (radio), a weekly program produced by the Passionist Fathers and Brothers of West Springfield, Mass., and carried by some 130 stations.

- *Sacred Heart Program* (radio and television), a Jesuit-sponsored program that has been on the air since 1939. One television program and 12 radio programs are syndicated weekly to more than 900 stations.

Also, the Department of Communication of the National Conference of Catholic Bishops/U.S. Catholic Conference consults with major television networks and helps produce several network programs, among them "Directions" (ABC-TV), "For Our Times" (CBS-TV), "Guideline" (NBC-radio), "On This Rock" (ABC-radio), and religious specials of NBC-TV, of which there are four one-hour Catholic specials a year, plus seasonal religious programs.

The principal national organization for Catholic broadcasters and allied communicators is *UNDA-USA*. (*Unda* is the Latin for "wave," and is used in the symbolic sense of the airwaves of communication.) Associated groups include Catholic Television Network, the Association of Catholic Radio and Television Syndicators, and the Association of Diocesan Directors.

- *Catholic Television Network* (CTN) facilitates the work of sees with closed-circuit educational television. As of 1984, these sees numbered at least seven: Boston, Brooklyn, Chicago, Los Angeles, New York, Rockville Centre and San Francisco.

Section V

Saints

SAINTS are the certified (canonized) heroes of Catholic history. Following are biographical sketches of a selection of them. A complete listing and sketching of all would require several volumes. What is offered here are biographical notes on some popular saints, and a few obscure ones. The feast days cited are those according to the calendar of the Roman (Latin) Rite.

St. Agatha was born in Sicily of noble parentage and martyred at Catania around the year 250, apparently because she refused to move in with the governor of Sicily, Quintian. She was tortured to incredible degree. She was ripped by iron hooks, and her breasts were cut off. When she was thrown on burning coals, Catania is said to have been rocked by an earthquake.

From earliest days, Agatha has been honored as a model of chastity, as indicated by the Introit prayer of the old Latin Mass for her feast day: "Let us all rejoice in the Lord, celebrating a festival in honor of Blessed Agatha, virgin and martyr, at whose passion the angels rejoice and give praise to the Son of God."

Because of the breast mutilation, St. Agatha was sometimes portrayed in medieval art with her breasts on a salver. Her feast day is February 5.

St. Agnes is revered as a virgin martyr of ancient Rome, going to her death in the year 304, after having declared herself a Christian. She was only 13. Legend has it that an angry judge threatened to consign her to a house of prostitution if she did not renounce her faith. She didn't. The judge made good on his threat. Agnes was taken to a brothel, where a young man is said to have turned a lascivious look on her, whereupon he was struck blind. Agnes was subsequently put to death, probably by stabbing.

St. Agnes' feast is January 21. Historically, on her feast day two lambs are solemnly blessed, and from their wool are made the cloaks, called pallia, which are sent by the pope to new archbishops of the world.

St. Angela Merici lived from 1474-1540, and was the founder of the Ursuline order of nuns. Her ideas were extremely advanced for their day. Angela Merici preferred that women of her order be without distinctive habit, without solemn vows, and without enclosure, living in their own homes or rooms. Then as now such ideas met with opposition from church officials, and finally legislation issued under Pope St. Pius V obliged the nuns to adopt what were called "canonical safeguards." They donned habits and moved into convents.

St. Angela Merici was born in Lombardy in northern Italy in 1474. Orphaned at 10, she was raised by an uncle and became a Franciscan tertiary in her teens. A devout person, she went to work teaching the poor children of Desenzano and Brescia. In Brescia, her example motivated a number of women to join her in her apostolate. This was the beginning of the Ursuline order. The year was 1535.

One of Angela Merici's favorite sayings was that "disorder in society is the result of disorder in the family." Valid or not, the principle inspired her to send her associates to teach girls in their own families. It was by educating children in the family milieu that she strove to effect improvements in social conditions. The work of the Ursuline sisters is more formal today, but the concern for education and the poor endures.

Her feast day is January 27.

St. Athanasius lived from 292-373. They were turbulent times for the church, and Athanasius was banished no less than five times from various church posts, including that of Bishop of Alexandria. One problem was that of the Arians, who denied the divinity of Christ, regarding him rather as a superior being and intermediary between God and the world. Athanasius' responses, at council and in writing, refuted the heresy and put his stamp on Catholic theology for all time. The Athanasian Creed is associated with him. The creed is the church's formal exposition of the doctrines of the Trinity (three persons in one God) and the Incarnation (the twofold nature in the one divine person of Jesus Christ). Athanasius' theologizing won for him the title of "Father of Orthodoxy" and he is ranked as one of the four great Fathers of the East (the others: St. Basil the Great, St. Gregory Nazianzen, St. John Chrysostom). His feast is observed May 2.

St. Anthony Claret is one of the church's modern saints; he lived in the 19th century, died at 62, and was canonized in 1950. He was a Spaniard who served as a missionary in Catalonia, as Archbishop of Santiago, Cuba, as confessor of Queen Isabella II, and as director of the Escorial, a famous educational center. But it is as founder of the Missionary Sons of the Immaculate Heart of Mary that Anthony Claret is best remembered. This is the order known popularly as the Claretians. In the United States the Claretians foster devotion to St. Jude and publish an assortment of Catholic books, magazines, pamphlets, and newsletters.

St. Anthony Claret preached some 10,000 sermons, published some 200 books and pamphlets in his lifetime, and founded publishing houses in Spain, the Canary Islands, and Cuba.

Two attributes of St. Anthony Claret commend him particularly: his realism and his practicality. His realism was grounded in a trust in God; his practicality in a facility to adapt to change both in his personal life and his professional career. His feast day is October 23.

St. Anthony of Padua was born in Lisbon, Portugal, around 1190 with the name Fernando de Bulhom. At 16 he joined the Canons Regular of St. Augustine and at 30 became a Franciscan, taking the name Anthony. His labors took him to Morocco, Sicily, Assisi, and Forli. But it was at Padua that he made his great reputation as confessor and convert-maker, and from Padua that he became celebrated as a preacher throughout Italy. As preacher he was in great demand. When word of his coming circulated, shops shuttered up, markets suspended business, law courts closed, and people flocked to hear him. As many as 30,000 people would gather. Anthony preached outdoors, as no cathedral or other edifice could accommodate the throngs he attracted. His favorite attack points were greed and luxurious living. His antidotes: concern for the poor and moderation in one's own living standard.

Hagiography has it that Anthony once held the Christ child, and this has been a popular artistic representation of the saint since the 17th century. He is also regarded as the patron of those seeking lost objects ("Anthony, Anthony, look around. Something is lost and can't be found"). His feast day is June 13.

St. Bernadette Soubirous is a saint who made a site famous. The site, of course, is Lourdes—a favorite pilgrimage objective for Catholics the world over.

The story of St. Bernadette and the Marian apparitions at Lourdes is a familiar one. It began February 11, 1858, when Bernadette, then only 14, set off with her sister and a friend to gather firewood from the common land by the banks of the river Gave. Bernadette fell behind the others, and as she was removing her shoes and stockings before crossing a mill stream near the grotto of Massabielle, she beheld a vision of a woman no bigger than herself, dressed in a white robe with a blue sash knotted about her waist.

The vision was of the Virgin Mary, and it was the first of 18 appearances of Mary to Bernadette. The two prayed the rosary together, and it was to Bernadette that Mary proclaimed, "I am the Immaculate Conception," a message that was to become a dogma of the Roman Catholic Church.

Bernadette paid dearly for the honor conveyed on her. She was bullied, cajoled, and cross-examined by skeptics. To escape the hostile and the curious, she went as a boarder to the convent of the Sisters of Nevers. She remained there eight years, finally taking the habit on July 29, 1866 as Sister Marie Bernard.

Her lot as a sister was equally difficult. The reverend mother and mistress of novices were strict to the point of harshness and allegedly took every opportunity to humiliate her. Superior General Marie-Therese Vauzou is recorded as having said: "Oh! She was a little peasant girl. If the holy Virgin wanted to appear somewhere on earth, why would she choose a common, illiterate peasant instead of some virtuous, instructed nun?" In Bernadette's own words, she was "ground like a grain of corn."

Lourdes and its continuing miracles have obscured the life of this remarkable saint, who, like the people who travel to Lourdes in such large numbers, was often ill. The story is told of how one day a visiting nun came to Bernadette's room and finding her in bed asked rather sarcastically what she was doing. Bernadette replied, "I am doing my job." "Oh," said the nun, "and what might that be?" "My job," said Bernadette, "is to be ill."

St. Bernadette's feast day is April 16. The feast of Our Lady of Lourdes is observed February 11.

St. Brendan is perhaps the Irish saint most widely known after Patrick. Brendan, whose life overlapped that of Patrick, was saint and scholar both. He was also a navigator of such fame that for centuries cartographers fixed on their maps a Brendan's Island, a true fantasy island.

The fictitious island grew out of a 10th-century account of Brendan's sea travels, *Navigatio Sancti Brendani*. The account concerned itself with the most spectacular undertaking in Brendan's lifetime: his expedition with 60 other monks to discover the legendary Island of the Blessed. Of course, he never discovered the Island of the Blessed, but he very well may have touched the Orkneys and Hebrides or, as some believe, America itself.

In any instance, there was no Brendan's Island, although it was not until the middle of the 18th century that Spanish and Portuguese cartographers were convinced and dropped it from their maps.

St. Brendan was a native of Kerry, born around the year 484. He founded a number of monasteries, including that at Clonfert in Galway. Tales of his piety and exploits were so great that the Irish gave his name to numerous landmarks about the country. Brandon Well, Brandon Point, Brandon Bay, Brandon Headland all recall St. Brendan.

Brendan lived to be 90, and for many the great lesson of his long life is bound up with the unpresumptuous way he faced death. He went to visit his sister Briga, Abbess at Annaghdown, and while there became ill. Knowing the end was near, he asked Briga to help him with her prayers. "What have *you* to fear?" she asked. "I am afraid of the loneliness on this dark journey to the unknown land," Brendan replied. "I fear the presence of the King and the sentence of the Judge."

St. Brendan's feast day is May 16.

St. Brigid was a 5th-century abbess, born in Ireland's County Louth. She became a nun at a time when nuns remained in their own homes. Brigid made history by gathering nuns together into a community life, and thus she is known as the pioneer of Irish feminine monasticism. In fact, she took the community concept a step further, founding a monastery in Kildare for monks and nuns both, under the joint rule of an abbot-bishop and an abbess.

She was known for her charity since she was a little girl, and would hand out from the family larder rashers of bacon or a sheep from the flock. She is also said to have given away her father's valuable sword. Hers was a warmth of heart which expressed itself in extravagant generosity.

Yet Brigid was no plastic saint. She has the reputation of being an excellent brewer of ale and of being something of a gourmand. Once she took two nuns with her to a friendly monastery to ask for a supply of corn to help her own monastery over a difficult period. On arrival, a feast of bread and bacon was laid out. It was Lent—the old Lent, when religious above all others normally abstained from meat. Under the special circumstances of the occasion, Brigid dug into the meal, bacon and all. Her two companions, however, abstained from the meat. When Brigid noticed this, she was on her feet. She seized her sister-companions by the shoulders and marched them from the room. Presumably she then finished her meal of bread and bacon in comfort.

Brigid lived to be 70 or so, and she was buried in Downpatrick, reportedly in the same grave as Patrick and Columkille. Her feast day is February 1.

St. Camillus de Lellis was born in 1550 in Bocchiancio, Italy. He was a giant of a man—six foot six inches tall, and built proportionately—perfect stuff for the army. And indeed at 17 he did enlist in the Venetian army, along with his father, then aged 67. An incurable disease in the leg ended Camillus' military career, and he wandered about something of a wastrel and a gambler.

At 25 he took a job as an orderly in San Giacomo Hospital in Rome, where he found patients who were left to rot in their own filth, who were beaten by attendants, who were often hurried off to the mortuary before they were even dead. The experience turned his life around.

Camillus became a reformer, and rose to superintendent of the hospital. Eventually he became a priest and founded a religious order whose members would bind themselves to help the sick, the plague-ridden, and the dying. These are the Camillans, long distinguished for their black habit with the red cross on the right of the breast.

Camillus' leg disease hampered him all his life, and it is reported that his feet were so calloused that he had to walk with the aid of a stick. Yet he combined the full duties of a priest with regular visiting and care of the sick, even to the extent of allowing himself but four or five hours sleep at night. He lived to be 64 years old. His feast is observed on July 14.

St. Catherine of Siena is revered as one of the greatest women of Christendom. She lived from 1347-1380. The youngest of 25 children, she became a Dominican tertiary at age 16, and three years later began to work in hospitals and with lepers. With her profound spiritual insights she soon attracted a large group of men as her followers. Charges of scandal were leveled against her, but these did not stand up against the evidence of her piety and commitment to the holy life. Catherine served as a peace-maker between the city of Florence and Pope Gregory XI, traveling to Avignon for that purpose and prevailing upon him to end the Avignon "Captivity" and return to Rome. Subsequently she devoted her life trying to end the great Western Schism that followed Gregory's death. Catherine of Siena carried the stigmata. She left behind some 400 letters and a famous mystical tract, *Dialogue*. She died in Rome in 1380, was canonized in 1461, and was declared patron of Italy in 1939. Her feast day is April 29.

St. Charles Lwanga and Companions are known collectively as the Ugandan Martyrs. They went to their death be-tween 1886-1887, victims of the rage of King Mwanga. The king's rage was triggered by Charles Lwanga's spurning of his homosexual advances. Charles Lwanga, a page of the king, was a convert of the White Fathers, who had arrived in Uganda in 1879, and he resisted the king's propositions on religious grounds. Infuriated, the king summoned all his pages to appear before him, and he commanded the Christians among them to step for-ward. Charles Lwanga was the first to move; others followed. Charles Lwanga and 12 companions were burned alive, reportedly over a slow fire, June 3, 1886. Nine more were martyred between May 26, 1886 and January 27, 1887. They are regarded as the first martyrs of black Africa. The 22 were beatified on June 6, 1920, and canonized by Pope Paul VI on Mission Sunday in October, 1964. Their feast day is June 3.

St. Christopher was one of those whose feast was dropped from the calendar of saints because their authenticity was questioned or because their feast seemed redundant on an otherwise crowded calendar. St. Christopher's feast was relegated to particular calendars because of the legendary nature of accounts of his life.

The story goes that Christopher was a huge man who, having found the faith, could not settle for prayer and fasting and went in search of something different to do with his life and his strength. He found his mission in helping pilgrims cross a difficult river by a notoriously dangerous ford.

Everyone knows the rest of the story: how Christopher one day was carrying a small child across the river, and the weight on his back grew so heavy that he feared both he and the child would drown. When they reached land safely, the child revealed himself as Christ, carrying the weight of the world in his hand. Christopher was sure he was dreaming, but when his staff of dry wood burst into leaf and flower, he knew otherwise.

To Anthony Ross of *The Tablet* of London, the story of St. Christopher is a kind of medieval *Pilgrim's Progress*, a simple outline of spirituality for Everyone. In Ross' words, Christopher "stands for every man and woman who finds prayer and fasting difficult, but who plods on in Christ's service, using whatever gift is available to help others through the river of life—or is it the river of death? He had size and strength, patience and perseverance. Patience with others, perseverance through weariness, and apparently unending, unrewarding effort, are virtues illustrated in the story of Christopher. The vision of the Christ-Child is not the end of the story in its final development but the beginning of a contemplative and apostolic period in the life of Christopher; patron not just of anxious motorists, but of all unassuming Christians whose work is their prayer and their way to God.''

St. Christopher allegedly died a martyr in Lycia around 251. His feast day was July 25.

St. Elizabeth Ann Bayley Seton is the church's first United States-born citizen to have been formally declared a saint. She was canonized in 1975 by Pope Paul VI, who thus honored a woman who was a convert, a New York socialite, wife, mother, and person of wide intellectual interests.

St. Elizabeth Ann Seton was born in 1774, daughter of a Columbia University professor and a stepsister of Archbishop James Roosevelt Bayley of Baltimore, also a convert. She was educated by her father and in 1794 married William Magee Seton.

As a young mother, Elizabeth Ann Seton was involved in charitable works, helping to found in 1797 the Society for the Relief of Poor Widows with Small Children. At age 29 she was widowed with five children of her own, but this did not handicap her in her life of good works. She founded a religious community, the Sisters of Charity of St. Joseph, and near Emmitsburg, Maryland, she opened a school for poor children that proved to be the beginning of the Catholic parochial-school system in the United States. Her feast day is January 4.

St. Frances of Rome lived from 1384 to 1440, an age when women married much younger than now. She wed at 13 and began raising a family. History records that Frances was a devoted wife and mother, and something more; she was a woman devoted to works of piety and charity. With sister-in-law Vannozza, she made regular visits to the poor and distressed, cared for the most difficult hospital cases, and worked heroically through a scary Roman plague. She was a woman of the home and of the world.

Frances of Rome lost two children in that plague, and she herself was sick for a time almost beyond hope. But she recovered and organized the religious group, Oblates of Tor de' Specchi, which became affiliated with the Benedictines. After the death of her husband, she entered the community and, against her wishes, was named superior. Her last years were marked by severe austerities and, it is said, by supernatural gifts which complemented earlier powers of healing. She was canonized in 1680. Her feast day is March 9.

St. Frances Xavier Cabrini is more popularly known as Mother Cabrini. The youngest of 13 children, she was born in 1850 in the town of Sant' Angelo Lodigiano in Lombardy, Italy. A devout but delicate young woman, she sought admission into two religious orders, and was refused by both for reasons of insufficient health. She secured work as director of a small orphanage at Codogno, where she spent six difficult years before the Bishop of Lodi decided to shut the institution down. His advice to Cabrini, who still wished to be a religious and preferably a missionary in the Far East, was to found a missionary institute of sisters herself, since he knew of none to recommend to her. This she did, naming the community the Missionary Sisters of the Sacred Heart.

It was the floodtime of Italian emigration to the United States, and there was great concern in Italy for the temporal and religious welfare of the emigrants. It was proposed to Mother Cabrini that she go to New York and work among these emigrants. At first she refused, but her mind was changed by Pope Leo XIII, who said to her, "Not to the East, but to the West.... You will find a vast field for labor in the United States." She shipped to New York and landed in March, 1889.

During the next 27 years, Mother Cabrini traveled across the United States opening schools and charitable institutions, and founding hospitals—two in Chicago, one in New York and one in Seattle. In the same period she also opened houses in Central America, Argentina, Brazil,

France, Spain, England and additional ones in Italy. Her order flourished, and her personal reputation for determination, organization and holiness grew in measure.

Mother Cabrini became a citizen of the United States in 1909 at Seattle. She died in Chicago December 22, 1917, and was buried in New York City. She was beatified in 1938 by Pope Pius XI and canonized in 1946 by Pope Pius XII, the first American citizen to be so honored. (Elizabeth Ann Bayley Seton was the first native-born U.S. citizen to be canonized, being elevated in 1975.) In 1950 Pius XII declared Mother Cabrini patron of emigrants. Her feast day is December 22.

St. Francis of Assisi is the saint associated with peacemakers. It is slightly paradoxical, because Francis originally aspired to a knight's career, and indeed was once a soldier, joining in an attack on Perugia, where he was taken prisoner and held hostage for a year. This was when he was a young man—before a memorable dream called him to Christ's service. Thereafter Francis abandoned family riches, rights, and possessions, even at times his own clothes. He devoted himself to the poor and the sick, and he founded the religious order that bears his name, the Franciscans. He eventually bore the stigmata of Christ's wounds.

Francis is thought of as peacemaker because he was such a gentle man. He conversed with the birds and animals of the field, and when he died larks reportedly collected around the roof of his hut, raising a song to heaven. What was remarkable about the dying incident is that the lark is a bird of the morning sun. Francis died in the evening, as the sun was setting.

Francis of Assisi lived from 1181(2) to 1226. He was only in his mid-40s when he died, but he left for all ages an exquisite example of the meaning of love for God and for humankind. His feast is October 4.

St. Francis de Sales lived from 1567-1622. Of French extraction, he served as Bishop of Geneva and became one of the outstanding figures of the Counter-Reformation, as a preacher and writer. Two of his books have been spiritual-reading classics for more than 350 years, *Introduction to the Devout Life* and *Treatise on the Love of God*. With Jane Frances de Chantal, he founded the Visitation Order of nuns, devoted to the care of children and the poor. He died in Lyons at age 55, was canonized in 1625, and declared a doctor of the church in 1877. His feast day is January 24.

Two details of his life especially are worth noting: his humility and his love of books (he considered books basic to the serious person).

St. Francis Xavier lived 46 years, being born in the Spanish kingdom of Navarre in 1506 and dying on the island of Sancian off the coast of China in 1552. He was one of the first recruits to the Jesuit Order, and he went to the Far East, where his missionary efforts were to become legendary.

Contrary to pious legend, Francis Xavier did not possess the gift of tongues. In fact, he relied on translators to articulate his message, and he was often sadly misled. Yet he converted thousands to the faith and left the mark of his missionary zeal and energy on areas which are Christian to this day, notably Goa, in India. His feast is December 3.

St. George is one of the most popular saints. He's the patron, for example, of England, Portugal, Germany, Aragon, Genoa and Venice. Notwithstanding, little is known about him. He was martyred at Lydda in Palestine, probably before the time of Constantine, but that is about all that can be pinpointed. Even the story of St. George and the dragon eludes documentation.

St. George is especially revered in England, and to this day symbols of St. George survive in the white ensign of the British Navy, in the flag flown on high holidays by English parish churches, and in the Union Jack itself. His feast—April 23—was a holy day of obligation in England from the Middle Ages until 1778.

The celebrated story of St. George's slaying of the dragon does not make its appearance in biographical accounts until the 12th century. Though the story acquired wide symbolic power and literary charm, appearing in tales as disparate as Spenser's *Faerie Queene* and the children's tales of the *Seven Champions of Christendom*, it seems to be more fable than fact.

The story alleges that the city of Sylene in Lybia was being terrorized by a dragon and the people pacified the beast with people from among their own community. One day the king's daughter was to be sacrificed to the dragon, whereupon George arrived on the scene, attacked the dragon, and subdued it. The dragon was taken captive, and subsequently George slew it on condition that the people be baptized. Embellishments of the story transform George into a knight of chivalry, who marries the princess. His feast day is April 23.

St. Isidore was born in Spain in 1130, and he worked the fields of an estate outside Madrid. He was a peasant farmer, yet he was able to give freely to the poor. He and his wife lived lives of such piety that both attained recognition among the special heroes of Christianity. Isidore was declared a saint in 1622; his wife, Maria de la Cabeza, was declared blessed in 1697. St. Isidore is the patron of farmers. His feast day is May 15.

St. Joan of Arc was born of peasant stock in 1412 in the French village of Domremy. She was the youngest of five children and completely uneducated. She could neither read nor write. A deeply religious girl, Joan was visited by "voices" beginning in 1425, voices which she subsequently identified as belonging to St. Michael, St. Margaret and St. Catherine. These voices urged Joan to seek out the French dauphin and inform him that she had been sent by God to lead his armies against the English occupiers of France, to rout them and thus rescue France from its national degradation.

Seventeen-years-old when she finally persuaded the dauphin of the authenticity of her mission from heaven,

Joan of Arc donned the armor of battle, fired French soldiers with unquenchable enthusiasm, and led them to a series of victories—some say miraculous—that loosened England's hold on France and made possible the crowning of the dauphin in Rheims Cathedral July 17, 1429. He became Charles VII.

But there was still fighting to be done, and so Joan continued at the head of the troops. On May 24, 1430 at a skirmish at Compiegne, she was taken prisoner by Burgundians, who sold her to the English, who in turn brought her to trial, in what stands as one of the most infamous legalistic exercises of the Middle Ages. She was condemned to death as a relapsed heretic and sorceress, and burned at the stake in Rouen May 30, 1431. The exact spot falls almost within the shadow of Rouen Cathedral's famous Butter Tower. Joan's ashes were cast into the nearby Seine River.

Twenty-four years after her death, a trial of rehabilitation was opened, and this led to Joan of Arc's complete exoneration. She was declared Blessed by Pope St. Pius X in 1909, and was canonized by Pope Benedict XV in 1920.

As warrior and saint, Joan of Arc belongs primarily to the age of nationalism, when wars could be fought without cosmic consequences. But she does have strong modern relevance as a woman who wore men's clothes (it was a major point of accusation at the trial which pronounced death upon her) and as a woman who functioned in the world of men. Her feast day is May 30.

St. Joseph was the husband of Mary and the foster father of Jesus. His profession was that of carpenter, and the presumption is that Jesus was an apprentice of sorts for him before he began his public life. Since there is no mention of Joseph being at the Crucifixion, it is likely that he died some time before.

Joseph figures prominently in several Biblical episodes involving the young Jesus, but curiously it is only in relatively recent centuries that honors have been accorded him by the church. He did not have an annual feast day until 1481, when one was finally declared by Pope Sixtus IV. Since then Rome has seemingly raced to erase the neglect. Pope Pius IX declared him Protector of the Universal Church in 1870, and Leo XIII singled him out as a model for the fathers of families. Benedict XV put workers under his protection; Pius XI cited him as the exemplar of social justice; and Pius XII established a second feast in his honor, that of St. Joseph the Worker, which is observed on May 1, as something of a counterbalance to the communist observance of May Day. St. Joseph's primary feast day, however, is March 19.

St. Joachim and St. Anne were the parents of the Virgin Mary. Their history is sketchy, but it appears they were married at an early age, and were childless for years—a cause for reproach in a time when childlessness was viewed as a sign of disfavor in the eyes of God. Joachim reportedly fasted in the desert for 40 days, and was visited by an angel who promised a child to the couple. The child was Mary. Their feast is jointly observed on July 26.

St. John is perhaps the best known of the four evangelists. He was the gentle apostle "whom Jesus loved," the one to whom at the crucifixion Jesus assigned the care of his mother. But he was also the "Son of Thunder," who with his brother James could ask Jesus to "call down fire from heaven" on the inhospitable Samaritans who would not welcome Jesus on his way to Jerusalem. They were reprimanded for the suggestion (Luke 9:52-55).

John the Evangelist wrote one of the most beautiful of the gospel narratives, a version simple in the style and vocabulary of fishermen but also mystical in the manner of a poet. It is to John and the opening chapter of his Gospel ("In the beginning was the Word...") that Christians owe the concept that God is love. Likewise it was John who stressed the concept of the "new commandment: love one another" (John 13:34).

John lived to an old age. After the Ascension, he attended the Council of Jerusalem in 49 A.D. and was probably present at Mary's death. He also wrote three Epistles and the Book of Revelation (the Apocalypse). His feast day is December 27.

St. John the Baptist was the son of Elizabeth and Zachary, a couple childless into old age, when they miraculously conceived and had a child. The event is obliquely alluded to in the Hail Mary, for it was the pregnant Elizabeth who spoke to the pregnant Mary the words of blessing and excitement, "Blessed art thou amongst women, and blessed is the fruit of thy womb."

John the Baptist was a hermit and preacher who demanded two rites of those who came to him: open confession of sins and physical washing as an outward sign of an interior change of heart. He baptized Jesus, but only with reluctance. "I should be baptized by you," he said, "yet you come to me" (Matt. 3:14).

John the Baptist would seem to have had large moments of doubt and impatience with respect to Jesus. Restless for the solemn manifestation of the Messiah, he once sent two of his disciples to Jesus to ask a question aimed at eliciting an explicit declaration of identity: "Are you 'He who is to come' or are we to expect someone else?" (Luke 7:19). Jesus refused to let John force his hand. The time for a formal declaration had not yet come. He merely pointed to the evidence of his miracles.

John the Baptist was beheaded at the order of Herod, acting under the spell of Salome's dancing. The entranced Herod promised Salome any request of her asking; she asked for the head of John the Baptist—which was delivered. John the Baptist's feast is marked on June 25.

St. John of the Cross was a Spaniard, who lived in the 16th century. He entered the Carmelite order and at the behest of St. Teresa of Avila introduced her reform among the friars. Inevitably he encountered opposition, and twice he was kidnapped and locked up—the second time in Toledo for nearly nine months. Here he wrote the *Dark Night of the Soul*, a classic spiritual time meditation whose title has since become a catchword for millions of Christians undergoing their own dark night of the soul, for which it sometimes seems no dawn will ever come.

St. John's dawn eventually came. The discalced Carmelites were recognized, and a separate province was established. St. John became a provincial, a prior, and the originator of several new monasteries. But he fell afoul of the Madrid chapter general, who deprived him of all offices and dispatched him as a simple monk to La Banuela. Another dark night of the soul. St. John's health gave way, and he died in Ubeda, Spain on December 14, 1591.

In popular hagiography, St. John of the Cross is perhaps best known for his austerity and his stress on nada—"nothing." It was John's catchword to drive home the principle that the soul that desires God must eliminate every other desire. His feast is observed on December 14.

St. John Vianney was a French parish priest, who was canonized in 1925. As a seminarian, he had such difficulties in his studies that he was not ordained a priest until he was 29. As the Cure of Ars, he was long scorned for his lack of advanced training. Superiors passed him over for promotion, and he was alleged to suffer from attacks by the devil. Still he became one of the most famous priests of his time, and in 1929 Pope Pius XI proclaimed him patron of parish priests.

St. John Vianney lived from 1786-1859. His sainthood derives from his priesthood. He was such a respected spiritual guide and confessor that Ars became a place of pilgrimage. John Vianney was in such demand as a confessor that he would spend from 16 to 18 hours a day in the confessional. His feast is August 8.

St. Jude was an Apostle and the brother of St. James the Less. How and when he came to be chosen by Christ is not known. According to tradition, he preached in Mesopotamia and then joined St. Simon in Persia, where the two were martyred. Before his death he wrote a short epistle that made its way into the New Testament. Otherwise little is known about him.

Confusion of names between St. Jude and the betraying apostle Judas effectively discouraged devotion to Jude for several centuries, but this was largely overcome in the 1300s when St. Bridgit of Sweden was reputedly told by Christ himself to turn to St. Jude in prayer with faith and confidence. "In accordance with his surname Thaddeus—the amiable, loving," said our Lord, "he will show himself most willing to give help."

In artistic representation Jude is shown with a medallion carrying the image of Christ, an imprint said to have been entrusted to him by the Lord. (Jude was a near relative or cousin of Jesus, and is said to have been a playmate of the young Jesus.)

St. Jude's feast is October 28, and he is known as the patron of seemingly hopeless causes.

St. Lucy was the daughter of an affluent Sicilian, who was martyred during the persecution of Diocletian in the year 304. Legend says that she was turned in to authorities for being a Christian by a rejected suitor. She was tortured and blinded, her eyes being plucked from their sockets. The Church of San Giovanni Maggiore in Naples claims to possess those relics. The blinding and the name —Lucy derives from the Latin word 'lux' for 'light'—have projected Lucy as the saint to be invoked by persons with eye problems. In the era of gaudy plaster statues, Lucy was depicted as a woman, demurely dressed, holding her eyes on a plate. Her feast is December 13.

St. Laurence was a Roman martyr and once one of the most popular of saints. The 6th-century Leonine Sacramentary assigned him no less than 14 Masses, and in the Middle Ages there were at least 34 Roman churches dedicated to him. He even became Rome's third patron.

According to tradition, St. Laurence was born in Spain and went with his family to Rome, where he became one of the seven deacons of the city under Pope St. Sixtus II.

During the persecution of Valerian, Sixtus was beheaded. Just before his death he told Laurence he would follow three days later. Laurence used those three days to distribute the church's property and precious vessels among the poor, and at the end of the three days he presented the poor to Valerian as the church's treasure.

Infuriated, Valerian ordered Laurence roasted alive on a gridiron. Several senators were so impressed by his actions and the heroic example of his death that they converted to Christianity. This is said to have marked the decline of Roman idolatry and the beginning of the conversion of Rome itself. The year was 258. St. Laurence's feast is observed on August 10.

St. Luke, the evangelist, was a Greek and by profession a doctor. To him Christians are indebted not only for a learned and literate narrative, not only for popular parables which might otherwise have been lost (the fig tree, the prodigal son, the good Samaritan), but also for prayers that are favorites of Catholic history—the Hail Mary, the *Magnificat*, the *Benedictus*, the *Nunc dimittis.*

Luke was neither bishop nor priest, but he played a prominent role in the early church as a member of Paul's mission through Asia Minor about the year 50. He stayed at Philippi as the Christian community's lay leader for six or seven years. He then rejoined Paul and was with him in Rome during the years of persecution which eventually led up to Paul's martyrdom in 66 A.D. Luke then went to Greece where, at 84, he died. His feast day is October 18.

St. Matthew, the evangelist, was a tax collector at Capernaum, and in following Jesus he probably took the greatest occupational risk of all the apostles. Peter and Andrew, for instance, could always return to their boats and fish the Sea of Galilee. It is extremely unlikely that Matthew would ever get his job back as tax collector.

Matthew wrote in Aramaic, and his Gospel account is ledger-like and mathematical in its orderliness and organization—which is perhaps to be expected of one whose training was in ledgers and numbers. There is, in his Gospel, a seeming fascination with combination figures: the seven parables of the Kingdom; the seven woes of the Pharisees; the seven invocations of the Lord's Prayer. The number five is also used often: the five disputes of the Pharisees; the five loaves; the five talents. He even divides his Gospel into five books. Maybe that's all coincidence— but not Matthew's special knowledge about money and taxes, down to technicalities like the difference between the indirect tax and the poll tax.

Matthew is said to have preached in Judea, Ethiopia, Persia and Parthia, where he was martyred. His feast day is observed on September 21.

St. Mark wrote the shortest of the Gospels and in many respects the bluntest. It seemed to be in keeping with his character. He is the only evangelist who acquaints readers with the faults and foibles of the heroes of the Gospel. Of course saints are known to have had human frailties. But even those who were physically close to Jesus?

Mark exposes vanity among some apostles: "At this they fell silent, for on the way they had been arguing about who was the most important" (9:34).

Mark suggests that perhaps the apostles were slow of wit: "On the contrary, their minds were completely closed to the meaning of events" (6:52).

And Mark reveals that in his human person even Jesus could be in error: "Observing a fig tree some distance off, covered with foliage, he went over to see if he could find anything on it. When he reached it he found nothing but leaves; it was not the time for figs" (11:13).

In addition to being an apostle, it is presumed that Mark was a Levite and from a wealthy family, for Peter used Mark's mother's house as a refuge after his escape from prison. That same house was large enough to accommodate sizable gatherings of Christians.

Mark traveled with Paul, but not everywhere. In fact he seems to have annoyed Paul by refusing to go with him to Tarsus. Paul accordingly declined Barnabas' proposal to take Mark with him on his second missionary journey. His feast day is April 25.

St. Mary, the Blessed Virgin, the mother of Jesus, is revered as the great saint, the most noble woman of Catholic Christianity. She was the daughter of Joachim and Anne, and as a young girl became betrothed to Joseph. Before vows were exchanged, she was visited by the Angel Gabriel, who announced to her that she had been chosen to be the mother of the Redeemer, which child had been miraculously conceived in her womb. In a word, hers would be a virgin birth. The account of the angel's appearance, Mary's bewilderment ("How can this be, for I know not man?"), her acquiescence ("Be it done unto me according to thy word"), is movingly laid out by Luke in 1:26ff., the same chapter that contains the prayer known now as the *Magnificat*.

Mary's story is central to the whole of the New Testament, for Mary not only gave birth to Christ and raised him, but also was close to him throughout his public life. When Jesus was crucified, Mary was at the foot of the cross. The Gospels portray Mary as a humble and unintrusive mother, but obviously she was one who could exercise the prerogatives of a mother, as of course happened at the wedding feast of Cana, when she prodded Christ into performing his first miracle, the changing of the water into wine (John 2:1-11).

Devotion to Mary has been strong in Catholicism since at least the 2nd century, when theologians first began to regard Mary as a counterpart to Eve—Mary's role in the Redemption remedying Eve's part in the Fall. The contrast between the two—Eve, the temptress; Mary, the respectful—is easily strained, nevertheless Mary became in Catholicism a kind of second Eve, the epitome of the new and perfect woman. She was never worshipped as a goddess, but there are those who would have her declared co-redeemer with Christ of humankind. Thus far the move has been resisted, though Mary clearly stands forth yet as model and exemplar of the totally virtuous person.

The calendar is crowded with feasts of Mary. Principal ones are:

January 1, the Solemnity of Mary, the Mother of God

February 2, the Purification

March 25, the Annunciation

July 2, the Visitation of St. Elizabeth

August 15, the Assumption

August 22, The Immaculate Heart of Mary

September 8, the Nativity of the Virgin Mary

September 12, the Most Holy Name of Mary

September 15, the Seven Sorrows of Mary

October 7, the Holy Rosary

October 11, the Motherhood of Mary

November 21, the Presentation in the Temple

December 8, the Immaculate Conception

A number of other feasts commemorate Mary's appearances, among them:

February 11, Our Lady of Lourdes (commemorating the visions of St. Bernadette Soubirous)

July 16, Our Lady of Mt. Carmel (commemorating the presentation of the scapular to St. Simon Stock)

August 5, Our Lady of Snows (commemorating the dedication of the Basilica of St. Mary Major in Rome, on the spot where Mary caused snow to fall as a sign of where to build)

September 24, Our Lady of Ransom (commemorating the establishment of the Mercedarians by St. Peter Nolasco)

October 7, Our Lady of the Rosary (commemorating the victory over the Turks at Lepanto in 1571, which headed off an invasion of Christian Eastern Europe)

(The Vatican lately placed in circulation a new 500-lire silver coin commemorating the 2,000th anniversary of the birth of the Blessed Virgin. Issued in 1985, the coin was dated 1984, and led to a speculation among some that the Vatican was dating Mary's year of birth as 16 B.C.— a year arrived at by mathematical deduction based on the then-custom of Jewish maidens being pledged in marriage about age 14, with marriage and a shared life following a year or so later. It is more probable, however, that the date on the coin represented an acceptable approximation, not a historical statement.)

St. Nicholas is the saint commonly associated with Santa Claus. It is an innacurate association. Santa Claus is a legend of pagan or pre-Christian creation, based on the legends of Thor, the god of fire in Germanic legend, who in turn was associated with winter and the yule log and who rode in a cart drawn by goats named Cracker and Gnasher. That is an imagery which has passed to reindeer and sleigh in the Santa Claus story.

St. Nicholas, on the other hand, was a native of Parara in Asia Minor, who gave away his possessions to the poor and the sick. He was elected bishop of Myra where he built up a legendary reputation for generosity. He arranged dowries for poor servant girls, tossed bags of money into homes where people faced starvation, and came constantly to the aid of impoverished sailors and prisoners.

He died around 350. In 1087 his relics were stolen and carried to Bari, which then became a major shrine. By the 13th century, St. Nicholas' fame was such that his feast was a gift-giving day in many parts of Europe. His feast is December 6, however, not December 25. St. Nicholas is the patron of Russia and Greece.

St. Patrick is a patron of Ireland and, by extension, the patron saint of people everywhere who possess a drop of Irish blood. He is known everywhere but as Irish scholar Thomas F. O'Rahilly has written, much of his life's story is obscure and only two events in his life can be dated, and these only approximately: his arrival in Ireland (circa 461) and his death (circa 492). No saint has more legends attached to him, but engaging as they are, most are nonverifiable and likely as not many are ahistorical. One such is the tale of his having driven the snakes out of Ireland.

Another popular story involving St. Patrick is of the dream that brought his return to Ireland as cleric. Ostensibly, an angel named Victor arrived in the dream with letters, one of which was for Patrick. It carried the inscription "The Voice of the Irish," and on opening it Patrick heard Irish voices—voices he actually knew—crying for him to come back to Erin.

The details of Patrick's life have been amplified from his *Confessio*, a document written late in life containing autobiographical material. From it the pious have deduced that Patrick was the son of a financially comfortable Roman collector of imperial taxes, who lived in Wales, near the mouth of the Severn River. The area was raided by pirates and Patrick, 16, was carried off to Ireland and sold as a slave. He labored as a swineherd in Antrim before he managed his escape, six years after his captivity. He returned to his home in Britain, then left for Gaul to study for the priesthood. He rose to the position of bishop, and was given charge of the mission to Ireland as successor to St. Palladius, who had recently died.

The rest is history. Under Patrick, Ireland was converted from paganism to Christianity. The faith flourished, and in time missionaries from Ireland were traveling to the known world as evangelizers.

St. Patrick's feast is marked, with gusto, on March 17.

St. Paul is the apostle and martyr, whose story is told in detail in the Acts of the Apostles. Originally he was Saul of Tarsus and he was bitterly anti-Christian, until one day traveling along the road to Damascus he was struck down and blinded, at the same time being censured by the voice of Christ: "Saul, Saul, why do you persecute me?" For three days Saul was blind, and he neither ate nor drank, whereupon Ananias, a disciple in Damascus, was sent to him by God to reveal God's plans for him. Saul regained his sight, was baptized, and his strength returned as he took food. Shortly thereafter Saul became known as Paul.

As Christ's personally designated Apostle to the Gentiles, Paul preached in Damascus, Tarsus, Antioch and Syria. He went to Jerusalem, where he was ordained with Barnabas in the year 44. Again he was on the road: to Cyprus, Perga, Antioch in Pisidia, Iconium and Lystra. He seemed never to stop, as he crisscrossed the known world.

His life was filled with adventure. In Damascus he escaped an assassination plot by escaping over the city wall with the help of disciples. In Philippi he was imprisoned with Silas, but escaped miraculously. He was shipwrecked on the shores of Malta, and was saved probably by clinging to debris from the ship, which debris carried him to shore. His good fortune ran out in Rome, where he was captured and imprisoned under Nero, and finally beheaded, perhaps on the Ostian Way. The year was 67 A.D.

Paul's zeal set an example for the other Apostles and disciples, and his numerous epistles brought an intellectual dimension to Christianity at a moment when doctrine might have been vitiated by vagueness and confusion. In a different era, some of his admonitions have about them a ring of male chauvinism; for example, Chapter 7 of the First Epistle to the Corinthians. But he wrote in the context of the times, and though new human emphases may render some passages anachronistic, the body of his work remains a cornerstone of the faith.

On January 25, the Church marks the Feast of the Conversion of St. Paul. Paul's feast day is June 29, a date he shares with St. Peter.

St. Peter, first among the apostles and the one selected by Christ to head his church (thus the first pope), was born in Bethsaida, son of Jonah. A fisherman by trade, he lived in Capharnaum on Lake Genesareth. Originally his name was Simon, and he was married.

It was his brother Andrew, also to be an apostle, who introduced Simon to Christ, and it was Christ who renamed him Cephas, Aramaic for "rock"; in the Greek the name translated to Petros, hence Peter. Peter was the first to acknowledge Christ as the son of the living God, immediately after which Christ named him head of the church and extended him full authority over it (Matthew 16:13-20).

Predictably, Peter figures prominently in the Gospel story. He was involved in the miracle of the great catch of fishes, was present at the Transfiguration, at the Agony in the Garden, and of course at the inquisition of Jesus. All four evangelists record Peter's denial of Christ, an event predicted by Christ and announced by the crowing of the cock.

Peter's leadership of the Apostles was no unchallenged thing, as Mark makes clear (9:33-37) in narrating the incident on the road to Caparnaum when the Twelve argued about who was the most important among the disciples, only to be rebuked by Christ for their self-concern. Peter's leadership firmed unmistakably, however, immediately after the Crucifixion. He presided over the assemblage in the "upper room" after the Crucifixion, and he presided over the selection of Matthias as the successor to Judas among the Twelve.

Details of Peter's life after the Ascension of Christ are recorded in the Acts of the Apostles, including his curing of the man lame from birth, and his capture and imprisonment by Herod Agrippa I, with his subsequent miraculous release by an angel.

Peter preached in Judea, Samaria, Galilee, Asia Minor and probably Greece before arriving in Rome. He was martyred in Rome during the reign of Nero, being crucified, head downwards. Tradition has it that he did not consider himself worthy to be martyred in the same way as Christ. The martyrdom occurred in the area of Nero's gardens at the foot of Vatican hill. His burial was on the site where St. Peter's Basilica was built. His tomb is held to be beneath the basilica's main altar.

Peter's feast days are February 22 (the Chair of St. Peter) and June 29 (the Feast of SS. Peter and Paul).

St. Peter Claver lived from 1581 to 1654. He was a Spaniard who went to Latin America in 1610 to help evangelize Spanish Colonies in the New World. He landed in Cartagena, Colombia, the city that was the heart of the slave trade from Africa. Appalled by the trafficking in the slaves and not in a position to suppress it, Peter Claver did what he considered the next best thing. He dedicated himself to the welfare of the slaves, declaring himself "the slave of the blacks forever."

He met the slave boats from Africa and carried food and delicacies to those aboard. He defended slaves from oppressors, and became the slaves' friend. He also welcomed blacks in his church, though the practice cost him the support and patronage of white men and women of Cartagena. In his lifetime it is said that he baptized 300,000 blacks. His feast is September 9.

St. Philip Neri (1515-1595) was a native of Florence who lived most of his life in Rome and with such sanctity as to become known as the Apostle of Rome. Rome was a loose and dissolute city in Philip Neri's time, but he did not withdraw from it, nor condemn it. He scarcely even criticized it, choosing instead to combat sin and mischief with the counter-attractions of holiness, purity, truth and gaiety. Above all gaiety.

He founded the Oratory in a church in central Rome assigned him and his followers by Pope Gregory XIII, and it became not only a center of devotion but also of talk and laughter and culture. The musical form we know today as the oratorio is said to derive from the musical programs conducted at the Roman Oratory.

As a priest, Philip Neri advocated frequent Confession and Communion—although as confessor there was nothing of the zealot in him. Once, when an over-earnest penitent asked Philip for permission to wear a hair shirt, Philip responded, "Certainly, provided you wear it outside your clothes." He recognized Confession (the Rite of Reconciliation, in the new liturgy) as a sacrament that is good for the psyche as well as the soul.

At one point in his life, Philip Neri thought of joining Francis Xavier in his mission to the Indies, but was advised, "Your Indies are in Rome." By coincidence Neri, the Apostle of Rome, was to be canonized with Xavier, the Apostle of the Indies, in 1622. St. Philip Neri's feast day is May 26.

St. Stanislaus was born at Szczepanowski, near Cracow, in 1030. He became a priest and eventually bishop of Cracow. When he censured the king, Boleslaus II, for his savagery and injustices, the monarch promised to reform. Instead, he kidnapped a noble's wife and brought upon himself the punishment of excommunication. Boleslaus then angrily invaded the bishop's chapel and slew Stanislaus as he was saying Mass. That was in 1079. Pope St. Gregory VII placed the country under interdict, and Boleslaus eventually fled to Hungary. Stanislaus was canonized in 1253, and his feast is observed May 7.

St. Teresa of Avila is associated with visions and cloisters—hardly a saint of interest it would seem, for those who are uncloistered and without visions. Yet for all those who look to saints for guidance in their spiritual lives, Teresa of Avila offers something uniquely feminine and holy, both in her life and in her spiritual classics: *Autobiography* (1565), *Exclamations of the Soul to God* (1569), *Way of Perfection* (1573), and *Interior Castle* (1577).

Teresa lived from 1515-1582. She had to overcome both illness and parental opposition before she was professed as a Carmelite in 1537. In 1555 she began to have visions and hear voices. At first these were thought to originate with the devil. After two years of spiritual desolation and inept spiritual advice, she came in contact with Peter of Alcantara, who also became a saint. He convinced her that her supernatural experiences were of holy inspiration.

Teresa subsequently founded a convent for nuns who wanted to lead a more spiritual life than was generally possible under the lax rules of the time. Because her nuns went without shoes, they were called Discalced Carmelites. Teresa in time established 15 more convents, and thus launched an order of women religious which thrives to this day. She died at 67 and was canonized in 1622.

It is said that few so perfectly united the contemplative and the active life as Teresa of Avila. It is said, too, that her writings comprise one of the most remarkable spiritual biographies—one with which only *The Confessions of St. Augustine* can compare. Her feast day is October 15.

St. Therese of Lisieux, the Little Flower, is another saint of modern times. She was canonized in 1925, and once was invoked as no other 20th-century saint. As Henri Petitot wrote, she was an unusual kind of saint and nun. She was not a nun devoted to the outward charity of the active apostolate, but rather was a young girl who entered the Carmel at 15, died at 24, and did nothing but pray, suffer, obey. She did not nurse the plague-stricken, the poor, the sick, the aged; she did not save her native France, as Joan of Arc had done; she did not bring the papacy back to Rome from Avignon, as St. Catherine of Siena helped to do. She did not do any great deeds, and yet she exerted an unparalleled moral influence throughout the world by the example of her life, as revealed in her autobiography, *The Story of a Soul*.

She became an example for the heroic way she dealt with physical suffering in her last years and for doing so when for years she had no sensible perception of God's presence. Her faith never wavered, and she went on to sainthood. Her canonization came only 28 years after her death. Her feast is observed on October 3.

St. Thomas the Apostle was surnamed Didymus, "twin," and was probably born in Galilee. Where and when he became one of the apostles is not known, but he was present at Lazarus' resurrection, at the Last Supper—and, to be sure, in the upper room where the apostles had collected in fear and uncertainty after the Crucifixion.

The upper room was the setting of the famous scene recorded in John 20:24-29—Christ inviting Thomas to touch his wounds, Thomas doing so, and then responding with the phrase immortalizing him in Christian history, "My Lord and my God!"

Thomas preached in Medea, Persia, and India, where he was martyred near Madras. His feast day is July 3.

St. Thomas Aquinas lived in the 13th century. He was Italian, a Dominican, and perhaps the greatest scholar in church history. His great achievement was to systematize Catholic belief. He took the tenets of faith and arranged them in orderly fashion, distinguishing between such things as revelation and reason, theology and philosophy. He drew conclusions from a reservoir of world thought, secular and Christian. He died in 1274, was canonized in 1323, and declared a Doctor of the Church in 1567. The title of Doctor is one reserved for the most learned and holy of saints.

An anecdote about Aquinas involves an incident in the monastery library. Aquinas was a huge man, over 300 pounds, it is said. He had to have a hole cut into his desk to fit his stomach. One day, brother monks decided to have a little sport with Thomas, and one of them excitedly exclaimed looking out the window, "Come quick, look at the cow flying!" Aquinas was up from his desk and across to the window like a young sprinter—to see nothing, of course. The monks had their laugh, but Aquinas had his historic rejoinder: "I thought it more likely that a cow would fly than that a monk would lie." His feast day is January 28.

St. Thomas More lived in 16th-century England, and was, as the playwright Robert Bolt typed him, a man for all seasons. Scholar, tutor to the future king, lawyer, family man, celebrated wit, and finally Lord Chancellor of the realm, Thomas More had everything—and sacrificed everything on a matter of religious principle. He refused to take an oath, provided in the Act of Succession, repudiating the Pope, recognizing the offspring of King Henry VIII and his second wife, Anne Boleyn, as heir to the throne, and declaring Henry's first marriage to Catherine of Aragon to be no true marriage. The action cost him his head.

Thomas More went to scaffold in 1535, wit to the end, commenting to the guard, "I pray thee see me safe up, and for my coming down let me shift for myself." On the scaffold he reportedly told his executioner, axe at the ready, to take care not to cut his beard since it, at least, was innocent of treason.

More was born in 1478 and lived 57 years. He was canonized in 1935, and his feast is observed June 22.

St. Vincent de Paul lived from 1581 to 1660 and left a legacy for charity that has been an inspiration and model for church and secular society for centuries.

He was the son of French peasants, who was once captured by pirates and sold into slavery. The experience fused the spirituality of the man. On his escape he went to Rome for seminary studies, was ordained, and named a chaplain to Queen Margaret of Valois in Paris. His sermons and his work with the poor attracted wide attention. In 1625 he founded the Congregation of the Missions (known as the Vincentians or Lazarists) to do missionary work among the peasants; and with Louise de Marillac, also later sainted, he founded the Sisters of Charity, whose work is in their name.

Vincent de Paul established hospitals and orphanages,

ransomed Christian slaves in North Africa, helped better priestly formation by founding new seminaries, and wrote widely on spiritual subjects. His life was devoted to the alleviation of human suffering and misery, and he left after him a network of charitable works and workers that endures to this day.

Vincent de Paul gave new meaning to the Catholic parish. He defined it as the center of the spiritual life and charitable and communal activity of its members. The spiritual dimension of parish life is the one most are all familiar with. The charitable and communal dimensions are elements now being rediscovered, as parishes shift emphases to adjust to a changing church scene. For instance, convents and schools are being closed, and in some places these empty properties are being converted into community centers for retired people, into homes for the aged, and in at least one instance into a halfway house for women leaving prison.

Vincent de Paul's feast day is July 19.

Famous Catholics of History

CATHOLICISM has never been a one-way street. People have moved into the church; some born-Catholics have moved out (James Joyce, Eugene O'Neill, F. Scott Fitzgerald, James T. Farrell, Theodore Dreiser); a few have moved in, then moved out again (Robert Lowell); some, allowing ecumenical sensibilities, might be said to have moved sideways (John Cogley). It has been going on for centuries. The sum of it is a church very many of whose members have made the world a richer place culturally and a better place socially, and on occasion even a holier place. Unfortunately, there have also been some Catholics that the world would have been better without. Still on balance the record is good. Famous Catholics have been prominently involved in all ages and in all fields of human endeavor. Some of the luminaries follow of the far and recent past.

Inventors

Blaise Pascal (1623-1662), French, the adding machine, 1642.

Guglielmo Marconi (1874-1937), Italian, the radiotele-graph, 1895.

Evangelista Torricelli (1608-1647), Italian, the barometer, 1643.

Allesandro Volta (1745-1827), Italian, the electric battery, 1799.

Johann Gutenberg (1397-1468?), German, movable type, 1450.

Galileo Galilei (1564-1642), Italian, the astronomical clock, 1634; the thermometer, 1593.

Jacques Etienne Montgolfier (1745-1799) and Joseph Michel Montgolfier (1740-1810), brothers, French, the *montgolfier* (hot-air balloon), 1783.

Thomas E. Murray (1860-1929), American, hydroelectric, steampower and radiator inventions; developed more than 1,100 patents, a number second at the time only to the patents held by Thomas A. Edison.

Discoverers

(The word is used in the generally accepted sense of one's having achieved something hitherto unseen or unknown to that part of the world then writing its history. Columbus, for instance, "discovered" the Americas, but the literal "discoverers" were those who evolved in the Americas or, as is more likely, who crossed to it from Asia via the Bering Strait in prehistoric times. More accurately, our "discoverers" were actually explorers.)

Christopher Columbus (1466?-1506), Italian, the Americas.

Marco Polo (1254-1324), Italian, continental Asia.

Juan Ponce de Leon (1460?-1521), Spanish, Florida.

Vasco Nunez de Balboa (1475?-1517?), Spanish, the Pacific Ocean.

Giovanni da Verrazano (c1480-1527?), Italian, the Atlantic coast of the United States and New York Harbor.

Pedro de Alvarado (1485?-1541), Spanish, the Yucatan, areas of South America.

Hernando de Soto (1500?-1542), Spanish, the Mississippi River at its mouth.

Samuel de Champlain (1567-1635), French, Great Lakes areas.

Pere Jacques Marquette, S.J. (1637-1675), French, the upper Mississippi.

Pere Louis Hennepin (1640-1701?), Belgian, Mississippi Valley, Niagara Falls, and the Falls of St. Anthony in what is now Minneapolis.

Rene Robert de La Salle (1643-1687), French, Lake Erie and Lake Superior regions; he was the first to travel the Mississippi from its upper waters to its mouth.

Louis Joliet (1645-1700), New France (Canada), the western country and Mississippi Valley; he was with Marquette on the trip that took them past the mouths of the Ohio and Missouri.

Scientists

Nicolaus Copernicus (1473-1543), Polish, mathematician and founder of modern astronomy.

Galileo Galilei (1564-1642), Italian, physicist and astronomer, who advanced the theory that the sun, not the earth, was the center of the universe.

Madame Curie (nee Marie Sklodowska) (1867-1934), discoverer with her husband Pierre (1859-1906) of polonium and radium. He, a freethinker, was born in Paris; she, in Warsaw.

Father Gregor Johann Mendel (1822-1884), Austrian botanist, discoverer of a law of heredity known now as Mendel's Law, which became a working basis of investigations into genetics.

Antoine Laurent Lavoisier (1743-1794), founder of modern chemistry who discovered the role of oxygen in plant and animal respiration.

Andre Marie Ampere (1775-1836), French, inventor of the astatic needle, which made the astatic galvanometer possible; the ampere, a unit of electrical current, is named for him.

Louis Pasteur (1822-1895), French, founder of the modern

science of bacteriology; the treatment of milk to kill impurities and known as pasteurization is named for him.

Artists

Johann Wolfgang Amadeus Mozart (1756-1791), Austrian, musical genius who began composing at age 4 (Mozart became involved in Freemasonry in 1784, and saw no conflict between this and his religious beliefs).

Thomas More (1779-1852), Irish poet and lyricist for songs such as "Believe Me If All Those Endearing Young Charms," "The Harp That Once Through Tara's Hall," "The Meeting of the Waters" and "Oft in the Stilly Night."

Ludwig van Beethoven (1770-1827), German-Austrian, composer of symphonies, minuets, sonatas, cantatas, etc., and a memorable *Missa solemnis*, among other masses.

Franz Peter Schubert (1797-1828), Austrian, composer of eight symphonies and more than 600 songs in a brief life of 31 years.

Michelangelo Buonarroti (1475-1564), Italian, painter, sculptor, architect, the very personification of the Renaissance man.

Raphael Santi (1483-1520), exquisite Italian painter; chief architect of St. Peter's after the death of Bramante.

Peter Paul Rubens (1577-1640), Flemish painter whose masterpiece "The Descent from the Cross" has decorated holy cards for centuries.

Georges Rouault (1871-1958), Parisian painter noted for his heads of clowns, satirical sketches of judges, and sad faces of Christ.

Dante Alighieri (1265-1321), Italian poet celebrated for the *Divine Comedy*.

Eric Gill (1882-1940), British sculptor and versatile artist; among other things, he designed ten type faces, including Perpetua and Gill sans-serif.

David Jones (1895-1974), British writer and artist, one of the "company of craftsmen" drawn together at Ditchling, in Sussex, as the Guild of St. Joseph and St. Dominic by Eric Gill; later an engraver for the Golden Cockerel Press.

Inigo Jones (1573-1652), British architect and designer of many of London's most distinguished buildings, including the Banqueting House in Whitehall, St. Paul's Church and the piazza in Covent Garden; he also added an Ionic facade to old St. Paul's Cathedral.

Ivan Mestrovic (1883-1962), Yugoslav sculptor who became an American citizen in 1954; he was the first living sculptor to be honored with a one-man exhibit at the Metropolitan Museum of Art in New York City.

Alfred Noyes (1880-1958), British poet particularly remembered for *The Highwayman*.

Georges Bernanos (1888-1948), French novelist and pamphleteer, whose *Diary of a Country Priest* (1936) became something of a minor classic. (Bernanos once explained his attacks on Catholics as an attempt to awaken them to their responsibilities.)

Political Leaders

Charles Carroll (1737-1832), American, signer of the Declaration of Independence and senator from Maryland.

Daniel O'Connell (1775-1847), first Catholic Lord Mayor of Dublin and champion of Irish causes in the British Parliament; known in Ireland as "the Liberator."

Charles Alexis Henri Maurice Clerel de Tocqueville (1805-1859), French jurist and later legislator and minister of foreign affairs, who came to the United States in 1831 to study its penal system and returned to France to write his memorable four-volume *Democracy in America* (1835-1840).

Konrad Adenauer (1876-1967), first chancellor of the West German Federal Republic in the recovery years after World War II (1949-1963).

Alcide De Gasperi (1881-1954), Italian statesman and premier from 1945-1953.

Charles de Gaulle (1890-1970), French general and statesman, president of the republic from 1958-1969.

Eduardo Frei (1911-1982), Chilean statesman, first Christian Democrat president of Chile, 1964-1970.

Gabriela Mistral (1889-1957), Chilean poet and diplomat; Nobel laureate in 1945; earlier was head of the Letters and Arts Committee of the Institute for International Cooperation of the League of Nations.

Theologians, Church Historians and Writers

St. Athanasius (297?-373), Doctor of the Church known for his defense of the Incarnation and Redemption.

St. Augustine (354-430), Doctor of the Church, whose more than 200 works, 300 letters and 400 sermons helped give definition to Christianity.

St. Justin (110?-165?), the first important Christian apologist, who opened a school of philosophy in Rome and was martyred, probably for having routed a Cynic philosopher in public debate.

St. Bede (672?-735), the "Venerable," who was one of the most learned individuals of his times and who had a major influence on literature in England.

St. Thomas Aquinas (1225-1274), Doctor of the Church, who systematized Catholic theology and thought.

John Duns Scotus (1270?-1308), who wrote commentaries on the Scripture and on Aristotle and became famous for his *Opus Oxoniense*, commentary on the Sentences of Peter Lombard, and *Reportata Parisiensia*.

Thomas a Kempis (1380?-1471), famous for his biographies, sermons, hymns, tracts on monastic life and an immortal book of spiritual meditation, *The Imitation of Christ*.

Francois de Salignac de la Mothe Fenelon (1651-1715), bishop and writer known for a remarkable eloquence, purity of style and a tender, mystic devotion.

John Baptiste Henri Lacordaire (1802-1861), an early lapsed Catholic who returned, became a Dominican, and achieved fame for his "conferences" or lectures at Notre Dame Cathedral which provided a bridge between religion and revolutionary zeal.

John Henry Newman (1801-1890), convert become cardinal, who was a leader in the Oxford or Tractarian Movement.

Ronald Arbuthnott Knox (1888-1957), convert become monsignor, famous for his writings, broadcasts, sermons, translation of the Bible, and ephemera, including a number of mystery stories.

Biographical Sketches

Following are biographical sketches of some 20th-century Catholics who have helped make Catholicism if not always a holier religion, then at least an interesting one. Some were born in the last century, but by and large their mark was made in this one. All of the subjects are deceased except for Graham Greene, who at 81 is still spicing the Roman-Catholic scene that he joined as a young man. Since Greene spans most of the century and has contributed so much, he is included. It is an arbitrary inclusion, which could easily have been extended to others.

Belloc, Hilaire (1870-1953), author. Born in France, educated at the Oratory School at Edgbaston (where Newman presided) and at Balliol College, Oxford, Belloc was historian, biographer, essayist, travel writer, poet, sometimes sketcher, indomitable controversialist and unblushing Catholic, who would argue in *Europe and the Faith* (1920) that "the Church is Europe: and Europe is the Church." He wrote with great speed, dispensing with references and detailed footnotes, a practice which exposed him to criticism from scholars and academics. To be sure, there was an unevenness in his work, but he had a huge following, and some of his books achieved a modest permanence, including *The Path to Rome* (1902), *A Bad Child's Book of Beasts* (1896), and a series of essays, *On Nothing, On Everything, On Anything, On Something, On* (1908-1911, 1923). Between 1927 and 1939 he undertook a modernization of Lingard's *History of England*. He wrote biographies of Wolsey, Cranmer, Milton and James II—and, out of his French background, Danton, Richelieu, Robespierre and Marie Antoinette. He was so prolific that once, in dedicating a work to Maurice Baring *(The Cruise of the Nona)*, he suggested that books ought to be numbered like the streets of America. In such a case, *The Cruise of the Nona* (1925) would have been Belloc 106. Belloc was a close associate of G.K. Chesterton, and Chesterton often illustrated Belloc's novels. George Bernard Shaw referred to the pair as ChesterBelloc, defining the term as an animal with four legs capable of doing infinite harm. Belloc became a British subject in 1903 and served from 1906-1910 in Parliament as the member for South Salford. He lectured widely and was a frequent visitor to the United States. (His wife was an American, Elodie Hogan, a native of Napa, California. They married in 1896 and had four children.) Belloc taught at Fordham and Notre Dame Universities. Boston College acquired his library and files in 1981, a mountainous collection of some 10,000 books and hundreds of thousands of papers. Throughout his life, Belloc was an aggressive defender of Catholic positions and Catholic interpretations of history, inducing the Sheed & Ward house organ, "This Publishing Business," to remark in May, 1939: "What Belloc writes goes *home*; they [his opponents] could no more ignore him than they could ignore a tiger on the doorstep." His Catholic attitudes were not matched by a similar solicitude for Jewish people, a circumstance which has left him open to charges of anti-Semitism. Belloc suffered an incapacitating stroke in 1946, and died in his home in Sussex, near West Grinstead, of burns suffered when he fell near an open fireplace.

Bloy, Leon (1846-1917), author. Born in Perigueux, Guyenne, France, of French-Spanish parentage, Bloy lost his faith as a teenager, but returned to the church toward the turn of the century. In the meanwhile, he fought in the Franco-Prussian War, served as secretary to Barbey d'Aurevilly, and achieved fame as a writer of critical essays (on Carlyle and others), pamphlets and other works attacking injustices. He wrote two novels, the second of which is considered his masterwork, *La Femme pauvre* (1897), translated into English in 1937 as *The Woman Who Was Poor*. The book was hailed as powerful in the manner of John dos Passos, yet spiritual in the manner of the Bible. Bloy was influenced by Huysmans, with whom he feuded, Beaudelaire and Father Tardif de Moidrey. A fiery genius, he also influenced others, including Jacques Maritain, his wife Raissa, and her sister, Vera Oumansoff. Their conversion to Catholicism was due in large part to Bloy. When the three entered the church in 1906, Bloy was their godfather. Bloy died November 3 in Bourg-la-Reine, France.

Chesterton, Gilbert Keith (1874-1936), author. Born in London, Chesterton was one of the great controversialists of his age, jousting constantly with government, the establishment and individuals like Kipling, Wells and Shaw—particularly Shaw. The two debated scores of times on platforms and in print, but retained a personal affection for one another. They were a study in opposites, physically as well as intellectually. Shaw was tall and bone thin; Chesterton, tall and heavy, weighing some 350 pounds. The story is told that the two encountered one another in a restaurant. "To look at you," remarked Chesterton, "people would think there was a famine in England." "And to look at you," countered Shaw, "they would think you were the cause of it." Chesterton was an essayist, critic, novelist, biographer, detective-story writer, and poet. Like Belloc, he frequently expressed his religious views in writing. Chesterton was a convert to Catholicism in 1922, but for years prior to that event he was an apologist for Christian theology. Asked why he became a Catholic, Chesterton responded, ''To get rid of my sins.'' His books include *The Man Who Was Thursday* (1908), *The Napoleon of Notting Hill* (1904), *Heretics* (1905), *Orthodoxy* (1908), and a series of detective stories beginning in 1911 and dealing with the adventures of one Father Brown. The character was molded after the priest who eventually received him into the Church, Father John O'Connor of Beaconsfield. Chesterton had moved there in 1909 into a country home called Overroads. Other books included *The Everlasting Man* (1925), an outline of history; biographies of St. Francis, St. Thomas Aquinas and Stevenson, among others; collections of essays, and *Autobiography* (1936). He was also active as an editor with the *New Witness* and later *G.K.'s Weekly.* Chesterton loved merriment, conversation and companionship, as might be deduced from his quatrain:

> And Noah he often said to his wife
>   when he sat down to dine,
> ''I don't care where the water goes if
>   it doesn't get into the wine.''

He died at Beaconsfield at age 62.

Coughlin, Charles Edward (1891-1979), radio priest. Coughlin was born in Hamilton, Ontario, son of a Great-Lakes American seaman and a Canadian mother. He was graduated from St. Michael's College, University of Toronto, and ordained in 1916. He taught for several years at Assumption College in Ontario before coming to the United States and being incardinated into the then-Diocese of Detroit in 1923. In 1926 he was assigned to establish a parish at Royal Oak, Michigan. He built the Shrine of the Little Flower (St. Therese of Lisieux), and proceeded to bring fame and notoriety to himself. The saga began after the Ku Klux Klan burned a cross in his churchyard, and Coughlin was extended time on Detroit's Station WJR to explain Catholicism. He quickly became a fixture on radio. Originally his was a children's program, but by 1931 he had his own private network, and he built an audience that grew to an estimated 40-million listeners as his broadcasts branched from religion to social and political issues. He sprinkled his texts liberally with quotations from papal social encyclicals, but Coughlin was neither theologian, economist nor astute political analyst. He blamed the depression on the bankers; castigated President Franklin D. Roosevelt; and found Communism everywhere. As war threatened Europe he became isolationist, pro-Nazi and anti-Semitic. (He harrangued on what he called the British-Jewish-Roosevelt conspiracy.) The reins on Coughlin were so loose during the decade of the 1930s that many wondered whether Coughlin spoke for the church. In 1934 Coughlin founded the National Union for Social Justice to lobby in Washington for legislation, and in 1936 he established the magazine *Social Justice* to promote the Union's principles. In 1936 he formed the Union Party with Congressman William Lemke of North Dakota as its presidential nominee, and he vowed to quit his radio program if Lemke did not receive 9-million votes. Lemke received only one-million, and Coughlin did go off the air. But he was back on a few months later, saying the program was being resumed according to the dying request of his bishop, Michael J. Gallagher. Gallagher had indeed been a supporter, but not so his successor from Rochester, Bishop Edward Mooney, later to become cardinal. Coughlin came under increasing pressure from Mooney and Rome, but curiously neither succeeded in silencing him. He was forced to abandon his radio program after the National Association of Broadcasters issued a code which forbade controversial broadcasters unless they were part of a panel; Coughlin, a demagogue, had to cancel his radio series for 1940-1941. Coughlin continued his crusade in the pages of *Social Justice,* but then the Government banned it from the mails for violating the Espionage Act. Coughlin was out of business. He stayed on as pastor of the Shrine of the Little Flower, retiring in 1966. He spent his last years in seclusion, breaking his silence only a few times to denounce Communism and Vatican Council II.

Day, Dorothy (1897-1980), social activist. Born in the Bath Beach section of Brooklyn of vaguely Protestant parents, Day grew up in Chicago, where her father was a sports reporter. The family moved briefly to San Francisco, but returned to Chicago after the earthquake of 1906 destroyed their possessions. She entered the University of Illinois at Urbana, but withdrew after two years and followed the family to New York, where her father had joined the *Morning Telegraph* as racing editor. Day worked at a series of jobs with the *New York Call, The Masses* and *The Liberator,* all left-wing journals, at the same time becoming caught up in radical issues. She was arrested in Washington in 1917 during a women's-suffragist demonstration. During World War I she was an ardent pacifist, a sentiment she would retain all her life. Her friends numbered Mike Gold, Max Eastman and Eugene O'Neill. Still groping for her life's objective, Day tried nursing, slipped off to Europe for six months, returned to Chicago (where she worked for the Communist cause), then located in New Orleans for a short stint with the *New Orleans Item.* Meanwhile, she wrote a play and a novel, the *Eleventh Virgin,* which was picked up by Hollywood for the then-grand sum of $5,000. With it she purchased a cottage on Staten Island and entered a common-law relationship with Forster Battingham, by whom she had a daughter, Tamar. She had the daughter baptized a Catholic, then entered the church herself in 1927, leaving Battingham in the process. In 1933 she met Peter Maurin, an impassioned Catholic social theorist, and together they launched *The Catholic Worker,* a newspaper that grew into a movement to help the needy and downtrodden. The movement grew to 60 Catholic Worker communities across the country and a few in foreign countries: farming communes, urban houses of hospitality, artisan colonies. Day lived in the house of hospitality that moved between addresses in New York's Bowery district, but she traveled regularly to Catholic Worker communities elsewhere, keeping a journal which she published in *The Catholic Worker* as the column "On Pilgrimage." She continued to witness for various causes, and as late as 1973, when she was 76-years-old, was arrested during a United Farm Workers demonstration led by Cesar Chavez. In the 1950s she had refused to participate in air-raid drills or to pay Federal taxes. The latter action eventually brought an Internal Revenue Service claim against her in 1972 for $296,359 in taxes owed. The outcry was such, including on the editorial page of *The New York Times*, that the IRS quietly folded its case. In all, Day spent 45 years in the Catholic Worker movement, supervising its soup kitchens, distributing food and clothing, providing free shelter and espousing a voluntary poverty, all in the name of Christian charity. She suffered a heart attack in 1975, and died five years later. Several of her books were reissued in 1978, including her autobiography, *The Long Loneliness* (1952). In 1972 she accepted Notre Dame University's Laetare Medal, but generally she spurned honors.

Feeney, Leonard (1897-1978), author, lecturer, priest. A native of Lynn, Massachusetts, Feeney entered the Jesuit Order in 1914, when he was 17. He enjoyed a sensational early career as a writer of poetry, short stories, biographies and essays, and by his mid-40s had a dozen books to his credit, notably *In Towns and Little Towns* (1927) and *Fish on Friday* (1934). He served as poetry editor of *America*, as president of the Catholic Poetry Society, as a broadcaster on the "Catholic Hour," as a professor at Weston, and as a preacher in St. Patrick's Cathedral in New York, where he called for an American saint ("How about a St. Barbara of Brooklyn, a St. Helen of the Bronx, and a St. Robert of Jersey City?") only to have *Time* magazine whimsically counter with a list of its own: a St. Francis, a St. Knute and a St. Joyce, after Father Francis Duffy of the Fighting 69th Regiment, Notre Dame football coach

Knute Rockne and poet Joyce Kilmer. In 1943 Feeney became permanent chaplain of St. Benedict Center, a gathering place in Cambridge for Catholics attending Harvard, Radcliffe and other nearby "secular" colleges. There he became a cult figure and controversialist because of his rigid insistence on the ancient but disowned Catholic adage, *extra ecclesiam nulla salus*—"outside the Church, no salvation." A strong anti-Semitism permeated his lectures and the center's literature. Protestants too were anathematized, as well as Catholics who associated with them. Soon Feeney found himself embroiled in a dispute which extended from Boston to Rome. He was dismissed from the Jesuits in 1949 and excommunicated by Rome in 1953. Meanwhile a small but zealous band grouped around him as the "Slaves of the Immaculate Heart of Mary." In 1958 Feeney and his community moved to a farm in Still River, Massachusetts. From there members of the community continued to distribute their literature, but as the years passed, they abandoned their inflammatory positions and became more conciliatory. In 1972 the ecclesiastical censures against Feeney were removed, and in 1974 most members of the community were reconciled with the church and accepted therein as the Pious Union of Benedictine Oblates of Still River. Feeney died in Still River four years later, on January 30.

Greene, Graham (1904-   ), English novelist and journalist. Oxford educated, Greene for decades has been one of England's most prolific and Catholicism's most controversial writers, though practically he has removed himself a distance from both. He resides in Antibes, France and he has spoken of himself as a kind of Catholic agnostic. Still his Englishness and his Catholicism have remained very much a part of his life and work. In 1941 Charles A. Brady wrote in *America* that "only Graham Greene, among contemporary melodramatists, fights the battle of Augustine in the mantle of Buchan and Conrad and Dostoievski." The same could be said in 1985. A convert to Catholicism, Greene has described himself not as a

Catholic author, but rather "a writer who happens to be Catholic," adding "I don't want to be a burden to the church." Nevertheless at times, some in the church have considered him a burden. A church censor once condemned *The Power and the Glory*, Greene's novel about a fugitive whiskey-priest in Mexico, only to have Pope Paul VI congratulate him on the same work years later. Greene had a brief flirtation with the Communist Party while at Oxford. He said he did it "for the fun of the thing" and also because he had hopes of getting a free trip to Moscow. When the trip did not materialize, he dropped from the group, but the association later troubled others. He became a prohibited immigrant to the United States under the McCarran Act, and in 1954 he was deported from Puerto Rico. He spoke of the incident as "an occasion I shall always remember with pleasure. Life is not rich in comedy; one has to cherish what there is of it and savor it during bad days." Greene has produced virtually a book a year. Many have been made into movies. His so-called theological novels (*The Power and the Glory*, 1940; *The Heart of the Matter*, 1948; and *The End of the Affair*, 1951) were favorite reading and intellectual exercises for Catholics in their time. At 81 Greene is still writing and making an occasional lecture appearance, as at Georgetown University in October, 1985. The university's Lauinger Library has an extensive collection of Greene material, including manuscripts of novels, first editions and letters, notably a 30-year correspondence with Evelyn Waugh. Greene is regularly passed over by the Nobel Prize judges, an action which speaks more about them than it does Greene.

Kennedy, John Fitzgerald (1917-1963), President of the United States. Born in Brookline, Massachusetts, on May 29, Kennedy belonged to a famous family, whose name he glamorized further by achieving the presidency of the United States, the first Catholic in history to do so. His father, Joseph P. Kennedy, was a wealthy financier and Ambassador to England from 1937-1940; his mother, Rose

Fitzgerald, was the daughter of a two-term mayor of Boston, John F. "Honey Fitz" Fitzgerald. Kennedy was educated at Choate and Harvard, graduating *cum laude* from the latter in 1940. His bachelor thesis, based on observations drawn while serving as his father's secretary in London, was published as *While England Slept* (1940), and achieved considerable success. Later a book written while recovering from a back operation won a Pulitzer Prize: *Profiles in Courage* (1956). Kennedy abandoned plans for graduate studies and enrolled in the Navy in 1941, serving as a PT boat commander in the Pacific. His boat was sunk by a Japanese destroyer off the Solomon Islands, and Kennedy suffered back injuries which troubled him the rest of his life. He entered politics in 1946 as a congressman from Massachusetts, and in 1952 he advanced to the Senate by unseating Henry Cabot Lodge Jr. Kennedy was not a particuarly visible senator, but his strong showing in his bid for the vice-presidency at the 1956 National Democratic Convention projected him in name and image to the country. In 1960 he won the presidential nomination itself, after a stunning primary victory in West Virginia, where his chances were held slim. He narrowly defeated Richard M. Nixon for the presidency, thus becoming the nation's 35th President, and at 43 the youngest ever elected. The campaign was highlighted by an appearance by Kennedy before the Houston Ministerial Association, where he laid to rest old biases about a Catholic being able to serve as President entirely free of Roman allegiances and entanglements. As President, Kennedy offered a program he called the New Frontier. It called for accelerated activity in space; broadened civil rights for blacks (Kennedy was the first President specifically to identify the race issue as a moral one); increased aid to education and depressed areas of the country; and a medical-care program for the elderly. Most were incorporated into President Lyndon B. Johnson's Great Society program after JFK's death. In foreign affairs Kennedy concluded the 1963 treaty with Russia banning the testing of nuclear weapons in space and underseas, but two crises involving Cuba caused apprehension world-wide. One was the Bay of Pigs invasion of 1961, a scheme to depose Fidel Castro that Kennedy inherited from the Eisenhower Administration and allowed to proceed despite personal doubts; the other was the Cuban missile crisis, which brought the United States into nuclear confrontation with Russia over the issue of ballistic missile bases in Cuba within easy range of the United States. On the first, Kennedy suffered a complete humiliation; on the second, he achieved a nervous success, when the missile bases were dismantled. In other areas of foreign policy, Kennedy established the Peace Corps, a volunteer program that continues in 1986, and an Alliance for Progress program to help Latin American countries. However, he deepened American involvement in Vietnam by expanding aid to its anti-Communist forces, a decision which would have disastrous consequences in subsequent years. Kennedy was assassinated on a visit to Dallas on November 22, 1963. He was only 46-years-old. The killing was done by Lee Harvey Oswald, who himself was assassinated by Jack Ruby while in police custody and being moved from one location to another. The bizarre sequence of events fed theories of a broad political conspiracy being at work, but a presidential commission report found otherwise.

Lavanoux, Maurice (1894-1974), architect. Born in New York City and educated in Montreal, at Columbia and Atelier Hirons in New York, Lavanoux served in World War I as an interpreter with the American Expeditionary Force in France in 1917-1918. He continued his studies at Atelier Laloux in Paris, then spent 15 years with architectural firms in New York and Boston. He was one of the founders of the Liturgical Arts Society in 1928, and from 1932 until its folding in 1972 for lack of funds he served as editor of the Society's distinguished quarterly, *Liturgical Arts*. Over those years he waged persistent, if gentle, warfare against imitative, tasteless and unimaginative church art. He wrote and lectured widely on church art and architecture, and was consulted on many ecclesiastical building projects both in the United States and Canada. However, when the Vatican established its Gallery of Contemporary Art in 1973, Lavanoux was not consulted, to his annoyance. "Why are Catholic sources slighted here and in Rome?" he asked in his diary. "Why are those of us who have worked and slaved for decades for a modern and religious art...so crudely bypassed?" Some felt that Lavanoux might have helped save the Gallery from becoming a "commercial affair" cluttered with secondary works by otherwise top-grade talent. In later years, Lavanoux edited the magazine *Stained Glass* and was closely associated with the Museum of Contemporary Christian Art in New York City. He was a Knight Commander of St. Gregory, honorary member of the American Institute of Architects, and holder of several honorary degrees. He died at 80, asleep in an armchair in his Queens home. The date was October 21.

Maritain, Jacques (1882-1973), philosopher and diplomat. Born in Paris, Maritain was baptized a Protestant, but converted to Catholicism with his wife Raissa Oumansoff Maritain in 1906 under the influence of Leon Bloy and the philosophy of St. Thomas Aquinas. Maritain became the leading neo-Thomist of his times, and played a leading role in the Catholic revival in France in the early decades of the century. In 1917 the bishops of France asked Maritain to prepare a manual of philosophy for use in seminaries, and the work, *Introduction to Philosophy*, resulted in his receiving the title of Doctor *ad honorem* from the Vatican's Congregation of Studies. Maritain opposed the political thought of Charles Maurras, and thus was on the right side of the 1927 Action Francaise controversy when Rome condemned the movement. Maritain traveled and lectured widely, and for years taught regularly at the Pontifical Institute of Medieval Studies in Toronto and at the University of Chicago. When France fell in 1940, Maritain was on a lecture tour in the United States, and he remained for the duration, teaching at Columbia,

Princeton, Toronto and Chicago until 1945, when he was named French Ambassador to the Vatican. It was an interesting appointment, as Maritain's father had earlier played an important role in French politics and was the defender of French interests in the peace negotiations with Germany at the end of the 1870-1871 Franco-Prussian War. Maritain served at the Vatican until 1948, whereupon he returned to the United States and a professorship at Princeton, a post he held to 1960. In 1958 Notre Dame University established a Jacques Maritain Center to further studies in areas of his philosophical thought. (Maritain believed that to think is to act, and that the person transcended the political community—hardly a presumption in the totalitarian period that coincided with much of his life.) Maritain wrote a steady stream of books, more than 50 in all. One of them, *True Humanism* (1938) became a kind of manifesto for the involved Catholic layperson of the mid-century through its careful distinction between action in the spiritual and the temporal orders ("to speak as a Catholic having a certain temporal position and to speak in the name of Catholicism are two very different things"). Maritain was long a folk-hero for Catholic liberals, but there was reassessment by some after publication of *The Peasant of Garonne* (1968), a bitter, caustic attack on the "new theology" and its alleged spawners, Teilhard de Chardin, Marx, existentialists and phenomenologists. Reviewing the book in the *New Republic*, Daniel Callahan recalled the Lenin maxim that the worst enemies of new radicals were old liberals. Traditionalists, on the other hand, saw the book as a clear-eyed reading of where Vatican Council II had led the church. Maritain died April 28 in Toulouse.

Maritain, Raissa Oumansoff (1883-1960), author. Born at Rostov-on-the-Don in Russia of Jewish parents, Raissa Oumansoff was raised in a strictly orthodox family in Rostov and later at Marioupol, a small town on the Sea of Azov, northeast of the Black Sea and connected with it by the Kerch Strait. When she was 10, her parents left

Russia to escape persecution of the Jews. The family settled in France where it was felt there would be greater opportunities for Raissa and her sister Vera. A brilliant student, Raissa enrolled at the Sorbonne, where she met Jacques Maritain, whom she married in 1904 and with whom she and her sister converted to Catholicism in 1906. At the Sorbonne, Raissa shared Jacques' disillusionment with the Sorbonne's scientism, and with him was caught up in an enthusiasm for St. Thomas Aquinas. She shared her husband's lifelong interest in Aquinas, and collaborated with him on books and other writings explicating the wisdom of Aquinas for the 20th century. She too was thus in the forefront of the French Catholic revival of the period. A frail but vivacious woman, Raissa Maritain joined with her husband in making their home in Meudon, outside Paris, a center for Catholic intellectual life with Sunday open-houses and a week's retreat each fall conducted by a Dominican. She also wrote a number of books of her own, including four volumes of poetry, a children's life of Aquinas, and the memoirs *We Have Been Friends Together* (1942) and *Adventures in Grace* (1945). She died September 12 in Paris.

Mauriac, Francois (1885-1970), author. Born in Bordeaux, Mauriac belonged to a pious and strict upper-middle-class family of landowners and vintners. Mauriac settled in Paris, but he did most of his writing in the Bordeaux region during his summer visits to the family estates. His first two books were volumes of poetry, but he turned to prose with the novels *L'Enfant Charge de Chaines* (1913) and *La Robe Pretexte* (1914). The novels were flawed, but Mauriac continued to write and in 1922 established himself as a major novelist with *Le Baiser au Lepreux (The Kiss to the Leper)*. In 1925 he won the coveted Grand Prix du Roman of the Academie Francaise. This was followed by election to the Academie in 1933, the year after the appearance of his masterwork, *Le Noeud de Viperes* (Viper's Tangle). In 1952 he was awarded the Nobel Prize for literature. Mauriac was preoccupied with the conflict between flesh and the spirit, and his characters were continually at grips with the problems of sin, grace and salvation. His viewpoint was essentially, though not evangelistically, Catholic. Of his faith Mauriac remarked: "I belong to that race of people who, born in Catholicism, realize in earliest manhood that they will never be able to escape from it, will never be able to leave it or reenter it....[F]or myself, I remained attached to the church as narrowly as a man to this planet; fleeing from it would have been as mad as trying to flee from this planet. I remember with what ardor I set about, at the age of 16, proving to myself the truth of a religion to which I know myself bound for all eternity." Mauriac's depiction of the underside of Parisian society shocked some readers, but, as he remarked by way of defense, "In the world of reality you do not find beautiful souls in the pure state. These are only to be found in novels and bad novels at that." Mauriac also wrote plays, four volumes of journals and three volumes of memoirs, but it was his novels that solidified his reputation. For many he was the greatest French novelist since Marcel Proust. An outspoken polemicist, he denounced the totalitarianisms of the 1930s, and during World War II he worked with writers of the Resistance. In post-war France he was a strong supporter of Charles de Gaulle. He lived to his 85th year, and died in Paris on September 1.

Merton, Thomas (1915-1968), Trappist, author. Born in Prades, France, of a New Zealand landscape artist and American Quaker mother, Merton was schooled there and in England. He spent a year at Cambridge before entering Columbia University in New York, where he earned both bachelor's and master's degrees. Merton had departed Cambridge under something of a cloud, and at Columbia he flirted with Communism, but in 1938 he converted to Catholicism and this stabilized his life and gave it its essentially religious direction. Merton taught at Columbia and St. Bonaventure, worked at a Catholic settlement house in Harlem, then in 1941 joined the Order

of Cistercians of the Strict Observance (Trappists) at Gethsemani, Kentucky. He was ordained in 1949 and took the
name Father M. Louis. As a monk Merton lived a life torn
between commitment to the monastic ideal and concern
for suffering humankind. He lived in a world of silence,
but wrote for a world that came to expect one or two
books a year from him, along with a flow of articles. Between 1944 and 1947, Merton published three books of
poetry, then stunned the literary world with an account
of family life and the forces which led him to the Trappists. This was *The Seven Storey Mountain* (1948), a run-
away bestseller that brought him fame, celebrity status,
and a readership that devoured future books, such as *The
Waters of Siloe* (1949), *Sign of Jonas* (1953) and *No Man Is
an Island* (1955). Though living in a monastery, he became
a leader in the struggle for civil rights and racial justice,
even writing a number of freedom songs for the movement. As a pacifist he troubled about the arms race and
the Vietnam war, and wrote fervently on the topics. He
was especially appalled at the tendency of the West to
wrap its cause in a mantle of crypto-messianism. He
feared that the West's "incentive to wipe out Bolshe-
vism...may indeed be the most effective way of destroying Christendom, even though man may survive." In
1968 Merton went to the Far East to study Eastern
mysticism. It was his first lengthy trip away from Gethsemani in 26 years. While attending a conference in Bang-
kok, Thailand, he was the victim of a bizarre accident,
an electrical fan toppling over on him as he rested in bed
and electrocuting him. To compound the ironies of his
life, his body was returned to the United States in a military plane bearing the remains of young soldiers killed
in a war he abhorred, Vietnam.

Murray, John Courtney (1904-1967), theologian. A native of
New York City, Murray joined the Jesuit Order in 1920
and was ordained in 1932. He received his doctorate from
the Gregorian University in Rome in 1936, and thereupon
joined the faculty of Woodstock College, as a professor

of dogmatic theology. In 1951-1952 he was a visiting professor of philosophy at Yale. Murray's theological and
intellectual specialty was the relationship of Church and
State, and for years he wrote in esoteric or specialized
journals of limited circulation, arguing that Church and
State not only could be separate, but also that in
separateness resided greater freedom and fuller theological health for the church itself, particularly in the
pluralistic state which guaranteed freedom of religion.
The proposition was one of great contention at the time,
and in 1954 superiors directed that Murray stop writing
and lecturing on the subject, which he did. In 1960, Murray's writings were published as the book *We Hold These
Truths*, subtitled "Catholic Reflections on the American
Proposition." The book was hailed as "probably the most
significant statement on American democracy ever published." It became a bestseller and propelled Murray to
the cover of *Time* magazine, for December 12, 1960. When
Vatican Council II came along, Murray was "disinvited"
as a *peritus* (consulting expert) by the Apostolic Delegate
to the United States, Archbishop Egidio Vagnozzi. However, New York's Cardinal Spellman rectified that at the
Council's second session, bringing Murray to Rome in
1963 as his *peritus*. There Murray played a major role as
architect of the Council's Declaration on Religious Freedom. Murray died of a heart attack while riding in a taxi
in New York City, two years after the Council's close.
At his funeral, Jesuit Father Walter J. Burghardt eulo-
gized: "Unborn millions will never know how much their
freedom is tied to this man. . . . how much the civilized
dialogue they take for granted between Christian and
Christian, between Christian and Jew, between Christian
and unbeliever was made possible by this man, whose
life was a civilized conversation."

Murray, Philip (1886-1952), labor leader. Born in Blantyre,
Scotland, of Irish immigrant parents, Murray left school
after the sixth grade and followed his father into the coal
mines as a laborer. The family moved to the United States

in 1902 and settled in Pennsylvania, where Murray continued as a coal miner. He was elected president of a United Mine Workers of America (UMW) local in 1904, following a strike triggered by charges of his against a company checkweightman for cheating. The strike failed, but Murray's career was launched as a labor leader. He advanced rapidly in the UMW, in 1920 being appointed vice-president by UMW president John L. Lewis. At the 1935 convention of the American Federation of Labor (AFL), Murray campaigned for the formation of industrial unions. When the craft unions rejected the idea, the UMW and seven industrial unions walked out and formed the Congress of Industrial Organizations (CIO), with Lewis as president. A brilliant organizer, Murray was named head of the Steel Workers Organizing Committee (SWOC) in 1936, and in that role he won the right to organize Big Steel and later, Little Steel, although not painlessly. A Murray recommendation to strike against foot-draggers resulted in bloody clashes, one of which left 10 workers dead at the Republic Steel in South Chicago in 1937. Murray meanwhile was seeking the reunion of the AFL and CIO, a prospect vetoed by Lewis in 1937. Three years later, Murray found himself CIO president, when Lewis followed through on a threat to resign if President Roosevelt was re-elected in 1940. Lewis and Murray, associates for more than 20 years, broke with one another in 1942, when Lewis removed Murray from his UMW vice-presidency, alleging that his involvements as SWOC chairman were inconsonant with his duties at the UMW. The UMW subsequently withdrew from the CIO; the SWOC became the United Steel Workers of America; Murray became its president, and he served in that post and as CIO president for the rest of his life. His headquarters were in Pittsburgh. In 1949 he expelled Communist-dominated unions from the CIO, an action which cost the organization almost a third of its members. Earlier he had formed a CIO Political Action Committee, which fought among other things for a guaranteed annual wage and union pensions, and vehemently opposed the Taft-Hartley bill, the Labor-Management Relations Act of 1947. Murray died on a working visit to San Francisco on November 9. *Commonweal* commented on his passing: ''...Mr. Murray viewed himself as a true patriot. He believed that the greatest contribution he could make to the well-being of his country was to build up the labor movement, to educate the union rank and file to their vocational and national responsibilities. He had great faith in their potentialities, in their innate good sense. If the demands of the workers he represented always came first in his mind, he did not ignore the effects of their attainment on the nation as a whole. He saw things decidedly as a partisan, from the workers' standpoint, but not exclusively so. It is symbolic that he died in the midst of his work.''

O'Connor, Flannery (1925-1964), author. Born in Savannah, Georgia, and reared from age 12 in Milledgeville, O'Connor ranks as one of the most distinguished writers of the century, despite an opus which is relatively small. She wrote two novels, *Wise Blood* (1952) and *The Violent Bear It Away* (1960); a number of short stories that were collected as *A Good Man Is Hard to Find and Other Stories* (1955) and *Everything That Rises Must Converge* (1965); and essays and lectures that appeared posthumously as *Mystery and Manners: Occasional Prose,* under the editorship of Sally and Robert Fitzgerald. Thirty-one stories, 12 of them previously uncollected, were published in 1971 under the title *Flannery O'Connor: The Complete Stories.* There was a pronounced preoccupation in O'Connor's fiction with the grotesque and the bizarre, but the point of her art was not to sensationalize, but explore the disorders which created these conditions. She was a profoundly moral, distinctly Catholic writer with a keen sense of grace, sin, free will and the individual's need and struggle for redemption. O'Connor was educated at Georgia State College for Women and the University of Iowa, from which she received a master's degree in creative writing. She lived for a few years in New York City, returning to

Georgia when her health began to fail. She suffered from disseminated lupus. In 1951 she moved to the family farm "Andalusia," outside Milledgeville. She died August 3 in Milledgeville, shy of her 40th birthday.

Sheen, Fulton J. (1895-1979), archbishop. A native of El Paso, Illinois, Sheen was baptized Peter, took the name John at Confirmation, then subsequently adopted his mother's family name, Fulton, as his given name, retaining it for the remainder of his life. He grew up in Peoria and in 1919 was ordained a priest of that diocese. He acquired several graduate degrees and doctorates following studies at the Catholic University of America, Louvain, the Sorbonne and the Angelicum in Rome. After teaching in Europe, he joined the faculty at Catholic University in 1926 and quickly attracted attention as a teacher, lecturer and preacher with both eloquence and dramatic flair. In 1930 he became the first regular preacher on radio's "The Catholic Hour," and as Monsignor Fulton Sheen he built up a following of millions of listeners on 118 NBC stations. In 1940, he conducted the first religious service to be telecast in the United States, and in 1951 he had his own network show, "Life Is Worth Living." It was televised on 123 ABC stations and broadcast over 300 ABC radio stations, reaching a combined audience of 30-million people each week. The program left the air in 1957, but in 1966 Sheen was back with another show, "The Bishop Sheen Program," which also enjoyed a huge success. In the meanwhile, Sheen was writing books (more than 60 in all); writing columns for the daily and the Catholic presses; editing magazines; winning awards (including an Emmy Award in 1952); and serving in various ecclesiastical capacities. In 1950 he became national director of the Society for the Propagation of the Faith, and during 16 years in the post he developed the Society into the church's principal fund-raiser for the missions. In 1951 he was named an Auxiliary Bishop in the Archdiocese of New York, then under Cardinal Francis Spellman. There was a keen competitiveness between the two men—of image and over control of the Society's treasury. On the latter issue, Sheen took his case to Rome in 1957 and is said to have been triumphant. In 1966 Sheen was appointed Bishop of Rochester, but he had a stormy administration there and resigned under pressure in 1969. He was named a Titular Archbishop of Newport (Wales), and retired to private life in New York City as a writer and teacher. His last appearances as a preacher were at the Good Friday *tre ore* (three hours) services in St. Agnes' Church in mid-Manhattan. By then he was aged and in failing health, but he still attracted large congregations. Ideologically Sheen was a fierce anti-Communist; ecclesiastically he was a traditionalist. Many of his books of spirituality were national bestsellers, among them *Peace of Soul* (1949) and *Lift Up Your Heart* (1950). Sheen died in New York City on December 9.

Smith, Alfred Emanuel (1873-1944), governor. Born on New York City's Lower East Side, Smith grew up in straitened circumstances. His father was a truck-wagon driver; his mother, a piece-worker in an umbrella factory. The father died when Smith was 12, and two years later, a month before completing the eighth grade, Smith was forced to drop out of school to help support the family. He worked at a succession of jobs—as errand boy, clerk at the Fulton Fish Market, boiler worker—before being named a process server for the commissioner of jurors in 1895. It was an $800 a year job, and it launched Smith into a career in the public sector. In 1930 he stood for election as Tammany Hall's nominee for the Second Assembly District seat. He won easily, and quickly rose to prominence in Albany. He became Democratic majority leader in 1911 and speaker of the Assembly in 1913, in the meanwhile gaining extensive media attention as a member of the committee that revised the New York City Charter and as vice-chairman of the special Factory Commission, which brought the sweatshop in America at last under public scrutiny. Smith moved steadily upwards with Tammany and in the Democratic Party, being tapped successively for the posts of sheriff of New York County, president of the New York City Board of Aldermen, and finally governor of the state. Smith served four terms as governor, being elected in 1918, 1922, 1924 and 1926. His were efficient, progressive administrations that won him the reputation as one of the nation's ablest governors. He lost bids for the Democratic presidential nomination in 1920 and 1924, but was successful in 1928, thus becoming the first Catholic to be nominated for the presidency by a major American political party. The ensuing campaign was rife with religious bigotry. Between that, an undistinguished campaign of his own, and an inability to shake his big-city image and Tammany background, Smith went down to defeat to Herbert Hoover. It was a landslide margin: 444 electoral votes to Smith's 87. Smith sought the nomination again in 1932, but lost to Franklin D. Roosevelt. Smith and Roosevelt had long been close political allies, and Smith stumped for Roosevelt in 1932. Eventually Smith broke with Roosevelt, and mystifyingly drifted ideologically far to the right. He accused the Roosevelt administration of being alien and socialistic, and in 1936 and 1940 he supported Roosevelt's opponents, Alf Landon and Wendell Willkie, respectively. His last years were spent as chief executive officer of the then-new Empire State Building, a position which paid a large salary ($65,000) but which some thought reduced Smith to the level of being just one more of the building's super-attractions. Smith received many honorary degrees and awards, including the Laetare Medal for 1929. Pope Pius XI named him a papal chamberlain in 1938. He died October 4 in the hospital of the Rockefeller Institute in New York City.

Spellman, Francis J. (1889-1967), cardinal. Born in Whitman, Massachusetts, Spellman was educated in public schools there and at Fordham University. He studied for the priesthood at the North American College in Rome as a seminarian from the Archdiocese of Boston. On his return to Boston he was assigned humbling positions, such as circulation manager of *The Pilot*, the diocesan newspaper, by an ordinary who did not particularly admire his style or ambitions. The ordinary was Cardinal William Henry O'Connell. Spellman managed to be asked back to Rome in 1925 as director of a playgrounds project funded by the Knights of Columbus. He was named an attache in the Vatican Secretariat of State and thus was launched on a spectacular career. When Pope Pius XI formally inaugurated Vatican Radio in 1931, it was Spellman who translated his words to the English-speaking world. When Pius XI wanted his encyclical *Non Abbiamo Bisogno* on Italian Catholic Action spirited out of Italy so that it could be released free of Fascist censorship, Spellman was chosen to be its courier to Paris. In the meanwhile, Spellman had struck a friendship with Pius XI's Secretary of State, Cardinal Eugenio Pacelli, and this proved crucial to his future. In 1932 Spellman returned to Boston and a furious Cardinal O'Connell as an auxiliary bishop (O'Connell's cable of greeting read: WELCOME TO BOSTON. CONFIRMATIONS BEGIN ON MONDAY. YOU ARE EXPECTED TO BE READY.). He served seven difficult years under O'Connell, then was propelled to New York as archbishop by two extraordinary strokes of fortune: the death of Pius XI before he could confirm the appointment of Cincinnati's Archbishop John T. McNicholas to the post; and the elevation of Pacelli to the papacy as Pope Pius XII. Pacelli tapped Spellman for New York in 1939. As archbishop, Spellman served as military vicar to the 11-million Americans in the armed forces during World War II, a high-visibility office which took him to the outposts of the world in that and succeeding conflicts as well. He carried out secret worldwide missions for President Roosevelt, at the same time supervising an energetic archdiocesan administration that brought the archdiocese out of a $28-million debt and made it one of the premier sees of Catholic Christendom. His administration was a model of efficiency and ingenuity, but his personal record was spotted by a number of controversial actions which undid some of the great good for which he was responsible. In 1949 he used seminarians in an effort to break a gravediggers strike. A rabid anti-Communism led him into an ideological flirtation with Senator Joseph McCarthy, and an equally rabid patriotism blinded him to the realities of the Vietnam war. He also involved himself in movie-censorship fiascos, and in a public dispute with Mrs. Eleanor Roosevelt that required a Canossa-like call to her Hyde Park home. At Vatican Council II, Spellman was the most frequent of American speakers with 131 oral and written interventions. He spoke on every conciliar schema. But his historic contribution was in bringing Jesuit Father John Courtney Murray to the second and subsequent sessions as his *peritus* (expert), thus opening the Council to Murray's influence in discussions on religious freedom. Spellman hosted Pope Paul VI's 1966 visit to the United States, and his offer of resignation that same year on his 75th birthday was refused by Paul. Spellman died of a stroke on December 2, while preparing for another of his Christmastime visits to American troops abroad, a custom he had begun in 1942. He wrote a dozen books, among them *The Road to Victory* (1942), *Action This Day* (1943), *The Foundling,* a novel, (1951), and *What America Means to Me* (1953).

Stein, Edith (1891-1942), philosopher and mystic. Born in Breslau, Germany, of Jewish parentage, Stein was educated at the university there and at Gottingen, taught in Breslau schools, and received a doctorate in philosophy from Freiburg in 1916. She became an assistant and disciple of the phenomenologist Edmund Husserl, and attained remarkable success in the male world of German philosophy. In 1922 Stein converted to Catholicism, taught at the Dominican convent in Speyer, and undertook translations of the works of St. Thomas Aquinas and Cardinal Newman. In 1932 she was named a lecturer at the Educational Institute at Munster, but lost the post because of her Jewish ancestry when the Nazis came to power. In 1934 she entered the Carmelite Order, taking the name in religion of Benedicta of the Cross. The Carmelites transferred her to a convent in Echt, the Netherlands, in 1938 to protect her against the Nazis. She was arrested there in 1942 after the Nazis overran the Low Countries, and was deported to Auschwitz when she refused to deny her Jewish heritage. Vigorously opposed to Nazism, Stein was anxious to affirm her solidarity with the suffering Jewish people at whatever cost to herself. She died in the gas chambers of Auschwitz, around August 10. Her religious meditations and writings on philosophy and education were collected and published after her death. Among her books are *The Science of the Cross* (1960), a study of St. John of the Cross, and *Writings* (1956), an anthology.

Teilhard de Chardin, Pierre (1881-1955), paleontologist, Jesuit. Born in Sarcenat, France, Teilhard's family was one of the oldest in the Auvergne; the family tree claimed Pascal on the paternal side and Voltaire on the maternal. (The "de Chardin" was an appendage that arrived via a 19th-century marriage.) Teilhard entered the Jesuit Order at age 18, did a teaching internship in Cairo, and was ordained in England in 1912, where he had gone for theological studies. He served in World War I as a stretcher bearer with the French army, and was decorated for his bravery. After the war, he taught at the Institut Catholique in Paris, at the same time earning a doctorate in paleontology from the Sorbonne, received in 1922. Thereafter Teilhard moved in the worlds of science and religion, propounding a complex theory that evolution was a continuing Christological process, with "man" (humankind) the very "arrow" of evolution. He reasoned that evolution was an irreversible process planned by God and converging ultimately on God, as the universe continued to perfect itself through the evolving intelligence of man. Teilhard posited a starting point (Alpha) and a goal (Omega); each in effect was God, so that what began in God returned in time to God. His theories developed out of research and study which took him to China (where he spent many years, then was sealed off by World War II), central Asia, the East Indies, Burma, Java and Africa's sub-Sahara, and which involved him in many adventures, including the discovery of Peking Man and other fossils that greatly enlarged scientific knowledge about the origin of life. Teilhard wrote extensively, but little appeared publicly in his lifetime because of a censorship born of Rome's regarding him as a pantheist and evolutionist. Teilhard resorted to what he called *clandestins*, privately circulated writings. As his reputation grew, so did Rome's nervousness. Teilhard was not only forbidden to publish, but was also denied teaching positions. It was widely felt that Pope Pius XII's 1950 encyclical *Humani Generis*, warning against attempts to distort Catholic truths, had Teilhard specifically in mind. Teilhard concluded that he had become "an embarrassment" to ecclesiastical officialdom, and he and his superior decided that a "shelter out of France" might be best for all concerned. Teilhard went to New York in 1951 and assumed a post at the Wenner-Gren Foundation for Anthropological Research in uptown Manhattan. But a lifetime of harassment had taken its toll. In New York he felt himself "a bird of passage, or something of a parasite," a feeling compounded by his not being "completely at home here in my Order." (Initally, he was "billeted" in the Jesuits' St. Ignatius rectory on Park Avenue, near 83rd Street, but he was asked to find rooms elsewhere when bedrooms became scarce because of a renovation project.) Teilhard suffered frequent bouts of depression before dying of a heart attack on Easter Sundy, April 10, in New York. Teilhard's prudence in making a will conveying his writings to a literary executor, Mlle. Jeanne Mortier, resulted in the posthumous publication of his works, notably *The Phenomenon of Man* (1957) and *The Divine Milieu* (1960). Rome responded by banning Teilhard's writings from Catholic bookstores in 1957 and issuing a *monitum*, or formal warning, in 1962 against uncritical acceptance of the ideas of Teilhardism. In 1981, Papal Secretary of State Cardinal Agostino Casaroli wrote a letter in the name of the pope (John Paul II) on the occasion of an international symposium marking the centenary of Teilhard's birth, which letter praised Teilhard's "vast vision" and the "richness of his thought." The Vatican Press Office made clear, however, that the *monitum* was still in effect.

Undset, Sigrid (1882-1949), author. Born in Denmark of a Danish mother and Norwegian father (the noted archeologist Ingvald Martin Undset), Undset was raised in Oslo, then called Christiana, in a home steeped in the legend, folklore and history of Norway. It was a rearing that served her enormously as a novelist, notably in her trilogy *Kristin Lavransdatter* (1920-1922), dealing with devout Catholic Norway in the 13th and 14th centuries. This was followed by the tetralogy *The Master of Hestviken* (1925-1927). By 1928 her fame was firmly sealed, and that year she was awarded the Nobel Prize for literature. In the trilogy, tetralogy and other novels, religious problems are dominant, and reflect Undset's own preoccupation with such questions. She converted to Catholicism in 1924, and thereafter solved matters by its prescripts, seemingly in real life as well as in fiction. Her marriage to the painter Anders C. Svarstad was dissolved in 1925, presumably in conjunction with her conversion, he having been married before and theirs therefore being an allegedly invalid marriage, since the first wife was still living. Undset's later novels were on contemporary social and psychological themes, but religion continued to occupy their concerns. After her great success as a writer, Undset moved into a restored house dating from around the year 1000, and surrounded herself with medieval Norse fixtures, even garbing herself as a Norse matron of the Middle Ages. The German invasion of Norway in 1940 forced her to flee to the United States, where she lectured and wrote in behalf of her country and its government-in-exile. She had additional reason to work in opposition to the Nazis, since her son Anders was killed by them in 1940. Undset told of her flight from Norway in *Return to the Future* (1942), and followed it with *Happy Times in Norway* (1943), a book about the country she knew and loved. Undset returned to Norway in 1945, and died in Lillehammer four years later, on June 10.

Waugh, Evelyn (1903-1966), author. London born and Oxford educated, Waugh wrote books of biography (e.g., *Edmund Campion*, 1935), travel (*A Bachelor Abroad*, 1930), and social and political study (*An Object Lesson*, 1939), but his fame is rooted in his biting satires of life among the aesthetes and socialites of England, particularly during the 1920s and 1930s. The most exceptional of these books was *Brideshead Revisited* (1944), the story of the decline of a landed British Catholic family and its recovery of faith in the years between the two world wars. Waugh converted to Catholicism in 1930, and *Brideshead Revisited* demonstrated the sincerity and depth of that conversion. When American critic Edmund Wilson objected to emphases in the book, Waugh responded in *Life* for April 8, 1946: "He was outraged (quite legitimately by his standards) at finding God introduced into my story. I believe that you can only leave God out by making your characters pure abstractions. . . . [Modern novelists] try to represent the whole human mind and soul yet omit its determining character—that of being God's creature with a defined purpose. So in my future books there will be two things to make them unpopular: a preoccupation with style and the attempt to represent man more fully, which, to me, means only one thing, man in his relation to God." Conservative to the point of reactionism, Waugh's politics were Jacobite and his Catholicism Tridentine. Pope Pius XII is reported to have once protested to charges by Waugh against the church with the comment, "But Mr. Waugh, I too am a Catholic!" During World War II Waugh served in the Royal Marines and as a Commando with the rank of major, narrowly escaping death on one occasion when a transport plane in which he was a passenger crashed and burned. Waugh participated in the abortive British strike against Dakar in West Africa, then in 1944 he joined in the British military mission to the Yugoslav Partisans, parachuting into Tito's headquarters with Winston Churchill's son Randolph. Waugh's *Men at War* trilogy—*Men at Arms,* 1952; *Officers and Gentlemen,* 1955; *The End of the Battle,* 1961—analyzed the character of the war in the context of the eternal struggle between good and evil, and the concomitant temporal struggle between civilization and barbarism. Scholars saw the trilogy as an attempt to temper victory with remorse, while pointing up the collective guilt for what happened. Waugh made occasional trips to the United States, and in 1948 lampooned Hollywood's death-style in a notable farcical satire, *The Loved One.* He died April 10 at Combe Florey, near Taunton, in Somerset.

Yon, Pietro Alessandro (1886-1943), organist and composer. A native of Settimo Vittone, Italy, Yon studied at conservatories in Milan and Turin, and at St. Cecelia Academy in Rome. Twice he served as substitute organist at the Vatican—from 1905-1907 and 1919-1921. In 1907 Yon emigrated to the United States, and was naturalized in 1923. He was organist and choirmaster at St. Vincent Ferrer Church on Lexington Avenue in uptown Manhattan from 1907-1919 and again from 1921-1926. In 1926 he was accorded the title of honorary music director of St. Peter's Basilica in Rome. The following year Yon became music director at St. Patrick's Cathedral on Fifth Avenue in mid-Manhattan, a post he held with distinction until his death. He also served as organist for the NBC Symphony Orchestra under maestro Arturo Toscanini. As a composer Yon had more then 70 compositions of sacred music to his credit, including 13 Masses, motets and oratorios, notably "The Triumph of St. Patrick" (1934). He died in Huntington, Long Island, on November 22.

Section VII

Miscellanea

ABBESS is the title of the female superior of a community of 12 or more nuns living in an abbey. In medieval times, abbesses of large and important communities were known to exercise great power and authority, sometimes in rivalry to bishops and abbots. The *Capitularies* of Charlemagne speak of "certain abbesses who, contrary to the established discipline of the Church of God, presume to bless the people, impose their hands on them, make the sign of the cross on men, and confer the veil on virgins, imploring during that ceremony the blessing reserved exclusively to the priests." Bishops were told to forbid such practices in their dioceses.

ABBEY is an independent, canonically erected monastery with a community of not fewer than 12 religious. Historically, abbeys have been known to develop into important centers of population, commerce and industry by gathering around them thriving permanent settlements. This was particularly true in Germany and England. Among the first guest houses and infirmaries for sick travelers were those established at abbeys.

ABBOT is the title given to the male superior of a community of 12 or more monks. The name derives from "abba," the Syriac form of the Hebrew "ab," and means "father." St. Benedict commented that "an abbot who is worthy to have the charge of a monastery ought always to remember by what title he is called" and that "in the monastery he is considered to represent the person of Christ, seeing that he is called by His name." Abbots are commonly entitled to pontifical insignia, like mitre, crosier, pectoral cross, ring, gloves and sandals.

ABJURATION is a denial, disavowal or renunciation of a heretical position made under oath by a penitent Christian. In some instances, abjuration has been accompanied by the imposition of hands, as a sign that due penance has been done, or by unction, or both. The church once required that converts, whose baptism was considered valid or who were rebaptized conditionally on reception into the Catholic Church, make a profession of faith which contained an abjuration of heresy. This has since been mitigated.

ABORTION from the Latin *aboriri,* meaning "to perish," is the expulsion of a non-viable fetus from the womb of the mother. Accidental expulsion, as in instances of non-induced miscariages, is without moral blame. However, induced or direct abortion, wherein the fetus is deliberately and intentionally removed from the womb, is considered by the church as a violation of the Natural Law and of the Fifth Commandment, and is punishable in church law by excommunication. This penalty applies not only to the mother, but also to all who cooperate in the abortion, such as doctors, nurses and counselors. Direct abortion, including therapeutic abortion (e.g. for the physical and/or psychological wellbeing of the mother; to avoid the birth of an abnormal child; or out of social, familial or community considerations) is never justifiable. Indirect abortion, wherein the fetus is expelled during a medical procedure on the mother for reason other than procuring the expulsion of the fetus, is permissible under the principle of the Double Effect. A case in point would be a medical procedure undertaken to save the life of the mother; the expulsion of the fetus in such a case must not be either directly intended or directly sought. Vatican Council II labeled direct abortion "an unspeakable crime."

ABSOLUTION is the forgiveness of sins in the sacrament of reconciliation by an authorized priest acting in his role as agent of Christ and minister of the church. The power to absolve is a priest's through ordination and is exercised by juridical faculties conveyed by the priest's proper religious superior. In emergencies, any priest can absolve, including priests under censure and laicized priests. By the same token, absolution may be received from priests of a separated Eastern (Orthodox) church in the absence of clergy of the Catholic confession.

ADORATION in the ecclesiastical sense is a religious act offered to God in acknowledgement of God's supreme perfection and dominion. It is expressed by prayers and by reverence, and by the offering of sacrifice—though today adoration is commonly an act of the mind and will. Adoration belongs to God alone, whereas veneration belongs to Mary and the saints.

ADULTERY is the act of sexual intercourse between a married person and another to whom the person is not married, whether wed or single. It is a sin against the Sixth Commandment.

Any sin of impurity involving a married person who is not one's spouse (e.g., to lust in one's heart for another) has the nature of adultery.

ADVENT from the latin *advenio*, "to come to," is the period beginning with the Sunday nearest to the Feast of St. Andrew (November 30) and embracing the four Sundays prior to Christmas. It is the beginning of the ecclesiastical year in the Western churches, and the period set aside as one of preparation for the anniversary of the Lord's coming into the world.

AGAPE, from the Greek meaning "love" or "love feast," designates the meal eaten at certain gatherings of early Christians, and by extended definition is sometimes used in describing the Mass as the Eucharistic banquet. Originally, Agape was the celebration of a funeral feast honoring the dead. The Last Supper itself fits into this historical perspective, Our Lord choosing the funeral feast, his own, as the occasion for binding together those remaining faithful to his memory. In the sense that the Mass reenacts the Last Supper in the breaking of bread and the consecration, the Mass becomes an Agape. In the early church, Agapes were observed in connection with the Mass, with a ritual that included prayer, the washing of hands, reclining on couches, a meal featuring talk on pious subjects, the singing of psalms and improvised hymns, final prayer and departure. The Council of Carthage (397) ruled against Agapes because of abuses that had grown up around them. By the 5th century the Agape had become of infrequent observance, and between the 6th and 8th centuries it disappeared entirely from the churches.

AGGIORNAMENTO is an Italian word having the general meaning of bringing up to date, renewal or revitalization. It was the word Pope John XXIII used to sum up the need and idea for Vatican Council II, and it has passed into the English language as descriptive of the process of reform and renewal in the church.

AGNOSTICISM in the philosophical and religious senses implies the limitation of human knowledge and correspondingly an inability to know phenomena other than what appears to the senses. Theologically this would mean that it is impossible therefore for one to acquire knowledge of God. Immanuel Kant was a proponent of agnosticism. Vatican Council I rejected agnosticism with the declaration that "God, the beginning and end of all, can, by the natural light of human reason, be known with certainty from the works of creation."

AMEN is a Hebrew word meaning "certainly, truly," and used at the end of prayers and in the reception of the Eucharist it adds the individual's assent to the minister's or leader's prayer or declaration. Example: "Body of Christ," "Amen"—it is true; this is the Body of Christ. The word is common to Jewish worship and the Old Testament, and its use in the Christian liturgy helps bridge the link between the two testaments of the Bible, the people of the Covenant and the people of the Cross.

ANATHEMA is the word adopted by the early church to designate the exclusion of a sinner from the community of the faithful, but its use was reserved chiefly for heretics. For several centuries anathema did not seem to differ from excommunication, but beginning with the 6th century a distinction was made between the two—excommunication separating an individual from the society of the faithful and anathema separating the person from the body of Christ, which was the church. The Latin phrase *anathema sit*, used by popes and councils, is intended to convey rejection and the penalty of excommunication.

ANCHORITES were members of the early church who shunned the world and lived in isolation, many going off into the desert, where they spent their lives in isolation. As such they were the precursors of monastic life and cenobites, who live, pray and work in common. One of the strangest groups of solitaries was the Stylites or Pillar Hermits, who mounted high columns and lived there for years, exhorting and instructing the crowd below. They are recorded primarily between the 4th and 10th centuries, with the asceticism of a few (e.g., Simeon Stylites the Elder and Simeon Stylites the Younger) winning for them the designation of saint.

ANGELISM is the denial of the embodied human condition. It is considered a heresy.

ANGELS are represented in the Bible as a body of spiritual beings intermediate between God and humans, and grouped into nine choirs. St. Thomas divides the nine choirs into three hierarchies relative to their said proximity to God. In the first hierarchy he placed Seraphim, Cherubim and Thrones; in the second, Dominations, Virtues and Powers; in the third, Principalities, Archangels and Angels. Scriptural names of individual angels are assigned only to Raphael, Michael and Gabriel. Fallen or bad angels are those who allegedly refused to serve God, fell from grace, and were banished to hell.

ANNULMENT is a declaration by competent church authority that no marital bond exists in what seems to have been a valid marriage. In other words, from the beginning there was no marrige because of the existence of an impediment, unknown or concealed. An impediment could be one of several kinds, such as minority of age, impotency, consanguinity, abduction, conspiracy, or the involvement of sacred orders or perpetual vows among one or both parties. The power to pronounce an annulment is vested in the main with diocesan marriage tribunals and the Sacred Roman Rota. An annulment is not to be confused with a divorce, which is a civil decree issued for civil purposes, and not affecting a valid marriage, which in the eyes of the Church still exists, the civil decree notwithstanding.

ANTEDILUVIANS were the people who lived before the great biblical flood. The Bible enumerates ten patriarchs of the period: Adam, Seth, Enos, Cainan, Malaleel, Jared, Henoch, Methusala, Lamech and Noe. The patriarchs are said to have been persons of extraordinary longevity, presumably because in the divine order of things God acted to increase the population and preserve the ancient tradition.

ANTICHRIST in the scriptural sense refers to the adversary of Christ, who will appear before the Second Coming and the end of the world. The word Antichrist occurs specifically only in the Epistles of St. John, though St. Paul's references in Second Thessalonians to the Great

Revolt, the man of sin, and the day of the Lord are also thought to relate to the Antichrist. Most agree that the Apocalypse refers to the Antichrist, but there is dispute whether the Antichrist is Satan, the red dragon, or one of several variously described beasts, like the beast with the seven heads and ten horns.

ANTIPOPE is the designation given to false claimants to the papacy, in opposition to the canonically elected pope. Thirty-seven pretenders or false popes have been recorded in history, the first being Hippolytus in the 3rd century and the last Amadeus of Savoy (Felix V), a pretender from November, 1439, to April 1449.

APOCALYPSE, from the Greek word "to reveal," is the name given to the last book of the Bible. It is also known as the Book of Revelation and the Apocalypse of John, and is primarily concerned with events hidden in the future, including the end of the world and a vision of a new heaven and a new earth.

APOCRYPHA, from the Greek word "hidden," designate works which allegedly were written by biblical personalities or persons associated with them. Examples would be the writings of the Shepherd of Hermas, the Epistle of Barnabas, the Didache, or Teaching of the Twelve Apostles. Though some apocrypha are held to belong to patristic literature, questions persist about the genuineness and canonicity of most apocrypha.

APOLOGETICS is the theological science which has as its purpose the explanation and defense of the Catholic religion and the reasons for beliefs through systematic use of reason, history, science, philosophy, comparative religions, etc. The word derives from the Greek word for apology or defense. Its adoption in the Catholic lexicon is not considered an altogether happy one because of the resultant defensive and/or reactionary implications. Justin and Irenaeus were noted apologists of the early church, and in the 19th century Cardinal Newman used the term "Apologia pro Vita Sua" in the autobiographical treatise defending his conversion from Anglicanism to the Roman Catholic Church. The tone of Apologetics has varied over the centuries, depending on the circumstances of the times, but its objective has remained more or less constant: the preparation for response to God in faith. As a theological science, Apologetics traditionally has fallen into three main divisions: study of religion in general and grounds for belief in a Supreme Being; study of revealed religion and grounds for Christian belief; study of the church of Christ and grounds for the Catholic belief.

APOSTASY in its etymological sense signifies the desertion of a post or giving up a state of life. Catholicism regards the word in a threefold sense: apostasy *a fide* or *perfidiae*, which is the giving up of the faith; apostasy *a religione* or *monachatus*, which is a religious' leaving of the religious life; and apostasy *ab ordine*, which is a cleric's abandoning of the ecclesiastical state.

APOSTLES' CREED is a formula expressing the fundamental tenets of Christian belief. The tenets number 12, and the coincidence of that number and the number of apostles helped foster the ancient theory that the creed was not only written by the Apostles, but that each apostle contributed one of the 12 articles. The theory is questioned by scholars who assign the creed's origin to the post-apostolic age. The common, current wording of the Apostles' Creed derives from the Council of Trent.

ASHES are a sacramental of the church, used on the first day of Lent, Ash Wednesday, to remind the faithful to do penance and to remember that into dust they will return. The ashes are secured from the burning of the palms of Palm Sunday or the Sunday of the Passion. The symbolic association of ashes with penance traces back to the Old Testament.

ATHANASIAN CREED is a terse exposition of the doctrines of the Trinity (three persons in the one God) and the Incarnation (the twofold nature in the one divine person of Jesus Christ), with a passing reference to several other dogmas. It is sometimes called the "Quincumque vult," from its opening words. The creed dates from the 4th century, and was long ascribed to St. Athanasius, a Bishop of Alexandria and Doctor of the Church. Later research, however, disputes that attribution of authorship, arguing variously for St. Hilary, St. Vincent of Lerins, Eusebius of Vercelli, Virgilius and others.

ATHEISM is the opposite of theism. It is a system of thought (speculative atheism) or a system of action (practical atheism) which denies the existence of God. Paradoxically the word has been used against any person or group calling into question the popular gods of the day. Socrates was accused of atheism, and Diagoras was called an atheist by Cicero. Not surprisingly, therefore, early Christians were called atheists by those now commonly regarded as pagans.

B

BEATIFICATION is the intermediate step between being declared Venerable and being canonized a saint. The beatification procedure involves investigation of the person's life, writings and heroic virtues, and the certification of at least two miracles worked by God through the candidate's intercession. A beatified person is entitled to be called Blessed, and may be honored locally or in limited ways in the liturgy.

BEATIFIC VISION is the sight and experience of God experienced by those who have achieved heaven.

BELL, BOOK AND CANDLE alludes to a solemn form of excommunication used in the medieval church. The procedure involved the reading of the decree of excommunication from the "book" of rituals; the casting down of a "candle," actually 12 candles, to symbolize the fall of the excommunicant from grace; and the tolling of the "bell" to accent the grave and somber nature of the occasion.

BIBLE SERVICE is a devotional exercise centered about prayer and the reading of Scripture, accompanied by a homily and meditation on the texts.

BIRTH CONTROL is the conscious planning of one's family. It may be either moral or immoral. Artificial birth control, or the use of medications, instruments or other mechanical means to prevent conception, is regarded by the church as contrary to natural and divine law. Natural birth control, such as use of the rhythm method, is a moral means of controlling conception, provided it is used for serious reason and with mutual consent. The church's birth-control position is based on the principle that the marital act must remain open to the possibility of the transmission of life.

BIRTHRIGHT is an independent nondenominational guidance and referral service offering pregnant women alternatives to abortion. Birthright was founded in Toronto in 1968 by Mrs. Louise Summerhill, and chapters have spread across Canada to many parts of the world, including the United States, Ireland, South Africa, Australia, New Zealand and England. Though not a specifically Catholic organization, its presence and commitment are welcomed and supported by many Catholic groups. Local chapters are listed in telephone directories.

'BROTHERS' OF CHRIST: Mark 6:3 speaks of "James and Joses and Juda and Simon" as the brothers of Jesus.

It is a reference which for some implies that Jesus had blood brothers (and sisters)—which, if actually so, would vitiate Catholic belief both in the virgin birth and in the perpetual virginity of Mary. It is conceded that the Greek word in the original texts means "brother," but Catholics contend that the Greek word is merely a carry-over from the Aramaic used by the first Christians, in which language the word is used to designate a closely defined group of people, such as cousins. Since Aramaic (like Hebrew) had no word for "cousin," it would be logical in the Catholic understanding of things to use the words "brethren" or "brothers" to identify cousins. One modern-day parallel would be use of the word "brothers" by black people as a generic term to designate members of their population group. Catholics reject the notion that Jesus had blood brothers (or sisters), and hold instead that he was the one child of a virgin mother.

BULL is a formal papal document having a *bulla* or seal attached. The seal has representations of SS. Peter and Paul on one side, and the designation of the reigning pope on the other. Bulls are used in the conduct of apostolic business, such as the conferring of episcopal titles, promulgations of canonizations, etc. A collection of bulls is known as a bullarium.

C

CANON is used ecclesiastically to designate: (1) the body of ecclesiastical law; e.g., the 1,752 canons in the 1983 revised Code of Canon Law; (2) the books of the Bible recognized as inspired by the Holy Spirit; (3) a portion of the Mass; (4) a religious dignitary, as the canon of a cathedral.

CANONICAL HOURS describe those eight parts into which the day has historically been divided by the church for devotional purposes, such as the recitation of the Divine Office and the scheduling of ceremonies in monasteries and churches. The Canonical Hours are:

Matins, originally observed before dawn but later anticipated the evening before;

Lauds, the morning prayer;

Prime, the first hour, sunrise, 6 a.m.;

Terce, the third hour, 9 a.m.;

Sext, the sixth hour, noon;

None, the ninth hour, 3 p.m.

Vespers, the evening service;

Compline, meaning "completion," the end of the day, bedtime.

The term "book of hours" applies to the book or collection which contains the prayers appropriate to each division.

CANONIZATION is the church's official declaration that an individual is already in heaven and worthy of public veneration and imitation. The process follows beatification and involves another investigation into the person's heroic virtues, writings, reputation for holiness, and miracles ascribed to the person's intercession since death. Miracles, however, are not required for martyrs. The pope may dispense from some of the formalities usual in the canonization procedure, and formal declaration of a candidate as saint is reserved to the pope. The first formal canonization for the universal Church was that of St. Ulrich by Pope John XV in the year 993. The canonization process has been reserved to Rome since 1171.

CAPITAL SINS are moral faults which are considered the sources of all sins. They are numbered as seven: pride, covetousness, lust, anger, gluttony, envy and sloth. Their opposite are the virtues humility, liberality, chastity, meekness, temperance, brotherly love and diligence.

CASUISTRY is the application of general ethical principles to particular cases of conscience or conduct. It is generally used in a disparaging sense; that is, the fallacious or dishonest application of said principles.

CELIBACY is the unmarried state of life, and is required of all candidates for Holy Orders in the Roman or Western Church. The discipline is different in the Eastern Church, where candidates for Holy Orders may marry before becoming deacons, but not after ordination, even when widowed; the celibate state is required for Eastern-Rite bishops. The tradition of celibacy in the Roman Church built on enactments of a series of local councils, beginning with one in Elvira, Spain, about 306, but the first comprehensive law making Holy Orders an invalidating impediment to marriage seems not to have been enacted until Lateran Council II in 1139. The Council of Trent confirmed this law in establishing current discipline on the subject in 1563. Exceptions to this discipline have been allowed by modern popes, beginning with Pope Pius XII (1939-1958). More recently, Pope John Paul II extended exceptions to a number of married Episcopalian (Anglican) clergymen, who converted to Roman Catholicism following the decision of their church to ordain women. Celibacy, thus, is a matter of church discipline and law, not a dogmatic formula. It is viewed by its champions as an instrument promoting total dedication to ministry and service in the church.

CENACLE is the upper room in Jerusalem where the Last Supper took place. The name also designates the retreat houses operated by the Congregation of Our Lady of the Retreat in the Cenacle, an order founded in France in 1826 and expanded to the United States in 1892.

CENSURE is the imposition of spiritual penalties on baptized persons for having committed certain grave sins. In the early ages, the church used the term to designate all its punishments, but since 1214 and the papacy of Innocent III, the term has applied to the penalties of interdict, suspension and excommunication. Absolution may be obtained from censure, though in some instances its granting may be reserved to a particular authority, such as the pope, the ordinary of a diocese, or a major superior. The penalty law of the church is detailed in Book IV of the new (1983) Code of Canon Law.

CHILDREN'S CRUSADE is the name given to the abortive Crusade of 1212, when great crowds of children rallied behind boy-preachers, who declared that young innocents would liberate Jerusalem from Islam by miracle. The principal preachers were a young shepherd of Vendome and a youth from Cologne. The movement spread through western Europe to Italy, where the Crusade eventually reached Brindisi on the Adriatic Sea on the southeast coast. The children waited for the sea to divide before them, so they could continue to the East. When the sea remained in place, the Crusade collapsed. Most of the children headed home, but many died en route of hunger and exhaustion. Some were seized by merchants and sold as slaves to the Moors. (See also Crusades.)

CIRCUMCISION is the removal of the prepuce, or foreskin, from the penis, and is a practice which some imbue with great religious significance and others regard as merely hygienic. In the Old Testament, circumcision was given to Abraham as a sign of the covenant between him and God, and even Christ was circumcised on the eighth day in fulfillment of the law and to indicate his descent in the flesh from Abraham. The religious necessity of circumcision concerned the early Fathers. St. Paul showed his freedom from the old legalities by not insisting on the circumcising of Titus (Gal. 2:3-4)—though he did subject his traveling companion Timothy to the rite (Acts 16:3). The Council of Jerusalem (A.D. 51) finally decided against the necessity of the rite. Nevertheless St. Thomas Aquinas in the 13th century would hold that circumcision was a figure of baptism and remitted both original and actual sins. Since Vatican Council II, new emphases have shifted attention during the Christmas octave from the rite of Christ's circumcision to Mary's role in the Incarnation, and the Feast of the Circumcision itself (January 1) is now known as the Solemnity of Mary or the Feast of Mary, the Mother of God.

CLERICALISM describes the use of clerical power or influence in matters extraneous to the clerical role; e.g., as in government, politics or the private lives of individuals. The word is used pejoratively.

CLOISTER is that portion of a monastery, convent or other religious house reserved for members of the order.

COLLEGIALITY is the principle that the bishops of the church in union with, but also subordinate to, the pope enjoy supreme teaching and pastoral authority in the church. This authority is exercised in Ecumenical Councils, as well as other ways approved by the pope. The collegial principle dates to apostolic times, but was diluted as authority became more and more centralized in the papacy, particularly with the declaration of papal infallibility in 1870. Vatican Council II (1962-1965) acted to restore historic concepts of collegiality, notably in the Dogmatic Constitution on the Church (*Lumen gentium*).

COMMUNION OF SAINTS is the doctrine expressing the spiritual solidarity which unites the faithful on earth, the souls in purgatory, and the saints in heaven. The solidarity embraces a number of inter-relationships in faith, prayer, merits, satisfactions, the sacraments and good works.

CONCELEBRATION is the offering of the liturgy by several priests, led by one priest of the group. The practice was common in Eastern Rite Churches from the beginning, but was long restricted in the Roman or Latin

Rite, being chiefly reserved for ordination of bishops and priests. This changed with Vatican Council II (1962-1965). Under new norms established by the Council, concelebration is now common in the Roman/Latin Rite.

CONCORDAT is a treaty or agreement between church and state concerning matters of mutual concern and having the force of law. The church has been party to some 150 concordats since the Concordat of Worms September 23, 1122, confirming controversial decrees of the First Lateran Council with respect to lay princes and their rights. A notable Vatican Concordat of recent date was that concluded with Italy on February 18, 1984. It continued the status of Vatican City as an independent and sovereign state but markedly lessened the influence of the Catholic Church on civil life in Italy.

CONSISTORY is an assembly of cardinals presided over by the pope. It may be one of three types: secret or ordinary; public or extraordinary; or semi-public. They are graded according to their exclusiveness. Only the pope and cardinals may attend the first; the other two are open to a wider body of participants, including laypersons. The formal elevation of a person to the cardinalate takes place at a public or extraordinary consistory.

CONSUBSTANTIATION is the theory that the substance of the body and blood of Christ coexists in and with the substance of bread and wine of the Eucharist. Also called impanation, the theory is incompatible with the doctrine of transubstantiation.

CONTRACEPTION: see Birth Control

COUNTER-REFORMATION describes the period following the Council of Trent (1545-1563) during which the church underwent extensive reform, much of it in reaction to the Reformation (although some Catholic historians argue that reform had actually begun before the

Reformation and that Martin Luther was a Catholic reformer before he became a Protestant). The period extends roughly from 1560 to the close of the Thirty Years War, 1648, and saw the emergence of several new religious orders. One, the Society of Jesus (Jesuits), continues as one of the great orders of the church. The Jesuits preached against heresies and carried the Gospel to Abyssinia, India, China and other far corners of the world. The three major reforming popes were St. Pius V, Gregory XIII and Sixtus V.

CREATION is the production of something out of nothing. It is a power reserved to God.

CREMATION is the reducing of a dead body to ashes by fire. It is a practice now tolerated by the church. Under Canon 1203 of the old Code of Canon Law, the practice was "reprobated," being regarded as a public display of irreligion and materialism. In 1963, however, the church relaxed this stricture and allowed cremation for good reason, such as national custom, control of disease, lack of burial space, and considerations of personal, hygienic or financial kind. A stated preference for burial was specified nonetheless. Canon 1176 of the new Code of Canon Law incorporates the 1963 decree but omits reference to a need for good reason. The canon reads: "The church earnestly recommends that the pious custom of burial be retained; but it does not forbid cremation, unless this is chosen for reasons which are contrary to Christian teaching."

CROSIER is the pastoral staff conferred on bishops as a symbol of their office, responsibility and authority. It is also conferred on mitered abbots at their investiture. The origin of the crosier is lost in antiquity. Some theorize that it is associated with the shepherd's crook. Others allege that originally it was nothing more than a walking stick adapted to assist prelates on their foot journeys and to be used as a support in churches before the introduction of chairs and pews. The crosier became the principal insignia of episcopal office as early as the 5th century.

CRUCIFIXION, Date and Year. The Crucifixion of Jesus Christ occurred on what is known as Good Friday of Holy Week. However, two Oxford University scientists, Colin J. Humphreys and W. G. Waddington, recently pinpointed what they say is date and year. By consulting historical and biblical sources, and by reconstructing the ancient Jewish calendar, they arrived at April 3, 33 A.D. Key clues were Peter's reference in Act 2:20 to Joel's prediction that "the sun shall be turned to darkness and the moon to blood," and other reports that after the Crucifixion the moon turned blood red. Humphreys and Waddington attribute this to a lunar eclipse during the reign of Pontius Pilate coinciding with Passover and the day before the Sabbath in the year 33. This figured to April 3.

CRUSADES, in the historical Catholic sense, were those expeditions undertaken over a 200-year period, roughly, to deliver the Holy Land from Islam. The period began with Pope Urban II's great exhortation to Christendom in 1097 to go forth and rescue the Holy Sepulcher, and extended to the fall of Acre in 1291, although in later centuries there were wars called crusades, such as those to push back invading Turks or quell the Barbary corsairs. When Christopher Columbus discovered gold in the New World his thought was that this might be used to equip an army to "free" Jerusalem, an idea supported by Queen Isabella, but never implemented. The Crusades have to be counted, in sum, as one of the great misadventures of Christian history. Whatever gains they achieved in terms of Christian access to places deemed holy, these were offset by new antagonisms and an alienation of East from the West, which persists to this day.

D

DEACON is the penultimate office in advancement to Holy Orders or the priesthood. (The offices of progression: porter, lector, exorcist, acolyte, subdeacon, deacon, priest.) In the early church, the office involved considerable and responsible duties, such as ministry to widows and the poor, instruction of catechumens, marshaling of congregations, and certain sacramental duties, notably relating to baptism. The duties and privileges of the office were such that many remained in it permanently (Permanent Deacons). By the 4th and 5th centuries, however, the office had lost its distinctive character and had come to be entirely regarded as a stage of preparation for the priesthood. The functions of a deacon were reduced, practically speaking, to ministration at High Mass and such incidental activities as exposing the Blessed Sacrament at Benediction. Vatican Council II's Constitution on the Church called for the restoration of the diaconate "as a proper and permanent rank of the hierarchy," and this exhortation along with a shortage of priests has helped return the office of deacon to something of its importance of earlier times.

DEACONESS is an office that had a distinct ecclesiastical standing into the 4th and 5th centuries. The New Testament speaks of Phebe as being a deaconess (Rom. 16:1-2), and it is considered probable that widows alluded to by Timothy may actually have been deaconesses (1 Tim. 5:3-11). The Council of Trullo in 692 is recorded as fixing the age of deaconesses at 40, while a 9th-century ordo mentions the place of deaconesses as part of the papal procession. Deaconesses engaged primarily in works of charity and in pastoral service to women. They were particularly prominent in the administration of baptism, when the sacrament involved immersion and the anointing of the whole body. Under the circumstances, propriety dictated the use of deaconesses when women were being baptized. With the turn to infant baptism and substitution of the pouring of water in place of immersion, the importance of the office of deaconess appears to have begun its decline. No record of the ministry of deaconess is found in the West after the turn of the 11th century, though the ministry lingered longer in the East. A modern revival of the office began in German Lutheranism in 1833, and there are those who would like to see its restoration in Roman Catholicism.

DEAD SEA SCROLLS, or more precisely the Qumran Scrolls, are those manuscripts found (beginning in 1947) in caves of the Desert of Juda, west of the Dead Sea. The scrolls, with one exception, are in Hebrew, and together they provide descriptions and insights into Jewish history and Hebrew literature particularly for the transition period between Old and New Testaments. They also confirm the time-fixing of certain books of the Bible of the pre-Christian era. Among other discoveries in the caves was a text of Isaiah dating from the 2nd century before Christ. Hitherto the oldest known Hebrew manuscripts dated from the 10th century A.D. Hundreds of scroll fragments have been found since the initial discovery by a Bedouin goatherd. The scrolls contain parts of virtually all of the Old Testament, together with texts of the Qumran sect and portions of apocryphal and pseudoepigraphical works. In 1985 Princeton University Press announced plans to publish three volumes of the Dead Sea Scrolls, a project that will include 91 scrolls and all of the major new documents discovered since 1947. The project has a completion date of 1991.

DEICIDE, which etymologically means killer of God, is the word under which, in the past, certain people were connected by some with the crucifixion of Christ. In general, this was the Jewish people, and the association, which resulted from implication rather than formal teaching, became a point of contention between Christians and Jews, and in the opinion of many a source of

Christian anti-semitism. The problem was addressed directly by Pope John XXIII, notably at a service in St. Peter's Basilica, when he demanded that a priest rerecite a prayer that spoke of the Jews as "perfidious," this time dropping the objectionable reference. The Deicide question was settled for Catholics, at least formally, at Vatican Council II (1962-1965) with the ratification of the Declaration on the Relationship of the Church to Non-Christian Religions *(Nostra Aetate)*. A passage of the document reads: "True, authorities of the Jews and those who followed their lead pressed for the death of Christ; still, what happened in His passion cannot be blamed upon all the Jews then living, without distinction, nor upon the Jews of today. Although the Church is the new people of God, the Jews should not be presented as repudiated or cursed by God, as if such views followed from the holy Scriptures" (4:7). The phrase "or guilty of deicide" was dropped from the latter sentence before final ratification, an action which spurred the charge that the deletion came under pressure from Arab governments. It was explained, however, that many Council Fathers asked for the deletion, feeling that the phrase was ambiguous and might even suggest to some people that the church no longer regarded Jesus as God.

DEISM is the belief in the existence of God on the evidence of reason and nature only, with rejection of supernatural revelation. It is a product of the rationalism of the 17th and 18th centuries. Voltaire and Rousseau were among its proponents.

DETRACTION is the making known of a true but hidden fault of a person without justifiable reason. It is a sin against the Eighth Commandment, which forbids the bearing of false witness. Detraction is related to:
  Defamation, which is any false statement which damages a person's reputation;
  Libel, which is a defamatory statement which is written, broadcast or otherwise publicized;

Slander, which is a defamatory statement which is
spoken;
Calumny, which is the harming of a person's name
and reputation by lies.

All are sins against justice, and demand restitution
when this is possible without further harm being done
to the offended person.

The moral principle behind such sins against truth was
exquisitely voiced by Iago in Shakespeare's *Othello*: "He
that filches from me my good name robs me of that which
not enriches him, and makes me poor indeed."

DEVIL (Satan) describes Lucifer, chief of the fallen
angels, and also any of the fallen angels who were banished to hell. Because they still possess angelic powers,
they are said to be capable of diabolical phenomena, such
as entering a person's body and exercising power over
the individual's faculties. They also are regarded as temp-
tors, leading persons to sin.

DEVIL'S ADVOCATE (*Advocatus Diaboli*) is the popular
name given to the official in the Vatican's Sacred Congregation of Rites, whose task it is to raise objections and
arguments against the elevating of one to the honors of
the altar, as in beatification and canonization causes. The
official's formal title is Promoter of the Faith.

DISCALCED derives from the Latin meaning shoeless
or without shoes. The word is applied ecclesiastically to
those religious who go barefooted or wear sandals.

DOUBLE EFFECT is the close relation of two results
from a single action. In instances where one result is good
and the other bad, the action may still be morally justified,
providing certain criteria are met. For instance, the action
must be good in itself; there must be proportionality between the good and bad effects; the bad effect cannot be
directly intended or sought. It is under the principle of
the Double Effect that it is possible for a pregnant woman

to have an indirect abortion. A textbook case would be a pregnant woman forced to undergo a medical or surgical procedure for a severe pathological condition, treatment of which cannot be deferred without risk of the pregnant woman's life. Though this medical procedure may result in the loss of life of the fetus, it may nevertheless be morally justified. The considerations: the pathological problem is life-threatening to the pregnant person; its treatment cannot be deferred without serious medical consequences to that person; the loss of the fetus is not directly sought. In other words, the loss of the fetus results not from a direct, deliberate procedure for the cure of the mother, but happens indirectly and as a secondary consequence of the medical procedure.

DOVE, a bird of the pigeon family, is the symbol of the Holy Spirit, perhaps because of its gentleness and purity of appearance. Matthew, in recording the baptism of Jesus by John the Baptist, identifies the Spirit of God as a dove descending on Jesus, while from heaven a voice blesses the Son in whom he is well-pleased (Mt. 3:16-17).

DULIA, from the Greek, is the homage or veneration extended to saints. It is different in degree and nature from the worship given to God.

E

EASTER is the feast commemorating Christ's resurrection from the dead. It is always observed on a Sunday, and it can come as early as March 22 or as late as April 25. Since the year 325, the formula has been to celebrate Easter on the first Sunday following the first full moon in the spring. Sunday was decided upon because ancient Christians believed Christ rose from the dead on the first day of the week.

ECUMENISM is the collective movement of Christians and their churches for the restoration of unity among those who invoke the Triune God and confess Jesus Christ as Lord and Savior. Ecumenism has several dimensions: spiritual or mutual prayer for unity; scholarship, involving a search for that which binds rather than divides; and activism or pew-level efforts aimed at furthering trust and cooperation between Christians of different persuasions. Vatican Council II's Decree on Ecumenism spells out the church's modern understanding on the subject.

EMBER DAYS belong to the pre-Vatican Council II church. They were days of fast and abstinence appointed by the church, beginning as far back as the 3rd century. Pope Gregory VII (1073-1085) prescribed Ember Days' observance for the whole church in the four seasons of the year, specifically on the Wednesdays, Fridays and Saturdays following: (1) December 13, the Feast of St. Lucy; (2) the first Sunday in Lent; (3) Whitsunday, the seventh Sunday after Easter; and September 14, the Feast of the Exaltation of the Cross. Ember Days were replaced by a 1970 Vatican instruction directing dioceses to observe "days or periods of prayer for the fruits of the earth, prayer for human rights and equality, prayer for world justice and peace, and penitential observance outside of Lent."

ENCHIRIDION INDULGENTIARUM is the name for the codification of the church's official list of indulgences. It is subject to frequent revision.

ENCYCLICAL is a pastoral letter addressed by a pope to the church and its members. Etymologically the word, from its Greek roots, means circular letter. The form was popularized largely by Popes Pius IX (1846-1878) and Leo XIII (1878-1903). Before their pontificates the encyclical letter was used but occasionally. Encyclicals are not necessarily *ex cathedra* pronouncements invested with infallible authority, but they do belong to what is called the ordinary magisterium of the church, and because issued by the pope they are documents of weighty importance. The authority of encyclicals is spelled out in *Humani Generis*, a 1950 encyclical of Pope Pius XII (1939-1958). Encyclical epistles are documents of more limited scope, being addressed to a section of the church, such as the hierarchy and faithful of a particular country.

EUCHARIST describes the presence of Christ, whole and entire, under the appearances of bread and wine. The Eucharist is one of the seven sacraments of the church, and results from the consecration at Mass of bread and wine into the body and blood of Christ with the celebrant's repetition of the words of Christ at the Last Supper: "This is my body...This is my blood," etc.

EUCHARISTIC CONGRESSES are gatherings of Catholics convened for the purpose of giving public adoration to the Eucharist. Eucharistic Congresses are held periodically at a place determined by a permanent committee with the approbation of the pope. Liturgical services and public ceremonies are planned about central themes aimed at increasing understanding of and devotion to Christ in the Eucharist. The first Eucharistic Congress was held at Lille, France, in 1881. Forty-two have been held since at the following locations: Avignon (1882), Liege (1883), Freiburg (1885), Toulouse (1886), Paris (1888), Antwerp (1890), Jerusalem (1893), Rheims (1894), Paray-le-Monial (1897), Brussels (1898), Lourdes (1899), Angers (1901), Namur (1902), Angouleme (1904), Rome (1905), Tournai (1906), Metz (1907), London (1908), Cologne (1909), Montreal (1910), Madrid (1911), Vienna (1912), Malta (1913), Lourdes (1914), Rome (1922), Amsterdam (1924), Chicago (1926), Sydney (1928), Carthage (1930), Dublin (1932), Buenos Aires (1934), Manila (1937), Budapest (1938), Barcelona (1952), Rio de Janeiro (1955), Munich, Germany (1960), Bombay, India (1964), Bogota, Colombia (1968), Melbourne, Australia (1973), Philadelphia (1976), Lourdes (1981), Nairobi, Kenya (1985).

Pope Paul VI attended the 38th Congress at Bombay in 1964 and the 39th Congress at Bogota in 1968. Pope John Paul II attended the 1985 Congress in Nairobi.

EUCHARISTIC MINISTERS are those who serve as special ministers of the Eucharist at communion at Mass and, outside Mass, on visits to the sick and shut-ins. They include both laymen and laywomen, and they function under the authorization of Pope Paul VI's 1973 instruction on facilitating Communion in particular circumstances *(Immensae Caritatis)*. Theoretically their presence is dictated by the need to furnish appropriate pastoral service when and where there is an insufficient number of priests and deacons to provide this service, but in effect many bishops and priests have used the permissions of the papal instruction to involve laity more intimately in the liturgy.

EUTHANASIA, or mercy killing, is the act of putting to death painlessly a person suffering from an incurable and painful disease or difficult condition, such as old age. It is a sin against the Fifth Commandment. Euthanasia is not to be confused with the withdrawal of life-support systems in instances where they are no longer in the best interests of a hopelessly sick person, and where a distinction has been drawn between the use of ordinary and extraordinary means in the continuation of life in the special circumstances of the one who is gravely and incurably ill. Extraordinary means are not always demanded in the care of such hopelessly ill persons, and one may legally and licitly switch to low-technology, comfort care, the effect of which may to be allow the inevitable to occur.

EX CATHEDRA is the Latin for "from the chair," meaning the chair of St. Peter. The term relates to the doctrine of infallibility and the understanding that the pope cannot err when he speaks on matters of faith and morals.

EXCOMMUNICATION is a penalty or censure which entails forfeiture of the spiritual privileges of ecclesiastical society, thus excluding the individual from the communion of the faithful. It results from committing and/or remaining obstinant in specified sins of a grave nature, and remains until the individual confesses, repents and receives absolution. Though excommunicated the individual is still bound to fulfill the normal obligations of faith as a Catholic.

EXISTENTIALISM is a philosophical theory involving a variety of themes, among them the tenet that individual existence determines essence, and that persons have absolute freedom of choice, even if there are not rational criteria serving as a basis for choice. The denial of objective truth is combined with the proposition that the universe is absurd. Existentialism is essentially atheistic, although some (Soren Kierkegaard, Gabriel Marcel) have sought to give it a Christian dimension. Pope Pius labeled Existentialism "erroneous" in the encyclical *Humani Generis* of August 12, 1950.

EXORCISM is a sacramental rite which aims at driving an evil spirit from a person or thing. Elements of the rite include prayer (Litany of the Saints, Our Father, creed, specific prayers of exorcism, *et al.*) and liberal use of holy water, crucifix and the Sign of the Cross. The use of exorcism has been reduced dramatically in modern times, but exorcism retains a place in the ceremony of baptism and among minor orders, the fourth of which is exorcist, empowering a person to exorcise evil spirits.

F

FAITHFUL ("the faithful") is the collective term used to describe all members of the Church, whether clerical, religious or lay.

FILIOQUE, Latin for "and the Son," is the term in the Roman Catholic version of the Nicene Creed that expresses double procession of the Holy Spirit from the Father and the Son. Rejection of the Filioque clause was one of the causes of the so-called Eastern or Greek schism. The doctrine of the Filioque was declared to be a dogma of faith by the Fourth Lateran Council (1215), the Second Council of Lyons (1274), and the Council of Florence (1438-1445).

FIRST FRIDAY is a devotion involving reception of the Eucharist on the first Friday of nine consecutive months. The devotion is said to have been communicated by Christ to St. Margaret Mary Alacoque in 1675, and promises the grace of final penitence to those who make the nine First Fridays. The devotion honors the Sacred Heart of Jesus and is offered in reparation for sin.

FIRST SATURDAY is a devotion involving confession and then, on the First Saturday of five consecutive months, reception of the Eucharist, recitation of five decades of the rosary, and 15 minutes' meditation on the mysteries. The devotion is said to have been communicated in the course of the Fatima apparitions of 1917.

FISH ranks among the most important of Christian symbols. It held for early Christians a particular significance, because the Greek word for fish *(icthus)* formed an acrostic describing the character of Christ and his claim on Christian worshippers; i.e., Jesus Christ, Son of God, Saviour. Symbol and word, accordingly, were an encapsulated profession of faith in the divinity of Christ.

FIXED FEASTS are those which occur each year on the same calendar date, as Christmas (December 25) and St. Patrick (March 17). They are the opposite of Movable Feasts. Among important Fixed Feasts: St. Joseph, March 19; SS. Peter and Paul, June 29; Visitation of the Blessed Virgin Mary, May 31; Assumption of the Blessed Virgin Mary, August 15; All Saints, November 1; Immaculate

Conception of the Blessed Virgin Mary, December 8. They are also known as Immovable Feasts.

FREE WILL is the ability to act freely or of one's own accord in a particular matter, when several alternatives are possible. That human action expresses personal choice; in other words, it is not determined by physical or other outside forces. The faculty of free will under-pins the matter of moral responsiblity.

FRIAR in the strict sense applies to one who is a member of a mendicant order; that is, an order in which members are without property rights and where they work or beg for their support. The practice of begging is restricted nowadays, but not totally disallowed. The Franciscans and Dominicans were the original mendicant orders, though in time others were extended the title and privi-leges of mendicant, including the Servites, Carmelites and Augustinians.

G

GALILEE is the ancient Roman province and sea in what is now northern Israel. It is where Christ was reared and where he spent much of his life preaching. All but one of the Apostles were from Galilee. The Sea of Galilee is really more the size of a lake. It is 15 miles long and six miles wide, and only 120 to 155 feet deep. The Sea of Gal-ilee was also known as Lake Gennesaret, from the plain at its northwest extremity, and the Sea of Tiberias, from the city of that name on its western shore. People still fish there for a livelihood, as they did in the time of Christ.

GEHENNA derives from the Hebrew for "Valley of Hinnom," a site near Jerusalem where ritualistic infant-sacrifices were practiced (2 Chronicles 28:3). The propitiatory sacrifices were made to the diety Moloch. Gehenna thus became a word synonymous with place of malediction, or hell.

GENUFLECTION is the act of bending the knee or knees in reverence or adoration. One genuflects before the tabernacle in church, touching right knee to the floor in acknowledgement of the Eucharistic presence. When the Eucharist is exposed on the altar, as during the Forty Hours devotion, the practice is to genuflect on both knees.

GOG AND MAGOG are the names assigned in Revelation 20:8 as symbols of the pagan nations. Gog probably derives from Gyges, King of Lydia. In Ezekiel 38:2 Gog represents a barbaric conqueror rising up to threaten Israel. He is portrayed as living in the land of Magog, among people on the shores of the Black Sea. Their ancestor would be Magog, son of Japheth (Gen. 10:2).

GRACE has a variety of meanings, including benefit, favor, benevolence. In the theological sense, it is the freely given, unmerited favor and love of God. In the plural (graces), it designates the supernatural gifts and help given to individuals by the Holy Spirit. Grace is essential for salvation. One achieves grace through the sacraments, prayer and good works. There are two kinds of Grace, Sanctifying Grace and Actual Grace.

Sanctifying Grace, or habitual grace, is that which makes persons holy and pleasing in the sight of God. It is grace which causes a state of holiness. Baptism and penance (the sacrament of reconciliation) convey this grace; the other sacraments increase grace in those already in the state of grace. Prayer and good works also contribute to the growth of this grace. (Graces which come through the sacraments are known as *Sacramental Graces.*)

Actual Grace is the supernatural help granted by God

for the performance of salutary acts, and is present and disappears with the action itself. It is not permanent as is Sanctifying Grace, and can be resisted or spurned.

GRAIL: see Holy Grail

GREGORIAN CALENDAR was the spectacular achievement of the reign of Pope Gregory XIII (1572-1585). It replaced the Julian Calendar, which went back to the time of Julius Caesar, but was so imprecise that by the 16th century the calendar year was running ten days behind the sun. Several councils, including Trent in its last session (1563), urged action to correct matters, since the ecclesiastical calendar was being affected. Nineteen years after Trent the puzzle was solved, thanks chiefly to Lilius, Clavius and Chacon (Chaconius). Adjustments were introduced, and on October 4, 1582, the calendar was jumped ahead so as to be followed by October 15. Some countries resisted change out of hostility to Rome. England did not adopt the Gregorian Calendar until 1751 and Russia held out until this century (with the curious result that "October" Revolution of 1917 actually took place in November). The key to the accuracy of the Gregorian Calendar was the rearrangement of leap years to offset the difference between the common year (365 days) and the astronomical year (365¼ days). As it is, the Gregorian year still exceeds the true astronomical year by 26 seconds, but scientists figure it will be 35 centuries before the difference amounts to a day.

H

HAGIOGRAPHY is the writing and critical study of the lives of the saints. Hagiography is a bona fide branch of learning, but frequently the word itself is used as a pejorative to label a writing or study as excessively and unreliably pious.

HALLOWEEN is a combination of holidays, some pagan, some Christian. The Romans celebrated the occasion as the festival of Pomona, goddess of gardens. The ancient Celts called the holiday "Samhain," or "end of summer," and observed the day as the end of the food-growing season. The Celts believed that ghosts of people visited the earth on Samhain (October 31), and they lit bonfires atop hills to scare the ghosts away. When the Celts became Christians, they and other Christian groups appropriated the holiday as a festive prelude to the day on which to remember deceased loved ones. All Saints Day (November 1) was known then as All Hallows Day, so inevitably the evening before was called All Hallows E'en, or holy evening. Eventually the term was telescoped to Halloween. The scary and spooky customs of Halloween are carry-overs from practices of the pagan Celts.

HELOISE AND ABELARD are classic representatives of star-crossed lovers, rather like Tristan and Isolde, Romeo and Juliet. Except there is nothing mythological or fictional about them or their love. Heloise was the niece of the medieval Canon Fulbert of Notre Dame Cathedral; Abelard was one of France's most celebrated 12th-century philosophers and theologians. They secretly married after Heloise gave birth to a son—though she in fact wished not to marry, sensing that Abelard's career might be ruined. She sensed correctly. An enraged Fulbert had Abelard emasculated. Heloise retreated into a nunnery, first at Argenteuil, later at Troyes; she became an abbess. Abelard took the habit of a Benedictine monk. The tender and passionate love-letters exchanged while Heloise was a nun and Abelard a monk are now a part of the world's great literature on the theme of love. Heloise is considered one of the remarkable women of the Middle Ages; Abelard's mark is historically less consequential, although he did bring to philosophy the Yea and Nay (*Sic et Non*) method subsequently developed by Alexander of Hales and St. Thomas Aquinas. This is the method which states the reasons for and against a proposition before proceeding to dialetical discussion.

HERESY, as defined by St. Thomas, is "a species of infidelity in men who, having professed the faith of Christ, corrupt its dogmas." Heresy is considered formal when there is persistent and obstinate adherence to an erroneous tenet. Heresy differs from apostasy, in the sense that an apostate *a fide* wholly abandons the faith of Christ, whereas a heretic retains faith in Christ. Heresy likewise differs from schism, in the sense that schismatics of their own will and intention separate themselves from the unity of the Church, whereas heretics do not necessarily consider themselves so separated.

HETERODOXY is the departure from true and established doctrine.

HOLY GRAIL is the cup or chalice which in medieval legend was associated with wondrous powers, especially the regeneration of life and, later, Christian purity. Allegedly the cup was the one Christ used at the Last Supper. St. Joseph of Arimathea supposedly preserved the Grail, along with some blood shed by Christ at the Crucifixion. The Grail was brought to England, where it disappeared. Another account has the Grail being entrusted by angels from on high to a body of knights, who guarded it on top of a mountain. When it was approached by someone of less than perfect purity, it disappeared from sight. Its quest was one of the adventures of the Knights of the Round Table, and was the subject of other literature, both ancient and modern.

HOLY MAID (NUN) OF KENT (Elizabeth Barton) was an English visionary who was executed at Tyburn on April 20, 1534. Was this domestic from Kent a martyr, a woman gifted with supernatural knowledge, or was she a fraud and impostor? History's answer is ambiguous. What is known is that she went into trances and related "wondrously things done in other places." Her utterances took on a strong religious character, and she became an outspoken opponent of the royal divorce of

Henry VIII from Queen Catherine. Her opposition was taken with great seriousness, as fame was hers after she was restored to health in the presence of a large crowd, allegedly by the Virgin Mary and true to her own prediction. In 1533 Cromwell slapped her into the Tower along with her confessor, Benedictine Father Edward Bocking, and others. Confessions of fraud and deception were extracted, and there was public penance at St. Paul's and Canterbury. Still the Maid of Kent, Bocking and five others went to their execution. The Maid of Kent is said to have repeated her confession before dying, but this and the other confessions are in doubt for emanating as they did through Cromwell and his agents. She died probably no older than 26, but she left a romantic stamp on the history of the period. James Joyce alludes to her in *Finnegans Wake*.

HOLY ROMAN EMPIRE was that confederation of central European states, extending from mid-Italy to the North Sea, which came into being with the crowning of Charlemagne in the year 800 and which existed, loosely or otherwise, until the abdication of Francis II (Francis I of Austria) in 1806. It was called "holy" for reason of the interdependence of Empire and Church, and its reportedly divine ordination.

HOLY SEE is (1) the diocese of Rome, of which the pope is head; (2) the office or jurisdiction of the pope; (3) the papal court and curia.

HOLY SEPULCHER is the tomb where the body of Christ was laid after the Crucifixion. Tradition fixes its current location in a cave under the Church of the Holy Sepulcher in Jerusalem.

HOLY YEAR in Roman Catholicism is a jubilee year during which Catholics are eligible for generous indulgences upon fulfillment of certain conditions. Traditionally they are held at 25-year intervals, the intervals coinciding with the quarter marks of the century (1900, 1925, 1950, etc.), although extraordinary Holy Years may be declared, such as those of 1933 and 1983-1984 commemorating the 1900th and 1950th anniversaries, respectively, of the death and resurrection of Christ.

HOSANNA is a Jewish expression for "may God save." It is used in the course of Jewish feasts, and of course is chanted in the liturgy of the Catholic Mass. It was the shout of praise that greeted Jesus on his entrance into Jerusalem, in its context meaning "long life."

HOUND OF HEAVEN, THE, is the best known of Francis Thompson's poems. Published in 1893, it depicts the pursuit of reluctant humankind by the grace and re- demption of a persistent God. The allegory is the chase of a hare by a hound. The playwright, Eugene O'Neill, harangued Dorothy Day with the poem one winter night in a saloon at Fourth Street and Sixth Avenue in Green- wich Village.

HYPERDULIA is the veneration offered to the Blessed Virgin as the most exalted of creatures. It is not to be con- fused with adoration, which is accorded only to God.

HYPOSTATIC UNION pertains to the union of the human and divine natures in the one divine person of Jesus Christ.

I

ICONOGRAPHY is the artistic science of the history, description and interpretation of traditional represen- tations of God, Mary, the saints and other sacred sub- jects—such as the anchor, dove, fish, lamb, Eucharist, etc.—whatever the medium, be it sculpture, mosaic, painting, stained glass, ivory, wood carving, etc.

ICONOSTASIS is the illuminated or decorated screen separating the sanctuary from the main body of the church, which is the main feature of Greek churches, both Uniate and Orthodox. It has three doors: the middle or great royal door leading to the altar of consecration; the deacon's door to the right; and the *proskomide* (preparation for the Mass) door to the left, as viewed from a seat in the congregation. The screens may be simple or extremely elaborate, but two pictures or icons must appear on each: that of the Lord on the right of the middle or royal door, and that of Mary upon the left.

ICONOCLASTS (image breakers) were reformers who made their appearance in the Eastern Church in the 8th century, and who opposed the use of visible representations of sacred objects, such as statues, icons and the like. They gave their name to the English language as those who attack cherished beliefs, traditions or institutions.

IDOLATRY is worship of any but the true God. It is a violation of the First Commandment, which requires persons to worship and adore God, and God alone.

IMMOVABLE FEASTS: see Fixed Feasts.

INCARNATION is the doctrine that the second person of the Trinity assumed human form in the person of Jesus Christ and is at the one time both God and man. It is a supernatural mystery coincident to Christ's earthly life and continuing in the eternal in Christ's concern with the Father for the salvation of humankind.

INCULTURATION identifies emerging forms of Catholicism which are simultaneously doctrinally orthodox and true to the culture of the region from which they are springing. An example would be the integrating of the Christian message with African culture.

INDEX OF PROHBITED BOOKS was the list of books and writings considered pernicious to faith and morals. The Index grew out of an impulse to safeguard truth, but itself grew pernicious, as various papacies applied the Index with particular severity. The Roman Index first appeared in 1559, and contained both the *Index Librorum Prohibitorum* (books absolutely forbidden to be read by Catholics) and the *Index Expurgatorius* (books forbidden to be read until certain parts were omitted or amended). Beginning in 1571 a separate department of the Curia, the Sacred Congregation of the Index, carried on the work of review and censorship of books and writings, and it existed into the 20th century. At times penalties up to that of excommunication were levied not only upon writers but also printers of their works. Some books were proscribed by name; others were prohibited under general norms of the Index. Complaints against the Index became mountainous, until finally, in 1917, Pope Benedict XV (1914-1922) turned the function of censoring publications over to the Sacred Congregation of the Holy Office, now the Sacred Congregation for the Doctrine of the Faith. In 1966 that congregation declared that the Index and related penalties of excommunication no longer had force of canonical law. Catholics are obliged nonetheless to take normal precautions with respect to writings in areas of faith and morals.

The Index disappeared with regrets by no one. However noble its purposes, it was an embarrassment to the church. For instance, Robert Bellarmine, later to be canonized as a Doctor of the Church, nearly landed on the Index for writing in *De controversiis* that in temporal matters the authority of the pope was not immediate and direct, but flowed indirectly from the pope's spiritual authority. Pope Sixtus V (1585-1590) was furious at the suggestion but died before he could enforce his decision to put the book on the Index. His successor, Pope Urban VII (1590), reigned for only 12 days, but long enough to order the matter dropped.

In 1619, the Servite theologian Fra Paolo Sarpi described the Index in his book *Istoria del Concilio Tridentino* as "the finest secret device ever invented for applying religion to the purpose of making men stupid." The book was quickly slapped on the Index. History, however, was to vindicate Sarpi.

INDULGENCE is the remission granted by the church of temporal punishment due to sins already forgiven. An indulgence does not take away sin, nor does it take away the eternal punishment due to grave or mortal sins. The Church grants indulgences in accordance with the power conveyed to Peter in Matthew 16:19 (" . . . whatever you shall loose on earth shall be loosed in heaven") and the sharing of spiritual goods in the communion of saints, or spiritual treasury. An indulgence is not a permission or license to sin, and no one can gain an indulgence who is not in a state of grace. An indulgence may be either plenary or partial, and can be applied to the dead by way of suffrage—the actual disposition resting with God.

INDULGENCE, PARTIAL: This does away with part of the temporal punishment due to sin. To be gained, a person must be free from serious sin, be sorry for one's sins, and perform the required action or good work. The intention to gain the indulgence can be either general or immediate. The *Enchiridion Indulgentiarum* of 1968 extends partial indulgences to those who raise their minds to God with some kind of prayer in the course of everyday life; to those who give of themselves or their goods to people in need; and to those who abstain from the enjoyment of things which are lawful and pleasing to them. Partial indulgences were once designated in terms of days and years, but no longer.

INDULGENCE, PLENARY: This does away with all of the temporal punishment due to sin. To be gained, a person must be free of all attachment to sin and fulfill the conditions of sacramental confession (Reconciliation), reception of Communion, and prayer for the intentions of the pope. The conditions may be fulfilled several days before or after the performance of the prescribed action, though it is considered fitting that the Communion and prayer for the intentions of the pope occur on the same day as the prescribed action. Among devotional practices qualifying for a plenary indulgence are the Stations of the Cross, a half-hour's devout reading of the Bible, adoration of the Blessed Sacrament for at least a half-hour, and recitation of the rosary in a church or public oratory, or in a group, such as with family, religious community or pious association.

INQUISITION was an ecclesiastical institution established for the combating and suppressing of heresy in the 13th century. A decree of Lateran Council IV (1215), providing for the confiscation of goods and banishment of heretics, set the stage for the establishment by Pope Gregory IX (1227-1241) of a special tribunal to deal with the matter. This came to be in 1233. Inquisitors traveled about discovering, investigating and punishing Catholics who had fallen into heresy. Many of the Inquisitors belonged to two new religious orders, the Dominicans and Franciscans. Methods of investigation included threat of death at the stake; confinement, possibly with curtailment of food; visits by tried men (accomplices), who would attempt to induce free confessions; and torture, by use of the rack. Abuses were so common that Clement V (1305-1314) finally ordered that inquisitors not apply torture without the consent of the local bishop. The Inquisition was most active in the second half of the 13th century.

INQUISITION, SPANISH: This too was a tribunal for dealing with heretics. The movement began during the reign of Ferdinand the Catholic and Isabella, who considered the faith in Spain threatened by so-called pseudo-converts from Judaism (Marranos) and Mohammedanism

(Moriscos). Pope Sixtus IV (1471-1484) approved the setting up of the Inquisition in 1478, and in time the institution reached to colonial Spain, with courts being established in Mexico, Lima and Cartagena. The first Grand Inquisitor of the Spanish Inquisition was the Dominican Tomas de Torquemada, whose cruelty is infamous. Thousands of Jews went to the stake as "impenitent sinners" under Torquemada, and thousands more suffered in other ways. It was mainly because of Torquemada that the Jews were expelled from Spain in 1492. The Spanish Inquisition fell into disrepute for its cruelty, its irregularities and its identification with the Spanish crown, yet it remained operative into the 19th century, when it was abolished at last by the Revolution of 1820.

I N R I is the inscription ordered for the top of Christ's cross by Pontius Pilate. The letters stand for *(I)esus* (N)azaraenus, (R)ex (I)udaeorum—Latin for Jesus of Nazareth, King of the Jews. The inscription was repeated in Hebrew and Greek.

INTERDICT is a form of ecclesiastical penalty imposed by the church. It is different from excommunication in that it does not involve the exclusion of the individual from the community of the faithful. A personal interdict prohibits an individual's taking part in certain liturgical services, as in administering or receiving certain sacraments. A local interdict applies this prohibition to certain places.

INTEGRISM is a term applied to a belief that most concessions to modern ways of thinking dilute and endanger the faith.

INTERREGNUM is the interval of time between the end of a sovereign's reign and the accession of a legitimate successor. In Catholicism, it is thus the interval between the death of one pope and the election of another.

ISCARIOT is a Hebrew word designating "man of Kerioth"—Kerioth being a small village of Judea. It was the place from which Judas came, hence his name: Judas Iscariot.

J

JACOBINS is a word which has described Dominicans in France. It derived from the Rue St. Jacques in Paris, where the Dominicans first established themselves in 1219. During the French Revolution the word identified members of a radical political club, which promoted the Reign of Terror, and which was active mainly from 1789 to 1794. They were called Jacobins after the Dominican convent in Paris where they originally met.

JANICULUM is the highest of Rome's seven hills (276 feet). It is the site of the "new" North American College, the residence and house of formation for seminarians from dioceses of the United States. The "new" college was opened in 1953. The college's graduate department is in the original North American College, renamed the Casa Santa Maria dell'Umilta on Via dell'Umilta.

JANSENISTS were a sect of Christians who subscribed to the preaching of Cornelius Jansen (1585-1638), Bishop of Ypres in West Flanders. Jansen's doctrines resembled Calvinism, particularly with respect to predestination; i.e., God's foreordaining of the salvation or damnation of individuals. Jansen taught the doctrines of "irresistible grace" and the "utter helplessness of the natural man to turn to God." His doctrines were condemned by Pope Urban VIII in 1642, Pope Innocent X in 1653, and then definitively by Pope Clement XI in the bull *Unigenitus* of 1705. The rigorisms of Jansenism persisted, however, especially in France.

JEBUSITES identified Roman Catholics in *Absalom and Achitophel,* Dryden's famous political satire published in verse in 1681. The association was with Jebus, the name for Jerusalem before the time of David.

JEREMIAD is a lamentation, a mournful complaint, so named after the Lamentations of the Prophet Jeremiah in the Old Testament.

JUDGMENT is related in the Old Testament to the covenant—kings and judges maintaining or reestablishing faithfulness to the covenant, which was the contract between God and the people of Israel. In the New Testament, the testament of the New Covenant, judgment interconnects with the work of Christ. The Day of Judgment is coming and individuals will be judged according to how they have lived and observed the Word. There is a *Particular Judgment* immediately after an individual's death determining the disposition of the individual's soul. There will be a *Last* or *Final Judgment* at the end of the world.

K

KENOSIS is the humbling of Christ and his renunciation of divine attributes through his taking on of human flesh and suffering for humankind.

KERYGMA, from the Greek to proclaim or preach, is the preaching of the Gospel of Christ in the manner of the Early Church, effective now as ever for salvation. The focus is on Christ and salvation.

KNOW-NOTHINGISM was a mid-19th-Century movement in American politics with strong anti-Catholic overtones. The movement began as a secret society in 1853 and reorganized in 1855 as the American Party. Its tag came about because in the beginning members would respond to questions about their group with the phrase, "I know nothing about it." Their objective was the repeal of naturalization laws and the restriction of all but native Americans from holding office. For a time their influence on states and individuals was real. John Jay, before becoming Chief Justice of the United States Supreme Court, succeeded in attaching to the New York State Constitution a provision which denied citizenship to foreign-born Catholics unless they first renounced allegiance to the pope in ecclesiastical matters. The Know-Nothings split on the slavery issue, and died out soon after 1856.

KORAN is the sacred text of Islam. It is believed to have been dictated to Mohammed by Gabriel. Moslems regard it as the foundation of religion, law, culture and politics.

KULTURKAMPF designates the bitter struggle between the German imperial government and the Vatican, which took place between 1872-1873 and 1886, primarily over control of educational and ecclesiastical appointments. For German Chancellor Otto von Bismarck the issues were insurance of the unity of the new German Empire and protection against outside interference. The phrase was coined by Ferdinand Lassalle, German socialist leader, and popularized by Rudolph Virchow, German anthropologist and politician, who argued the struggle involved not only religion but also all human culture. The struggle was triggered when members of the sect known as "the Old Catholics" were not permitted to teach in the universities and were excommunicated by Rome. "Old Catholics" were followers of Johann von Dollinger, the learned Bavarian priest who rejected the dogma of papal infallibility pronounced by Vatican Council I (1869-1870) and seceded from the church.

L

LACHRYMA CHRISTI is Latin for "tear of Christ." It is also the name of a Neapolitan wine—as *Liebfrauenmilch* is the name of a Rhine wine. *Liebfrauenmilch* translates as "milk of Our Lady, the Virgin Mary." Neither of the wines' names is considered blasphemous, but rather a reflection of an age more graphic in the expression of belief.

LAICIZATION is the ecclesiastical process by which a person in Holy Orders is relieved of the obligations of his Orders, and returned to the lay state.

LAITY are members of the church who do not belong to the clerical or religious states. At the same time they are persons with active, distinct roles in the liturgy, evangelization, social action and the carrying out of the church's mission in the world. Vatican Council II's Decree on the Apostolate of the Laity specified this, declaring that the laity should be "well-informed about the modern world...[and be] an active member of...society" (Ap. 29), adding that "as sharers in the role of Christ the Priest, the Prophet, and the King, the laity have an active part to play in the life and activity of the church" (Ap. 10).

LAW is any written or positive rule or collection of rules governing the behavior or activity of persons. In ecclesiology it has several specifics, among them:
Natural Law: This is the law imprinted by God in the minds and hearts of individuals having the use of reason enabling them to know the difference between right and wrong, as by instinct. For instance, murder or the direct taking of life is a violation of the Natural Law.
Divine Law (Revealed Law): This is the amplification of Natural Law, as in the Ten Commandments and the two precepts of charity, love of God and love of neighbor.

Church Law: These are the rules and regulations in use in the church for the spiritual welfare of the people and the orderly conduct of the church's affairs. They are spelled out in the Code of Canon Law, as well as in decrees of the pope and the various Vatican congregations.

LENT is the 40-day period (Sundays excluded) prior to Easter, which the church observes as a penitential season. It begins on Ash Wednesday (which can occur any time between February 4 and March 11, depending upon the date of Easter), and it concludes with the Passiontide, the two-week period during which the church's liturgy follows Christ's activity closely through the final stages of his life on earth. These two weeks are called Passion Week and Holy Week. It was once claimed that the Lenten practice was of apostolic origin, but historians fix its establishment at a later date, probably the 5th century. Catholics are required to fast and are urged to adopt other penitential modes during the season.

LIMBO describes the state or place of rest and natural happiness, said to surpass any earthly happiness but to be short of heavenly happiness because those there lack a face-to-face vision of God. It is alleged to be a place reserved for deserving but unbaptized persons, such as infant babies. The theory for a Limbo traces to the Apostles Creed and the phrase "descended into hell," but the existence of Limbo has never been formally defined by the church. The word has acquired popular non-theological usage to describe a place or state of suspension, restraint, confinement or exclusion, and has been widely used in literature, as in Shakespeare's *Henry VIII,* where in Act V, Scene III, the Porter speaks of having in *Limbo Patrum* youths "that thunder at a playhouse and fight for bitten apples." The scriptural reference to "Abraham's bosom" is thought by some to refer to Limbo. St. Peter called Limbo "a prison."

LITANY is a form of prayer comprising a succession of salutations followed by a responsive petition. Example from the Litany of the Blessed Virgin: Tower of David, pray for us; Mystical Rose, pray for us, etc. A number of litanies have been composed, as of All Saints, St. Joseph, the Holy Name and the Litany of the Dying.

LORD originally simply meant "sir," a common title of respect. In the 3rd century B.C., the Jewish people replaced the ineffable *Yahweh* with *Adonai*, meaning Lord, in biblical contexts. Applied to Jesus by the early Christians, the word Lord thus became an expression and affirmation of Jesus' divinity.

M

MAGI in the Old Testament are associated with sorcerers and diviners. In the New Testament they are the three Wise Men, the Three Kings who followed the star to the stable at Bethlehem, where they paid homage to the Infant Jesus. Their names were Caspar, Melchior and Balthasar—though these names do not appear in historical records until the 8th century. There is no mention of their names in the Gospels—nor, for that matter, any mention of their number. It is figured they were three, because the gifts to the Infant were three: gold, frankincense and myrrh. Records in the East indicate that their number could have been as many as 12. Also, it is extremely unlikely that the visitors from the East were kings.

MAGOG: See "Gog and Magog."

MANICHAEANISM is sometimes spoken of as a heresy, though more properly it is the religion founded in the 3rd century by the Persian Mani. It claimed to be the true synthesis of known religious systems, but contained only superficial elements of Christianity, which it abhorred for its mysteries. Manichaeanism professed to be a religion of pure reason. Salvation came through knowledge; ignorance was sin. It built on the dualist principle of powers of good and evil being operative in creation and life. The world was created by the power of evil. There were ten commandments, which forbade idolatry, mendacity, avarice, killing, fornication, theft, seduction to deceit, magic, hypocrisy (secret infidelity to Manichaeanism) and religious indifference. Religious duties were essentially prayer and fasting, though Manichaeans probably had a form of baptism and eucharist.

MARDI GRAS (literally in the French, "fat Tuesday") is the day before the beginning of Lent, and in many places is celebrated as a day of carnival before the 40 days of austerity and deprivation slated to begin with Ash Wednesday.

MARTYR derives from the Greek word for witness *(martys)*. It describes one who chooses to suffer death rather than renounce faith or other Christian virtue; e.g., feminine virginity. The problem is that not all deaths for the faith turn out to be exactly so. St. Maria Goretti died at 12 in 1902, for resisting advances against her virginity. She was canonized for her purity in 1950. In 1985, a book, *Poor Saint, Poor Assassin: The Story of Maria Goretti,* by Giordano Bruno Guerri, reported that Maria Goretti had yielded to her killer's sexual advances on several occasions in order "to save her life." The Vatican convoked a commission not to call into question Maria Goretti's sanctity but to "reaffirm the fundamental theology of sanctity and investigate the inaccuracies in the book."

MERCY KILLING: see Euthanasia

MIRACLE is an effect or extraordinary event in the physical world which surpasses all known human or natural powers and is ascribed to a supernatural cause. Christ worked some 35 miracles, raising people from the dead (Lazarus, Jairus' daughter, and the son of the widow of Naim), healing the deaf, the speechless and the leprous, and of course, changing water into wine at the wedding feast of Cana. Christian history is also rife with the stories of miracles worked through the intercession of the Blessed Mother and the saints.

MISSION has several meanings within Catholicism. (1) It can apply to a certain work or assignment, as St. Francis Xavier's mission to the Indies. (2) It can apply to a territory, where the Gospel has been preached but where the Church's presence is not strongly established. (3) It can apply to an ecclesiastical jurisdiction, usually one with but basic or small canonical organization. (4) It can apply to a chapel or church with a visiting as distinct from a resident priest. (5) It can apply to the devotional exercise which is a series of sermons and spiritual practices usually held in parishes over several days' time.

MODERNISM is the name given to the so-called synthesis of heresies, which appeared around the beginning of the 20th century and which were condemned by Pope St. Pius X, first in the decree *Lamentabili Sane Exitu* (July 3, 1907) and more formally in the encyclical *Pascendi Dominici Gregis* (September 8, 1907), the two documents comprising his Syllabus of Errors. Among other things, Modernism made ecclesiastical decisions subject to the judgment of scientific scrutiny, while questioning dogmatic definitions such as the divinity of Christ, the Resurrection as an historical event, the origin of the Sacraments, and Christ's conscious founding of a church.

MONTH'S MIND is the devout practice of remembering a loved one with a liturgy on the thirtieth day after death. Like other customs surrounding death, including the laying out of the body and the funeral banquet, the Month's Mind replaced a corresponding pagan usage or custom. In some places, as in 10th-century England, the Month's Mind *(moneth's mynde)* was the memorial of constant prayer for the dead person during the month following his or her decease.

MOTU PROPRIO is a document issued by a pope on his own authority and theoretically without counsel from others.

MOVABLE FEASTS are those which fall on variable calendar dates, depending on the date of Easter or the calendar date of a Sunday. Examples: Ascension Thursday, which falls on the fortieth day after Easter; and the Sundays of Advent, which fall on the four Sundays before Christmas. The calendar dates for movable feasts will vary from year to year. Septuagesima Sunday, Ash Wednesday, Easter, Pentecost and Corpus Christi are among the Movable Feasts. Movable Feasts are the opposite of Fixed Feasts or Immovable Feasts.

MYSTERY in the theological sense is a revealed truth that is beyond the power of human understanding, and which would not be known except for God's revelation. The Trinity would be one example of a mystery. Another would be the presence of Christ, whole and entire, under the appearances of bread and wine in the Eucharist.

N

NEIGHBOR in Old Testament contexts means brother, countryman, fellow tribesman, member of the same race. The Israelite was directed to love these people. In the New Testament, Christ said that everyone was one's neighbor, including the hostile. The point was made in the parable of the Good Samaritan (Luke 10:29-37).

NICENE CREED is the profession of faith common to the Catholic Church and recited at Mass. Its formulation began with the Council of Nicaea (325 A.D.), which condemned Arianism for denying the divinity of Christ, and was completed at the Council of Constantinople I (381 A.D.). Over time the creed was adopted as the proper profession of faith for candidates for baptism.

NOVEMDIALES is the nine-day period of mourning for a deceased pope. The word comes from the joining of the Latin words *novem* (nine) and *diales* (days).

NOVENA is a devotional practice, public or private, of nine consecutive days (or nine weeks, in which one day a week is specially observed) for purposes of obtaining special graces. The word derives from the Latin *novem*, nine. Though permitted and encouraged by ecclesiastical authority, novenas do not have a proper and fully-set place in the liturgy. In general, there are four kinds of novenas: of mourning, of preparation, of prayer, of indulgenced petition. Wide popularity of novenas occurred in the 19th century with the Church's concession of indulgences to them, and carried through the first half of this century before waning.

NOVICE is a person, male or female, who has entered a period of trial and formation (novitiate) in preparation for membership in a religious order or institute. A novitiate may last from 12 to 24 months, at the conclusion of which the novice professes temporary vows of poverty, chastity and obedience. A novice is not bound by the same obligations as a professed member of the order or institute, and is free to leave at any time—or, for that matter, be discharged by competent authority. A novice's immediate superior is known as master or mistress of novices.

NUN: See *Sister/Nun.*

O

OATES' PLOT is named for Titus Oates (1649-1705), the English imposter who alleged to have discovered a "Popish Plot" to massacre Protestants and burn London. The allegations were spurious. Oates, for a time a national hero, fell out of favor. He was convicted for charges preferred against the Duke of York and imprisoned. He was pardoned, however, on accession of William and Mary.

OATH is the calling on God to witness to the truth of a statement. In solemn oaths, the hand is placed on a Bible, and the individual swears to the honesty of his/her statement with such words as "So help me God" or "As God is my witness." Solemn oaths are usually taken before ecclesiastical or civil authorities, with an official present. A simple oath is one taken between individuals under less formal circumstances.

OCCASIONS OF SIN are external circumstances, whether persons, places or things, which because of their nature and the frailty common to humanity or peculiar to an individual, incite or entice one to sin. Occasions of sin may be proximate or remote. The individual is under obligation to remove the former and take precautions against the latter.

ORDO is the booklet containing short and abbreviated directions for liturgical functions of each day of the year. The Ordo does not include the texts of liturgical prayers. These are contained in separate books, such as the Sacramentary, Antiphonary, Psalter, etc.

ORIGINAL SIN is the sin of Adam (Gen. 2:8 - 3:24), personal to him but passed on to all born since as a deprivation of grace. Original Sin is said to descend from Adam, not Eve, since he was the first and head of the human race. Adam's sin was to eat of the forbidden fruit

(Gen. 3:1-13). The scriptural basis for the proposition of Original Sin is based strongly on St. Paul (Rom. 5:12-21 and 1 Cor. 15:21). The sin is remitted by Baptism and incorporation in Christ. Fundamentalist belief is that with Original Sin humans became subject to disease and death, and that Baptism restores the right to heaven which Adam lost.

OXFORD MOVEMENT, also called the *Tractarian Movement*, was a movement within the Church of England toward High Church principles, which began at Oxford University in 1833 in opposition to liberalizing and evangelical tendencies. It emphasized the principles of primitive and patristic Christianity, as well as the historic and Catholic character of the church. Leadership of the movement gravitated to a young Anglican clergyman named John Henry Newman, who, on a stormy October night in 1845, stunned colleagues and disputants by resigning as the Anglican vicar of St. Mary's and converting to Roman Catholicism. He was ordained a Catholic priest in 1846 and elevated to cardinal in 1879.

The name *Tractarian Movement* derived from the theological and liturgical papers published at Oxford between 1833 and 1841 and known both as "Tracts for the Times" and "The Oxford Tracts." The series was terminated at the request of the Bishop of Oxford, ending with Newman's Tract No. XC, "On Certain Passages in the XXXIX Articles." Many Tractarians followed Newman into the Roman Catholic Church. Many others stayed in Anglicanism, devoting their lives to the movement's original purposes.

P

PACIFISM is a principle or policy professed by those who, on spiritual, moral or humanitarian grounds, or combination thereof, refuse to participate in activities of organized violence, particularly war.

PAGANISM describes the state of one who is neither Christian, Jewish nor Muslim; that is, one who is not a member of a revealed religion.

PALMER is another word for a religious pilgrim. In the Middle Ages, it identified in a particular way pilgrims who had returned from the Holy Land, in token of which they bore a palm branch.

PALMS are a sacramental of the church, blessed and distributed on the Sunday marking Christ's triumphal entrance into Jerusalem. This would be Palm Sunday or, as now known, the Sunday of the Passion. Ashes from burned palms are used in the ritual of Ash Wednesday for the signing of the foreheads of the faithful.

PARABLE is a short allegorical story designed to convey a truth or moral lesson. It was a favorite teaching form for Jesus, and the Gospels record more than 30. Parables are divided into the dogmatic (e.g., the Pearl of Great Price, Matthew 13:45-46), moral (e.g., the Barren Fig Tree, Luke 13:6-9), and prophetic (e.g., the Ten Virgins, Matthew 25:1-13).

PARACLETE is one called on to aid; an advocate or intercessor. In Christianity, it is another name for the Holy Spirit, the Comforter.

PAROUSIA, in Platonism, is the presence in a thing of the idea after which it was formed. In Catholicism it refers to the Second Coming of Christ, an event which will mark the end of salvation history and the coming of God's kingdom. It is an event set for the end of the world.

PASCAL'S WAGER is named for Blaise Pascal, French religious thinker, author and mathematician who lived from 1623-1662. His wager related to the existence of God. One believed, because if God existed, one had everything to gain; if God did not exist, nothing was lost by having believed. The theory is consistent with Pascal's exaltation of faith above reason, enunciated in his *Thoughts on Religion.* Among his other works was *Provincial Letters,* which defended the Jansenists in their controversies with the Jesuits.

PATERNOSTER is another name for the Lord's Prayer, and comes from the first two Latin words of the prayer, *Pater noster,* Our Father. The combined Latin words arrived into the language in curious ways. Paternoster is the name, for instance, for a fishing tackle, in which hooks and weights are fixed alternately on the line, somewhat in the manner of a rosary. Similarly, paternoster is the name for an elevator having platforms or shelves which rise and drop on an endless moving chain—again the notion of a rosary. The usage is more European than American. Paternoster Row in London is thought to derive its name from the area's once having been a center for rosary—or paternoster—makers. Another theory is that funerals on their way to St. Paul's began their paternoster at the head of the Row.

PENTATEUCH is the name for the first five books of the Bible: Genesis, Exodus, Leviticus, Numbers and Deuteronomy. The books enjoy a special reverence among Jews as "The Torah" or "The Law," and are regarded as the concrete expression of God's will in their regard.

PEOPLE OF GOD is the term designating Israel and its people throughout the Old Testament. They are the people chosen by God to be his very own (Deut. 7:6). God dwells among them (Ex. 25:9). They are a people set apart (Levit. 20:26). The term is appropriated in 1 Peter 2:9 to describe Christians as a chosen race, a royal priesthood, again a people set apart. The passage even speaks of a consecrated nation, but eschews a particular nationalism. With Vatican Council II, the term has taken on yet another meaning, one embracing all who believe in Christ, and the Catholic faithful in particular. People of God has thus become synonymous in popular Catholic understanding with the church's membership, God's People, the new People of God.

PERMANENT DEACON is the office restored in the modern church by Pope Paul VI with the 1967 document *Sacrum Diaconatus Ordinem,* issued by way of implementing the desire of Vatican Council II for a return to emphases originally associated with the diaconate. Under Paul VI's guidelines, the holy order of Permanent Diaconate may be conveyed on qualified unmarried men who are 25 or older (they may not marry after ordination) or qualified married men 35 or older (consent of the wife is necessary, and these men may not remarry after the death of a spouse). Preparation involves study and formation over at least three years. Candidates who are not Religious must be affiliated with a diocese, and once ordained Permanent Deacons must practice their ministry under the direction of a bishop and with the priests with whom they are associated. As of 1985, more than 140 dioceses in the United States had instituted Permanent Diaconate programs or were in the process of doing so, and there were 7,425 ordained Permanent Deacons and 2,263 in training. Seventeen dioceses had 100 or more Permanent Deacons, accounting for 41 percent of all American Permanent Deacons.

PETER'S PENCE is the collection taken up among Catholics each year for the maintenance of the pope and his charities. The collection originated in England, and draws its name from the penny contribution or tribute expected from each householder with land of a particular value, deliverable on St. Peter's day. Today the collection occurs on the Sunday in February anticipating the Feast of the Chair of St. Peter. The collection dates from the 8th century, and one early record states the money was to be applied to relief of the poor and for lights for the churches of Rome.

PHARISEES were a religious sect, said to have numbered about 6,000 in the time of Christ. They formed a school of ascetics, who sought to regulate their lives by the letter of the law. Christ rebuked them for their insincerity (Matthew 23:25; Luke 11:39; 18:9-14). The pejorative use of the word derives from the Pharisees' regarding themselves as holier than other persons.

PHILISTINES were non-Semitic invaders of Palestine of ancient times, who occupied its southwestern plains. They were subdued by David, and disappeared after the time of the Maccabees. The Philistines were looked down upon as ill-behaved and lacking in culture. Their name thus has entered the language to describe one who is hostile or smugly indifferent to culture or aesthetic refinement. It was first used in this context, it is said, by Matthew Arnold, 19th-century English essayist, poet and literary critic.

PILGRIMAGE is a journey, especially a long one, taken to some sacred place as an act of devotion. The practice has a long and noble tradition in Catholicism. One of the first and enduring places of pilgrimage was to the Holy Land, where Christ lived and died. Later, as the cult of martyrs developed, pilgrimages to their shrines (places of death or burial) came into vogue. Chaucer used the pilgrimage as the literary vehicle for his *Canterbury Tales*, a book comprising stories told by pilgrims on their way to the Shrine of St. Thomas a Becket at Canterbury. At one time, pilgrimages were primarily acts of penance, and confessors even directed penitents to travel to Rome to seek forgiveness there; in recent years, however, pilgrimages have become the rationale rather than the primary reason for travel. At one time, also, a distinction was made between major and minor pilgrimages. The major pilgrimages were those to Canterbury, Compostela in

Spain, Cologne (to the shrine of the Magi), and Rome (the Holy Land being inaccessible for most). Other objectives were minor holy places. Today the distinction between major and minor pilgrimages is no longer made.

PILGRIMAGE OF GRACE describes not a devotion, but a religious uprising that took place in central and northern England in 1536. The uprising extended over five counties, was led by Robert Aske, and was caused by "spreading of heretics, suppression of houses of religion, and other matters touching the commonwealth"; also, an "especially great grudge [existed] against the lord Crumwell." Aske's insurgents entered York and arranged for the return of expelled nuns and monks. As Aske's following grew to between 30,000 and 40,000 men, a worried Henry VIII promised a general pardon and a parliamentary session to be held at York within the year. Aske trustingly dismissed his followers only to find himself betrayed by the king's promises. He was arrested, convicted of treason, and executed—and the uprising was effectively crushed. The Pilgrimage of Grace was the subject of H.F.M. Prescott's historical novel *The Man on a Donkey*.

POPE JOAN is the name of the fictitious person who is alleged to have occupied the papacy from 855-858. In fact it was a time that Benedict III reigned as pope. The Pope Joan myth appears to have been born in the 13th century, and is not taken seriously nowadays. According to the myth, Joan harbored a consuming passion for the monk Folda, and in order to be near him assumed the monastic habit. Being shrewd and popular, she achieved the papacy, succeeding Pope Leo IV (855). Her deception was discovered when she gave birth to a child, as fate would have it, during a solemn papal ceremony.

"POPE JOHN XXIII"—there were two. The Good Pope John XXIII is well known. He was the Pope (1958-1963) who convened Vatican Council II and initiated the modern renewal of the church. The other John XXIII was an antipope, who claimed the papacy from May 17 (25), 1410, to May 29, 1415. His formal name was Baldassare Cossa and according to history he was so dishonest and inept that the Emperor Sigismund forced the calling of the Council of Constance (1414-1418), not only to rid the church of that John XXIII, but also to bring order to the church. There were then three claimants to the papacy, and it was thought that without a Council there would have been four. Appreciating the precariousness of his position, the spurious John XXIII fled Constance with the intention of revoking the Council's convocation and starting a counter-movement to that of his opposition. However, he was caught, arrested and tried on a variety of charges, including simony, maladministration of church property, and corrupt stewardship in matters spiritual and temporal. He was deposed May 29, 1415. Angelo Roncalli's choice of the name John XXIII on his election to the papacy on October 28, 1958, was seen as a move to rehabilitate the name and return it to the list of acceptable name-possibilities for future popes.

PRINCE OF THE CHURCH, the honorary title conveyed to a cardinal, is a recognition whose origins are not in Roman protocol, but in the Congress of Vienna, 1814-1815. The Congress was convoked with the eclipse in power of Napoleon by the four powers allied against him (Great Britain, Austria, Russia and Prussia), and it met in Vienna under the patronage of Prince Metternich. Its principal purpose was to restore all legitimate kings and princes to the power they enjoyed before the *coup d'etat* that brought Napoleon to power in 1799. Among other results was the restoration of the Papal States to its old dimensions (except for Avignon and Venaissin, and a strip of frontier territory in the Ferrara district which went to Austria). The historic rights of Italian princes were recognized, and it was proclaimed that henceforth cardinals of the Roman Catholic Church would be known as Princes of the Church. The agreement was considered a triumph of diplomacy on the part of the Vatican's

Secretary of State, Ercole Cardinal Consalvi. In other business, the Congress under the urging of Great Britain declared that slave trade was to be abolished; provided for the free navigation of international rivers; and guaranteed the neutrality of Switzerland. The final act was signed June 9, 1815—just a few days before the Battle of Waterloo.

PURGATORY is held to be a place or condition of temporal punishment for those who, having died, are in venial sin or have not satisfied God's justice for mortal sins already forgiven. Catholic belief in Purgatory is rooted in such passages as Revelation 6:9-11 and decrees of the Council of Florence (1438-1445) and Council of Trent (1545-1563). The Purgatorial principle has also been located in the Jewish tradition that the soul of the deceased for 12 months after death was allowed to visit its body and the places or persons especially loved. In Dante's *Divine Comedy*, Purgatory is a mountain rising from the ocean and divided into terraces, at the top of which is terrestrial paradise. From this summit the poet ascends through the planetary heavens, the fixed stars, and the "primum mobile" to the empyrean or seat of God. Thomas Merton used Dante's image of a seven-tiered mountain as the symbol of the modern world in his 1948 autobiography *The Seven Storey Mountain*.

Q

QUO VADIS? is a term and a novel which speaks to Christian values. It is the title of the 1895 historical novel by the Polish writer Henryk Sienkiewicz dealing with the Rome of Nero and the early Christian martyrs. The title is drawn from an incident reportedly involving Peter. After most of the Christians have been killed by Nero, Peter flees the city for safe refuge elsewhere. As he is leaving the city, he has a vision of Jesus. Peter falls to his knees and exclaims, "Quo vadis, Domine?" (Whither goest thou, Lord?). Jesus responds, "As thou art deserting my people, I go to Rome to be crucified for a second time." Smitten by these words, Peter wheels and returns to Rome, where he works among the Christians until he is arrested and put to death. Sienkiewicz's novel was made into a film starring Charles Laughton as Nero. Pope John Paul II quoted Sienkiewicz's message in his inauguration Mass as pontiff in 1978.

One of the most celebrated landmarks along the Appian Way is where the alleged confrontation of Peter by Christ is said to have occurred. The small chapel of Quo Vadis marks the spot. Divine footprints are said to remain on a paving stone.

R

RASH JUDGMENT is the attribution of something harmful to another's character without sufficient reason. It is a violation of the demands of justice and charity, and a sin against the Eighth Commandment.

RED-LETTER DAY is a term alluding to the old tradition of marking saints' feastdays and other special occasions with a red letter on church calendars. From the practice came the expression "red-letter day," meaning a particularly fortunate or happy day.

RELICS are objects associated with a saint of the church, and thus deserving of veneration. A first-class relic would be a physical remain of the saint, such as a fragment of bone; a second-class relic would be something closely associated with or touched by the saint, such as an article of clothing. The veneration of relics traces back to the earliest days of Christianity, when St. Ignatius of Antioch was thrown to the lions and his bones were gathered up by two companions who came by night to rescue them. The Council of Trent (1545-1563) affirmed the practice of veneration of relics, saying that "through these [bodies of the saints] many benefits are bestowed by God on men." At times, relics have been subject to grave abuses, as in the 9th century, when the export of relics of martyrs from Rome took on the dimensions of commerce. Enthusiasms for relics were once so extravagant and the claims grew so robustly that the authenticity of many relics (e.g., the boards from Christ's crib in the Basilica of St. Mary Major in Rome) is now open to question. Today the discipline relating to relics is controlled by the Vatican's Congregation for the Causes of Saints.

RELIQUARY is a repository or receptacle for the preservation or display of a precious relic.

RESCRIPT is a written answer to a query or petition submitted in writing to the pope or one's ecclesiastical superior. Provisions of a rescript relate only to the parties involved. By way of example, a papal dispensation is issued in the form of a rescript.

ROBBER SYNODS are unlawfully called church councils. They are termed *conciliabula, conventicula,* or *latrocinia*—i.e., "robber synods." The Council of Ephesus of 449 is classified as a Robber Synod. Its acts were declared null by Pope St. Leo the Great. He also excommunicated all who took part in the event, and absolved all whom it had condemned, but one—Domnus, Bishop of Antioch. Domnus agreed in the first session to the acquittal of the Archimandrite Eutyches, who was charged with denying the two natures in Christ. Then, pleading illness, he refused to appear again at the council. Domnus retired to monastic life which, it is said, he left years before with regret.

ROGATION DAYS belong in something of the same

pre-conciliar category as Ember Days, which is to say they have been displaced by other practices. Rogation Days, as distinct from Ember Days, did not call for fasting. Mainly they were days of special prayer for a bountiful harvest, for protection against calamity and for penance for sins. A Major Rogation day was observed in April, and there were three days of Minor Rogation immediately preceding the Feast of the Ascension. Rogation Days were observed as far back as the 5th century. They have been replaced by special days of prayer designated by the local bishop, in conformity with a 1970 instruction of the Congregation for the Sacraments and Divine Worship.

ROMANITA is an Italianate word used to describe a clergyman who has an instinctive sense of what is acceptable in Rome. It is attached as a rule to clergy of whatever rank who are stationed in Rome, dependent on Rome for position and favor, or aspiring to same in or of Rome. Romanita is generally used derogatorily.

S

SABBATH is the seventh day of the week (Saturday) observed as a day of rest and religious observance by the Jewish people and some Christian groups (Sabbatarians). The name is sometimes loosely and incorrectly applied to Sunday, the day of religious observance for Christians generally.

SACRAMENTALS are holy objects or actions instituted by the church for the promotion of devotion among the faithful. They are not necessary for salvation. Some common sacramentals include blessings, holy water, crucifixes, palms, scapulars, medals, rosaries, images, holy pictures, and prayers and ceremonies of the Roman ritual. The chief benefits of sacramentals are said to be actual graces, forgiveness of venial sins, remission of temporal punishment due to sin, protection from evil spirits, and health of body and material blessings.

SACRAMENTARY is the liturgical book containing the celebrant's prayers for the Mass and the rites for administration of the sacraments. The first sacramentary dates from the 6th century, and was known as the Leonine Sacramentary. The Sacramentary currently in use is the Roman Missal.

SACRAMENTS are outward signs instituted by Christ to give grace. They are the primary channels of grace in the church, and they receive their power to give grace from God through the merits of Jesus Christ. They number seven: Baptism, Confirmation, Holy Eucharist, Penance (Reconciliation), Extreme Unction (the Anointing of the Sick), Holy Orders and Matrimony. (The Sacraments are described individually in the section titled "The Basic Tenets of Belief.")

SAINT SWITHIN'S DAY is marked on July 15. Swithin is known as the Weeping Saint, because of the tradition that rain on July 15 means rain for 40 days. The legend is that Swithin, a 9th-century Bishop of Winchester, asked to be buried in the churchyard so the "sweet rain of heaven might fall upon his grave." When he was canonized, the monks decided to honor Swithin by transferring his body to the choir. The day chosen was a July 15. But it rained on that day and for 40 days after. The monks interpreted this as a message from Swithin to abandon their idea and leave him alone—which they did.

SATAN: See devil.

SCAPULAR (from the Latin *scapula*, shoulder) is a part of the habit or religious dress of certain monastic orders and religious congregations. It consists of a shoulder-wide piece of cloth worn over the tunic and falling front and back almost to the feet. Because of its shape, it is said to symbolize the cross and yoke of Christ.

Small scapulars, usually consisting of two squares of cloth joined by strings and worn front and back, were introduced for lay persons for devotional purposes and as a sign of their association with a religious order, spiritually and materially. Scapulars are classified by the church as sacramentals.

There are at least 18 kinds of scapulars, the best-known of which are those of Our Lady of Mt. Carmel (brown), the Holy Trinity (white), Our Lady of the Seven Dolors (black), the Passion (red), and the Immaculate Conception (blue). Several scapulars may be attached to the one string. In instances where the above best-known are attached, the combination is known as the "fivefold scapular."

SCAPULAR MEDAL is a medallion worn or carried by an individual already invested with a scapular. The medallion, having a representation of the Sacred Heart on one side and Mary on the other, was authorized by Pope Pius X in 1910. Only small scapulars (not the large) may be replaced by such a medal.

SCAPULAR PROMISE expressed belief in the intercession of Mary in one's salvation. It originates in the pious tradition that the Virgin Mary appeared to St. Simon Stock, then general of the Carmelite Order, on July 16, 1251 in Cambridge, England, and scapular in hand promised that everyone who wore it in holy fidelity would be safeguarded in dangers and would escape damnation. The promise to those who wear this brown scapular of Our Lady of Mt. Carmel is extended indirectly to the scapular confraternity generally on the theory that all who wear Mary's habit or badge are affiliated in effect to the Carmelite Order. The church has never spoken officially on the St. Simon Stock legend.

SCHISM in canon law and the theological sense is the rupture of ecclesiastical union and unity by disassociation or separation from the social organization or mystical body of the church. "Active" schism is the deliberate detachment from the body of the church by renunciation of the right to form a part of it; "passive" schism relates to those whom the church itself has rejected from its unity by excommunication.

SCRIBES were Palestine scholars and teachers of the Jewish law and tradition, active from the 5th century B.C. to the 1st century A.D. They translated, edited and interpreted the Bible. Like the Pharisees, they were held to be prideful, and they too were rebuked by Christ (Matthew 23:2ff; Mark 12:38-40; Luke 20:46). However, there were Scribes who were quite admirable, notably Nicodemus and Gamaliel.

SEPTUAGESIMA is the period of preparation for Lent. It lasts two and a half weeks, running from Septuagesima Sunday to Ash Wednesday, and thus includes three Sundays, respectively called Septuagesima, Sexagesima and Quinquagesima (70th, 60th, 50th). In the early Church, many Christians began fasting 70, 60 and 50 days before Easter.

SHROVE TUESDAY is the English term for the Tuesday before the beginning of Lent (Ash Wednesday). The term derives from the verb "to shrive," that is to hear confessions or confess oneself. *Ecclesiastical Institutes,* translated by Abbot Aelfric in 1000 A.D., illuminates the background: "In the week immediately before Lent every one shall go to his confessor and confess his deeds, and the confessor should so shrive him as he then may hear by his deeds what he is to do (by way of penance)."

The English custom of eating pancakes on this day is traced to the economy of using up the eggs and fat, once forbidden dietary items during the Lenten season. The expression Pancake Tuesday or Pancake Day originated with this custom.

SIMONY is the purchase and/or sale of ecclesiastical offices, spiritual goods or material goods so closely related to the spiritual that one is indistinguishable from the other. It is an offense that is considered a sin against the First Commandment, and in some cases is subject to Censure. The name derives from Simon Magus (Simon the Magician), who attempted to purchase the power of the Spirit from SS. Peter and John (Acts 8:4-24).

SISTER/NUN are words that are often used interchangeably. There is, however, a distinct ecclesiastical difference of meaning between the two. Traditionally the word nun has defined a woman religious in solemn vows *(moniales)*, such as a contemplative or one living in an enclosed group. Those, on the other hand, in simple vows are more properly called sisters *(sorores)*. Generally, sisters belong to the so-called active orders, such as teaching or nursing communities, or other communities whose works are carried on outside the convent or enclosure. Most of these communities or institutes were established during or since the 19th century. At one time a careful distinction was made in the use of the words nun and sister, but of late they have become virtual synonyms for one another.

SITUATION ETHICS is the ethical theory that behavior may be initiated and governed in response to immediate situations. The system is both subjective and individualistic, and thus operates apart from binding norms of law and morality. It relies on internal judgment and illumination of the mind to decide what is to be done in a concrete situation. The system is rejected by Catholic authority.

STOLE FEE is an offering made to a priest for administering or presiding at a sacrament or rite; e.g., baptism, wedding, funeral, month's-mind Mass. The purpose of the fee is the support of the clergyman. It is not a charge for the priest's services.

SUSPENSION is an ecclesiastical penalty usually applicable to a cleric, and involving the withdrawal of power and/or authority to exercise some or all of the individual's orders and jurisdiction. It can also extend to the right to accept the financial support of one's benefices.

SYLLABUS OF ERRORS: Actually there were two Syllabuses. There was the Syllabus of Pope Pius IX (1864) and the Syllabus of Pope St. Pius X (1907).

The first was issued on December 8, 1864, in conjunction with the encyclical *Quanta Cura*, with the wordy title, "A Syllabus containing the most important errors of our time, which have been condemned by our Holy Father Pius IX in Allocations, at Consistories, in Encyclicals, and other Apostolic Letters." The Syllabus of Pius IX contained 80 theses, grouped as follows: Pantheism, Naturalism, Absolute Rationalism (1-7); Moderate Rationalism (8-14); Indifferentism and False Tolerance in Religious matters (15-18); Socialism, Communism, Secret Societies, Bible Societies, Liberal Clerical Associations, Errors Regarding the Church and its Rights (19-38); Errors on the State and its Relation to the Church (39-55); Errors on Natural and Christian Ethics (56-64); Errors on Christian Marriage (65-74); Errors on the Temporal Power of the Pope (75-76); Errors in Connection with Modern Liberalism (77-80). Opponents of the Syllabus regarded it as a rejection of modern culture and a declaration of opposition to the modern State because of its claims on a general separation between Church and State.

The Syllabus of Pius X, issued July 3, 1907, as the decree *Lamentabili Sane Exitu*, condemned the chief propositions of Modernism in 65 propositions. The condemnations fell into six categories: The doctrine of the Modernists on ecclesiastical decisions (1-8) and Holy Writ (9-19); the Modernist Philosophy of Religion (20-26); Modernist

Christology (27-38); theories of the Modernists on the origin of the Sacraments (39-51); theories of the Modernists on the evolution of the Church with respect to its constitution and doctrine (52-65). The Syllabus of Pius X was soon formalized by the encyclical *Pascendi Dominici Gregis* of September 8, 1907. (See Modernism for further information.)

SYNOD, DIOCESAN is an assembly of representative members of a diocese (priests, religious and laity) with the bishop or ordinary of the diocese on matters affecting the life and mission of the local church. Diocesan Synods are called by the bishop, and he alone is the legislator having the power to authorize synodal decrees. The status of persons taking part in Diocesan Synods is thus merely consultative. Canon Law calls for all dioceses to convene a synod every ten years.

SYNOD OF BISHOPS is a central ecclesiastical institute, permanent by nature, chartered by Pope Paul VI in the document *Apostolica Sollicitudo* of September 15, 1965. Synods are convened on a periodic basis to deal with matters of moment in the church. Among their purposes are: "to encourage close union and valued assistance between the Sovereign Pontiff and the bishops of the entire world; to insure the bishops that direct and real information is provided on questions and situations touching upon the internal action of the church and its necessary activity in the world of today; to facilitate agreement on essential points of doctrine and on methods of procedure in the life of the church." In theory, the concept is to promote collegiality in the church. The reigning pope is the president of the Synod of Bishops, and to him is reserved the right to appoint the general secretary, special secretaries, and up to 15 percent of the membership of a Synod. Most of the remaining members are elected by national or regional conferences of bishops. Synods of Bishops are also directly subject to the pope, whose authority it is to call the Synod into session, assign its agenda, and confirm its deliberative and advisory authority.

Synods fall into three categories: Ordinary Synods, such as those held in 1967, 1974, 1977, 1980 and 1983; Extraordinary Synods, such as that called in 1985 to review developments in the church since Vatican Council II; and Particular or Special Synods, designed to deal with problems in a particular region, such as the 1980 Special Synod of the Dutch bishops aimed at resolving divisions in the Dutch Church.

T

TALMUD is the collection of Jewish law and tradition, consisting of the Mishnah and the Gemara. The Mishnah consists of the collection of oral laws edited by Rabbi Judah ha-Nasi (A.D. c135-c210). The Gemara consists in the main of commentary on the Mishnah.

THEISM is a system of thought based on belief in the existence of the Supreme and Infinite Personal Being known as God, and by extension the possibility of divine revelation. Theism is generally monotheistic, but being based as a rule on philosophical rather than theological principles, it does not include specific doctrines of the Christian faith, such as the Resurrection and the Trinity.

THEOLOGY is the field of study, thought and analysis that treats of God, his attributes and relations to the universe. In Catholic context, theology concerns the truths of faith, real and theoretical, and their application. It subdivides into five fields: Dogmatic Theology (including Christology and Soteriology—Christ and the doctrine of the work of the Redeemer), Moral Theology, Pastoral Theology, Ascetical Theology and Mystical Theology.

TITHING is the contribution, often by pledge, of a fixed portion of one's income to the church, for support and charity. The practice derives from the ancient biblical method of support for sacred ministers. The Israelites contributed one-tenth of the yield of crops and of the increase of animals for this purpose. Tithing is mentioned 46 times in the Bible. Tithing is not a fixed principle of Catholicism, although the fifth of the so-called Chief Commandments of the Church requires Catholics to contribute to the support of their church. Many Catholic parishes have tithing programs, with percentages varying on the portion of income that one is expected to contribute. Percentages usually range between five and ten.

TITULAR SEES are ancient ecclesiastical jurisdictions, which exist now in title or name only. Generally speaking, they are located in areas of the world where the church once flourished, but which it was forced to abandon or flee, as the areas fell under the influence of non-Christian elements. The Latin terminology for the areas is *In Partibus Infidelium*, "in the lands of the unbelievers." To preserve the memory of these sees, their names are assigned to auxiliary bishops in missionary countries.

"TOTIES QUOTIES" is the Latin term indicating that an indulgence may be gained as often as one recites a particular prayer or performs a particular act. In other words, the indulgence is granted with no limitation as to the number of times it may be gained.

TRANSUBSTANTIATION, as applied to the Eucharist, is the conversion of the whole substance of the bread and wine into the body and blood of Christ, only the external appearances of bread and wine remaining.

TRINITY describes the dogma of three divine persons, separate and distinct, in the one and same God. The first person of the Trinity is God the Father; the second, God the Son; the third, God the Holy Spirit. The three persons are perfectly equal to one another and each is God. The doctrine of the Trinity is classified as a strict mystery; that is, it cannot be learned nor understood completely from reason.

TRIDUUM is a three-day period of prayer and devotions, public or private.

TRUE CROSS is the rood or cross on which Christ is said to have been crucified on Calvary. It was found in 326 A.D. by St. Helena, mother of the Emperor Constantine, in a search of the crucifixion site. The true cross ranks among the holiest of Christian relics, though skeptics allege that the relics are so numerous as to make its weight implausible, a charge which immediately brings into question the authenticity of many of these relics. This is countered by others who claim that if all relics of the true cross were brought together, they would make up but one-sixth of a cubic foot. (One authority calculated that, presuming the true cross were made of pine wood, it would have a volume of 178-million cubic millimeters, whereas the known portions of the cross amounted to 4-million cubic millimeters.) The largest relics of the true cross are found in Jerusalem, Brussels, Ghent and Rome. The finding of the true cross and the recovery of a major portion of this cross from the Persians, circa-629, are marked by a special feast day: the Triumph of the Cross, September 14.

U

ULTRAMONTANISM, for some, is a term denoting integral and active Catholicism, in that it recognizes the authority and leadership of the pope who, for the greater part of Europe, resides beyond the mountains (*ultra montes);* that is, beyond the Alps. For others it is an opprobrious word whose meaning is bound up with an increasing and enhancing of the power and authority of the pope and his curia.

USURY is the charging of excess interest on the loan or use of money, and is considerd a violation of the Seventh Commandment concerning stealing. The topic of usury and money-lending has figured prominently in the polemics of recent years as an example of how doctrine can evolve in Catholicism. In the early church it was held contrary to mercy and humanity for one to demand interest on money from a poor or needy person. The 12th canon of the first Council of Carthage (345) and the 36th canon of the Council of Aix (789), for instance, declared it reprehensible for laity to make money by lending at interest. This reasoning continued into the Middle Ages, theologians and canonists holding that the loan of money or items for immediate consumption did not legitimize as such a demand for interest, and that any interest exacted must be returned as having been unjustly claimed. Pope Benedict XIV endorsed this position in the document *Vix pervenit* of 1745. Eventually the church reversed itself and recognized the legitimacy of loans, even for ecclesiastical property, the rationale being that a fair interest is justified to compensate the lender for the risk of losing his or her capital or for the positive loss of income which would otherwise have been had if the money were not on loan. Polemicists see the evolution of doctrine with respect to the loan of money as typifying possible evolution in other doctrinal areas.

UTOPIA is the name of the imaginary island in the political romance of the same name by Sir (St.) Thomas More, published in 1516. In Utopia everything was perfect—the laws, politics, morals, etc. The word has thus come into the language as a synonym for a place or state of political or social perfection.

V

VATICAN, the name, derives from the site on which it stands. Some say the name originated with a vanished Etruscan town called Vaticum. In any instance, in Roman times the area was known as *Ager Vaticanus* (Vatican Field). It was a low, marshy area, and not particularly desirable; Emperor Aurelian did not even bother to include the area within the ancient city walls of Rome. In time, the name became attached to the hill which rose from this low, level land near the Tiber River. In the Middle Ages, popes bought up large tracts of this Vatican Hill, thus opening the area up for development as the headquarters of the Catholic Church. Between 848 and 852, Pope Leo IV surrounded the area with a wall, segments of which survive to this day.

VENERABLE is the title allowed one whose cause for beatification has been accepted by the Vatican's Congregation for the Causes of Saints. Beatification, when a person is declared "blessed," is one of the final steps before being declared a saint.

VENERATION, as distinct from adoration, is the reverence accorded the Blessed Virgin, angels, saints, relics and the like. It is of a degree and kind different from the adoration or worship accorded God.

VIATICUM is the Eucharist given to those in danger of death. The word derives from the Latin "something for the journey," and in spiritual context represents that which supplies strength and comfort to the dying, enabling them to make the journey into eternity with confidence and a stronger feeling of security.

VIRTUES, CARDINAL, number four: prudence, justice, temperance, fortitude. For St. Augustine the cardinal virtues were the "order of love." They are also called moral virtues.

VIRTUES, THEOLOGICAL, number three: faith, hope and charity. According to St. Thomas they are so called "first, because their object is God, in as much as they direct us rightly to God; second, because these virtues are infused in us by God alone; third, because these virtues are not made known to us, save by divine revelation, contained in Holy Scripture."

VOTIVE OFFERINGS are those things vowed or dedicated to God or to a saint by way of petition or in thanksgiving. Example: King Edward I of England made the offering of a falcon in wax to the shrine of St. Wulstan, when, by the intercession of the saint, his favorite bird was cured of a malady. Votive Offerings commonly take the form of money and valuables.

VOW is a conscious, deliberate promise made to God by which the individual binds himself/herself under pain of sin to do some moral good. Nonfulfillment of a vow may be grave or minor depending upon the importance of the matter. Among the most common vows are those of poverty, chastity and obedience taken by those joining a religious order. A vow differs in kind from a promise or resolution, neither of which binds under pain of sin.

W

WEEPING CROSSES were crosses beneath which penitents offered their prayers in ancient times.

WORD within Catholicism has the special meaning conveyed by John in the opening of the fourth Gospel: "In the beginning was the Word, and the Word was with God, and the Word was God" (1:1-2). Word, thus, designates the Son of God. The usage may have derived from Greek philosophers, who used the word Word to describe a mediator between God and creatures. It is theorized, that with his use of the word Word, John wished to indicate that Christ, the Word of God, was the mediator of creation and the divine life. The opening segment of St. John's Gospel was the concluding prayer of the pre-Vatican II Mass (before the appendage of the Leonine prayers at the foot of the altar).

WORSHIP in the general sense is the homage paid to a person or thing. In Catholicism, it is the homage paid to God in the Trinity of God the Father, God the Son and God the Holy Spirit. In Catholicism worship is paid only to God. The Blessed Virgin is venerated. So are the saints.

Y

YAHWEH is the personal name of the God of Israel, the "I am who am" of Exodus 3:14-15. Out of reverence for the name, the word Adonai, "My Lord," was later substituted, Yahweh being reserved as a word too sacred to be pronounced.

Index